VIDEO COMMUNICATION

From the Wadsworth Series in Mass Communication

General

Media/Impact: An Introduction to Mass Media, Updated First Edition by Shirley Biagi

Media/Reader by Shirley Biagi

Mediamerica: Form, Content, and Consequence of Mass Communication, Updated 4th, by Edward Jay Whetmore

The Interplay of Influence: Mass Media & Their Publics in News, Advertising, Politics, 2nd, by Kathleen Hall Jamieson and Karlyn Kohrs Campbell

Technology and Communication Behavior by Frederick Williams

When Words Collide: A Journalist's Guide to Grammar and Style, 2nd, by Lauren Kessler and Duncan McDonald

Interviews That Work: A Practical Guide for Journalists by Shirley Biagi

Mass Media Research: An Introduction, 2nd, by Roger D. Wimmer and Joseph R. Dominick

Computer Graphics Applications: An Introduction to Desktop Publishing & Design, Presentation Graphics, Animation by E. Kenneth Hoffman with Jon Teeple

Radio/Television/Cable/Film

Stay Tuned: A Concise History of American Broadcasting, 2nd, by Christopher H. Sterling and John M. Kittross

Movie History: A Survey by Douglas Gomery

Working Cinema: Learning from the Masters by Roy Paul Madsen

World Broadcasting Systems: A Comparative Analysis by Sydney W. Head

Broadcast/Cable Programming: Strategies and Practices, 3rd, by Susan Tyler Eastman, Sydney W. Head, and Lewis Klein

Immediate Seating: A Look at Movie Audiences by Bruce A. Austin

Radio Station Operations: Management and Employee Perspectives by Lewis B. O'Donnell, Carl Hausman, and Philip Benoit

Broadcast and Cable Selling, 2nd, by Charles Warner and Joseph Buchman

Advertising in the Broadcast and Cable Media, 2nd, by Elizabeth J. Heighton and Don R. Cunningham

Copywriting for the Electronic Media: A Practical Guide by Milan D. Meeske and R. C. Norris

Announcing: Broadcast Communicating Today by Lewis B. O'Donnell, Carl Hausman, and Philip Benoit

Modern Radio Production, 2nd, by Lewis B. O'Donnell, Philip Benoit, and Carl Hausman

Writing for Television and Radio, 5th, by Robert L. Hilliard

Writing the Screenplay: TV and Film by Alan A. Armer

Institutional Video: Planning, Budgeting, Production, and Evaluation by Carl Hausman

Video Communication: Structuring Content for Maximum Program Effectiveness by David L. Smith

Television Production Handbook, 4th, by Herbert Zettl

Electronic Moviemaking by Lynne S. Gross and Larry W. Ward

Audio in Media, 3rd, by Stanley R. Alten

Directing Television and Film, 2nd, by Alan A. Armer

Sight-Sound-Motion: Applied Media Aesthetics, 2nd, by Herbert Zettl

Electronic Cinematography: Achieving Photographic Control over the Video Image by Harry Mathias and Richard Patterson

VIDEO COMMUNICATION

Structuring Content for Maximum Program Effectiveness

David L. Smith

Xavier University

Wadsworth Publishing Company
Belmont, California
A Division of Wadsworth, Inc.

To my wife, Linda, and daughter, Jennifer

Senior Editor: Rebecca Hayden
Editorial Assistant: Sharon Yablon
Production Editor: Sandra Craig
Managing Designers: James Chadwick / Cynthia Schultz
Print Buyer: Karen Hunt
Art Editor: Marta Kongsle
Permissions Editor: Bob Kauser
Designer: Peter Martin
Copy Editor: Janet Brown
Compositor: G & S Typesetters
Cover: Peter Martin
Signing Representative: Steve Simmons

Printed in the United States of America   19

1 2 3 4 5 6 7 8 9 10—95 94 93 92 91

Library of Congress Cataloging in Publication Data

Smith, David L. (David Lee), 1941–
    Video communication : structuring content for maximum program effectiveness /
    David L. Smith.
        p.   cm.
    Includes bibliographical references and index.
    ISBN 0-534-13146-8
    1. Video recordings—Production and direction.   I. Title.
PN1992.94.S6   1990
791.45'0232—dc20   90-44444
                                                                              CIP

About the Author

· ·

David L. Smith is professor of communication at Xavier University
in Cincinnati. Since joining the faculty in 1981, he has served as
director of the Television Center, which is both a teaching and production facility. He teaches courses in program design and development, television directing, lighting, and advanced production.

Formerly he was production manager for WNEO/WEAO, the
public television station at Kent State University. He was a pro-
ducer for WKRC-TV (Taft Broadcasting Company—now Great
American Broadcasting), where he also did assignments for ABC-
TV, including *Wide World of Sports* features. For WCPO-TV
(Scripps-Howard Broadcasting) he served as cinematographer, pro-
ducing commercials, documentaries, and corporate presentations.
Prior to that, he served as director-cinematographer for K&S Films
Incorporated in Cincinnati.

He received a degree in photography from the Rochester Institute of Technology. At the University of Cincinnati he completed a
degree in broadcasting, followed by a master's degree in communication with an emphasis in anthropology.

Mr. Smith has produced more than 500 television commercials,
dozens of broadcast documentaries, profiles, and feature stories,
children's programs, public affairs series, corporate image and training tapes, dramas, comedies, and a variety of "talk" formats. He
was awarded an Emmy (cinematography) for *The Eyes Have It,* a
documentary about blindness. He has also received awards from
the Chicago Film Festival, the American Advertising Association,
and Action for Children's Television (ACT). In addition to various
organizational and corporate grants, he was awarded a program development grant from the National Endowment for the Humanities.

He cofounded the World Good News Network with futurist/
author Barbara Marx Hubbard and served for several years on the
board of the Association for Responsible Communication. His focus
is on the fostering of excellence and innovation in the development
of socially responsible programming.

Contents in Brief

Contents

· ·

PART **III**

Designing Program Content   168

Chapter 8   Developing Program Content   193

PART **V**   **Making It Good**   266

· ·

Preface

· ·

One of television's pioneers, David Sarnoff, commented that television's technology had far outdistanced our capacity to use it. With the proliferation of portable video equipment in the last decade or two, and with increased access to production technologies, more and more people are turning to video to communicate. Unfortunately, many of their efforts fail, largely because they may know a lot about equipment but very little about how to communicate.

Video Communication is for people who want to design, develop, and produce quality media programs, in particular for video and television. Students and public access producers, beginners and professionals—all who want to complement their equipment operation proficiency with effective communication skills—will find this book helpful.

To tie effective communication and skillful use of the technology together, video producers need to apply substantive attention to the organization of ideas and issues; critical thinking to promote good decision making; expanded perception to encompass a broader view of the subject matter; and thorough analysis of one's audience to develop content that's relevant and expressive. In every phase of a project, it's the marriage of quality thinking and quality use of the technology that leads to effective programs.

Approach

This work represents a synthesis of my own studies, professional experience, and observation of other professionals producing television and video programming. As a producer, I want to make meaningful, entertaining programs that have a measurable effect on audiences. In my work with experienced producers and directors over the years, I've encountered various theories and gained insights that help explain the success or failure of certain techniques. I have adopted those that work and dropped those that don't, and I continue to experiment. This practical experience is at the root of the book.

As an academic, my inquiry centers on the anthropology of communication, especially visual communication. My passion is to understand the way people effectively communicate their attitudes, values, feelings, and beliefs through the media. How are these elements communicated visually? How can a producer achieve maximum message impact with a particular audience? What symbolic or literal, overt or subtle cues operate in media communication? The search for answers to these questions, I believe, helps artist-producers working in a visual medium to increase the quality and impact of their work.

My goal for this book was to blend my professional practice and theoretical understanding into a unified approach. Not only is such an integrated perspective new, but in my opinion it's the most effective method for approaching video communication. Although I have attempted to be analytical and objective in the presentation of material, my conclusions are often subjective. My purpose is not to demonstrate that a theory or technique is correct but to stimulate and empower producers to realize their own visions. Test the ideas and accept only what works for you.

Organization of This Book

For the most part, the subjects covered in the book are not steps along a particular production path. Rather, the six parts of *Video Communication* are arranged sequentially as they relate to program *content*—not production. This is not a production book; it is a communication book!

Part I, "Setting the Stage," looks at the overall subject matter and approach. Part II, "Planning the Project," focuses on video as a communication medium and presents a method for project planning. Part III, "Designing Program Content," and Part IV, "Making It Work," are concerned with planning program content for effectiveness. Part V, "Making It Good," addresses production values and quality. Part VI, "Doing It Right," discusses ethical issues that affect media communication and decision making. In addition, the appendixes provide examples of selected production documents and forms and discuss in more detail the VALS 2 typology and the Prizm Cluster Model. A glossary offers brief definitions of important video terms for quick reference.

Using This Book

Don't expect to use *Video Communication* as you would a cookbook, combining specific ingredients and following the recipe through a sequence of acts and techniques to create a program. Video is an eclectic, malleable medium and every project is unique.

Instead, use the book to stimulate your own ideas and innovations and as a reference work to help you answer questions and solve problems as you create programs. Read with a highlighter in hand to mark ideas for quick reference or later consideration. Think about where to apply what you're reading. Then, each time you develop a new project, refer to Chapter 6, "Planning the Project," and let it guide you to other sections as appropriate.

Acknowledgments

First I want to thank my students, especially those with a sincere enthusiasm for video. Their creativity, hard work, and search for greater effectiveness showed me that this kind of book was needed. I also want to express gratitude to my teachers at the Rochester Institute of Technology—including Charles Arnold, William Shoemaker, Minor White, Hollis Todd, and Richard Zakia—and at the University of Cincinnati—Michael Porte and Roger Fransecky. Thanks also to my professional friends and colleagues in broadcasting: Bernie Bordon, Marty Ducheny, Jim Ellis, David George, Bob Gerding, Judy Zarick, Patrick Griffin, John and Dan Guntzelman, Jack Robertson, and Oscar and Mindy Welsh.

Special thanks to Sandy Cole and Lolly DuMont, who provided clerical support; Tim Broering, Jeff Feld, and Gary Templeton for their general assistance; Tom Cooper, Barbara Coffman, Alan Hammond, Stan Grindstaff, Beatrice Bruteau, Dee and Mike Lococo, Jim Somerville, Barbara Marx Hubbard, Irvin Laszlo, and Beaumont Newhall for their inspiration; and Xavier University for providing its resources. I owe special thanks to my wife, Linda, who was the first to edit the manuscript.

Thanks are due also to those who made a contribution to the work in other ways: Bunny Arszman, Tom Hayward, Julie Smith, Michael Hagen, Kathy Henry, Patrice Wilson, Paula Price, Charles Carey, and Reverend Gordon Hall, Jr.

To the reviewers of the manuscript I owe a great debt of gratitude. Their comments have been a substantial contribution toward refining the work. I offer my special thanks to: Ira R. Abrams, University of Texas, Austin; Stan Denski, Indiana University, Indianapolis; William H. Lloyd, Clarion University; Robert G. Main, California State University, Chico; Robert Musburger, University of Houston; and Val Sakovich, San Francisco State University.

Thanks also to the Wadsworth staff for their care and attention during the production process.

David L. Smith

VIDEO COMMUNICATION

PART I

SETTING THE STAGE

S tarting a new project is always exciting. The idea is fresh and enthusiasm is high. Likewise, we love to complete a project, especially when it "works." But it's what happens between these two points that really matters. Program effectiveness and production quality come not from visions of glory or the thrill of accomplishment but from a disciplined enthusiasm for, and focus on, every detail of the process. If you maintain a **process** (rather than goal) orientation and perform each part with an eye toward excellence, you will contribute to the quality of the whole.

In a video or television project, the challenges can be enormous, given the complexities involved. The process is so complex, in fact, that we need both an overall framework for understanding the process and tracking systems to monitor every detail and ensure that each is handled competently

and at the right time. This requirement applies to what goes into the program (message and content), how the message is expressed (creativity), the people who do the work (production team), where and when production occurs (location and time frame), and the technologies (equipment and facilities) that are used. Each of these areas contains its own complexity, but, more to the point, all of them are interrelated into a totality—a video project.

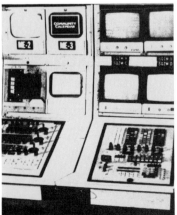

By far the more important and challenging aspect of producing a program is communication. Marty Shelton put it this way in a recent issue of *Corporate Video Decisions* magazine:

> *What counts is* communication. *Are the client's messages communicated to the target audiences? And communication means the target audience receives the message. Understands it. Accepts it. Assimilates it in the context of their perceptions. And, most important, the audience does, says, acts or thinks as the client wishes to accomplish the goals set for the audiovisual. It's imperative that we always keep to the fore that we are in the communication profession rather than the video, film or whatever medium profession.*[1]

A program fails if it doesn't communicate—no matter how interesting the material, exciting the presentation, or large the budget. To help us ensure that our planning and practice is effective, we'll build on a foundation of some relevant communication theories because they can help us to better understand how communication works. We'll also look into systems theories, which provide a framework for ensuring that a production unfolds efficiently.

In Part I we'll examine these *theoretical perspectives*. Then we'll walk through the *production process* to get an overview of what's involved in a video project. This walk-through will also underscore the importance of a process orientation. And, finally, because every video production relies on subject matter (program content), we'll take note of our starting point— a personal inventory of who we are and what we know in relation to our program content. I refer to these insights as *consciousness*. We can't properly map the way to a destination without knowing the starting point.

These three areas, theoretical perspectives, the production process, and consciousness, set the stage for the rest of the book. Their integration in mind and practice are the necessary foundation for the efficient production of effective video programs.

CHAPTER 1

Theoretical Perspectives

· ·

The most neglected art in the world is communication.

—*Norman Cousins*

had been working as a commercial producer in a television station for a year before I got my first opportunity to create a whole program on my own. A priest who was a friend of mine had been awarded a small grant from his archbishop to produce a program for use in high school classrooms to promote discussion on human values. He asked if I could produce the program with his assistance on weekends as a private venture. With visions of "making a difference" (and possibly winning awards), my wife, Linda, and I developed the program concept and an outline over dinner one night. They quickly approved the idea, and shortly after I completed a script for a thirty-minute morality play that we called *The Tender Clay.*

Our leading man was on a journey through the forest (life's path) and along the way he encountered individuals who represented a variety of values: money, power, sex, food, knowledge, and so on. The hero is finally assaulted by a motley bunch of "antiestablish-ment" types who try to prevent him from continuing his journey. He is mortally wounded (death is a part of life), and the film ends in the rain with a hooded figure who picks him up and walks away from the camera. As a butterfly (symbol for metamorphosis) comes into the shot, the frame freezes. We used no voices or narration, just music, because we wanted to keep the symbols "open" to interpretation.

Although the concept was fine, what we did with it was disastrous! Audiences who viewed the program were confused from the start. Where was the protagonist going? Why? Who was he? What was happening? Where did he come from? What was the time period? Where is this forest? Why is he alone? The imagery and camera movement were beautiful, but we even failed to communicate that the piece was intended to be symbolic. Viewers grew restless right away. "How come we couldn't hear the voices?" "Why such strange music [originally written and recorded]?" We were so close to the concept, so delighted by the opportunity, and so absorbed in the symbolism that we didn't anticipate these responses. We forgot—no, we weren't aware of—the necessity to provide the essential contextual and content cues necessary for the audience to understand what was happening.

Our production problems were equally disastrous. The entire program took place in a forest, but why I chose such a dense one (trees blocked the light all the time) and a site so remote (sixty-five miles round-trip) is beyond my comprehension now. We worked every weekend for an entire summer, carrying very heavy equipment and props down a half-mile ravine and then up again each time, in difficult terrain. Considering the light, the weather (we couldn't shoot when it rained), the trek, the extensive (and heavy) props and costumes, not to mention the equipment, including portable lights, large reflectors, and food for the five to eight members of the team, it was a miracle that we accomplished anything.

Aside from these logistical problems, we faced constant equipment problems: batteries not fully charged; essential pieces of equipment left behind, which caused delays; dampness effects; broken tripod parts, which caused me to fall into four feet of water—fortunately, I held the camera high enough that it didn't get wet— and that's how it went week after agonizing week!

What we have to show for it is a thirty-minute, beautiful but boring program that sits on the shelf. Maybe a hundred people have seen it at the most. While the client and production team loved the concept at the time, we had overlooked essential steps both in our thinking and in our performance. Most of all, we forgot who we were communicating to.

Communication—that's what video is all about, whether the format is entertainment, documentary, event coverage, news, training, or drama. For this reason, much of this book deals with communication, its theories and especially its implications, and techniques for producing a high-quality program. Effective program production first requires effective thinking and communication.

In the situation just described, effectiveness and efficiency broke down as a result of inadequate planning communication, and systematic organization. There was no communication about who the audience was, much less what they would respond to. There was miscommunication about the equipment that would be needed and when. We spent more time discussing whose diet required special consideration at lunchtime than audience cues. We wasted at least an hour of every working day on lugging equipment to and from the location. We just didn't have enough experience to know better. Had we understood some basic communication principles, and had we taken the time to think and plan systematically, these breakdowns would not have occurred. *Communication* and *systematic thinking* then are absolutely necessary if a production is to be both effective and efficient.

Communication Theories

Although a number of communication theories exist, most fit into two primary orientations, which are represented by the post office model and the transactional process model. Both have relevance for media production.

Post Office Model

The "post office" model treats communication as a commodity to be sent back and forth. A message originates with a sender, who passes it through a medium to a receiver, who in turn offers feedback. I send, you receive. Then you send, and I receive. The interaction goes back and forth. The process could be diagrammed by connecting the participants with straight lines to show the direction of information flow.

This model views a message as something that is sent from a source to a receiver, much as we send a letter to a friend. Theories based on this model, also referred to as "transportation" theories, seem to give greater power to the source (producer) by putting him or her at the beginning of the equation: source, message, medium, receiver, feedback. In media production, this perspective too often results in the source (producer) operating under the mistaken impression that he or she has more power in the process than is actually the case. In a model in which communication is viewed as something that is sent, it's easy to see how the sender can become the center of every transaction. For instance, many talk-show hosts focus attention on themselves rather than on those they interview because they view themselves as the source, the person with something to say or something to offer the audience. But this perception may be inaccurate. Do people watch Phil Donahue because they want to know what Phil thinks about the issues he presents? Does the Johnny Carson *Tonight Show* audience show up to see his guests or him?

Television broadcasts at first glance seem to be very one-way. Producers put forth their progamming messages with the attitude that the audience is there to receive them passively. "I send. You receive. And if you don't like what I send, you'll likely call the station to complain. That's one way we'll learn what you (the receiver) want. And perhaps your response will be factored into our future programming plans." Maybe, maybe not. What if the receiver doesn't pay attention to the program or decides not to accept the message? Are the viewers actually receiving if their minds are closed to the message? Does communication still occur? Of course it does, because more is going on than simply linear exchanges of information, which leads us to another category of communication theories.

Transactional Process Model

Theories based on the transactional process model view communication as a process in which participants are involved in complex negotiations of meaning. The message, sender, medium, receiver, and feedback are continuously interacting to arrive at meanings that fulfill the objectives of sender and receiver. This model cannot be diagrammed easily because the process is more a "field," or complex of interacting forces, rather than a flow of information from point to point.

Although it was perhaps relevant and influential in the past, the post office model has been largely replaced by these transactional process theories, which give equal weight to sender and receiver. James Carey, in his article "Communication and Culture," cites the transactional process perspective as a "ritual" where communication is "not directed toward the extension of messages in space, but the maintenance of society in time; not the act of imparting information, but the representation of shared beliefs."[1] Communication then becomes a matter of mutual interaction, with participants sharing responsibility for what happens. In transactional theories, the rigid roles of sender and receiver collapse. The *active* character of the media audience is stressed, and the role of the audience (as receivers) is regarded as complex and interdependent.

Television and video are not simply one-way processes, as they appear. Viewers (audiences) participate in the communication because they already have cognitive perspectives, feelings, and preferences that are actively perceiving, selecting, and rejecting information as they watch. The communication is not "in" the messages sent but "among" the people involved. So communication occurs as long as the TV set is on and someone is present. (This is not to say that the participants agree about what is communicated or even like the communication.)

If television and video programming is a field of cognitive and emotional interaction rather than a series of messages for the viewer to observe, the producer's perspective changes. Instead of seeing and treating communication as information to be provided, we as producers begin to see it as a vibrant exchange among the participants—the design and creative team, the audience, the delivery system, and even those who promote the program. Like ecological chains that bind animals together in the same natural environment, we in our communication environment are bound in a field of interactive forces.

Most of the time we are unaware of this interaction. However, you may have noticed occasionally that as you were speaking to someone, you began to alter your message and presentation, depending on the listener's body language, facial expression, and attention. How listeners respond to you makes a difference as you continue to speak. If they are rejecting your message, for instance, you may soften your tone or potential content differences to maintain the relationship or the congenial atmosphere. Many actors prefer performing on the stage to performing in front of a camera because they can sense the audience's responses better and modify their performance accordingly.

To indicate how responsive the communication field is in media, often neither the speaker nor the listener has to speak or consciously send a message to influence the communication. Sender and receiver need merely to be present and sensitive to each other. For example, no dialogue is necessary for a love scene to convey powerful emotions. In fact, some of the most communicative moments on the screen are simply facial expressions or other bodily reactions—the quick glance, the long penetrating stare, or the abrupt turn. As every experienced drama writer knows, behavior and action speak much louder than words, especially on the screen. It takes some discipline, but you can look at any element (person) who is part of a communication field (the person who designed the set, the lighting director, the production assistant) and see his or her influence in the expression, whether in a video or in any other media event.

The orientation of this book then is toward the transactional process perspective because, in my experience, at every level of content design and expression, it works. Also, transactional process theories fit beautifully into the systems framework (to be discussed next) because they focus on relationship and interaction rather than on separate and isolated events. Communication never happens in isolation.

Nor do effective program content and efficient production occur accidentally. They result when members of the production team understand the significance and relationship of each participating element and ensure that each is well organized, informed, and handled according to its needs. In fact, one of the best ways to tell if communication is effective, whatever the medium, is to see whether or not the goal of the participants has been realized. If the participants have found meaning, communication has occurred. As we go along, you'll begin to see that meaning is central to, if not the motivation for, most communication. Aside from *communication, meaning* may be the most important word for the producer who values effectiveness.

Once we understand that effectiveness comes from communication, we need to develop a way of thinking and performing that efficiently encourages communication in the context of a production. This is where systems theories can be a tremendous asset.

Systems Approach

Communication is the broadest context of our subject matter. Within it we need to view a media project in such a way that the complexities of message, audience, medium, and production become manageable. Without such a framework, our effort would be chaotic and destined to fail. In my experience, both as a producer and as a teacher, *general systems theory* can bring order and efficiency to a project by illuminating the relationship of the parts to the whole.

System

A **system** is an interactive, interdependent group of elements that form a unified whole that has a purpose. A wristwatch is a system designed to tell time. An automobile is a system designed to transport human beings. Your body is a system designed for life experience. The equipment used on a remote shoot can, taken together, constitute a *technical* system designed to produce images and sounds on tape or film.

Each individual piece of equipment, such as the camera and **video tape recorder** (VTR), is a system in itself and a *subsystem* of the total production system. The parts that make up a subsystem are referred to as *elements.* For instance, a camera (as a system) contains these elements: viewfinder, lens, battery, pickup tube (or electronic chip if it's a **CCD,** or charge-coupled device, model), and so on. If we took the camera completely apart and laid out every piece on the floor, we could refer to each part as an element. As isolated parts, they are functionally inert. Put them together according to a specific design and they become a system capable of a purpose—generating pictures. So a camera can be conceived of and referred to as a "system," a "subsystem," or an "element," depending on the context. The point of reference for all systems is the functional whole that has no apparent higher role to play as a part in any other system.

All the people involved in a video project, taken collectively, constitute the production's *social system.* Each member of the team is an element. Typically, there are several subsystems within each social system made up of people with the same function. These might be the members of a camera crew, writers, engineers, or actors ("talent").

Another system of prime importance to our topic is the **content system.** This term refers to the specific ideas, information, and other elements that carry the program's subject matter, including its expression, within a format. By thinking about programs as a whole, the producer gains a perspective of the end product that shows how the parts (content) should be organized and presented to lead to the desired communication result (the system's purpose).

The Tender Clay failed partly because the content system was out of sync with the program's intended audience. It didn't offer ways for the audience to relate to the main character. The lack of a voice track, instead of being a device to hold attention, became an obstacle to acquiring meaning; an emphasis on looking "creative" diffused the power of the message. And the symbolism, although obvious to the producers, was obscured by our not communicating that the audience was supposed to be looking for symbols. These and other elements of the content system—which seemed like good ideas at the time—were based on ignorance and erroneous thinking. The content system's purpose, although we were unaware of it, was to appeal to the producers rather than to the program's target audience—a mistake of the first order. Had we thought more about who our audience was and what they would respond to, the content would have worked. We had overlooked a major element of the content system.

The producer's challenge is to handle myriad personal, social, technological, and creative elements so that everything happens as it should, on time, and in a qualitative manner. It's a big job to ensure that proper planning and preparation take place There are just too many details to rely on memory or instinct alone. And, when you're surrounded by people needing your focused attention, the problems can quickly become compounded.

The beauty of the systems approach as a way of perceiving and acting is that it can be applied to any medium and any size project. The initial requirement is to understand *all* the elements that make up each subsystem, and then to make sure each is addressed to maximize its function and relationship to all the other parts of the program. Once that is done, the system then requires management to keep it functioning optimally.

System thinking thus provides an efficient and secure means of designing, planning, and implementing a project. By viewing the program (whole) as the result of the interaction of scenes, which in turn depend on a variety of elements (lighting, props, background, talent), it is much easier to design and manage each step of the complex production process. When you know all the parts, you can more easily make sure that each one receives the attention it needs. And, when you know the parts are fully functioning, you can be confident that the product will be what you intended.

The price you pay for these benefits is, of course, being organized. Complex systems require management, which requires organization. The more complex the system, the more organization will be needed to manage it effectively. If you're not normally an "organized" person, don't worry—the systems approach imposes its own discipline. It requires that you (as the producer) identify all the parts while maintaining the vision of the whole. Naturally, without responsible follow-through the entire exercise is wasted. Daily organization and management of the smallest details get the job done well.

The Trial-and-Error Alternative

The "trial-and-error" method is a different approach from systems thinking. Instead of seeing elements as interrelated, the producer treats them as isolated incidents or problems to be solved, usually sequentially. You try something. If it works, fine; if not, you try something else. Because its strength is in helping a person attend closely to a single element at a time, the trial-and-error method is most often applied to equipment troubleshooting rather than to social or creative situations.

The weakness of this approach is that, in situations where the elements are highly interdependent, chaos and time loss occur. For instance, you get all your equipment together for a shoot, trying to remember everything. Then, out on location, you find you forgot the power cord to the camera a/c power supply and you don't have a battery. The error requires a trip back to the studio. A systems approach prevents such occurrences because you develop an equipment checklist in your mind by seeing every element in relation to the others. You can't set aside the camera power supply without thinking about the power cord as well. Whether the element is people, equipment, or subject matter (program content), or how content is expressed, a systems approach saves time and money because energy is not wasted on elements or actions that turn out to be useless.

Systems Management

. . . .

The key to managing the design, planning, and production of a program is *attention to detail*. Each individual element of every subsystem requires focused attention, and no element is too small to be regarded as unimportant. A good producer never assumes that details will take care of themselves. They don't! It is through meticulous attention to the smallest elements that great works are produced. However, it can take years of experience to reach this conclusion because our tendency is often toward the path of least resistance.

Something going wrong with a piece of equipment should be a signal that the elements involved require even more attention. The way to fix a flat tire is not to kick it, blame the tire, or look for help but to move into thoughtful action, attending closely to the tools and process of replacing the tire. If an element still doesn't work, then it means you're not attending to it closely enough, or properly, or both.

Each element of a system, at every level, has its own **integrity;** it fits appropriately with the other elements. When any element cannot fulfill its function—because it is missing or broken, for example—then the next level of the system is just that strong—or weak. For instance, beginning camera operators often forget an essential part—a tripod base plate, the bolt for the base plate, or whatever—and have to return to the studio, thereby holding up production. On one out-of-town shoot, the camera person forgot to bring the raw film stock, and it took an entire Saturday to repurchase the 400-foot rolls of film.

As I mentioned earlier, one substantial payoff of systems thinking is that a person develops a detailed, accurate mental checklist. When you see the elements as part of a system, you can quickly develop this checklist and integrate it into your professional life-style.

People make mistakes for a reason—they don't know something, they don't think about it, or they don't follow instructions—or a combination of these. The trick is to keep mistakes to a minimum, which requires *listening, learning,* and *thinking.*

Paradoxically, during a production, directors will often inform interns or production assistants that they have to make all the "right" mistakes. And this is true because, until a person has encountered specific problems and breakdowns, that person will not focus attention on them. When mistakes are made, learning occurs, and the likelihood is greater that, during the next production, each of those details will be checked and double-checked. Mistakes are bad only when they don't result in learning. And hiding mistakes is even worse. Everyone in this business knows that a learning curve is involved, so beginners should never be afraid to admit they don't know something or that they broke something. Better to err on the side of more and honest communication than on the opposite side.

Attention to detail is critical and takes constant discipline. It's the only way that Murphy's Law (if anything can go wrong, it will) can be overcome. As you learn to see a program and its production as a whole and develop a feeling for all the parts and how they relate, the process will become easier for you; you will use time more productively; and there will be less headache and confusion among those involved. When you attend to the battery charge, give a courtesy call to the talent the night before a shoot, or run through the spelling of the TelePrompTer script before the shoot, you are, in essence, ensuring that at the most fundamental level the system will work. Then, when the production moves to the next level—for example, a shooting session—every element will function as it should, and the success will be compounded.

Attention to detail, as the key to managing systems, applies equally to all three subsystems of a program: technologies, personnel, and program content. To produce effective programs, you must understand and manage all three subsystems. Each of these subsystems of program production is an area of study that can, and should, go far beyond this book. Effective producers are always searching for greater understanding of and appreciation for the fields of technology, psychology, interpersonal communication, sociology, anthropology, rhetoric, and drama as they relate to communication, media, and advertising. Knowledge and experience in these areas give a producer a substantial competitive edge (read: effectiveness, fulfillment, power, money, jobs).

Characteristics of Systems

. . . .

Systems scientists and theorists are most often found in fields involving computers, business management, engineering, or the "hard" sciences. Each field has built on earlier, more fundamental assumptions, thereby interpreting relationships between part and whole in ways unique to its own discipline. Media production is no exception. If you were to research thoroughly the underlying assumptions of general systems theory, the physics and math could be intimidating, to say the least. And there are critics of the systems approach. But I haven't found an alternative framework that even comes close to being as effective in practical terms. So let's look now at some of the theories within systems thinking that have particular relevance for the media producer.

Entropy

The scientific definition of **entropy** relates to the **second law of thermodynamics** and is overly technical for our consideration. However, in the field of information theory (computer science, cybernetics, communication), the term is more practically used to designate the capacity of elements to undergo spontaneous change that leads to disorder and chaos. In essence, things break or things die, and their raw material is recycled back into the ecosystem (the earth). This applies to all matter without exception. Entropy may even turn out to be the cause of Murphy's Law. Yet entropy is no cause for discouragement or despair. It can be overcome.

Neg-entropy (the opposite of entropy) refers to acts that create order and organization. Brushing your teeth, for instance, overcomes the entropic tendency for gums to deteriorate. Oiling metal surfaces and joints keeps them from rusting. Maintaining a video recorder keeps the parts in good working order. So, although it's normal for equipment to break down, it's also possible to keep it functioning by performing those neg-entropic acts that lead to optimal performance.

Order is the operative word when it comes to managing entropy because, by definition, it's the opposite force. As we bring order, and thereby organization, into any system, we increase the system's ability to continue functioning. This rule applies to "hard" systems (such as a camera, an amplifier, or an edit controller) and to "soft" systems (communication, personal relationships) as well. Caring for the sick, a positive mental attitude, punctuality, and cooperation are examples of neg-entropy in soft systems. The video producer needs to understand that, if they are left alone, both human beings and equipment will tend not to work very well, and the only way to overcome this tendency is to design into the production process thinking and acting that promote order (organization).

Five to ten million years of human evolution provide us with outstanding evidence that, in spite of entropy, life still "works," even thrives, on this planet. This net gain over entropy should provide us both with confidence that equipment and people can be (and are) effective and with an important lesson in how the greater system works—through organization and cooperation.

Simplistically, one difference between a video engineer and a producer is that, when equipment breaks down, the engineer assumes it to be a normal occurrence—entropy is having its way—that requires more attention to its parts, but the producer sees the breakdown as a problem that should never have happened. Which perspective is potentially more productive? The former, because once we understand that it's the natural tendency of equipment to break down or of people to get hungry or tired, it's easier to maintain an attitude of composure when these events interrupt our production. Breakdown is a fact of video life, but one that can be managed when it's understood as a systems challenge. The solution is to see every element's relation to the whole, recognize all the parts of each subsystem, focus attention on each element at the appropriate time to ensure its proper functioning, and emphasize solutions that contribute to increased order (organization).

Feedback

All dynamic systems require **feedback** to continue functioning. In other words, a system needs information about its performance to adjust to changing circumstances—just as we shift the focus of an interview toward the interviewee's individual experience.

Feedback can be positive or negative. The pathway along which information flows is referred to as a "feedback loop." These loops amplify or depress the dynamics of a system, depending on whether the information is negative or positive. Negative loops inform the system that it's moving too fast or too slow, doing too much or too little, going too far or not far enough, exceeding a limit of tolerance. In contrast, positive loops inform the system that its current level of activity is "OK," operative within the tolerance limits.

Often, beginning camera persons spend a great deal of time and energy on a shoot without playing back the tapes they recorded on location. This is a big mistake, because they're not taking advantage of a feedback loop to tell whether or not the scene has in fact been recorded or that it works as it should. So it is highly advisable to get into the habit of playing back at least a portion of every scene immediately after recording it. It's much more efficient to reshoot while the equipment (system) is set up than to reschedule another shoot. Likewise, every time you duplicate a tape, you should check the beginning, middle, and end to make sure the recording is right before delivering it to a client or customer.

Feedback is not merely a means of determining that the equipment works. It's equally important to invite human feedback as part of the production process, from team members—"How's it going?"—and especially from the client or members of the target audience. Advertisers, as standard operating procedure, conduct **focus**

group sessions so a new product or service can be sampled by representatives of the target audience before it's distributed. It would be highly wasteful for a manufacturer to go into production on a new product based only on the opinion of the product designers. The entire procedure of market testing is, in essence, a feedback loop, which ensures that, when the product is distributed, customers will buy it. In this way, businesses use feedback to reduce financial risk.

Media producers do the same. When a program is produced, we need to know ahead of time that it will work and that it will actually be used. Work done for a client should never be kept a secret to be unveiled when the production is complete. That's asking for trouble. For this reason, commercial production companies use a step-by-step procedure that allows the client to become part of the process by periodically reviewing completed program elements. Sometimes the client even "signs off" on these elements so the production house is no longer responsible if changes occur later. The continuous application of feedback assures the producer that the work is acceptable. And, if not, it's easier to do something about it in the production stage than when the piece is completed.

Finally, feedback should be part of the development of content as well. The producer or writer or both should invite content resource people to check the accuracy of the facts and their expression. The outline, treatment, and script should be reviewed by those in a position to provide constructive criticism.

Naturally, we get nervous about how well we have performed, but that should never inhibit us from seeking feedback. The more feedback loops involved, the more control we will have and, therefore, the more order that can be put into the system. Feedback—the more the better—increasingly ensures effectiveness.

Quality In–Quality Out

Computer professionals use the term *garbage in–garbage out* to indicate that the information available from any computer system depends on the quality of the information put into the computer. If the data is garbage, that's what's available. If the information is good, then the opposite prevails: *quality in–quality out.*

This idea is based on the systems principle, more formally known as the principle of **equifinality.** It states that "the final state [of a system as a whole—a program, for instance] is unequivocally determined by the initial conditions. . . . If either the initial conditions or the process is altered, the final state will also be changed."[2] Simply put, this means that every decision I make (or do not make) influences the end product. Although *equifinality* is not a term likely to come up at the next production meeting, there is nevertheless a tremendous lesson in this principle as it applies to the production of a video program, beyond the idea that input equals available output.

Each semester I review several music videos that students produce in their video production and technology class. As we screen and discuss their projects, I have them compare the final video with what they originally envisioned. The principle of equifinality pops up every time. Invariably students give reasons why the entire video or a particular scene is different from what was intended—for example, "I didn't have the right color gel for the lights"; "I wanted a beautiful sunset but it didn't happen that day"; "the scene didn't run long enough so I did a series of repeat edits"; "I asked the talent to wear a tie and he showed up in a T-shirt"; "we tried to simulate a dolly shot with a shopping cart and it didn't quite work"; "we forgot to white-balance." These circumstances occurred because some element deviated from the plan. And, as a consequence, the end product was different from what was expected.

Sometimes—often, in fact—happy accidents occur, and for those we are grateful because the piece is enhanced. But it is critically important to realize that the details that altered the initial conditions during the production process were precisely those points of dysfunctionality or alteration that *we let happen*. When we let something happen (instead of what we wanted, saw, hoped for, or expected), that's a decision that changes the outcome and, therefore, the program. Beginners often make these decisions easily and quickly—usually because of expediency. But it's precisely during these points in time that the quality and effectiveness of a video break down. And don't forget: *Not to decide is a decision.*

When I don't clean off the lens smudge, I'm deciding in favor of reduced sharpness in that area. When I let the actors read lines their way because they're making a fuss about where the emphasis should be, the result of that decision is what the audience will hear. When, as editor, I select a scene that has unintentional camera movement—rather than taking the time to reshoot or reedit—I send a subtle but significant message to my audience.

The principle of equifinality tells us that, if we change *any* element in the system—no matter how small it may seem—the outcome will be changed. It has to be changed. And the extent to which this factor operates is amazing. "Quality in–quality out" implies that, for the program to be effective, the work that goes into the production must be top quality. Every element of the system must be well managed. We're faced with so many choices that we sometimes forget (or don't care) that every decision counts.

Equifinality suggests that what we *allow* has equal weight with what we purposefully select. It's relatively easy to choose elements, but it's a much greater challenge to change situations that don't add to the quality of the program. All too often, expediency, cost, timing, personalities, and even the weather put pressure on us to let the program be less than we envision. In each instance, the choice is not mundane because, whichever way you go, that's what will show up on the screen. Entropy operates constantly within all physical systems, so each time you face a decision, choose a direction that overcomes entropy. I admit that it's not always easy, but you should consider the decision alongside what's at stake in program effectiveness.

Often in small productions, where there is sometimes little concern for or interest in the subject matter, where the project is being done just to get a grade, or where the budget is insufficient or absent, producers seem more apt to make expedient decisions. On the other hand, we see the quality of expression that the major network producers achieve and wonder how they do it. How do they consistently bring in high-quality programs? It's easy to attribute their success to money. Certainly that's a consideration, but, more important, there is a producer behind each production who did not settle for light that wasn't right—who didn't make do for any reason. If the script, design, or vision specified a pink elephant, she would not make do with an orange one simply because it was more readily available or cheaper. If the choice came down to an actor's ego or better camera action, she'd choose the camera action.

So the final product (program) is a result of the sum total of the decisions made throughout the production process. It's up to each of us as producers to determine if and when the vision of the whole can be sacrificed for expediency. The systems approach warns us in advance that not only must equipment have integrity (work well) but so must those who make the decisions, small and large, creative and mundane, to change any element of the production. Become determined that *all* decisions will contribute to the quality and effectiveness of every element, and encourage everyone else on the team to do the same. This is the basis for a true and substantive commitment to quality.

The Social System

Video is a social medium. Its production usually involves more than one person and sometimes hundreds of people who must interact with one another. The production team, as a **social system,** constitutes fully half of the determinant of the quality of the result. The other half is how well the technological system is managed, which we'll look at later because, during a production, people concerns should always come first. People—not equipment or scripts—produce programs.

The Weakest Links

You have probably heard that a chain (whole system) is only as strong as its weakest link (element). This systems theory, applied to video, means a program is only as good as the performance of the people who work together to co-create it. If the crew is highly skilled and talented except for the character generator (CG) operator, then that is the link in the social chain where the program will likely break down. This is why, when industry executives are putting together production crews, they select the very best (competent, experienced, responsible, creative) people they can get. Only when each person on the team is able to perform effectively is the producer confident that the outcome of his or her creative effort will be the desired one. Strong systems are always, and only, a result of strong elements.

Strangely enough, we sometimes don't choose the best person for a particular function. We'll use a friend, or someone who needs a favor, or a person who's been bugging us for the experience, or someone who's great fun to have around. If you select crew based on these parameters, you should be aware of the systemic implications for the program. It's fine if you want to make compromises, but do so with a clear understanding of how they will affect the outcome.

The Strongest Links

When you select people to work on a production, look not only at their ability to operate equipment (competence) but also at their ability to interact effectively with others. It makes no sense to have a technical director who is an excellent operator of the production **switcher** but who tends not to listen to the director.

The producer who genuinely cares about the quality of his or her program puts personality, glamour, and even money second to the substantial decisions relating to the qualitative performance and contribution of each element. Everything and everyone is evaluated on the ability to maximize functioning excellence. That may sound cold, but the program has your name on it alongside the others' names, and all your reputations are on the line. More important, you want the program or series to be as good (effective) as it can be. That's what being responsible means, and sometimes we have to make hard and unpopular decisions to get there.

Select the best-qualified people you can find and put them in the positions where they can perform best. Camera persons need to have an aesthetic "eye"—already. That's not something a person can acquire in an hour or so. Audio technicians need to have a sensitive "ear"—for nuances, details, and noise. And a CG operator needs a sense of composition as well as the ability to spell.

Sometimes people can be trained to be effective operators. For instance, floor managing and VTR (video tape recorder) operation are relatively easy to teach to newcomers. But it would be unwise to invite into a crew a person who cannot communicate or behave professionally.

Attitude

Bad attitudes kill effective interaction as nothing else can. On professional projects, it is not uncommon for a person who is exhibiting a bad attitude to be dismissed summarily. Nothing effective can happen unless the social system involves people who can work together effectively.

We'll encounter the importance of attitude again, but, in the context of selecting people who will be involved in a project, this factor directly relates to the quality of the production. When people get along, their attitudes and interaction support the production effort. When they don't get along, the work can easily be undermined. People want to feel good when they work with others, whether their motive is personal, financial, or altruistic. In fact, part of the benefit of working on projects is that we enjoy the work. It's fun—or at least it should be. If it's not fun, then something is wrong in the social system, and each member of the team should be reevaluated.

When a car is sputtering, and we discover that the problem is a dirty carburetor, we have two choices: Fix it or replace it. The car (whole system) will not function effectively without a carburetor that works. This rule is also true in a production. The decision must be made to fix the attitude or other personal problem or to replace the individual. A producer who has program excellence clearly in mind as a system can more readily see the implications of each possible social decision and make the appropriate choices.

A friend of mine from high school developed a video sideline from nothing into a multimillion-dollar business. Whenever he dealt with a prospective client, his conversation would include brief anecdotes about how much fun he and his crew had had on previous shoots. And because his clients had a good time interacting with him, the quality of their work was better. Clearly, he was attracting clients on the basis of both their need for quality and their desire to have a good time. We all want to have a good time, but how many of us can incorporate it into our day-today work? People are intuitively attracted to a system that functions in a positive manner.

In the final analysis, it is people who, through their *cooperative interaction,* produce a video. By regarding the participants as elements of a greater whole, the producer can better structure, plan, and evaluate their contribution throughout the production process. Seeing people as elements is not as dehumanizing as it sounds—quite the opposite, in fact. The way to maximize cooperative interaction is by friendly, warm, personal dealings. I always try to make a friend first because I would prefer to end up working with my friends but also because these relationships go well beyond the function we perform for the production. The people we work with are the people who influence our lives. Seeing them as elements of a system is just a convenient device for remembering that our effort together is directed toward a common goal.

The Content System
. . . .

It may sound strange to refer to *program content* as a system given that it deals with ideas, images, sounds, and words—software, as opposed to the more tangible objects already described. Not only is the systems framework applicable to content; for me, it has also proven to be an invaluable way of seeing content relationships. This is because the program concepts, subject matter, and their expression also constitute subsystems of a whole body of content. A story has a beginning, middle, and end, with many other subsystems, including theme, plot, dialogue, conflict, and climax, to name a few. A commercial message also has elements: the hook, the pitch, the appeal, and the context. And a training program contains narration, interviews, testimonials, data, graphics, and so on. Every program is made up of content elements that require identification (What will be included in the program?), organization (What will be the order of its presentation?), and expression (How can it best be presented?). The effective management of the *content system* involves seeing how the elements relate to each other and to the total program. As stressed earlier, systems theory's greatest contribution to media production is the way it highlights and reveals relationships.

The Technical System
. . . .

Another subsystem of a production involves the equipment and facilities used. Again, the key to the effective management of the **technical system** is attention to detail. Professional photographers have developed a rule of thumb concerning their equipment, materials, and processes: The only way to know for sure that any element will work is to test it. This may sound elementary, but a person must exercise discipline and patience to make these tests each time he or she uses new materials or equipment. It's a lot easier to pull something off the shelf and hope it works. After years of experience with missing parts and unchecked systems, we realize that, in the long run, it's more cost-effective, less time-consuming, and much less frustrating to pretest each item.

If you expect to run into the studio, grab a camera and deck (VTR), and then run out to the location for a shoot, you can also expect that, on most occasions, something will malfunction. And, for unexplainable reasons, breakdowns always seem to happen at the most critical and embarrassing moments. Taking the time beforehand to set up the camera, make the appropriate connections, and test the system for audio and video signals is a time investment well worth making. When you test in advance, you learn in time if something is missing or broken.

The trial-and-error approach discussed earlier works exceptionally well for physical elements such as hardware. In fact, pretesting is the only way you can be fairly certain that the equipment will function when needed. Even with pretesting, breakdowns can occur. In the process of moving the equipment from the studio to the location, parts can be jiggled loose; temperature can change the alignment of camera tubes, resulting in misregistration; bulb filaments can break due to excessive vibration; and dust or smoke can damage tape heads in a video recorder. But if you test the equipment before taking it out, it is more likely to perform well.

As we saw earlier, the more complex the system, the more management, and, therefore, organization, is needed to keep equipment functioning properly. Look inside a video tape recorder or a camera. The complexity is boggling. A shoot using one camera and two crew members is less complex, as a system, than a shoot involving three or more cameras and a crew of eight. Some productions require a full-time video engineer to set up and operate the equipment, and others need little or no technical personnel. However, the fact that a shoot seems simple does not mean—ever—that you can skip pretesting.

We pretest and double-check equipment primarily to gain confidence that the system will operate when it needs to. There is a good reason why this is necessary, and it has to do with "nested" systems. The more subsystems there are in a system, the more complex the system is. Therefore, more organization and information is required to keep the subsystems working. In the example of the camera mentioned earlier, each subsystem has a unique function that is part of the original design of interactions that, when put together, result in a video image. All these elements come together as a result of an **organizing principle**—the original vision and intention of the design engineers who created the camera in the first place. Most of us who use that camera don't care about who designed it or the organizing principles involved, because our purpose is to make pictures. But if we're to manage this nested system so it does in fact make quality pictures consistently, it helps immensely if we understand something about how the elements are organized.

For instance, you take the camera out for a big shoot. You pretested before you left to ensure that the camera was working. It's Sunday and you're the only stringer covering the Super Bowl game for your local cable channel. The station wants its own talent on camera at the game (you and he were flown in just for this). It's two hours before the game; you're set up in a great spot; the light is perfect; the environment is exciting. You turn on the camera and discover the registration is way out of alignment. The image is unusable. What do you do if you don't know how to register the camera? Of course, you look for help or try to find another camera. Or you press every button on the camera, hoping it will magically correct the problem. Meanwhile, the clock ticks down to kickoff, and you're anxiously trying to fix the camera when your mind should be poised for the shoot. You will probably come away with bad pictures or none at all.

I heard about a situation in which a camera operator missed shooting an entire event. Later, back in the studio, he learned that the reason the camera "wasn't working" was that the brightness control knob on the viewfinder was turned completely down so no picture appeared in it. He didn't know that the camera was working perfectly except for this minor problem. He assumed the camera had died and thus lost the coverage of a onetime event.

These kinds of situations happen all the time. The only way to ensure they don't happen to you is to make sure you understand each subsystem with which you're dealing and how to adjust or otherwise troubleshoot its common problems. One of the best ways of doing this (without a degree in engineering) is to study. You should sit down and read, cover to cover, the operations manual for every piece of equipment you use. Learn the function of every part. When you take equipment into the field, *always* take the operation manual along. If you have access to a video engineer or someone with technical expertise, try to take advantage of their knowledge and have them show you how to manage these systems. You should be prepared for any kind of breakdown, because entropy (and Murphy's Law) never rests.

It's one thing to be able to operate a piece of equipment and quite another to understand it. It takes an hour or so to learn how to connect a camera and then operate it, but it takes a great deal of experience using the camera to understand it well enough to troubleshoot problems and quirks. You'll probably never forget to white-balance once you've seen the off-color results after an intensive and difficult shoot that has been negated because you didn't white-balance. I've seen people change careers because they were unable to cope with simple technical breakdowns. Even seasoned professionals sometimes marvel at how many occur when they are attempting the simplest of productions. The equipment is not at fault. It's just doing what comes naturally. The solution is to see the problems differently and take steps to ensure their management. Increased order, information, and pretesting make living with equipment quite comfortable.

When the content, social, and technical systems are well coordinated, marvelous things can happen. I worked for a few years as a cinematographer on a four-person team for an industrial motion picture production company. On one shoot we produced a documentary-style film showing the process of meat packing from the hoof to the market, plastic wrap and all. It was grueling work for a solid week of thirteen-hour days. It was cold and the odor of the packing house was terrible. There was blood all over the place, and we waded through running water constantly. It was a miracle that our power cords, wet and covered with animal fat, didn't cause an electrocution. This nightmarish experience was only made bearable by the fact that we performed as a precision team. Each member knew what to do and did it. There were entire setups with almost no verbal communication between us. The noise of the machinery forced us to yell when we did talk, so we were strongly motivated to use hand signals and body language. And although the physical environment was horrible, I remember most the exhilarating feeling of the high-level teamwork. We were a well-oiled (pun intended) production machine, and that feeling was so strong that it became part of the motivation for every project that followed. Once you've tasted a high-performance experience, you strive for it every time.

Summary

Media production is a highly complex endeavor involving the interaction of subject matter, people, and technologies. To ensure that this interaction is efficient and effective, a sound theoretical foundation is essential. The theories described in this chapter are grounded in professional practice.

Communication is what video is all about. It's the word that applies to all media projects, irrespective of subject matter, expression, or complexity. A program works when it communicates. When it doesn't communicate, the program fails, even if it's well done.

There are two primary orientations in communication theory. The post office model regards communication as something sent (message) from a source (sender) through some medium to a relatively passive receiver. While these theories find good application in some contexts, such as business and computers, theories that view communication as a transactional process in which the parties involved negotiate meanings are more useful for media production.

According to the transactional process model, the role of the receiver is very complex and as significant as the role of the sender. A good way to look at this model is to see communication as a field of dynamic, interacting forces. All of the participants—the message, sender, medium, receiver, and feedback—are part of this field, and all are continuously changing.

When we apply the model to video, we see that communication occurs constantly as the audience watches a videotaped program, even though the producer is not present (her message is) and even though the audience appears simply to be receiving. In fact, the role of the audience is much more active than it appears because viewers constantly select, evaluate, and discriminate among the images and sounds they experience.

To learn how to manage the complexities of the production process, we also examined general systems theory, which provides a view of the whole and how parts relate to it and each other. The parts, variously referred to as "subsystems" or "elements," make up the total system. By ensuring that each element is operating well, we make the entire system more reliable. Systems become manageable when we pay close attention to detail. When each element works as it should, it is in proper functional relationship to the other parts and the whole. Inevitably, then, the system (program) depends for its viability on this elemental integrity—ensuring that all the parts work.

Several other principles relate to the systems approach. *Entropy* refers to the fact that all material components tend naturally to a state of disorder and chaos. As solid as the world seems, everything we can sense is in a state of decay, returning to a pure energy state—it's just a matter of time. Neg-entropy, the opposite of entropy, is any action that creates order or organization in a system. Organization, therefore, is necessary to keep things going. *Feedback* is the way a system discovers how well it's functioning so that the operator can alter the system appropriately—usually by adding some form of order, organization, or information.

Equifinality is a fancy word for the principle of "garbage in–garbage out," and for our purposes this phrase has been transposed to "quality in–quality out." All decisions, especially the seemingly small ones, change the outcome of the product, including a decision not to decide.

In this chapter we elaborated somewhat (and there will be more as we continue) on each of the primary subsystems of a video program production. The *social system* is the total production team. If a member of the team is incompetent or has a negative attitude or other problem, the system is weak (and therefore vulnerable) at precisely that point. For this reason, producers should select the best people they can find.

The *content system* consists of programming elements, including subject matter, format, information, entertainment, and so on. And the *technical system* consists of the equipment and facilities used to create the program. When every element of every subsystem is working, the program "works"—it communicates!

How well a system is managed communicates.

Notes

1. James Carey, "Communication and Culture," *Communication Research,* April 1975:177.
2. Ludwig von Bertalanffy, *General System Theory* (New York: George Braziller, 1968), 40.

Suggested Readings

Bertalanffy, Ludwig von. *General System Theory: Foundations, Development, Applications.* New York: George Braziller, 1968.

Fitzgerald, John M., and Ardra F. Fitzgerald. *Fundamentals of Systems Analysis.* New York: John Wiley, 1973.

Haken, Hermann, ed. *The Dynamics of Synergetic Systems.* New York: Springer, 1980.

Jantsch, Erich, and Conrad H. Waddington, eds. *Evolution and Consciousness: Human Systems in Transition.* Reading, MA: Addison-Wesley, 1976.

Laszlo, Ervin. *Introduction to Systems Philosophy.* New York: Harper & Row Torchbooks, 1973.

Littlejohn, Stephen. *Theories of Human Communication,* 3rd ed. Belmont, CA: Wadsworth, 1989.

Miller, James Grier. *Living Systems.* New York: McGraw-Hill, 1978.

Ramo, Simon. *Cure for Chaos.* New York: David McKay, 1969.

Ruben, Brent, and John Kim, eds. *General Systems Theory and Human Communication.* Rochelle Park, NJ: Hayden, 1975.

Schramm, Wilbur, and Donald Roberts. *The Process and Effects of Mass Communication.* Urbana: University of Illinois Press, 1971.

Senge, Peter M. "Systems Principles for Leadership." In *Transforming Leadership: From Vision to Results,* edited by John D. Adams. Alexandria, VA: Miles River Press, 1986.

Severin, Werner, and James Tankard, Jr. *Communication Theories: Origins, Methods, Uses.* White Plains, NY: Longman, 1988.

CHAPTER 2

The Production Process

· ·

*When you construct anything,
do it as though you had a thousand years to live, and as if you
were to die tomorrow.*

—*Shaker philosophy*

seasoned producer for whom I worked once remarked, "Life is too short to learn production adequately." I believe him, but I have learned that production excellence can occur when the process is well managed. If it were up to just one person, a production would probably never get started. But video is a cooperative medium. Video (and television) is still in its infancy. The future belongs to those who understand the medium, who can tell stories (communicate) with it, and who can manage the production process efficiently and effectively. We will discuss the production process in this chapter. Subsequent chapters will discuss the other topics.

If we look at program production as a system, we can break it down into logical stages. These stages are various activities that are composed of the elements that need to be managed. By giving significant attention to the details of each element, by maximizing order through organization, by stressing the need for lots of clear communication, and by making good decisions, each action will build qualitatively on the others, resulting in a program that works. The systemic challenge then is to constantly hold the vision of the completed program while attending carefully to the smallest details of each phase.

Video production is a *cumulative* process. Each activity results in materials and influences that build on one another, so that the quality of the whole depends on the quality of the parts (equifinality).

Before we get into the details of these production elements in other chapters, it's important to have an overview of the process, especially for those readers who may not have completed a whole production. A program as a whole can be treated as a system. A program can also be viewed as a subsystem of the production because a program is the result of the production process. (I've purposefully repeated these systems perspectives—and will do so occasionally—as a way to strengthen your ability to see their applications in various other contexts.)

The industry (broadcast and nonbroadcast) identifies four phases of production:

Design

Preproduction

Production

Postproduction

Every production is unique. Therefore, every step is not necessary or the same for each project. The sequencing can, and frequently is, different from what we'll discuss here, so the material covered and the order of its presentation is based on a pattern of how a "typical" production flows. This is not a "how-to" chapter on video production techniques. Rather, we'll walk through each of these primary phases of the production process to gain an overview of the objectives and activities involved in each.

One of the most confusing aspects of a video production for the beginner is the issue of scale. Each production has a different level of complexity. It's not like working on an assembly line, where each step, procedure, and tool is identical. In video, almost nothing is identical from production to production except perhaps the equipment. Every production entity (company, department) has its own unique history, purpose, and structure. And the way a production is constituted in terms of equipment, content, and personnel will influence the timing and sequencing of each step. Because "form follows function," it makes sense to approach each phase and its steps according to the functions dictated by the circumstances (people, a location's availability) and resources available.

If you are currently involved in the development of a video project, do not initiate the steps indicated in this chapter yet. Because this is an *overview* of the production process, the details that relate to it are discussed in chapters yet to come.

Phase I: Design

The first step in the production process is designing your project by outlining your ideas and planning your approach.

The Idea/Purpose/Outline

The design phase begins with an idea for a program. At some point a communication need, desire, or vision will come to mind, suggesting that a video should be produced. While excited about the new idea, we mentally scan the possibilities of what the program could be. Underlying this creative outpouring is already a sense of purpose against which the details of the idea are being measured. Should the program/video do this or that? What should it contain? To whom will it be directed? Why do it at all? Answers to these questions are accepted or rejected based on your newfound purpose.

Ideas seem to come to me late at night. Even if it's two o'clock in the morning, get out a pencil and pad and discipline yourself to express your purpose in one or two sentences. As you do this, go over it repeatedly, asking the question: Is this true? If every phrase, especially the verbs (*to express, to give, to focus, to excite, to inform, to entertain*), truly represents what you want, and the total statement is true, then you have at least a "working" purpose statement. If the program is being designed for a client, find out what the client's purpose is.

At the same time, put down everything that comes to mind that relates to the idea—no matter how silly, remote, or abstract, write it down. Then, take advantage of what researchers have learned about creativity—put your notes aside for several hours to let the ideas germinate in your unconscious and come back to them fresh. Take your idea notes, sit in a comfortable and quiet place, and write out the purpose and associated ideas again, modifying them as you feel appropriate. (I like to type up the notes at this stage so the ideas begin to take on the appearance of a professional-looking presentation.) After this, sketch out the program in broad strokes. This will help you see what is already in your "mental computer" relating to the topic. At this early stage it is important to get the ideas out. Don't worry about form or spelling or anything else—you should just get the ideas in writing.

The Project Plan

At this point, you begin to map out the project. In preparation for working on the design, it's wise to spend some quiet time taking an inventory of what you already know about the subject matter (more on this step in Chapter 3). Take notes so that your ideas are in front of you when you begin to design in earnest.

Chapter 6 provides a needs analysis, a methodical approach to answering the key project design questions. The issues include

Purpose statement

Target audience

Communication objective

Program content

Format

Program elements

Program use

Financial matters

Technology

Locations

Personnel

Time frame

Evaluation

The first seven of these categories constitute a *program* needs analysis and the remaining issues relate to a *production* needs analysis. All of these issues are addressed in the design stage (see Chapter 6), allowing the producer to sketch and plan what the program is about; who it is for; how it will be used; where, when, and how it will be produced; and who will be involved under what arrangements. In some instances responses to these questions can be co-created by the production team, which is an excellent practice to further integrate and strengthen the team.

It's important to note that the design phase relates to the design of both the **program** and the **production.** Taken together, these are referred to here as a "project." Needs analysis is not only an effective way of planning a project; it also provides all the information needed for obtaining funding through grants.

Previsualization

When you address the issue of program content during the planning process, it is highly desirable to be able to see what the program will be like. This is necessary so you will be able to express the program concept to others in terms they can appreciate. It also provides more content and expression alternatives (ideas) than those that first came to mind. *Previsualization,* the application of creative imagination, is a way to envision what the program will be like when it's finished. Chapter 8 ("Developing Program Content") provides a previsualization technique.

Previsualization is not hard, it just requires some time without distractions. It is one of the most direct aids in creating program content and expression. After you have previsualized your program, the writing of an outline or a treatment is much easier. Writing down what you previsualized is essential because others (potential investors, crew, funders, agents, clients) need to be able to see what the producer or writer has in mind.

The Preliminary Outline

Once the program concept is crystallized in your mind, it's time to write a **preliminary outline.** It gives specificity to the program and shows how the content relates to the format sequentially. Additionally, the outline helps in developing a content shopping list, indicating those elements that will require further research or coordination. The outline also helps in planning transitions between segments as continuity options begin to become apparent.

Remember that the outline, although a way to communicate the rough idea of the program and its content to others, is primarily a worksheet for you. Leave lots

Title: The Potentialists   Length: Series of 8 half hours
Producer: D. Smith   Date: 11-28-88

Use: To be offered to national cable networks for Sunday schedule

---

OUTLINE

GENERIC OPEN	Slo-mo montage: people realizing their goals in sports, health, business, art, education, performance. Peak experiences — artfully photographed (emphasize backlight). Music and voice-over establish the series context and program theme (subject matter); define the term *potentialist*.
STUDIO	Man/woman (field producers) sit at working edit console (off-line) and tell the audience about three individuals that will be featured. They specify the qualities that these potentialists have in common as a continuity thread relating to the theme. Then they set up the first segment; put a tape in the machine.
PROFILE 1	Preproduced profile package of potentialist. Show her challenge, goal, vision or dream; make it important; show her approach to realizing it; show the physical, emotional, mental, spiritual struggle; show the outcome; get her formula for success. (Do in-depth voice interview with audio recorder.)
STUDIO	Intro. next segment.
PROFILE 2	Same process as in profile 1 but with different person, different field of interest.
STUDIO	Intro. next segment.
PROFILE 3	Same as above.
STUDIO WRAP	Hosts encapsulate the key points and commonalities in the profiles (VO) that relate to the program theme. Visuals consist of dynamically edited montage of the best images from each feature. (Stylized shooting and editing give the show its unique look and texture … profiles shot on film originally.) Hosts ON CAMERA, show clips of next week's potentialists and give the address where viewers can write for assistance in their own endeavors to develop their potential, realize their dreams.
CREDITS	Voices of potentialists with FI/FO of credits over white background.

FIGURE 2.1
Program Outline

A preliminary program outline for a series of programs titled The Potentialists. *The series is designed for cable networks.*

of space on the pages. This makes it easy to add notes and make changes as research reveals other content options. The outline is a working blueprint of the structure of the program and, as such, every element in it is subject to change. The content will not be "locked in" until the final version of the script is written. Even then, changes occur.

Outlines vary considerably depending on the medium and the nature of the production. The preliminary outline just described works well for most commercial, industrial, and other private (nonbroadcast) projects. But television drama and movie screenplay outlines require a different approach. An outline for a TV drama, for instance, is often your first presentation to a prospective producer and can be from two to forty pages long. A teleplay outline is usually extracted from an already written script. In the motion picture business, production companies will make initial decisions on either an outline or a treatment. It's not uncommon for a studio to purchase a treatment along with rights to produce it so they can use their own writers instead of the person who wrote the treatment. So be sure to consult a current book on writing for television or for the movies before you waste effort. Know the protocol and procedures of the industry to which you're appealing. Figure 2.1 is an example of a preliminary outline for a cable series. It is solely intended to be an aid to the producer, the first written expression of the program content. Figure 2.2 contains an outline for a teleplay (drama for television), illustrating the difference between a preliminary outline for the producer and a presentation for a production company.

The Treatment

Although the outline lays out the format and the organization of content elements for you, the **treatment** is prepared as a narrative description of the program for others. The treatment should be between four and twelve pages long. Dramatic screenplay treatments for television and film can be as long as sixty pages. The treatment's purpose is to give the reader the best possible experience of the program. It should create emotion, provide information, elicit the entertainment value, sell the product, or persuade. Whatever your communication objective, the reader should understand it.

You should write treatments in prose, never in outline form. On the first page, indicate the program title, writer, and producer and, in one paragraph, establish the context and content of the program. Hook the reader in this paragraph in the same way that the video itself will command attention at the beginning. Get the reader immediately interested in the content and how you intend to create it. After this paragraph, begin the body of the text on the next page. Use visual language throughout. Be specific, but don't be too detailed. Describe the content in broad strokes and in sequence. Occasional reference to camera angle, movement, and other screen directions may be appropriate for certain types of programs, where these elements are intrinsic to the design. But avoid them in any program that has a story line, such as a drama or news story. You don't want to do anything that will distract the reader from the story.

If the treatment contains humor, include specific lines and present them in a manner that will evoke a humorous response (not an easy thing to do in print). If you are wondering about whether to include or exclude material, favor excluding it—keep the treatment as brief as possible. Leave the reader wanting more. And, especially at the end, structure the presentation so the reader feels the same emotion or gets the same idea as the viewers will have when the program is over. You want to leave your readers with as definite an impression as possible of what the program is supposed to accomplish. Work on the treatment until it approximates the fulfillment of the communication objective (discussed in Chapter 6); then it will have accomplished its purpose.

The treatment provides the team with the best available description of the pro-

YESTERDAY'S DREAMS

by Bunny Arszman

Lindsay Oliver, 38, madly and passionately in love with a man she has never met and can never have, tries to continue with her life. The pain never eases or diminishes. Falling in love with Paul Jamison when she was only 16, she has tried to keep him out of her head, but has never been able to keep him out of her heart.

Lindsay's marriage is in shambles. She has always felt needed ... but never loved. Her husband resents her career. The higher she rises at Fortune Records, the more unhappy he becomes. He seeks solace with other women and she struggles to keep their family together. Suddenly she finds that Paul Jamison is again very much in her thoughts.

Paul Jamison, 46, survives in a fish bowl. Every move, every statement, is known instantly around the world. Unable to cope with the constant surveillance, he dropped out of the rock music scene 15 years ago. Bitter and cynical, but longing to make music again, Paul signs a three-record deal with Fortune Records, agreeing to an American tour of which Lindsay is put in charge.

Molly Bergesch, 40, also loves Paul Jamison ... and Rod Stewart, and Mick Jagger, and anyone else she can get to.

She's desperate, lonely, and tired of being tossed out of hotel rooms at 3:00 in the morning. She figures she's ready for the big time. She deserves to be a part of Paul Jamison's life, whether he wants her or not.

Their lives become progressively intertwined. During the tour, Lindsay conceals her true feelings for Paul when he is devastated by his closest friend's death from a drug overdose. Molly cunningly stalks Paul with a gun, wanting to possess him ... if not in this life, then possibly in the next.

On the climactic evening in San Diego, during a live press conference, Molly's assassination attempt is foiled by Lindsay. Lindsay, unable to deny her feelings any longer, rushes to Paul's open arms. News of their affair spreads across the tabloids, and Lindsay reluctantly decides that she must return to her family. After an emotional good-bye, Paul departs by chartered jet and Lindsay returns home in the family station wagon.

This is a story of choices. The choice between the dreams of yesterday and the responsibilities of today.

FIGURE 2.2
Teleplay Outline
A formal outline for potential producers. (Courtesy of Bunny Arszman.)

gram. As a polished presentation, it can be used as part of a fund-raising effort. The program could even be sold as a product in itself if it fits the interests of one of the major-league broadcast/cable companies. One of my students is an example. When he was twenty-three years old, he was offered $10,000 for a screenplay treatment (though he chose instead to find independent financing for the film and direct it himself). Practically, the treatment will be useful as a way to promote wider interest

THE HAMILTON COUNTY JUVENILE COURT
(20-minute orientation video for new employees)

Treatment
Writer: Janet Steele
Producer: Jeff Feld

New employees need to become familiar with the faces, locations, and operating procedures of the court. In this program two judges (on camera) tell the story of how the court system works by providing a tour through its various functions. The program uses a board game to simulate case situations so viewers can see the different procedures for various cases. Cards are picked that contain symbols directing the player through certain procedures. In this way the employees encounter every kind of situation the court is designed to handle. They also become acquainted with the associated paperwork and its flow. The tour and game end with words of welcome from the judges.

FIGURE 2.3
Treatment

The first part of a four-page treatment for an employee orientation tape is shown on these two pages.

in your program, making its production more feasible. As with outlines, treatment styles vary with the medium and the format, so again consult one or more of the books listed at the end of this chapter. Appendix A includes the first four pages of a treatment for "Hurricane," a program in the *Nova* series produced for PBS. On the nonbroadcast level, Figure 2.3 shows a partial treatment for an employee orientation video that we proposed (and produced) for our local juvenile court system.

Project Feasibility

The next step is to determine whether the project is feasible to produce. Given your personal circumstances, is the production financially and logistically ready to go? So far the design has only required an investment of time and creativity. As it costs nothing to design, you haven't spent any money. But as soon as the design becomes feasible to produce and steps are taken to move into the next phase (preproduction), money and time will be required. So at this stage the question is whether or not one can get the program produced, and often this decision rests on the availability of equipment and funds.

Just as in the business world, an idea or a design is only a possibility. The idea becomes a **project** when dollars are made available for its implementation. In essence there is no project until someone decides to make a financial commitment to implement the idea.

Some projects move steadily from design to preproduction because there is an established commitment in place. The entire design phase may last just a few days. Other productions may require some research into economics, distribution factors, and other considerations. Any obstacles will become readily apparent in the process of completing the project needs analysis (Chapter 6).

The program opens with two 20-second introductions by the judges, then fades to black. Fade in on hands shaking dice, releasing them onto a board labeled "Juvenile Court." Music comes up and the narrator explains that the game of life is not easy; that the children whose lives they are about to enter already know this. A hand moves a token to the "abused child" square on the game board. Crash cut to video of a girl with a black eye and swollen lip. She stares, is hurt and frightened. A hand moves a token to the "traffic offender" square. Cut to video of teenage boy tossing beer can out of a car window. He looks at the camera and laughs, squeals out past a stop sign. Another hand moves a token to a square marked "delinquent child." Cut to video of teenage boy and girl leaning against brick wall smoking pot. Both level hard stares at the camera.

The narrator's hand picks up the dice from the board, and the narrator addresses the camera: "As a duly sworn officer of the Juvenile Court, you're now a part of their lives. And, for them, it's no game." As he continues to speak about the responsibilities of employees, we begin a visual tour of the facility beginning at the door with its "Juvenile Court" sign. Imagery is well composed, camera moves on a dolly through the spaces where people are working. Clerks are busy, lots of movement.

The narrator talks about how offenders enter the process as we see a referee during an actual hearing. Cut to sounds of the court room proceedings briefly. Dissolve back to the game board as the narrator sets the stage for specific types of cases. A card is selected that tells the player to go to the "Clerk of Court" office. Cut wide to the office and then to a form that is identified and shown full screen.

...

Sometimes the timing is just not right; perhaps the right person needs to come along and get excited about the program. In any case, there needs to be some research and attention to the question of feasibility before preproduction can begin. Just because a program idea is exciting or desirable doesn't mean that it should or can be produced. Like me, most producers probably have a file of production folders marked "completed" and "not completed." Guess which one is the thickest? Ideas always outnumber realizations.

Phase II: Preproduction

. . . .

The preproduction phase officially begins with the financial commitment to produce. This commitment may be expressed with a check, a verbal agreement, the signing of a contract, the award of a grant, or simply by an informal acknowledgment that the project is going forward. Unlike the design phase, at some point in the preproduction phase, it's likely that some money will need to be spent. Depending on the scale of the production, this could amount to under $100 or go upward into the thousands.

In cities where major productions are commonplace (Los Angeles, New York, Chicago, Orlando, London), there are companies that, for a fee, will take your treatment and project needs analysis and develop a detailed budget (in the preproduction phase). They will take from two to eight weeks to do this, and it will cost between $2,000 and $15,000. So I strongly recommend you do your own budget. If you do you'll at the least have expenses for parking and photocopying, and probably some legal fees for drawing up and coordinating any contracts or agreements that may be involved (for talent, crew, music providers, copyrights, and so on).

Library Research

Once you have developed a needs analysis and a treatment, you are ready to delve into the subject matter of the program in detail. No matter how much one may

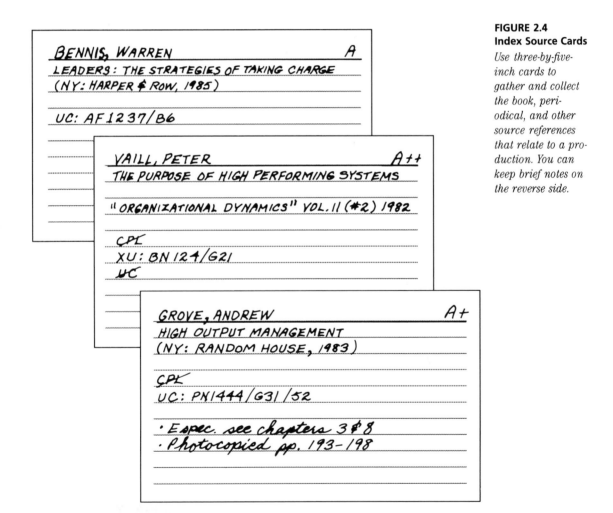

FIGURE 2.4
Index Source Cards
Use three-by-five-inch cards to gather and collect the book, periodical, and other source references that relate to a production. You can keep brief notes on the reverse side.

know about a topic, there's always more to learn. The more you can bring to your program, the better it will be. Investing time and money in upgrading what you know about a subject is the best insurance for program effectiveness—even if you're not the writer.

Some people gravitate to video in the first place because it affords them an opportunity to gain some expertise in subject areas they would otherwise never explore or experience. Some programs don't require library research, but most require at least some familiarity with the topic's background and current status.

For some people the word *research* is a turnoff. It conjures up images of boring hours or days in a stuffy library poring over reams of material to find a few useful nuggets of information. You don't have to make a career out of researching for a production, as long as what you do is *focused* and *organized*.

Take your needs analysis and treatment and write down the key words in your topic. Librarians refer to these as "bullets." Don't use sentences, just one word or a phrase. Take this list to the card catalogue (or computer) at the library and see what books are available on each of your bullets. (Do this alphabetically—it saves time.) Use the *Reader's Guide* index or selected computer databases to find periodicals with articles relating to your bullets as well. You will probably find the most recently published material on your topic in periodicals. Look under the current or previous year. Take along three-by-five-inch cards and write out a *source card* for each book, article, or journal you think may be useful. Figure 2.4 shows the format I've adopted based on the way the card catalogue is organized.

Select only those titles that seem to be *directly* relevant to your subject matter. If there are thirty, select the best three. Keep your effort focused. Don't overload yourself at any one time or it will sour you on the process of discovery. Within a half hour you can end up with several cards relating to your bullets. You shouldn't necessarily expect to cover all the bullets in one visit. Check out the best five to eight books. Copy one to three articles (just the essential pages) and, during the next few days, in a more comfortable environment, scan them (don't read for detail until you find something really germane).

When you find something that you want to keep for incorporation into your program, mark it with a scrap of paper, highlight it, or use a Post-it note.

Put your best notes on the back of the three-by-five-inch source cards. You'll be able to find information fast, and it will be related to its source. Computers, especially portable ones, also work well. Everyone organizes information differently, so do what you find most comfortable and efficient for you. But the information must be easily retrieved over time.

I prepare a three-hole loose-leaf binder at the outset of every production. The title of the program or series is put on the spine. Inside the binder are separators with tabs (see Figure 2.5).

All paperwork relating to the production is hole-punched and put in the binder, except for invoices, which can get quite bulky. Content research goes under "content," correspondence under "contacts," and so on.

For every production I also make a file box for three-by-five-inch source cards that relate to the content research (Figure 2.6). I take the file box to the library with me. It has separators so I instantly know the status of any source:

Search	(Sources to find)
Review	(Sources to be reviewed)
Re-search	(Items needing further search)
Periodicals	(Periodicals to review)
File	(Sources to be filed elsewhere)
Interlibrary	(Consult other libraries)
Copy	(Make copy of selections)
Quotes	(Relevant quotations)

I always rate the usefulness of sources by assigning a grade in the upper right corner. "A+" indicates that the source (and pages from it that I have copied or noted) is so good that it contains something for the program directly. A's are useful and will probably be used. B's may or may not get used. And C's do not get used. Nonetheless, I keep all the cards because they may be suitable for a future production.

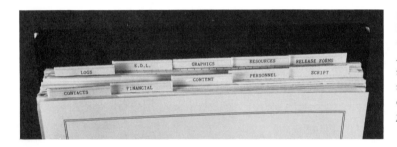

FIGURE 2.5
Production Binder and Tabs
Hole-punch all the information relating to a production and put it in the production binder.

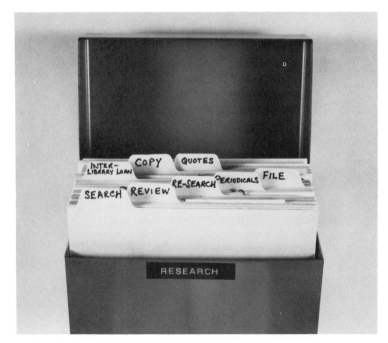

FIGURE 2.6
File Box and Tabs
Keep source cards in a file box with tabs so the status of each card is apparent. The file can be taken to the library easily.

When the production is over, the binder goes on the shelf and the file box is emptied into a larger file for the three-by-five-inch cards under the title of the production.

This system is simple, compact, and efficient, and, best of all, I can easily retrieve the information and nothing gets lost over time. All it requires is the time to set up the system initially—each time a production begins—then a commitment to maintain it with a binder, a three-by-five-inch file box, some index cards, and a three-hole punch.

Some experience in data gathering is needed to catch on to what is important to keep. But creative people need to find ways of becoming comfortable with the research process. Spending time experimenting with innovative ways of handling information efficiently is highly productive because it saves time in the future.

Personal Research

Personal research is needed because much of what one needs to know about a topic cannot always be found in books or other materials. We will often need to talk to others who have some connection with our topic. For most producers, this kind of research is the most rewarding because it affords the opportunity to meet and interact with people who have some real experience or expertise in the content area.

As a young producer, I was somewhat hesitant to contact celebrities and other notables, but I later discovered that most people love to share what they know, especially if it will be used in the context of a media project. Over the years several close friendships have developed as a result of a "cold call" to ask for an interview.

News producers think nothing of calling a celebrity or her agent in order to get information, a story, or an interview. Some radio interviews are even conducted on the initial phone call. One person I met on the phone later became a regular client. You never know what will happen as a result of a personal connection, and content research is an excellent context for building relationships.

Before making a personal contact, identify the individual(s) who can make the best contribution to your project. Look for the most authoritative, the most experienced, the most enlightened people you can find. Then learn as much about them as possible by reading their books or other writings. Find out what motivates them, what their relation to the topic is, what experience they have. Then write a letter introducing yourself and the project, indicating how you see them participating. The objective of this letter is to get an interview either by phone or in person—whichever serves you best. A personal visit is always preferred because it provides an opportunity to make a friend. Additionally, audio or video can be recorded on the spot. In the letter, say that you will call within the week. Then do so and ask for an interview. After making hundreds of interview requests, I can't remember being turned down once. So stay confident. People love to talk about what interests them. If your time frame is short, phone them instead of writing and just let the conversation flow. Before you call, know exactly what you want from them—and what they might get from helping you.

Don't underestimate what can come from a phone interview. Tell the person that you would like permission to audio record the interview at the time you make the appointment for a phone interview. At the beginning and at the end of the interview, it's common practice to ask permission to use the interview or information from it in your program, as well as to thank the interviewee.

Information gained from authorities and other notables, whether over the phone or in person, can be invaluable to your project. In some instances you may use selections of the interview recording as a voice-over. More often, however, you can enrich the content of your program with the information. After establishing a relationship with the expert, it is appropriate to ask for an on-camera interview or other performance if that is warranted by your program format.

You'll find that personal contacts with content experts will substantially contribute to the richness of your programs. Often these people will invite you to sample their environment to help you further understand their perspective. People with business experience strongly advise beginners in business to get jobs working behind the counter, dealing with the public, operating a cash register, and getting the feel of the life-style. Direct experience is the best teacher. If your next project is a story about veterinary medicine, go to work for a veterinarian for a while; volunteer if you have to, but get this firsthand experience.

Team Building

At this point in the preproduction process, you should put the team together. Selecting crew members, writers, talent, and support services is dependent on the scale of the production. In smaller productions, this may be a relatively easy task, but in larger productions, it can become a full-time job. The social system is one of the most significant factors in realizing an effective production. There's a tendency to invite people to join a production team simply because they are friends, friends of friends, or available, but that is not the way to build a successful team. The evaluation parameters should include

> Positive attitude
>
> Competency
>
> Integrity
>
> Team skills
>
> Professional experience

Early in the preproduction stage, call a team meeting to begin building enthusiasm. Don't wait until all the positions are filled. The team spirit is generated by those who hold the vision of the program. Initially this can be as few as two; as others are added, they will catch the spirit and contribute their own uniqueness to it. Build the team as soon as preproduction begins, when you are certain that the project is going to happen.

Script Writing

With the materials and energy gathered thus far, script writing can begin. Who will write the script? Nonbroadcast scripts are rarely written by committee. More often they are written by two collaborators, a content expert and a production expert, for instance, and their work can be checked or edited by others.

If you are not going to be the writer, how do you find one? Ask anyone in the production business; they usually have several connections. Individuals and companies write scripts exclusively for corporations and other entities. Many scripts are written on a freelance basis. Advertising agencies frequently have people on their staff who focus on script writing—even for noncommercial subjects.

You can also find writers and other specialized people by attending local trade meetings. And you can watch the credits of programs similar to the one you intend to produce to find writers.

Engaging a friend or relative to write a script because he knows something about the subject matter is a mistake that's often made. Effective script writing is a very different skill from expository or creative writing because it requires a *working* knowledge of media techniques, technologies, and processes. On the other hand, a competent scriptwriter can be engaged to write a script on a subject that is totally new to her or him. Scriptwriters can learn about a topic and express it effectively but a content expert often cannot. This is why writing teams frequently consist of a scriptwriter and a content expert.

Different programs require different scripting formats. The format for scripting a *teleplay* (TV drama) or *screenplay* (movie) as seen in Figure 2.7 is highly standardized.

Most producers won't even consider reading a script when they see it's not in the standard form. The Writers Guild of America can provide you with format guidelines as well as salary scales. Its address is given at the end of the chapter. The full-page format is the only one used for dramatic productions, and it's also used for some other types of programs. Figure 2.8 shows the full-page format applied to a documentary where the intent was to provide the director with specific visual recommendations. The same format is used in Figure 2.9 for a *Nova* documentary, but the director is given complete creative control over the visuals.

The two-column format shown in Figure 2.10 is most commonly used for institutional training and sales presentations, children's programming, TV commercials, and news (see Figure 2.11) and for most other business- or issue-related programs. The benefit of the two-column format is that visuals are related to audio in a sequential manner, so the director and editor can more quickly track the progression of scenes. Also, there's plenty of room to elaborate on visual descriptions if the scriptwriter wants to be more detailed about the look of the program in advance. You can vary the two-column format by adding a third column when the audio track is complex, as in the multimedia production shown in Figure 2.12. Use the format that best meets the needs of those who will actually use the script.

Because script writing is such an essential part of video production, I highly recommend you consult one or more of the writing texts indicated at the end of this chapter. There is not enough room here to do the subject justice, but the samples provided will be a good start. For the serious student, writer, and producer, college courses in script writing are a wise investment.

If you're thinking about a career as a producer, it's important to know that there's a difference in educational requirements and experience for those who want to produce programs and those who are primarily interested in a subject area (sciences, religion, politics, business) and want to use video to present that subject more widely. The former requires a more technical orientation, while the latter needs an emphasis

FIGURE 2.7
Drama Script Format
The first page of Act II of a teleplay, Yesterday's Dreams, *by Bunny Arszman.*

ACT II

FADE IN

1. EXT. FORTUNE RECORDS. DAY.

Snow is falling. Christmas decorations surround the entrance of the building. LINDSAY makes her way through the front door, carrying a grocery bag.

2. INT. FRONT OFFICE. DAY.

Fortune Record employees are partying to the hilt. Empty beer and wine bottles line the desks. There is laughter everywhere. LINDSAY enters.

> OFFICE EMPLOYEES
> (cheering)
> There she is!

> LINDSAY
> Don't worry, reinforcements are here!

LINDSAY sets the grocery bag down. Anxious employees begin pulling out bottles of wine and beer. PETE, an office worker, hands Lindsay a bottle of wine.

> LINDSAY
> No thanks, Pete.

> PETE
> Aw, come on Lindsay, it's Christmas!

> LINDSAY
> Well ... I ... oh well, what the hell?

LINDSAY takes the bottle and enters her office, while the party continues.

> DISS TO

3. INT. LINDSAY'S OFFICE. NIGHT.

The wine bottle, now empty, is sitting on Lindsay's desk. LINDSAY is gazing out of the window. MARK enters.

> MARK
> You still here? The van left an hour ago. I thought
> you'd be home, wrapped in your bathrobe by now.

in writing, communication, aesthetics, and organization. If your career is centered on communicating in a particular subject area, you need to focus on that area primarily and on communication as a support. If, however, you just love to produce television or video no matter what the subject, then your orientation should be toward the tech-

TEILHARD
(VOICE-OVER)

Progress, if it is to continue, will not happen by itself. Evolution, by the very mechanism of its synthesis, is constantly acquiring greater freedom.

What steps must we take? I see two, summarized in five words: *a great hope held in common.* Our hope will be operative if it is expressed in greater cohesion and human solidarity. The future of the earth is in our hands. How shall we decide? ...

(DISSOLVE to ZOOM IN, EXT. of St. Ignatius Rectory in New York ... DISSOLVE to NARRATOR in guest room at St. Ignatius Rectory, which TEILHARD once occupied.)

NARRATOR

In his last years, TEILHARD lived in this guest room at St. Ignatius Rectory in New York. ... Anonymous, largely unknown even to the members of the community with whom he dined, still generally unknown to the world outside. He died of a stroke on Easter Sunday 1955.

(NARRATOR picks up sheaves of papers, then CUT to detail.)

NARRATOR

None of his writings perished, however. He made arrangements for them to be published after his death. And, bit by bit, over the past 25 years, his thought has become public....

(Cut to NARRATOR at Teilhard's grave site ... TILT DOWN to modest tombstone.)

Only a few weeks before he died, TEILHARD wrote, "As I look around me, how is it possible that I find myself entirely alone? Why am I the only one who sees...?"

nical and aesthetic aspects of communication and these media, especially in terms of production. This is why many people who write for the screen have master's degrees, while producers often do not. Are you in video because you have something to "say," or is video something you want to "do"?

FIGURE 2.9
Documentary
Script Format
Without Direc-
tor Cues
A page from a Nova
*documentary
script titled "Hur-
ricane" that gives
neither camera
direction nor direc-
tor cues. The intent
is to allow the di-
rector complete
creative control.
(Courtesy of WGBH,
Boston, and* Nova.*)*

Aboard, a small group of scientists will man sensors and advanced radar designed to probe deep inside the hurricane. For the next ten hours they'll crisscross the storm, reading its vital signs, and sending them back to forecasters in Miami.

The lead scientist, Hugh Willoughby, believes the key to predicting the behavior of these deadly storms lies in subtle changes in wind and air pressure patterns within the hurricane's core.

Hugh Willoughby

The biggest mystery is how does the hurricane interact with its surroundings, with the surroundings in the atmosphere. That controls the motion and in a big way it controls the intensity. And I think that's a solvable problem.

And I feel that the hurricane, when all is said and done, is going to be one of the most forecastable things that happens in the atmosphere. There's a lot of hope that the way the equations work out, we are going to be able to predict hurricanes more accurately, well say as accurately as we predict day to day weather.

Narrator

But so far hurricanes have proven notoriously unpredictable.

And no one knows better than forecasters at the National Hurricane Center in Miami. Information about hurricane Gilbert is now pouring in from advanced weather satellites, aircraft, and remote weather stations.

Storyboarding

A **storyboard** is a visual representation of the sequencing of shots within a program, usually containing sketches with associated words (see Figure 2.13). You should prepare a storyboard soon after the script is finalized. Doing so before a final draft of the script is available is risky because changes will most certainly occur, and there is no sense in redoing a storyboard. We usually prepare storyboards for presentation to others who may not be adept at visualizing a program from a script. In some cases it can be a necessity, where grand-scale and highly complex productions involve many people and disparate locations. In these instances, the storyboard is the best way for everyone to stay on the same track as the production elements (audio and video) are developed. The participants can best maintain and refer to the common vision of the program by using the storyboard.

cut to CU: Various computer screens ECU: Different icons	COMPUTERS ARE A VERY SOPHISTI- CATED MODE OF COMMUNICATION REQUIR- ING THE COORDINATOR TO HAVE A BACK- GROUND IN CURRENT MEDICAL TERMINOL- OGY, SYMBOLS, AND ABBREVIATIONS BECAUSE THEY FUNCTION AS LIAISONS FOR PHYSICIANS, NURSING PERSONNEL, ANCIL- LARY DEPARTMENTS, PATIENTS AND VISI-
cut to MCU: Unit Coordinator reading physician's orders	TORS. IN USING THE COMPUTER, THE COORDINATOR MUST POSSESS THE SKILL OF READING AND UNDERSTANDING THE PHYSICIAN'S ORDERS AND MUST BE CA- PABLE OF TRANSLATING THE ORDER INTO A LANGUAGE ACCEPTABLE TO THE COM-
cut to MCU: Unit Coordinator punching in info CU: Keyboard CU: Printer	PUTER. USE OF THE COMPUTER ALSO REQUIRES INPUTTING INFORMATION, THUS SENDING MESSAGES, ORDERING, SCHEDUL- ING, AND THEN RECEIVING THE RESULTING COMPUTER PRINTOUTS FOR THE PATIENT'S PERMANENT RECORDS.
dissolve to ECU: Order transcription	IN ORDER TO PERFORM ANY PATIENT PROCEDURE OR SERVICE, A PHYSICIAN'S ORDER MUST BE OBTAINED. THE ORDERS
dissolve to Registered nurse talking with physician	MUST BE WRITTEN BY THE PHYSICIAN OR VERBALLY OBTAINED BY A REGISTERED NURSE FROM THE PHYSICIAN.
cut to MCU: Physician & Unit Coordinator	THE PRIMARY FUNCTION OF THE UNIT COORDINATOR IS TO READ AND UNDER- STAND ...

FIGURE 2.10   Two-Column Script Format

A page from a hospital training program script showing the two-column
style that is commonly used for information and lecture-type programs.
(Courtesy: Jeff Feld, Bethesda Hospital, Cincinnati, OH.
Written by Shirley Walker-Powell.)

```
ANIMALS INTRO                      — — — — — LIVE — — — — —
:49
LIVE ONCAM                         DO YOU KNOW THAT THERE ARE HUNDREDS
                                   OF ANIMALS AROUND THE WORLD IN
                                   DANGER OF BECOMING EXTINCT? WELL,
                                   NOW THERE IS ONE MORE.
                                        AN INTERNATIONAL DELEGATION AN-
                                   NOUNCED THIS WEEK THAT THE FAMILIAR
                                   AFRICAN ELEPHANT IS OFFICIALLY AN EN-
                                   DANGERED SPECIES. AMY LYONS HAS
                                   MORE.

Take VTR FULL                      — — — — — SOT — — — — —

     SUPER CG: (:18-28)
          THANE MAYNARD
          ASST. CURATOR, CINTI ZOO        (OUTCUE: "… its last habitat")


HIT & RUN                          — — — — — LIVE — — — — —
:20
LIVE ONCAM                         POLICE ARE STILL SEARCHING FOR A
                                   DRIVER INVOLVED IN A HIT-AND-RUN
                                   ACCIDENT LATE LAST NIGHT. BARBARA
                                   WOLF OF PRICE HILL WAS WALKING SOUTH
                                   ON EMMETT AVENUE AROUND MIDNIGHT
                                   WHEN SHE WAS STRUCK BY A SPEEDING
                                   CAR. SHE DIED LATER AT BETHESDA HOSPI-
                                   TAL. WITNESSES SAY THE DRIVER WAS A
                                   YOUNG WHITE MALE, WITH A DARK BEARD.
                                   HE WAS DRIVING A RED, EARLY MODEL
                                   CAMARO.

Take FULL SCREEN CG                — — — — — VO — — — — —
     CINCINNATI POLICE             IF YOU HAVE ANY INFORMATION REGARDING
          352-3040                 THIS ACCIDENT, PLEASE CALL THE CINCIN-
                                   NATI POLICE AT 352-3040. THAT'S 352-3040.
```

FIGURE 2.11 News Script Format

*A page from a newscast that indicates the timing, director's cues, roll-in
material, CGs, and narrative. This script will be used in the control room
by the director and taped into a long roll for the TelePrompTer.*

THE GLASS HALF FULL

SCENE	VIDEO	TIME	NARRATION	SOUND EFFECTS
1. Black			NARRATOR (VO)	Music fades up slowly & builds to a "swelling" point.
2. CU a glass shaped like the earth (or with meridian lines etched on it) half filled with wine.			IS THE GLASS HALF EMPTY … OR HALF FULL?	
3. Super title: <u>THE GLASS HALF FULL</u>				Theme music up
4. MONTAGE: HEADLINES (TV & Newspaper) -TV screen dot pattern image -newsprint dot pattern image -super this symbol:				Anchorperson (VO) TV Anchorpersons read negative story headlines that correspond to visuals.
⊘			NARRATOR (VO)	
-wider image of breakdowns in -economy -crime -government -human rights (the effect is that the breakdown symbol is stamped over most of the ordinary TV & newspaper stories).			THE WORLD IS AT A CRITICAL CROSSROAD. ON THE ONE HAND, UNPRECEDENTED CRISES COULD LEAD TO MASSIVE DESTRUCTION. ON THE OTHER HAND,	
5. MONTAGE: HUMAN POTENTIAL -healing/health -robotics -space -alternative energy -computer			UNPRECEDENTED POTENTIAL COULD LEAD TO GENUINE TRANS-FORMATION, A POSITIVE FUTURE FOR THE WHOLE HUMAN RACE.	Music fade in softly under images.
6. MONTAGE: MEGA-CRISIS -overpopulation -pollution -crime -energy			THE FACT IS, WE HAVE A MEGA-CRISIS: A SERIES OF PROBLEMS THAT ARE GLOBAL, INTERRE-LATED, AND COMPLEX.	Music segue to somber.

FIGURE 2.12   Three-Column Script Format

A page from a multimedia presentation in which the sound track is specified in some detail because of its complexity.

BORDEN-CREMORA
CREMORA LITE TV
14244T

"BREAKFAST COUPLE" :15
12/15/89 rev.

Video: Audio:

We see woman, about 42
years old, looking very attractive and professional. She sits
at table, reading morning
paper. Cremora Lite and
coffee cup are in front of her.

She is joined by husband—   MAN: Honey?
also attractive and profes-   Why did you buy
sional. He sets coffee cup on   Cremora Lite?
table.

Close up of Cremora being   WOMAN: Because Cremora Lite
stirred into coffee.   has 70% less satu-
                                            rated fat than Coffee-
(SUPER POSITION MAY   mate Lite.
VARY):
Both contain less than one
gram saturated fat per serving.

Man is trying to be humorosly   MAN: So you did it because
sarcastic.   you care?

FIGURE 2.13 Storyboard
Storyboard for a 15-second TV commercial.
(Courtesy of Sive Associates, a Y&R Company.)

FIGURE 2.13   Storyboard (continued)

Finally looks at husband over top of newspaper, smiling.

WOMAN: No.
                   Because I'm smart.

SUPER ANNOUNCER:
Cremora Lite.

SUPER:
Coffee-mate is a registered trademark of Carnation, Inc.

ANNCR: New Cremora Lite.
              Less saturated fat.
              No cholesterol.

Budgeting

Budgeting can only be done after the script has been completed and a schedule projected. That is, you must estimate participants' time investment in the production closely enough to make the budget realistic. In small-scale productions, budgeting may be a simple matter of estimating the cost of time, materials, equipment rentals, personnel fees, and any other expenses. On larger productions, every detail will have to be researched.

The budgeting procedure begins with the **script breakdown** process, which analyzes the scope of the production by specifying the work to be done, the workers involved, and the time investment (Figure 2.14). This information is transposed onto a *script breakdown summary* sheet (Figure 2.15), which is used for developing the budget because it shows every item for which a cost needs to be figured. The summary includes some information that's not on the breakdown sheet, including an estimate of the materials that will be needed, which is usually tape stock but could also include any special rentals or other out-of-pocket expenses. Using the script breakdown summary sheet, I can then go through every page of the budget form and figure the costs. Figure 2.16 shows a typical budget page. If I find a category where I can't estimate the cost, I call around to get more information. Proceeding this way through the entire budget, I can then total the sections and enter them on a *budget summary* page (Figure 2.17). An additional budget summary is provided in Appendix B, and a complete budget prepared for a National Endowment for the Humanities grant is included in Appendix C.

Each project has its own budgetary context and constraints. Again, because this is an overview, the reader can refer to the list of excellent books on budget prepa-

SCENE	PAGE	DESCRIPTION	INT/EXT	CREW	TALENT	EXTRAS	SETUPS	PROPS	SPECIAL EQUIP.	TIME
1	1	STUDIO OPEN w KATHY	I	1 CAM – AUDIO – T.D. – FLOOR – DIR	K. HUNTER	–	2	WORKOUT PADS	DOLLY	2 HRS.
2	1	INTRO. ASSISTANTS	I	''	K. HUNTER J. KLEIN S. WELLES	–	2	PADS	DOLLY	2 HRS.
3–5	1	EXERCISES: SET 1 (WARM–UP)	I	2-CAMS + CREW OF 4 DIR	K.H. J.K. S.W.	–	4	• CHART • X-RAY LIGHT BOX	DOLLY	4 HRS.
6–8 15–21	(1) (2)	FOREST CUT-A-WAYS	E	(EFP) DIR • J.K.–CAM • P.J.–AUDIO • ?–GRIP	–	–	10	–	• WIDE-ANGLE LENS • FOG FILTER	1 DAY
9–14	½	EXERCISES: SET 2 (LOW IMPACT) AEROBICS	I	2 CAMS AUDIO T.D. FLOOR VTR DIR	K.H. J.K. S.W.	–	6	LONG STEM ROSE	• FOG FILTER • DOLLY	1 DAY
22–23 24–28	(2) (3)	EXERCISES: SET 3 (UP-TEMPO)	I	2 CAMS AUDIO T.D. FLOOR VTR DIR	K.H. J.K. S.W.	–	7	HUMAN SKELETON	DOLLY	1 DAY
29–30	3	MICROSCOPE CUT-A-WAYS	I (LAB)	(EFP) • J.K.–CAM • P.J.–AUDIO • GRIP DIR	–	–	2	✻ CLOSE-UP ADAPTER	–	3 HRS.
30–37	4	EXERCISES: SET 4 (ON THE FLOOR)	I	2 CAM'S AUDIO T.D. FLOOR VTR DIR	K.H. J.K. S.W.	–	8	ELECTRONIC KEYBOARD	DOLLY	1 DAY
38–39 40–43	(4) (5)	GUIDED VISUALIZATION	I	2 CAM'S AUDIO T.D. FLOOR VTR DIR	K.H. J.K. S.W.	–	6	ELECTRONIC KEYBOARD	DOLLY	5 HRS.

SCRIPT BREAKDOWN "FITNESS ..." Page: 1
Date: 7/89 Producer: G. ZARICK Director: D. SMITH

FIGURE 2.14
Script Breakdown

With the script in hand, the director breaks down every element of the production into its sections. Each section can be cut out and put into various orderings, depending on how the work will be organized. These sheets are used for scheduling, coordinating, and budgeting.

ration provided at the end of the chapter. These books contain other examples of budget formats. And there are some excellent computer programs (advertised in video and film trade magazines) that provide production spreadsheets.

To find current prices, contact the various services and suppliers you will be dealing with during the production. Write for equipment and rental catalogues. Obtain the rate cards for the production and postproduction resources you intend to use. In budgeting personnel rates you can write to various unions and guilds (selected addresses at the end of the chapter) to obtain standardized rates. The U.S. De-

SCRIPT BREAKDOWN SUMMARY

"Fitness From..."

PERSONNEL	ROLE	ACTIVITY	TIME
G. ZARICK	PRODUCER	TOTAL PRODUCTION	35 DAYS
D. SMITH	DIRECTOR	TOTAL PRODUCTION	35 DAYS
J. ZARICK	ASSOC. PROD.	TOTAL PRODUCTION	27 DAYS
K. HUNTER	TALENT	ON CAMERA	5 DAYS
K.H. /D.S.	WRITERS	WRITE SCRIPT	3 DAYS
K,H. /D.S.	WRITERS	WRITE TREATMENT/PROPOSAL	4 DAYS
J.Z. /D.S./G.Z.		SCOUT LOCATIONS	2 DAYS
G.Z.		BUSINESS ARRANGEMENTS	12 DAYS
J.Z. /D.S./G.Z.		SCHEDULING	1 DAY
J.Z. /D.S.		ORGAN. & SECURE EQUIP.	2 DAYS
J.Z./D.S./G.Z. + 5 CREW		STUDIO SHOOTING	6 DAYS
J.Z. /D.S./ + 3 CREW		FOREST SHOOTING	1 DAY
J.Z. /D.S./ + 3 CREW		LAB SHOOTING	½ DAY
D.S. /G.Z. + OPERATOR		COMPUTER GRAPHICS	2 DAYS
D.S. /G.Z.		OFF-LINE EDIT (INCL. PREP.)	4 DAYS
D.S. /G.Z.		ON-LINE EDIT (INCL. PREP.)	1 DAY
J.Z. /M.H. /T.J.		MUSIC PRODUCTION	4 DAYS
D.S. /J.Z. /G.Z. /T.J.			1 DAY
D.S. /J.Z. /G.Z. /		LAY-BACK /DUPLICATION	1 DAY

TRAVEL/LOCATIONS: (ALL LOCAL)
— MT. AIRY FOREST — STUDIO [XU TV CENTER]
– U.C. MEDICAL COLLEGE
– P.P.S.

PROPS:
- ROSE (LONG STEM)
- HUMAN SKELETON
- X-RAY LIGHT BOX
- EXERCISE MATS
- 4 LARGE PLANTS
- DESK + CHAIR
- HAIR DRYER
- MATCHING COSTUMES FOR 3

MATERIALS & SUPPLIES:
- PHOTOCOPIES (200)
- PHONE (ALL LOCAL)

ONE-INCH TAPE – (6) 60's
A ROLL   – (1) 60
B ROLL   – (1) 60
MASTER   – (1) 60

RELEASE   – (6) T/20's
3/4" SAFETY – (1) 60
3/4" T.C. DUBS (6) 60's

SPECIAL EQUIPMENT:
- MICROSCOPE ADAPTER FOR CAMERA LENS
- DOLLY (NO TRACK) + RENTAL
- WIDE-ANGLE LENS
- FOG FILTER
- ELECTRONIC KEYBOARD
- WIRELESS MIKE (1)
- TELEPROMPTER (2)

OTHER:
- LUNCH (STUDIO) ON 6 DAYS – 8 PEOPLE
- 3 LARGE SHEETS OF POSTERBOARD (WHITE)

FIGURE 2.15   Script Breakdown Summary

A summary of the elements involved in a production including scheduling. This sheet gives the director a clear indication of the scope of the production, and it is also used to develop the budget.

CODE	DESCRIPTION	SUB-TOTAL	EXTERNAL	INTERNAL
	PRODUCTION PERSONNEL-VIDEO/FILM			
	STAGE MANAGER			
	TECHNICAL DIRECTOR *MIKE TOEPKER* $100/d x 3		300.	
	LIGHTING DIRECTOR *DAVID SMITH*		(INCL.)	
	AUDIO TECHNICIAN *TIM BROERING* $300/d x 3		900.	
	VIDEO TECHNICIAN *GARY TEMPLETON* $300/d x 3		900.	
	TELECINE OPERATOR			
	VIDEOTAPE OPERATOR			
	CAMERAPERSON(S) 1: $400/d x 3 2: 400/d x 3 3: 400/d x 3	1200 1200 1200	3600.	
	BOOM OPERATOR $200/d x 3		600.	
	CRANE OPERATOR $100/d x 3		300.	
	CHARACTER GENERATOR OPERATOR $100/d x 3		300.	
	MAINTENANCE			
	GRIP(S) 1: 50/d x 3 2: 50/d x 3 3: 50/d x 3	150 150 150	450.	
	16 MM FILM CINEMATOGRAPHER(S)			
	16 MM AUDIO TECHNICIAN			
	ASSISTANT CAMERA			
	PRODUCTION PERSONNEL-VIDEO/FILM		7350.	

FIGURE 2.16   Budget Page Format

Page 3 of a production budget. The page that precedes this one also relates to "production personnel," and the summary is shown on the bottom of page 3. On page 4, a new category begins, and so on. This particular budget is sixteen pages long.

PROGRAM BUDGET ANALYSIS
Summary Sheet

PROGRAM/SERIES TITLE "FITNESS FROM THE INSIDE OUT"

NUMBER OF PROGRAMS: 1   EACH LENGTH: 60 min   FILM/TAPE/LIVE _____

PRODUCER: Highlight Productions, Inc.   UNIT MGR. D. Smith

DATE SUBMITTED: 7-16-86   TARGET START DATE 2/87

SUMMARY OF PROGRAM COSTS

	Page	EXTERNAL	INTERNAL
PROJECT STAFF	1.	$19,700	
TALENT/ARTISTIC PERSONNEL	2.	5,844	
PRODUCTION PERSONNEL (VIDEO/FILM)	3.	7,350	
STAGING & DESIGN PERSONNEL	4.	1,650	
OTHER PERSONNEL COSTS	5.	200	
PRODUCTION FACILITIES	7.	9,740	
SUPPLIES/MATERIALS	10.	7,516	
TRAVEL/MILEAGE	11.	100	
OTHER PRODUCTION EXPENSES	12.	1,440	
POSTPRODUCTION — PERSONNEL	13.	6,400	
POSTPRODUCTION — FACILITIES	14.	3,840	
ROYALTIES/CLEARANCES	15.		
PROMOTION & ADVERTISING	16.	800	
TOTAL PRODUCTION COSTS:		$64,580	
CONTINGENCY 5 %		3,229	
TOTAL EXTERNAL & INTERNAL		$67,809	
GRAND TOTAL:		$68,000	

FIGURE 2.17   Program Budget Summary
When the budget sheets are completed, the subtotals of each category are entered on the summary sheet and then totaled after adding a contingency fee (to allow for cost fluctuation). The summary page then becomes the first page of the budget when it is presented.

partment of Labor has extensive, current information on many of the positions listed in Figure 2.18. Various industry periodicals, such as *Video Systems* and the ITVA (International Television Association) newsletter, provide salary surveys and other personnel rate charts. If I've exhausted all other resources, I'll even call a facility where a similar position is filled and say, "I'm preparing a production budget and I need to know the daily rate you would charge if I employed your (job title)." Sometimes I'll call a facility in a comparable market if I don't feel like asking someone local to disclose proprietary information.

You can organize budget information in a variety of ways. Select a format that includes the categories you are most likely to encounter, and then use it as a guide to develop your own budget preparation sheets. This can be done on a typewriter or computer.

With the research involved in finding accurate prices, a simple production budget might take hours to complete, whereas a complex production budget might take weeks. Budgets for grant proposals vary considerably depending on the funding organization. Some foundations just want a general estimate (those awarding $5,000 or less) but, for larger grants, the production budget must be very detailed.

It took me three weeks to prepare the budget for the National Endowment for the Humanities grant because we had to anticipate and detail every expense. Obtaining the prices was the easy part. Understanding what costs would be involved required an effort comparable to doing the production itself because we had to complete the script and then do a detailed breakdown. We had European travel, filming in several American cities, animation, and other complexities, which was quite a challenge to budget. This is where methodical preparation of the project needs analysis and previsualization of the final program become a major asset.

Funding/Financing

Assuming that your project is of sufficient scale to require a budget, and having prepared a summary of the costs involved, the next step is to acquire the funds. Monies for producing a video or television program will likely come from one of these sources (or a combination):

- A company's departmental budget or in-house allocations
- A foundation or other granting organization (in the case of nonprofit situations)
- Investors (individuals hoping for a return on their investment)
- A sponsor (corporate or other interested party)
- A production or distribution entity that perceives a profit to be made by distributing or licensing the finished program
- Yourself, friends, and relatives

Producers who already have an organizational framework within which to operate—such as universities, hospitals, corporate video departments—have a clear path to financing. The independent producer, however, must carefully strategize finding the most appropriate source(s) and how funding can be received. One option is to set up a nonprofit production company specifically for the purpose of producing a program or series. This process will involve an attorney and, therefore, legal

Executive producer
Obtains financing, celebrity talent, literary or story (script) property; person who makes the project possible.

Senior producer
Has overall authority for hiring and securing all production resources; final decision maker when several producers are involved such as in a TV magazine series.

Producer (or line producer)
Has overall management responsibility for the production. Determines content, participants, and budget. Makes sure all production elements are on hand for the director. Administers the budget (decides how money will be spent).

Associate producer
Has a close-working partnership with the producer; the nearest implementer for the producer.

Supervising producer
Assumes producer responsibility for a part or section of a production (rather than the whole program); usually a "field" producer.

Assistant to the producer
Handles the detailed paperwork, people contacts (phone calls), and scheduling of the producer (not secretarial tasks but details relating to production).

Executive in charge of production
A title most often applied to executives high up on the corporate ladder under whose jurisdiction the program is being produced.

Segment producer
Has responsibility for producing a segment or story.

Special projects producer
Oversees a department called "special projects."

News producer
Has management responsibility for a newscast operation and program.

Director
Has overall creative responsibility for transforming a script into a program; has final creative decision-making authority.

Assistant director
This is the "right-hand" person for the director, handles production details.

Segment director
Directs only a segment or story for a program.

Director of operations
Responsible for the day-to-day communication and activity of a production unit: makes sure that the equipment works, the people show up, the set is ready for the director, and so on.

Casting director
Helps select cast; makes recommendations to the director; makes arrangements between talent and director; handles contractual terms; secures the talent for a production.

Preproduction director
A director whose energy is focused on making preparations for production, mostly relating to the script.

Floor director (floor manager)
The director's representative in the studio: sees that the studio and all its elements are under control; cues the talent; implements the director's decisions in the studio when she's not present.

Writer
Writes the program or series (script).

Actor (talent)
Performs a role in front of a camera.

Managing editor
Manages stories—usually in a news or magazine-type format; has final decision over stories.

Story editor
Reads stories and makes appropriate changes in either the script or the program accordingly.

Assignment editor
Receives stories from variety of sources and assigns them to be produced.

Videotape editor
Operates an editing system.

Technical director
Operates a production switcher.

Marketing director
Analyzes the market for a program and designs strategies to maximize the program's sales/rental/licensing.

Script supervisor
Manages the script throughout the course of a shoot and production; ensures its accuracy and keeps track of what has been done and what remains to be done.

Postproduction supervisor
Management responsibility for the people and equipment (or facilities) involved in the postproduction of a program or series; overall authority second only to the director.

**FIGURE 2.18
Personnel
Roles and
Responsibilities**
A listing of some of the more commonly used titles and their roles.

FIGURE 2.18 Personnel Roles and Responsibilities (continued)

Choreographer
Designs and implements all dance elements.

Research supervisor
Management responsibility for those who invest time and energy researching program content, legalities, and other information.

Production coordinator
In charge of securing props and other physical items; handles the production scheduling day to day; makes arrangements between the studio and the outside world.

Production supervisor
Overall supervision of production activities—makes sure everything is happening smoothly.

Production secretary
Available to the director for making notes, keeping track of every scene and its related details, and then putting this information into a usable form.

Production manager
Secures the equipment, facilities, and locations: oversees the scheduling of crew and talent; ensures that every element the director needs is in place for the shoot.

Unit production manager
Handles production management for a field (or studio) unit that is working independently from the main operation.

Key grip
Supervises the grip team; makes final decisions about grip equipment.

Grip
Sets up and maintains equipment relating to the physical and lighting needs of a production; manages lights and stands, dollies and cranes, flags, dots, silks, and a host of other items. In small-scale productions, the grip carries equipment.

Hospitality coordinator
Makes sure the crew and talent have food, shelter, and other comforts to make the production situation as pleasant as possible.

Wrangler
Responsible for keeping horses in good condition; often provides training in horsemanship and riding tricks.

Location manager
In charge of the location preparations and permits; makes sure the location is returned to its former condition after the shoot.

Set designer
Designs sets.

Set decorator
Provides the finishing touches to a set, such as wallpaper, painting, carpeting, ceiling tiles, in addition to the props.

Set construction supervisor
Works from plans provided by the set designer to construct the set.

Research staff
Conducts the research.

Art director
Designs the look of the program including the way the sets, costumes, titles, and locations interact. In small-scale productions, the art director is in charge of graphics.

Stunt coordinator
Works closely with the director and stunt performers to plan and execute stunts.

Graphic designer
Designs the titles, credits, and any other graphics to be used in the program.

Graphic artist
Implements the designs of the graphic designer by creating the graphics as either flat art, paintings, or computer images.

Clearance supervisor
In productions where much of the material will be borrowed from other creative sources, clearances are negotiated. A *clearance* is permission to use something.

Music composer/producer
Writes the music.

Music coordinator
Finds appropriate music for the program.

Musicians
Perform the music.

Promotion coordinator
Designs and coordinates a promotion strategy.

Production assistants
Available for whatever needs to be done, which ranges from going for coffee for the crew to managing a large crowd of extras waiting for a cue from the director.

Maintenance supervisor
Has management responsibility for maintaining the equipment and sometimes the set.

Announcer
Offers a vocal performance for a program.

FIGURE 2.18 Personnel Roles and Responsibilities (continued)

Dolly operator
Handles the setup and movement of a dolly.

Boom operator
Handles the setup and movement of a mic on a boom arm.

Gaffer
Handles the setup and operation of lighting equipment and other electrical needs.

Best boy
This is a go-for position for the most part.

Sound effects supervisor
Oversees the production of sound effects.

Videotape operator
Sets up and operates a video tape recorder (VTR).

Audio recordist
Sets up mikes and records sound.

Director of photography
Determines the location of the camera and the dynamics of each shot.

Camera operator
Operates the camera.

Videographer
A camera operator who determines the camera placement and dynamics for each shot.

Camera assistant
Assistant to the camera operator who may set up the camera, transport it, run follow focus, assist in camera movement on a dolly or crane, or take light meter readings and set the lens diaphragm.

Costume designer
Designs the costumes.

Wardrobe
Keeps track of costumes; makes sure they are in good condition; dispenses and collects them when appropriate.

Makeup
Provides makeup services to the talent.

Hair stylist
Provides hair styling services to the talent.

TelePrompTer operator
Operates a TelePrompTer.

Consultant
This is a content expert who helps the producer and/or writer to understand the subject matter.

Driver
People who drive vehicles in front of the camera.

fees, but, once established, any contributions to this entity become tax deductible (in whole or in part depending on current law) for the contributors. Another option is to set up a for-profit entity (sole proprietorship, partnership, or corporation) and develop a prospectus to describe the rate of return for yourself and any investors. Any investment in a video product (for sale) constitutes purchase of a security and is strictly regulated by both state and federal securities laws—hence a formal prospectus is always needed for this type of investment. A limited partnership is another way to structure the financing of a production. Whenever a project involves income to individuals, it's advisable to consult an attorney to make sure the financial structure and arrangements fit both the needs of the production and the people involved.

Traditionally, independently produced television programs have not been very profitable ventures. Many do not earn back the cost of their production. This is why, from an investment standpoint, television program investment is considered a "high-risk" venture. With the advent of home video and more diverse opportunities for program distribution, this situation is beginning to change, mostly in cases where a program has some definite marketability. You gauge your program's approximate financial potential by asking the question: "If this program were sitting on a shelf in a video store, how popular would it be as a sales item?" In your financing strategy you want to be very clear about the prospects your program has for generating income. You would have thought about the issue of distribution in the needs analysis stage, so by this point it should be clear just how your program will reach its intended audience and whether revenues will be generated in the process.

The funding/financing stage, which is the final one in the preproduction phase, is critical. Its success often makes the difference between programs that get produced and ideas that end up in the "not completed" file. So take the time to plan the very best way to obtain funding for your production. Then implement your plan as quickly as possible while enthusiasm is high.

Whether your structure for receiving funds will be not-for-profit or for-profit, the outcome of this stage should be getting the money you need. For that to happen, you usually need to develop some form of documentation to communicate to others what you intend to do. This might take the form of a **proposal,** a document that requests funds from a foundation or other granting entity, or a **prospectus,** a detailed presentation that describes your business arrangements along with a program description, budget, resumes, and other pertinent information. Again, if you seek investors, a prospectus is required.

Phase III: Production

The production phase begins when funds have been secured and shooting begins. In this phase you begin the process of creating the audio and video elements of the program. A small-scale production may move into this phase without much effort. Medium- to large-scale productions, however, require some further steps that are discussed in this section. These steps mostly involve putting the organization in place, setting up an operations center, building a team, scouting locations, scheduling, recording the audio, and shooting the scenes.

Establishing the Operations Center

Production companies and entities within larger organizations almost always have studio facilities. If not, a place can be set up temporarily to serve as a base. While this is fairly straightforward in most circumstances, it can become quite a challenge for extensive productions, particularly if most of the production will be done on remote location, far from the organizational headquarters.

A major motion picture company on location is an example of how complex an operations base can become. It will usually have several trailers, each dedicated to a particular purpose (grip equipment, accommodations, makeup, electrical equipment, lighting, props, costumes).

Although this step in the production process may seem obvious, on several occasions, I have seen situations where there was no production office or even a central base. These instances mostly involved independent producers who had little or no funds available for an office, much less a secretary. The producer was on the road so much that a home answering machine was the usual method of making connections with the outside world. Although this can work at a "bare bones" level, it is inefficient and unprofessional, and I don't recommend it from a practical standpoint. The producer is just too busy with production concerns to have to answer the phone, write correspondence, and handle the myriad other details involved in the day-to-day operation.

Sometimes the production doesn't need to be scheduled tightly. It may fit into the context of other productions going on simultaneously, which is normally the case in a production company or corporate studio situation. Or there may be a flexible deadline for the project so that things can get done in a relaxed fashion. In these instances, there will generally be an office with personnel or at least a resource-sharing situation where communication and coordination can be handled.

When a production is relatively large, however, you will usually find an intensive effort, focused during a specified period of time, so that everything can happen efficiently. In these situations, a base of operations is essential.

Making Legal/Insurance Arrangements

In productions with strong financial resources, where the participants will be earning wages, it is common practice to draw up formal agreements or contracts. When the details of each individual's role, responsibilities, rate of compensation, and time frame are specified before the work begins, there is little room for confusion or misunderstandings later on. As legal documents these agreements and contracts are usually created by an attorney. People who draft their own usually have an attorney go over them to make sure the language is clear, comprehensive, and accurate. They should at least be witnessed and signed by a notary if an attorney is not involved.

Other legal issues that arise in the course of a production could include copyrights for visuals, musical compositions, or performances; ownership rights to the final product (program); business arrangements between partners or investors; special permissions for shooting in restricted or unionized areas; and so on.

On larger-scale productions, especially where employees will be away from home, it is customary to provide liability insurance so everyone is covered in case of accident, disability, or death. Additionally, producers usually secure production insurance to protect the program owner(s) should anything happen to the original shooting materials (film or tape). Should the originals (or, later on, the master) somehow be accidently destroyed or lost, the insurance would provide sufficient funds for the program to be reshot or reproduced.

Making Crew Assignments

One of the major reasons for breakdown on a production is confusion surrounding the roles and responsibilities of crew and other participants. Figure 2.18 provides a list of personnel roles and responsibilities, but it can only be a rough outline because people have their own title preferences and there is lots of room for lumping roles together.

Usually the producer has been clear enough with individuals at the outset that each is aware of his or her role within the production context. But frequently members of the team do not know what has been agreed upon by the others. These issues should be addressed at the initial production meeting, with all members in attendance. The objective is to make people aware of their own, and everyone else's, roles and responsibilities, detailing gray areas where there may be confusion or overlap.

For instance, individual directors feel differently about creative decision making. Some are open to suggestions from other crew personnel and work in an egalitarian manner. They promote open communication and spontaneous interaction by inviting input. At the other extreme are directors who see themselves as best qualified to make creative decisions, and they don't want to take precious time debating options. They want few or no suggestions from others. In between these extremes are most directors (in my experience), who reserve the right to make final decisions but invite creative suggestions when appropriate (when it does not interfere with the production or schedule). Even then, most directors are careful about who may make these suggestions. These are the kinds of issues that need to be dealt with at the beginning of a production. Otherwise feelings can be hurt, assignments confused, gossip circulated, criticisms suppressed, and rivalries inflamed.

By the time of the initial production meeting, all jobs should have been assigned. If there is uncertainty about which person would be the best for a particular position, the decision must be made before this meeting so everyone in the room can be fully informed. The impressions and attitudes that color the entire production begin with this meeting. So it's important that everyone involved be there. By providing an open, honest, and fully communicative experience at the beginning, the team members will assume that they are free to continue in like manner throughout the production period.

Coordinating

Coordination refers to activities and scheduling designed to supply the production team with everything needed, when and where it is needed. The more complex the production, the more coordination will be required. Larger productions employ full-time coordinators or production managers responsible for handling scheduling, acquisitions, communication with outside agencies, and other details that relate to the team's needs.

The essential skills of coordinators are resourcefulness and initiative, and they should be outgoing. They must be able to take a list of items and find and acquire them quickly, with every detail correct and on time, secured under clear conditions and agreements (trade, purchase, rent, loan). This is not a job for everyone, but those who do it well are among the most appreciated persons on the team because they regularly make things happen that often seem impossible.

In very large productions, specific areas are handled by several coordinators: the schedule coordinator, talent coordinator, wardrobe coordinator, and so on. On medium to small projects, one person, often the production manager, will handle all the coordination.

At the time of the initial meeting, the coordinator can ask for a listing from each member indicating their needs (in detail) with their time requirements. Usually these requests are made in writing so there is a paper record of every detail.

Scouting Locations

Even for the simplest shoots, scouting locations is necessary. Unless you have been to the site, you cannot anticipate accurately what you will encounter when the crew shows up fully equipped and ready to go. Whether the location is near or far, it makes sense to take some pictures (Polaroid or otherwise) to refer to and share with other team members. **Electronic news gathering** (ENG) shoots might not require scouting because the conditions of the environment aren't as important— you take what's given. Figure 2.19 shows a typical *scouting checklist.* Considerations for the scouting checklist include:

Lighting

What kind and quality of lighting is optimal?

What is the amount and direction of the ambient light?

What is the best time of day or night to shoot?

How many lights will be used? Where?

Is the color quality of the light consistent or mixed?

What specific lighting equipment will be needed?

How broad an area will need to be lit?

Are color-correction gels or filters needed?

Does the location lend itself to special effects?

Electrical

Where are the circuit panels?

How many circuits are available and where are they?

Where can extension cables be run? How many are needed?

Where should the production equipment be placed?

Is a power generator needed? What are the power requirements?

Will an electrician be needed? Union or nonunion?

Space

Is the room temperature appropriate?

What is the capacity of the space (fire code)?

What are the access and exit routes?

How will cables be distributed or hidden?

If there's an audience, how will it be placed?

Is there adequate water supply, and are restrooms nearby?

Is there a specified emergency exit plan?

What is the normal traffic-flow situation?

Can the space be reserved, blocked off, and secured?

What are the clean-up arrangements?

SCOUTING CHECKLIST

TITLE: _____ JOB NO. _____

AGENCY & PHONE _____ AGENT _____

LOCATION & PHONE _____ LOC. CONTACT _____

BEFORE LEAVING THE OFFICE:

_____ Production envelope

_____ Scout bag, including Polaroid camera, director's finder, compass, tape measure, film, and light meter

_____ Still camera, film, filters, tripod, lights, and gels

Directions to the location: _____

_____

_____

WHEN AT THE LOCATION:

_____	Travel time	_____	Available light
_____	Interior or exterior or both	_____	Type of light
_____	Power box type	_____	Foot-candles
_____	Volts	_____	Ceiling height
_____	Amp rating of panel	_____	Surface
_____	Distance to shooting area	_____	Suitable for dolly

Surface obstacles. Explain: _____

_____

_____

Sound problems. Explain: _____

_____

Location accessibility. Explain: _____

_____

Ideal off-loading area. Explain: _____

_____

_____ Permission to shoot and fee

_____ Polaroids or slides of shooting area

Special items and notes: _____

_____

_____

_____

Draw map on reverse side of location, including compass direction, dimensions, location of power, off-loading area, surface obstacles, camera angles, and other appropriate information.

FIGURE 2.19   Scouting Checklist

A sheet used on location to ensure that all location details are managed.

Acoustics

How "live" or "dead" sounding is the space?

What is the nature of the reflective surfaces?

What mics are needed?

How many mics are needed, and what will be their placement? Any baffling?

How will the mic cords be strung? What path?

Is an audio mixer needed?

Is there noise that may need to be turned off?

Access

Are permissions needed? Keys? Supervisors?

Where can equipment be unloaded most efficiently?

Are there any hidden expenses in getting there (tolls)?

Who will make arrangements for scheduling? When?

Is insurance of any kind necessary?

By handling these and other issues ahead of time, efficiency is increased, planning becomes easier, and, in the long run, money is saved.

Scheduling Personnel

Because of the complexities and frequency of changes, scheduling is best handled by one individual. It's important that one person's calendar be the single indicator of who's doing what, when, with whom, and where. This approach is efficient because the entries on the schedule are also understood contextually by one person, who can easily resolve questions and confusion.

A weekly schedule (Figure 2.20) works well when the production will be on-going for weeks or months and when the same key people will be working together throughout the production. A daily schedule (Figure 2.21) is more appropriate for short-term productions and when different people will be filling the various roles.

Whatever the form and format of the production schedule, it should be available (on a bulletin board or wall chart) for others to scan to see the status of various days and times. Then they can ask the schedule keeper, usually the production manager or coordinator, to make entries. The criteria for "bumping" others off the schedule, and the person with authority to do so, should be clear to everyone. It can be very frustrating to show up for an appointment to find that you have been bumped without being informed. This is another good reason for having one person handle the schedule—communication between parties who are competing for the same time can be facilitated.

Every member of the production team should be able to contact everyone else. You or the production coordinator can prepare a list of everyone's contact informa-

TAILWIND

Week	1	2	3	4	5	6	7	8	9	10	11

Production Activity

Stock ftg search
Landscape shots
Hotel exteriors
Limo exteriors
Limo interiors
Car chase
Downtown misc.
Nature scenes
Ending reveal
Music selection
Graphics (CG)

(- = day)

Week __3__

MONDAY _NOV. 7_	TUESDAY _NOV. 8_	WEDNESDAY _NOV. 9_
8:00 CREW CALL — STUDIO 10:00 SHOOT SCENES: 27-30/41-42/50-55 AT THE HOTEL JULIE - SET UP MEETING w/ AUDIO STUDIO T.B./G.R SCREEN LANDSCAPE FTG. & TIME-CODE	10:00 CREW MEETING TO PLOT LIMO SHOOT J.S. MAKE CALLS RE: STOCK FOOTAGE T.B. CHECK EQUIP. FOR TOMORROW'S SHOOT ★ CHARGE 750 BATTERIES OVERNIGHT (3)	8:00 CREW CALL - STUDIO 10:00 SHOOT REMAINING SCENES AT HOTEL 2:30 M.H. PICK UP DOLLY & 18' TRACK AT M.D.I. DELIVER TO HOTEL 3:00 J.S. MEETS W/ GRAPHIC DESIGNER

THURSDAY _NOV. 10_	FRIDAY _NOV. 11_	SATURDAY _NOV. 12_
T.B. TIME-CODE & DUB ALL REMAINING TAPES G.T. RETURN DOLLY & TRACK TO M.D.I. 2:00 SCOUT LIMO LOCATION (M.H. & P.P.)	T.B. LOGGING J.S. FOLLOW-UP CALLS ON STOCK FOOTAGE 7:30 L.S. DINNER w/ CH 7 PROGRAM MGR.	SUNDAY _NOV. 13_

NOTES

• WIRELESS MIKE IS OUT FOR REPAIR

• CREW MEETING NEXT TUE. @ 10 AM

Larry	745-3461	453-7564
Tim	745-3526	453-3655
Gary	745-5748	677-4632
Mark	745-7786	453-9898
Paula	756-9987	
Julie	745-5534	677-7772

FIGURE 2.20 Weekly Production Schedule

A form that displays a week at a time with the relative time frame of each production phase indicated at the top. These pages are kept in the schedule binder.

PRODUCTION SCHEDULE

Production Title: _____   Production Date: _____

Client/Agency/Project: _____   Location: _____

CLIENT PRODUCER: _____   PHONE: _____

PRODUCER: _____   PHONE: _____

DIRECTOR OF PHOTOGRAPHY: _____   PHONE: _____

DIRECTOR: _____   PHONE: _____

ASSIST. CAMERA: _____   PHONE: _____

VIDEO OPERATOR: _____   PHONE: _____

ENGINEER: _____   PHONE: _____

SECRETARY: _____   PHONE: _____

KEY GRIP: _____   PHONE: _____

DOLLY GRIP: _____   PHONE: _____

GRIP: _____   PHONE: _____

GRIP: _____   PHONE: _____

BOOM: _____   PHONE: _____

PROD. ASSIST. _____   PHONE: _____

PROD. ASSIST. _____   PHONE: _____

PROD. ASSIST. _____   PHONE: _____

AUDIO: _____   PHONE: _____

LIGHTING DIRECTOR: _____   PHONE: _____

MAKEUP: _____   PHONE: _____

WARDROBE: _____   PHONE: _____

WRANGLERS: _____   PHONE: _____

DIRECTOR: _____   PHONE: _____

OFF-LINE EDITOR: _____   PHONE: _____

PROPS: _____   PHONE: _____

FLOOR MANAGER: _____   PHONE: _____

GRAPHIC ARTIST: _____   PHONE: _____

CAMERA OPERATOR: _____   PHONE: _____

CAMERA OPERATOR: _____   PHONE: _____

TALENT: _____   PHONE: _____

TALENT: _____   PHONE: _____

CREW CALL: _____   CREW WRAP: _____   Checklist Mgr.: _____

CAST CALL: _____   CAST WRAP: _____

Type of Production: Lunch to be: Dress Code:

_____ Exterior   _____ Brown Bag   _____ Professional

_____ Interior   _____ Fast Food Rest.   _____ Casual

_____ Studio   _____ Other   _____ Old Clothes

Directions to Location: _____

FIGURE 2.21   Daily Production Schedule

Daily production schedules are filled out by the director or coordinator.
They are tacked to a bulletin board, where the crew can see them easily.

tion and make sure each member has a copy for his or her production binder. This list should be posted near the master schedule and by every phone.

On large-scale productions, "call sheets" are used to indicate which actors are being used, when they need to show up for makeup, their set call, the locations, and the scenes to be shot for each production day. For Hollywood-scale productions, I suggest you refer to *The Primal Screen,* by Bob Shanks (listed in the chapter's Suggested Readings), which illustrates a large number of production forms including a call sheet.

For practical reasons, most location shooting is scheduled before studio shooting. This allows some of the primary footage to be gathered so everyone can get a sense of how things are going in terms of efficiency and quality. If enough people are involved, the studio shooting can be done simultaneously, but in smaller-scale situations studio work is usually done after the bulk of the location work is completed. In this area the scale of a production and the nature of various organizational structures will result in different approaches.

Often a significant part of scheduling involves making arrangements between the crew and talent, making arrangements for rental equipment, scheduling the studio or other spaces that need to be rented, and scheduling travel time and holiday work. Among other reasons, schedule forms are not standardized because production entities, and their work styles and requirements, differ considerably.

Scheduling Facilities

In the needs analysis, you will decide which facilities will be used for the production. At this point, facilities (studio space, post house, special locations) should be scheduled. All studios have a schedule (Figure 2.22) that indicates bookings. Most operate on a first-come, first-served basis. Experience has taught me to reserve a backup date and time for every booking because, if for some reason the time doesn't work out, you don't have to wait a week or more to get back into the studio. And, if I see I won't need a time I've reserved, I'll call the facility immediately so they can offer it to someone else—and so I won't be billed for the time.

Choosing Equipment

The equipment you'll use probably depends on what is available or what you can afford given the budget. "Vidiots" (people crazy about video equipment) at every level of the business enjoy discussing and debating which tape format and brand is better. In the end it usually comes down to cost versus the quality demand of the production. Figure 2.23 describes the more popular formats.

In the needs analysis include specifications relating to equipment—resources, availabilities, and costs. Most important, the total production system (all equipment) should be checked out (tested) to ensure that each component is functioning optimally. This is also a good time to make sure you have copies of manuals to accompany the equipment. This is also the time—just before shooting—for testing, troubleshooting, or repair work that may need to be done.

When you rent equipment there are usually specified terms and conditions (see Appendix C) that protect the owner from liability and explain the renter's responsi-

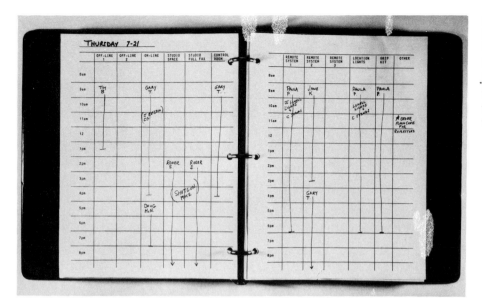

FIGURE 2.22
Facilities Reserva-
tion Schedule
*This is the kind of
form rental houses
use to keep track of
who will be using
what and when.*

bility. Become familiar with these for each rental company you deal with; if they don't offer these guidelines, ask for them.

Photographing

All the shooting is done in this period so that, before the next stage, all the visual materials (original tapes) will be on hand to prepare for postproduction. Shooting includes photographing any special flat art, stills, tabletop setups, animation, or other special visual material. After recording, the original rolls should have their red buttons removed so there is no chance the tapes will be recorded over. Label each tape and its case, clearly specifying them as "original" rolls. Other useful labeling information includes the title of the production, the number of the roll in terms of the sequence of shooting, the location of the audio (track 1 or 2, or both), the camera operator, the director, and the date.

A systems management practice that saves time and headaches is to phone everyone (crew and talent) the day before a shoot, confirming the time and double-checking details relating to their roles. We include phone numbers on our daily production schedule (Figure 2.21) for this purpose. We also use production crew cards (Figure 2.24) to keep track of everyone who wants to work for us and to quickly access our personnel options.

By pulling the cards, we can determine a person's availability and contact information. Calling people the day before a shoot prevents that nightmarish situation where people you expect to be present either show up late or not at all. Production time is not the time to chase people down because they forgot to tell you they couldn't make it. Assume nothing—and take responsibility for everything—if you prefer to produce in an atmosphere of confidence and calm.

FIGURE 2.23
Videotape Record-
ing Formats

VIDEOTAPE RECORDING FORMATS

"D" Format	Highest quality available to date Faster setup and editing time Greater reliability Little/no generation loss
Type "C" One-Inch	Broadcast quality (standard) Variable tape speed (slow motion and freeze frame) Picture displayed during forward and rewind
MII	Similar quality to one-inch Time compression and FM recording Metal particle tape Available as camcorder
Betacam and Betacam SP	Competitor of MII Camcorder Component signal processing
¾ in. U-matic and ¾ in. U-matic SP	NTSC (composite) signal processing Standard for nonbroadcast studios SP gives better picture quality
S-VHS	(Super VHS) Component processing Available as camcorder High-quality original recording Uses T-120 tapes Industrial and commercial use
Hi-8	Competitor of S-VHS Uses very compact cassettes Industrial, commercial, and consumer
VHS	Consumer grade; very portable Approximately 50% less resolution compared with S-VHS
8 mm	Consumer grade Extremely portable

*Some of the most
common video re-
cording formats.*

Also, be sure to obtain a **talent release form** (Figure 2.25) for anyone who will be on camera—it's the law!

Phase IV: Postproduction

. . . .

We will discuss postproduction in terms of communication values in greater detail in Chapter 14. Here we'll discuss postproduction's various phases from a technical standpoint.

PRODUCTION CREW

NAME: _____ ROLE: _____

PHONE: (H) _____ (W) _____ DATE: _____

ADDRESS: _____

CAREER OBJECTIVE: _____

AWARDS: _____

SPECIALTY/RESOURCES: _____

COMPENSATION REQUESTED: _____ WILL VOLUNTEER: YES NO

LEVEL OF EDUCATION & FIELD: _____

PLEASE INDICATE THE HOURS YOU CANNOT WORK:

	8	9	10	11	12	1	2	3	4	5	6	7	8	9	10	11
MON.																
TUE.																
WED.																
THU.																
FRI.																
SAT.																
SUN.																

Experience
(Check roles you have performed)

Camera	( )	Director	( )
Audio	( )	A.D.	( )
Switcher	( )	Typing	( )
Floor Mgr.	( )	Photog.	( )
VTR Operator	( )	Artist	( )
Char. Generator	( )	Talent	( )
Narration	( )	Other _____	

**FIGURE 2.24
Production Crew
Cards**

To keep track of the many people who want to work on crew, we use these cards and keep them up to date.

The Posting Design

As the production process unfolds, you will develop a postproduction design—a plan of how the program master tape will be created. Throughout the production process, you will have made certain decisions based on how the program will be edited. Therefore, before going into the posting phase, it's wise to meet with the principals who will be involved in the actual editing. The director (or producer) usually calls the shots while an editor operates the machines. Go over each detail to make sure the editing process is understood and agreed upon by those involved. This is also a good time to secure the costs relating to postproduction.

The postproduction design should specify the exact procedure, the editing equipment (system) to be used, format transfers, time-code considerations, transitions (cuts only? dissolves? effects?), and character generated (or other) graphics. Will it be advisable to edit a **rough cut** (work print)? Will there be any special computer effects? What kind? How long? How will the various audio tracks be mixed, and where? How long will posting take—a factor based on the number and complexity of edits in the show. **Post houses** commonly base their rate estimates on the anticipated number of edits, so it's good to have a sense of this in advance of your meeting. A recent 30-minute documentary contained 460 edits.

Organization of Materials

In some instances, the editing may be done using the original rolls, such as in news work or when the video will be used just a few times. More often, however, the

TALENT RELEASE FORM

Production Company: _____

Production Title: _____

Location: _____

     In consideration of one dollar ($1.00) or other consideration
_____ , I hereby release the production company,
producer, and its employees from any legal responsibility in
relation to videotape, film, or other media materials containing
my recorded image and/or voice or property. I understand that all
rights as to the use of such tapes or other materials is given
freely to the production company.

     I hereby waive any right to inspect or approve the finished
product or the copy that may be used in connection therewith. And
I release and discharge the production company and its personnel
from any liability whatsoever that may occur or be produced in the
taking, processing, distribution, or publication of such images.
The undersigned accepts employment as an independent contractor
on the terms and conditions set forth herein.

     It is also understood that any such materials (video, audio,
film, slides, etc.) will be used with the highest integrity and
discretion, with the intent to communicate responsibly and
ethically, the subject matter contained therein.

NAME: _____ (Please print)   Time in: _____

ADDRESS: _____   Time out: _____

_____   Paid: _____

PHONE: (H) _____ (W)_____   Check # _____

SIGNATURE _X_____   Date: _____

WITNESS _X_____

PARENT SIGNATURE: _____

NOTES:_____

_____

FIGURE 2.25   Talent Release Form

practice is to go to great lengths to protect (and not use) the original rolls. Every time a tape is played, it is degraded microscopically, and the opportunity increases for dust to accumulate and tape aberrations to occur. So in cases where the program will be duplicated and used widely, it's advisable to perform all preliminary, decision-making work on dub rolls (copies made from the original rolls).

Whatever the case, each tape needs to be logged in preparation for editing (Figure 2.26). **Log sheets** are always printed on (not written on in script) with a felt tip pen to provide better copying quality and quick reading by others.

If time-coding is to be done, it will be recorded onto the original rolls simultaneously with the dubbing. Sometimes, if a portable time-code reader/writer is available, time-code numbers can be recorded on the original rolls in the field. Hour, minute, second, and frame numbers are "burned into" the dub for visual reference. Then the logging can be done from these **window dubs** without any harm to the originals. It's good practice to make a time-coded dub of each of the original rolls and then use the dub rolls for all subsequent viewing. If the material is to be edited on-line with a computer-type edit controller, time-code numbers are necessary to maintain frame accuracy.

You can structure the editing process in a number of ways depending on the format of the original rolls, the equipment available, cost, generational quality considerations, and special effects. Figure 2.27 shows some of the most common postproduction strategies.

Off-Line Edit Decision List

An off-line **edit decision list** (EDL) is prepared using the log sheets and/or a VTR to make scene placement decisions. Log sheets show which scene and "take" is best and where it is located on the roll. The window dub rolls give the exact numerical location of every frame, so it's simply a matter of writing down the "in" and "out" points for each scene—in the desired sequence. In most instances the sequencing of scenes will closely follow the order of the shooting script.

I use two kinds of EDL forms depending on whether or not the editing will be done with time-code numbers. When I'm building a program master using just the footage counters on the VTR instead of time-code numbers, I'll use the off-line edit decision list form (Figure 2.28). This way is faster but not better, especially when the program will contain dissolves, effects, or character generated material. This kind of EDL is for a cuts-only situation such as in news and event coverage. If the editing will be done with the original rolls only, this list is fine for designing the program master. It is also useful as a first step toward preparing a rough cut so time-code numbers can be derived.

I use the other form, an *on-line EDL,* when time-code numbers are known or available and when the posting will involve the integration of dissolves and other effects. The form shown in Figure 2.29 is typical of what would be used in any professional postproduction house. When people refer to an EDL, they usually mean this kind of format.

VIDEO LOG

THE NEW RELATIONSHIP

Program Title (Thursday AM: ASSEMBLY)

REEL __12__
PAGE __1__
DATE __2/88__

Scene #	Take #	Audio	Evaluation	Start at . . .	End at . . .	Notes / Zero counter at first video after bars
—	1	2	C	:00	:47	EXT. OF CAPITAL BLG. Z/1 (MED. SPEED)
	②		A	:48	1:20	" (SLOW ")
—	1		B	1:22	1:40	PEOPLE WALKING AROUND FOUNTAIN (FOLLOW)
				1:52		HENRY BOROVICK
			(A+)			— NATURE NEEDED MILLIONS ... YRS...
						CAN WE ALLOW... DESTROY THIS PROCESS
						NO !
						— UNREQUITED LOVE
			(A++)	3:18		— "LET'S NOT EXPECT MIRACLES — LET'S
					3:50	MAKE THEM "
—	1	—		3:58	4:25	CONVERGENCE CENTER SIGN — PAN TO ACTIVITY
				4:50		BARBARA MARX HUBBARD
—			(A)			— INVITED TO SOVIET EMBASSY ... ONE FAMILY
			(A++)			— NEW RELATIONSHIP IS NOW! ... PROCESS IS BIG
			(A++)			— CREATE TOGETHER; "CO-CREATE" THE NEW
			A			— TASK FORCES: "WHAT DO YOU WANT TO DO?"
						: TV CAMERAS BELONG IN THE PROCESS
			(A++)			: CHANGE THE CONCEPT OF NEWS
					12:20	: 300 DELEGATES ... INTEGRITY
—				13:05		INTERVIEW: BRIAN O'LEARY (ASTRONAUT)
			(A+)			— MISSION (w/SOVIETS) TO MARS
			A		17:40	— US/SOVIET ASTRONAUT/COSMONAUT EXCHANGE
—			A+	17:50	20:18	PERFORMANCE: DAVID POMERANCE
						("FARAWAY LANDS — FARAWAY PLACES")

FIGURE 2.26   Video Log Sheet

A form such as this is filled out for every tape that is shot. Kept in the production binder, these sheets indicate a tape's content and quality.

LEVEL I: CUTS ONLY. FOR NEWS AND OTHER VIDEOS WHERE THE EDITED MASTER COPY WILL ALSO BECOME THE PLAY-BACK TAPE.

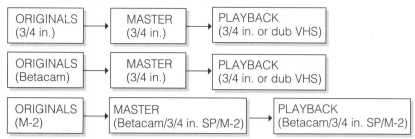

LEVEL II: DISSOLVES, WIPES, AND VISUALS (INSERT) EFFECTS. FOR BUSINESS, INDUSTRIAL, PSA, AND LOCAL COMMERCIAL PRODUCTIONS WHERE QUALITY IS NECESSARY AND/OR MANY COPIES OF THE PROGRAM WILL BE DISTRIBUTED.

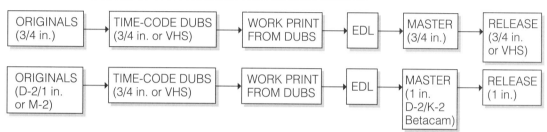

LEVEL III: AUDIO AND VIDEO HANDLED SEPARATELY. FULL VIDEO EFFECTS. HIGHEST QUALITY ATTAINABLE. FOR BROADCAST AND NATIONAL COMMERCIAL PRODUCTIONS. ORIGINALS CAN BE VIDEO OR FILM.

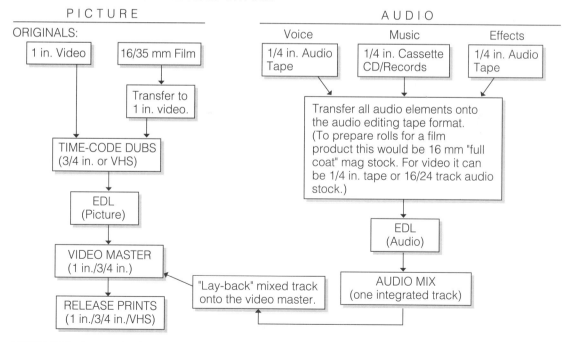

FIGURE 2.27 Postproduction Strategies

Level I strategies are the simplest. Level II strategies are of medium complexity.
Level III strategies are the most complex—and the most expensive. Level III
also indicates the use of film as the camera original. Each facility, due to
unique equipment capabilities, will approach editing differently.

	OFF-LINE EDL					"THE NEW RELATIONSHIP" — SOVIET-AMERICAN CITIZENS' SUMMIT—
Event	Scene	Log	Reel	In	Length	Description
1					:30	BARS + TONE
2					:05	BLACK
3		60.2	60	21:13	:20	G. TOSSING SINGS "A MEETING OF THE HEARTS"
4		13.2	13	19:02	:07	R. MULLER: "WE SHOULD...(NOT KILL)...NATION OR RELIGION"
5		12.1	12	5:25	:20	D. POMERANCE SINGS "FARAWAY LANDS"
6		23.2	23	38:12	:12	P. ELLSBERG: "MUTUAL REGARD ... RULE OF LAW"
7		47.2	47	21:40	:20	A GRADSKY SINGS "MARIA"
8		21.1	21	14:20	:12	G. ALFERENKO (ON GORBACHEV REVOLUTION)
9		52.2	52	19:10	:20	EXTERIOR OF CAPITAL BUILDING (Z/IN) —MUSIC—
10			CG		:05	SUPER TITLE: "THE NEW RELATIONSHIP" —MUSIC—
11		20.1	20	8:15	:06	KIDS PLAYING AROUND FOUNTAIN (VO) —MUSIC—
12		21.1	21	10:40	:06	FACES IN A CROWD (NAT. SOUND) —MUSIC—
13		20.1	20	4:14	:08	SOVIET AIRPLANE LANDING (NAT. SOUND) —MUSIC—
14		20.1	20	15:10	:20	SOVIETS ON BUS TO HOTEL (NAT. SOUND)
15		31.2	31	20:25	:40	B. HUBBARD (BKGND. OF CONFERENCE) INCL. INTRO. OF R. VERNON
16		12.1	12	7:28	:58	R. VERNON WELCOME, CITIZEN DIPLOMATS ... CUTAWAY TO
17		28.2	28	11:00	:40	INT. SOVIET EMBASSY (PEOPLE MILLING AROUND)
18		30.1	30	16:05	:32	AUDIO SITES AT EMBASSY 1) H. BOROVICK

(Scene column annotated vertically: NOT SCRIPTED, spanning events 4–14)

FIGURE 2.28 Off-Line Edit Decision List

An EDL used in the off-line process using VTR footage counters, instead of time-coding, to reference scenes.

EDIT DECISION LIST

PRODUCTION: BOOK OF CO-CREATION
DIRECTOR: D. SMITH EDITOR: J. ZARICK
DATE: 8/89
PAGE: 1 OF: 1

EVENT	REEL	TRAN	PLAYER IN	PLAYER OUT	DURATION	R START	R STOP	
1					20 00	00 00 10 00	00 00 30 00	BARS + TONE
2	(CG)				08 00	00 00 32 00	00 00 40 00	CG (INTRO)
3	23 A	F/I	19 21 43 02	19 22 25 06	42 04	00 00 42 00	00 00 42 46	STAR FIELD Z/I
4	1 B	DISS	00 28 01 21	00 28 08 26	07 04	00 00 42 46	00 00 50 00	EARTH (NASA FTG.)
5	LA 2A	DISS	02 17 39 12	02 17 39 14	05 02	00 00 48 00	00 00 55 04	OPEN SEA
6	LA 3B	DISS	00 02 38 02	00 02 47 05	09 03	00 00 55 04	00 01 04 07	SURF
7	(CG)	SUPER			05 00	00 00 57 04	00 01 02 04	CG (TITLE) *
8	LA 8A	DISS	08 19 32 18	08 19 57 22	25 04	00 01 02 04	00 01 27 08	FOOTSTEPS Z/O TO
9	27 B	FI/FO	14 20 00 04	19 20 23 08	23 04	00 01 03 02	00 01 26 06	ANNCR. VO "AUDIO ONLY"
10	27 B	CUT	08 02 16 30	08 02 17 50	01 20 00	00 01 26 06	00 02 46 06	SOT - AUDIO ONLY
11	LA 9A	CUT	12 13 04 00	12 13 08 13	08 13	00 01 28 14	00 01 36 27	(INSERT) HANG GLIDER
12	LA 2B	CUT	04 21 12 10	04 21 15 20	03 10	00 01 36 27	00 01 39 37	(INSERT) BIRD

* FONTS = DISC 1 P.25
DISC 2 P.24
DISC 3 P.24 MURRAY HILL BOLD (COLOR # 140008)

FIGURE 2.29 On-Line Edit Decision List

An EDL used in the on-line posting process. Every scene is exactly specified by its time-code numbers.

Audio/Music Production and Mixing

Any audio or music elements that have not already been gathered or produced must now be recorded. Frequently you will need to do additional audio work such as sound effects or **Foley** effects (footsteps, running) or **rerecording** (looping) of voices to improve the sound quality. The music should also be available, whether it is from a copyright-cleared source (needledrop) or originally produced. The audio-tape format depends on the format of the equipment to be used, but eventually you must be able to record the audiotape onto the videotape program master.

On small-scale productions you may simply transfer the audio elements to the master tape, using one or more of the audio tracks on the videotape. More often, the music, sound effects, and voice tracks will be patched through a mixing board so that the combined "mix" becomes an integrated whole that is then transferred to just one of the tracks on the master videotape.

In more complex productions, you may need to transfer the voice track on the edited master videotape to multitrack audiotape so it can be mixed with music and effects tracks in sync. This **layoff** allows the speech track to be on the same audiotape (16- or 24-track) as the sound effects and music. Another of these audio tracks is allocated for the time code, which maintains sync throughout. Using time codes the operator knows each frame of every track she is dealing with and can set up the mixing board accordingly. (A *sound effects log* is shown in Appendix D.) As each audio element appears, its level will be appropriately assigned. Once all of this editing and alignment is complete, to the satisfaction of both the director and the audio engineer, the final audio mix can be done. The mixed track, still on audiotape, is "laid back" onto the master video tape, with **SMPTE** time code on both machines (video and audio), thus keeping everything in perfect sync.

In the past television producers concentrated on the quality of the picture, almost to the exclusion of audio quality. Because TV sets had small, single speakers, even good-quality audio got substantially reduced. Today, with high fidelity and stereo sound capabilities in TV receivers, most producers give equal attention to audio quality.

With major improvements in audio technologies in recent years and their widespread availability, producers now consider audio **sweetening** to be a necessary part of the total mix. Sweetening improves the quality of originally recorded audio (whether recorded on an audio or video recorder). The background noise can be reduced. Hiss and hum—any sound that is constant—can be reduced or eliminated. You can alter the frequency response substantially to increase highs or lows, change the timbre or resonance of a voice, or strengthen the rumble of a drum. You can alter the duration of a sound by expanding or compressing it. Off-mike accidental sounds can be eliminated. Reverberation can be added to voice or music to make the audio space seem more expansive. And you can dampen sounds to drop off immediately, making the recording space feel closer. With computer-assisted digital recording and processing, audio time, space, and quality are completely controllable.

Off-Line Editing

The term **off-line** refers to the way a video editing system is wired or configured with other equipment. An off-line *system* is not connected to a production switcher (used to make video transitions). It stands alone, only having the capacity to transfer audio and video to a recorder. Off-line editing is used to make cuts-only transitions with no other inputs (from a **character generator** or other source). In practice, however, editing systems are wired in a variety of ways to maximize capabilities, and so off-line editing has come to mean any editing *process* that is preliminary to making the final program master. A master tape can be made off-line, but the program will be restricted to cuts-only transitions.

Off-line editing then, as part of the posting process, refers to the use of an edit system to make edit decisions concerning scene placement and timing. It's usually a preparatory step to on-line editing, where dissolves and other transitions (wipes, special effects) are added.

Computer-based edit decision listing is making the process of developing an EDL fast and easy. I know someone who used to offer EDL services to independent producers. He worked out of his home with only a VCR, a PC (personal computer), and a listing program. He would give the client a disk that could then be taken to a post house along with the original rolls. The disk would then control the machines, making the right kind of edit at exactly the right places, in perfect sequence. A high-end (expensive) variation of this technique is to put every scene on a videodisk and have an EDL, also on disk, that manipulates it to produce a master tape. With a videodisk there is virtually no time lost in rewinding or fast-forwarding. In- and out-points are available instantly anywhere on the disk, and there is no generational loss of picture quality.

On-Line Editing

On-line editing always refers to compiling scenes using an integrated editing system to produce a program master tape. Postproduction houses are primarily in the business of doing on-line editing. They expect producers to have done all their off-line work (edit decisions) and organization before they show up for the editing session.

To go into an on-line session, you will need all the original rolls. You'll also need an EDL (Figure 2.29), which specifies the exact location of every scene on the original rolls, the in- and out-points (time-code numbers) of these scenes, their order of placement in the program, the type of transition (in and out) for each scene, and the length of each scene.

Don't make creative decisions now—not at around $350–$600 an hour—that's the purpose of off-line editing. Nonetheless, as the program comes together scene by scene, the producer and the editor will be making some fresh decisions based on how well or poorly they think it's going. There is ample opportunity to make changes, but the fewer changes, the more time and money saved. Transitions, character generated (and other) graphics, and special effects will be mixed into the program at this point.

All that remains are any transfers to other formats for distribution purposes. The post house customarily makes a **safety** copy, which they keep on file should your program master tape meet with disaster or be lost.

Summary

For beginners and others who may not have experienced a complete production, this chapter provides an overview of the production process. We focused on the four production phases: design, pre-production, production, and postproduction.

In the design stage use the needs analysis questions (Chapter 6) as a guide to the unfolding of the production process. The program should be previsualized and an outline prepared. The outline becomes the working structure of the program. When you need others to see what the program will be like, a treatment is written to describe it in visual language. The treatment, because it's intended for others, is carefully crafted to accomplish the program's communication objective for the reader, providing a vivid impression of the program. If the program is to go forward, it will need money, and so in this stage a feasibility study is done to see if in fact the program will become a real project. If it does go forward, the point at which the preproduction phase begins is when the commitment (usually financial) is made.

Preproduction involves preparing for production. This phase includes library and personal research relating to the program content, building the production team including the talent to be used, writing the script, storyboarding if needed for presentation or accuracy purposes, and budgeting and all other financial arrangements including the preparation and signing of legal agreements between the principal parties.

In the production phase, all the program elements—audio and video—are produced. Initially a base of operations is established where crew assignments, scheduling, bookkeeping, and coordination can occur. If not already handled, all legal documents, including those concerning production insurance, should be signed. Scout every location before the actual shooting to understand the existing and desired environmental, logistic, and lighting conditions. The various shoots are then scheduled with the appropriate personnel, facilities, props, and equipment, and these are coordinated to converge at the proper time and location. The taping (or filming) takes place. You label the original rolls appropriately in preparation for the next phase.

Postproduction involves editing the program either from the original rolls or from dubs made for working purposes. The original tapes are dubbed, possibly time-coded, and logged. You'll prepare an edit script from the log sheets to describe the location of each scene in the program. Audio and music elements are recorded, mixed, and sweetened. An off-line edit using either the original rolls or the time-coded window dub rolls results in an edit decision list. You'll then use the EDL as the script for putting together the final program. An on-line edit system, a keyboard editor or edit controller connected to a series of video recorders, a switcher, a character generator, and other machines (for computer graphics and special effects) are then used to compile the scenes onto a virgin roll that becomes the edited program master.

How you produce a program communicates.

Suggested Readings

DiZazzo, Ray. *Corporate Television: A Producer's Handbook.* Boston: Butterworth (Focal Press), 1990.

Hauge, Michael. *Writing Screenplays That Sell.* New York: McGraw-Hill, 1980.

Shanks, Bob. *The Primal Screen: How to Write, Sell, and Produce Movies for Television.* New York: Fawcett Columbine, 1986.

Van Deusen, Richard E. *Practical AV/Video Budgeting.* White Plains, NY: Knowledge Industries Publications, 1984.

Wiegand, Ingrid. *Professional Video Production.* White Plains, NY: Knowledge Industries Publications, 1985.

Wiese, Michael. *Film and Video Budgets.* Westport, CT: Michael Wiese Film Productions, 1984.

Addresses

Directors Guild of America
7950 Sunset Blvd., Los Angeles, CA 90046

American Society of Cinematographers
1782 North Orange Dr., Hollywood, CA 90028

American Women in Radio and Television
1321 Connecticut Ave., N.W., Washington, DC 20210

Writers Guild of America
8955 Beverly Blvd., Los Angeles, CA 90048

Associated Musicians of Greater New York
330 West 42nd St., New York, NY 10036

Producers Guild of America
292 South La Cienega Blvd., Beverly Hills, CA 90211

Script Supervisors, Production Office Coordinators
Local 161, I.A.T.S.E.
34-31 35th St., Astoria, NY 11106

National Association of Broadcast Employees & Technicians
1776 Broadway, Suite 1900, New York, NY 10019

Screen Extras Guild, Inc.
3629 Cahuenga Blvd. West, Los Angeles, CA 90068

International Photographers Guild (Motion Picture Industry)
7715 Sunset Blvd., Suite 150, Hollywood, CA 90046

Screen Actors Guild
1700 Broadway, 18th Floor, New York, NY 10019

Motion Picture & Videotape Editors Guild
7715 Sunset Blvd., Hollywood, CA 90046

International Television Association (ITVA)
6311 N. O'Connor Rd., LB-51, Irving, TX 75039

CHAPTER 3

Consciousness

· ·

A leader uses only one tool: him or herself. Like any other tool, the more we know the tool's potential and limitations, the more effectively we can use it. Leadership is therefore dependent on self-knowledge and awareness.

—Christopher Meyer[1]

In this chapter, I refer to "self-knowledge" and "awareness" as **consciousness,** a word that fits our study well. Philosophers, poets, and mystics have defined *consciousness* variously, and it still defies specificity outside a particular context. In Sanskrit, an ancient east Indian language, there are over twenty diverse meanings for the word, each expressing a nuance or way of thinking distinct from the others.

We know that humans are endowed with the faculty of being aware of their own existence. We also realize that how we think directly influences (some would say determines) our individual capabilities, potentials, dreams, values, and behavior. But consciousness goes beyond merely what we think; it's more *how* we are or *who* we seem to be to ourselves. It's intimately connected to our identity.

Our thoughts are the center of our world and no one else sees the world exactly as we do. Consciousness, as the source of one's unique viewpoint, is the basis of one's personal reality. And although video communication is a collaborative activity, every writer, producer, and director—in his or her leadership capacity—must bring to the project a consciousness that encompasses technical knowledge, creative vision, and content expertise.

Consciousness provides the building blocks for all program content and its presentation. In essence anything that comes from us finds its greatest potential and limitation within us, as individuals. By expanding that potential, we can increase the quality and effectiveness of our creative output.

In Chapter 1 we laid a solid foundation for our subject by adopting an interactive field perspective of communication as well as a context within which to manage it—the systems approach. In Chapter 2 we widened our perspective to see the production process as a whole. Now we're ready to focus on the individual producer to consider his or her point of reference. From this point we'll include other people and examine the importance of attitude and the potential for interacting effectively with others. These personal issues profoundly influence a project. The energy in a production moves from the producer at the center through the entire social system.

How You See Determines What You Get

Each of us is unique. We view life differently. Consider the probable differences in consciousness among a rock musician, a corporate executive, and a monk. Each lives out a variety of ideas, expectations, and goals based on certain assumptions and values that relate to life and living. Their decisions and behaviors conform to the way they see the world and how they choose to relate to it. The musician might make decisions that lead in the direction of increased fame and creative opportunity; the executive's choices might lead in the direction of increased profits and power; and the monk might invest his time and energy in developing his inner self. As they each pursue what they value, the process of seeking offers feedback (successes and failures) to suggest whether they are on the right track toward the fulfillment of their dreams. While life is not this black and white—rock musicians, for instance, might have goals other than fame and opportunity—it illustrates that *how we see* directly influences what we get. Our viewpoint significantly influences program content, how it's expressed, how we get along with others on (and off) the set, and ultimately the success of the program.

Our individuality is the foundation of our creative potential. Too often we undervalue our unique perception, passing it off as "weird" or "unconventional." But we can choose, as most successful people do, to claim uniqueness as an asset. What we do with our potential is completely up to us. For instance, if two different individuals were to write, direct, and produce a program on the same subject—say, drug abuse—the programs would differ significantly according to each producer's unique perspective (or consciousness). One producer, perhaps an occasional drug user, might choose to focus on life-style by shooting the program in an environment where drugs are commonly abused. The program might be coarse and depressing as the producer tries in his way to dissuade the audience from using drugs. Another person, involved in law enforcement or drug abuse education, might choose to do library research and focus on statistics and legislation. The sensibility in this program might be more cerebral than emotional. In each case, the individual's consciousness is the source and cause of everything that follows.

A finished program is a direct reflection of the consciousness of the team that produced it. They made the small and large decisions that resulted in the program as it is. Look, for example, at the differences among *20/20, 60 Minutes,* and *West 57th.* Each of these newsmagazine programs used the same format, the same kinds of technology, and the same time frame, but there are significant differences in terms of the kinds of stories presented and the approach taken to each.

20/20 is oriented toward stories of the human situation, often focusing on a person or group overcoming difficulties or the personal implications of mismanaged monies or practices. The producers seem to say, "Our program should partly up-lift your spirit or at least have some constructive relevance to your own life." *60 Minutes* takes the hard-news, investigative approach, striving for "objectivity" and an appearance of factual, informative journalism. Their program context says, "Our job is to keep you informed." So the stories we get are comparatively harsher in relation to those seen on *20/20.*

West 57th selected stories for their emotional value, hard edge, and glamour. These producers wanted to move the audience emotionally, and so they used pro-duction techniques and a storytelling style that created that response. The style of the lighting and camera angles, for example, on the *West 57th* generic open would not be used by the producers of *60 Minutes* or *20/20.* The differences in how the respective producers see themselves, their role in the show, their respon-sibility, and the audience directly determine the subsequent differences in sub-stance and style. Consciousness is the causal factor, giving every program its unique viewpoint.

With this in mind we can work backward as a way to understand our own view-point—we can study (not merely watch) programs more closely. Archaeologists derive an understanding of ancient civilizations and their context from the close examination of artifacts. Just so, we as video producers can become sensitive view-ers of television and other media in order to evaluate programs produced by others, especially by attending to the details of programs we like. It's easy to criticize, but the greater challenge is to see what works and then analyze why. Answering the "why" question is a matter of looking at the *thought* behind the form.

What are the program elements? How are they organized within the format and why? What production values (lighting, camera movement, graphic effects, pacing) are evident and why? What makes the presentation interesting and why? What appeal or other persuasive devices were used and why? By studying the decisions made by producers of programs that work, we can begin to see the connection between what appears on the screen and how the producers think. As we develop a habit of watching television as a visual anthropologist would, relating content and its expression in form to consciousness, it becomes easier as producers to see how each of our own decisions contributes to, or detracts from, our purpose. This pro-cess of analysis leads to a more conscious and purposeful way of working, and it stimulates creativity because more options are seen.

Self-Knowledge

Expression begins with an individual viewpoint. So the better we know ourselves, the more we can realize our potential. This is the hard part. But that is no reason not to begin. There are many techniques and exercises that can help us understand "where we're coming from." I have indicated some resources and two exercises at the end of this chapter that will be especially helpful.

Self-knowledge is a process of exploring our consciousness to see what can be brought forth to support our purpose. We also want to learn about those areas that seem to be limiting or blocking our progress toward achievement. Our mind is the most important tool we'll use on a production, so it makes sense to begin there.

If a program, perhaps ordered by a client, contains material that is contrary to our own thinking, we may be inclined to give it less attention. We may think the subject matter is wrong, but in reality it's just that our perspective is different. Perhaps we need to understand the client's perspective better.

Frequently, because we're used to our comfortable way of seeing and working, we overlook an idea or possibility that could make the difference between doing an adequate job and a sensational one. It's easy to get caught up in the frenzy of activity, which often results in more frequent breakdowns. One friend put it this way: "I need to slow down so I can get more done." This "slowing down" means reserving quiet time to be alone and calm, to take a walk in the woods, to work in consciousness. Then, once we have an understanding of the context, needs, or challenges, we can take the appropriate action, allowing the form to flow naturally from quality thinking. This is "working smart."

Assuming that a particular subject is easily within our grasp or that it can't be very interesting might make us reject possibilities that could lead to a better way of seeing. Although we sometimes have deadlines that urge us into immediate action, quiet time exploring inner resources is always the best investment we can make at the beginning of a project. Stay open to all perspectives; put yourself in the client's consciousness and stretch a little. Instead of seeing problems, see opportunities. Instead of leaping into action, be still and allow your intuition time to engage.

Many producers enjoy a challenge because it allows them to extend their limited viewpoint. A program's topic can be a motivation for further introspection, research, and personal experience with the subject matter. David George, a writer-producer and friend with whom I worked for several years (now at CNN), became so knowledgeable about health care issues as a result of a series he wrote that he could converse comfortably with doctors and technicians using their professional language. The award-winning series *A Matter of Life* clearly reflected David's intelligence, but it also carried his genuine interest in expressing the leading-edge thinking surrounding the topic. One of the producer's goals should always be to incorporate the highest-level thinking that can be achieved, and that begins with introspection first and then research. Only when I know who I am and what my work is about can I effectively understand and convey the subject matter.

Space scientists have a saying: "In order to know where you're going, you have to know where you are." I think this applies to every kind of creative expression.

Subject Knowledge

· ·

Professionals in the video and television production industries would probably agree with the adage "It's not so much what you know, but who you know that counts." That's because media production is a people-oriented business and, without contacts, progress would be slow. But that doesn't mean a successful career in these fields can be based on connections—it can't.

It is more important for the producer to have something to say. Too many programs are barely able to express anything useful, let alone make it interesting or entertaining. Watch public access, where you'll find people who want to produce video because it's fun or interesting but who do not pay enough attention to *what* is being expressed. These producers have yet to learn that technique is secondary to substance.

An axiom I've found helpful is this: "Earn the right to communicate." If I don't earn that right, the audience will sense my weakness. If you're already an expert on the topic, produce what you know. If not, become an expert.

When we set out to research content, we naturally gravitate to those ideas and issues that interest us, the ones that fit our unique perspective—or our client's. But it's best to keep an open mind. Research broadens the data base and often presents possibilities not previously imagined. Immerse yourself in the subject.

Professional actors often engage in personal research so they can get "into" the characters they will portray. Producers should do the same when preparing for a production, because not only do tidbits of helpful information come along but it is the research experience that reveals the sensibility and leads to a feel for the subject. Often indefinable, intuitions, feelings, and insights are the deciding factor in great works. Look at any powerful movie—*Amadeus,* for example—and you will see that the consciousness behind the camera (the director) was attuned to an essence—in this case, the love of music—that permeates the presentation. James Cameron, director of *The Abyss,* spent years researching deep-sea diving technologies before he undertook the project in earnest. This close identity with and understanding of the subject can only come from direct and intense experiences with it.

Attitude Is Everything

. . . .

How we see, and what we know of ourselves and our subject, will become the basis for our productions. The producer establishes the climate for whatever happens. But the producer is not alone. We create an attitudinal climate when we work together that also significantly influences the outcome. This applies to all productions and all members of the team, whatever their role, expertise, or experience.

"Attitude is everything" is a phrase commonly heard in the film and television industries. It is usually expressed when an attitude has in some way interfered with production quality or efficiency. A person with a negative attitude can depress an entire production, and, conversely, a person with a cooperative, enthusiastic, and flexible attitude can do just the opposite. A person's attitude is an expression of consciousness, and it can either limit or enhance the task at hand. People cooperating toward a common goal need to be able to work together comfortably.

When interviewing people to work on a project, it is not unusual to ask them to work with the team on a trial basis. The trial can be for as short a time as a day or as long as a week, given availability and budget constraints. Within a relatively short period, one can ascertain competence and whether a negative attitude is an anomaly or a pattern. No production can afford a bad attitude. Allowing such energies amounts to planning for weakness and breakdown.

In terms of the system, it's not enough to decide *not* to be surrounded by people who exhibit a negative attitudinal pattern. One must identify and work with people who exhibit attitudes that support the process at every level.

Managers in both broadcast and nonbroadcast environments have identified specific attitudes that are especially helpful in the production context, as follows:

- *Responsible:* "They're asking me for 100% effort, so I'll give them 110%. They will continue to want me around; they'll be getting a good value and I'll build a good reputation."
- *Competent:* "I'm good at what I do. If I don't know something, I'll learn. I'm capable of doing well the job I've been given, and I look for opportunities to demonstrate that this is true."
- *Professional:* "I'm a professional and as such my total expression contributes to what I do. My professional demeanor reflects positively on the organization and the project. I am on time every time. I am dependable."
- *Enthusiastic:* "I genuinely enjoy this work and this project. No detail is too small to give my undivided attention. It's a privilege to be able to be involved with this project and these people. I welcome responsibility. I'm having fun."
- *Positive:* "The impossible just takes a little longer. Anything is possible. No matter how many breakdowns, re-do's or whatever, it will all work out in the end. I and the team will succeed."
- *Flexible:* "So what if it didn't work out the way I expected, I can shift quickly to what will work. I'm not attached to any single way of doing things or even thinking about them. I can adapt quickly to any change that increases the quality or effectiveness of our work."
- *Helpful:* "I notice what needs to be done and handle it before I'm told to do it. [Radar O'Reilly on *M*A*S*H* had developed this to a high level.] As soon as I see something that needs to be done I'm on it—even if no one else is noticing me do it."
- *Assertive (but not aggressive):* "I'm not afraid to jump in when I see a way to improve things. At the same time I know when not to interfere. When given responsibility I can handle it with grace and dignity. I'm neither pushy nor shy."
- *Cooperative:* "I enjoy working within the team context. I'm eager to work with others so we can accomplish the goal. I want to blend with them as much as possible, as opposed to providing resistance to their ideas and activities."

Team Consciousness

A constructive attitudinal climate is a prerequisite to efficient and effective interaction. Yet there is more to team effectiveness. Once you identify team players with positive attitudes, the next step is to get them to cooperate. Human interaction today is dramatically different from the past because of the needs of our more complex society. Being paid is only one kind of compensation. Other considerations include life-style, personal fulfillment, ethical working conditions, and providing a genuine service to the community or humanity.

Business is the context in which most individuals join with others in a daily commitment to a project or enterprise. Most of the theories relating to effective group interaction come from the academic communication fields, but their application is most abundant in business. Almost all universities have courses on group behavior, management theory, group communication, performing in groups, and high performance. It's no wonder that this area of study has created an army of consultants offering seminars, books, and videos, because anyone striving for excellence realizes the challenge involved in bringing people together for a common purpose.

Considering our present focus on consciousness and the importance of team interaction, we'll examine in some detail two approaches to teamwork that have been the most useful in my own experience—synergy and resonance.

Synergy

Synergy, simplistically defined, is "cooperation" or working together.[2] Largely because of the application of the term in living systems theory, *synergy* came to connote more than merely people cooperating. Its expanded meaning includes a quality of interaction that is dynamic, effective, and smooth-flowing. A synergistic social system is effective. The individuals within it are well coordinated, and the process moves along steadily toward its goal. Because of this kind of effectiveness, we assume that synergistic teams can achieve goals involving greater complexity.

In the early 1980s, businesses began using the term to sell clients on the effectiveness of their teams. Because of its potential power to generate sales, *synergy* quickly became the buzzword of the decade. Eventually its now-common usage evolved—to express a condition of effective human interaction where the team's capability as a whole is "greater than the sum of its parts." This implies that the product of synergistic interaction is better than it would be if the team members merely worked together to get the job done.

A cooperating team becomes synergistic because of common caring, that is, concern for the same outcome or goal. This mutual care, concern, or love for the result of their labor, for one thing, helps ensure people's attention to detail. Each person feels connected to the others, the project, and the outcome, and the participants behave responsibly.

Synergy is a useful concept in the video production context because it presents the possibility of higher-level functioning. Some organizations, including grade schools, high schools, hospitals, and businesses, now use video for the specific purpose of building synergy. Anyone who has worked on a synergistic production team will appreciate the personal bonds that are formed. Lasting friendships often result from such interaction, especially when the product of the effort is successful.

The story of another producer with whom I worked will help illuminate this. Oscar's objective was to produce for broadcast a television series of thirteen half-hour children's programs called *Max B. Nimble*. He wanted the series to appeal to both parents and their kids so they would watch together. After getting approval from the station management (along with a budget), Oscar assembled the eight-member team. He had private discussions with each person, telling us that he thought we were the best available, that he chose us because this production required the very best.

Essentially he bolstered our egos and set up a high level of expectation. Then he called everyone to a meeting, and for the first time we met as a group around a conference table. Oscar went around the room introducing each person, identifying each as highly competent in his respective area. He took time to describe each person in glowing terms. As we sat there listening, we began to get a picture of the others. I remember thinking what an honor it was to be included, and how wonderful it was going to be to work with these talented people.

Then he described the series, again emphasizing that this project was so intensive, so creatively demanding, so important that only the best of the best could pull it off. We didn't get to speak to all the others that day, but our relationships grew in the context of the work. Synergy began among us at that meeting. Each person saw the others as highly competent, creative, and intelligent (even though none of us saw another's resume or work samples). Each of us felt we were in the company of giants. I knew that if I were to stay on the team I would have to perform at or above their level of expectation, which by then had grown significantly in my mind.

I didn't know it then, but everyone else's experience was similar. I don't think anyone felt he or she deserved to be on the team. It was intimidating, yet grand at the same time.

The process was exhilarating and intensive. We all worked hard because we wanted to. We had daily script readings and weekly evaluations. We discussed every detail down to the sandbags that held up the set flats. No detail was too small for consideration and elaborate discussion. Each day we were eager to get to work to see what was happening.

We all did our very best, and, when each element of the show was submitted, we were lavished with praise from everyone else on the team. For instance, when I finished a film segment and showed it to Oscar, others would gather, make positive comments, and celebrate what a fine job it was. I remember feeling that the praise was overdone, but, nonetheless, for whatever I (we) did, there was overwhelming approval. Now I realize that the celebration of each completed element was not so much a sign of individual achievement but an acknowledgment that the team was working.

Suffice it to say that we completed the thirteen programs on schedule and management loved them, but we were not prepared for the series to be renewed three times, or for the series to win national and regional competitions, or for the success of the series in terms of sales and syndication.

We were a synergistic team. The project result was significantly greater than the sum of its parts, and that happened primarily because of the consciousness of the producer, who demanded the best people and equipment and who convinced each member of the team that it was a privilege to work together for his vision. He fostered caring, painted a grand vision of the goal, expressed it as a team challenge, and created a dynamic environment that included feedback and positive reinforcement.

To create synergy, you need to build a team where each member

- Is respected, admired, and needed.
- Is uniquely qualified to be part of the team.
- Is competent to do the work involved.
- Cares very much about the goal.
- Is given creative opportunity and responsibility.
- Knows that his or her contribution matters.

You also need to create a commonly held vision of the goal, which includes the ideas that

- The project is important to do, worthwhile, and meaningful.
- The project requires high levels of cooperation and performance.
- The process will be fun.

Every team leader (producer) tries to create this synergy. It begins in consciousness and proceeds through attitude and expression to create something you can feel.

If the feeling stays fairly constant through each phase of a production, the process is moving synergistically. If the chemistry is off, however, the producer must notice it and do something about it. Communicate; find out if the reason is serious or trivial. Can changes be made? It may sound cold, but if a person's attitude is "off" and nothing can be done to balance it, then it may be best for that person to drop out or be dropped from the team unless he or she can be helped or trained into alignment. This applies to every position—writer, director, crew, talent— without exception. A production with weak links in the social chain is structured for breakdown.

Resonance

Another, more recent concept takes synergy one step further. **Resonance** is a vibrational alignment between elements having a common orientation. In addition to bringing people together cooperatively in an atmosphere of focused caring, resonance theory[3] suggests that alignment with others having the same personal, and often vocational, goals will lift the group endeavor to even greater effectiveness.

If a team member has a deep vocational urge to work in a certain way and she is invited to do so, more of the self is invested. What starts out as the team project now becomes her project; she "owns" it because it's in perfect alignment (resonance) with her purpose. It's easy to see how such a person would perform better than another whose aspirations are in a different area.

People who work in resonance know when an idea, issue, or solution is out of resonance with the group purpose. They openly discuss the occasions when resonance is absent or faltering, when the idea or suggestion somehow doesn't "feel right."

A resonating group, or "resonating core," depends on open and honest communication. *Feelings* toward the issues as well as toward people are as valid as thoughts or ideas. It's a whole-person approach, calling for the integration of left and right brain, head and heart. As the production process unfolds, we frame issues and questions in the context of each member's deep personal purpose and intuition. If the idea or plan supports that purpose, there is resonance and the process is smooth. If not, there is further work to be done.

Resonance can be demonstrated physically. We could prop up a set of tuning forks, one for every note on the musical scale. Then, by tapping a separate "C" fork, the other C fork would begin to sound (resonate—*vibrate*) while all the others remained silent.

Socially, the same thing happens. We stimulate and attract others who resonate to our purpose and expression. To extend the analogy, imagine a video production team in which each individual sounds the same note. The result is a focused field of coordinated energy that is extremely potent. Like a laser, the energy moves in parallel and is extremely ordered.

A "resonating core"[4] is more like a family than a team made up of individuals. The group moves this way or that based on a collective sense of what best contributes to its common purpose. The individual's sense of purpose is usually deeply felt, such as a vocational goal, but it could include any deep personal commitment.

Resonating cores are not formed in the same way that a producer finds talent and crew personnel to fill positions. Instead, their coalescence is more amorphous, usually beginning with a deep-level agreement between two or more individuals. The agreeing parties begin to express their vision, plans, and objectives openly and, through their vibration, others are attracted. If the attraction is genuinely associated with prior internal commitments and there is agreement all around, then the new person is acknowledged already to be "in resonance." There's no "welcome aboard, fill out our form" kind of decision. Rather, the person has found her family, a group of like-minded people already working on the same goals. One usually finds resonance operating in projects that deal with human values, social and environmental issues, or other subjects to which people can commit their lives.

The elements of a resonating core include a commonly shared vision, individuals' deep commitment to the vision, open communication, rigorous honesty, enthusiastic cooperation, trust, flexibility, and group harmony.

Resonant functioning also has its problems. Sometimes an individual is in resonance with the group but is not competent to do the work required. It then becomes the responsibility of the person (if he sees this) or the group (if the person in question does not) to move that person into a position where he can be more effective.

And there are people who become part of a resonating core who are interested only in performing the work they enjoy, reluctant to carry out tasks the organization or group needs to have done. Some people only want to do camera or audio work or be talent, and if they don't happen to be selected for a particular shooting session, their attitude goes sour. Resonance comes at a cost—the need to be flexible to the demands of the endeavor and willing to serve the group sometimes in ways that are different from our preferences.

One can always tell when resonance is operative in a working group because the activity of the group feels less like work and more like play. Frequently time seems to stand still; no one is looking at the clock. And there is little or no separation between working on the project and being "away" from it. For these reasons, resonant functioning is not only a highly effective way of producing a program, it can also be the most fun and fulfilling.

Expansion and Qualification

Consciousness expands. None of us thinks exactly the same as we did just a week ago. As Buckminster Fuller said, "You can't learn less, you can only learn more."[5] Human beings are learners, and, as we learn, our way of viewing ourselves, others, and the world changes. Every video production is an opportunity for learning. At the end of a project, producers often say that, given another chance, they would do it differently. Their consciousness has expanded as a result of the production.

Television programming itself can provide a powerful demonstration of expanding consciousness. Some programs deal with the lives of people who are absorbed almost exclusively in the material world. The characters are into drugs, alcohol, violence, and other less harmful things like dancing, sex, food, and exercise. Their experience is sensual. Commercials appeal especially to people living in a predominantly physical reality. They exhort people to buy this or that, to improve their looks, or to experience life more fully or comfortably. Smell good, feel good, "go for the gusto." We could say that this consciousness is "physically qualified" because it is a materialistic view of life.

The term *qualify* in this context means to invest energy, to give attention and value to an idea, perception, or behavior. To be qualified one way or another is not a value judgment. It's just a perception. For example, while some might criticize materialism, it has nonetheless been responsible for many of the good things that have made life easier and better. On the other hand, an argument can be made that a preoccupation with getting "stuff" is not the best way to find happiness and fulfillment. Physically qualified characters, however, act as if that is so.

TV characters, especially in made-for-TV movies, who are struggling with personal or social problems reveal another qualification of consciousness (not better, just different). The issues of their concern may be the AIDS virus, battered women, child pornography, learning disabilities, or increasing gang violence. These people don't care about what's in fashion and so on—their focus is a mental/emotional one. They're absorbed in an idea or an ideal such as health, quality of life, or relationships, and they can be said to be "mentally qualified" because their reality is defined primarily in psychological terms.

The central characters on the sitcom *Designing Women* are examples. Their interest is centered on subjects in the realm of relationships, ideas, values, or motives. A mental orientation does not exclude physical or material experience; it includes them but places more emphasis on concerns of the mental and emotional aspects of life. In this sense, mental qualification is an expansion of physical qualification.

To take our examination a step further, let's consider a monk. Clearly he doesn't approach life in physical terms, even though his work may deal with meeting physical needs. And, although his worldview may incorporate an ideal such as selflessness or love of neighbor, his highest preoccupation and motive is so extended that it's no longer earthbound. Ask him what he's doing, why he does what he does, and he'll likely respond, "To build the kingdom of heaven or to achieve nirvana," not a corporate empire, security, democracy, or middle-income housing for the poor. His "spiritually qualified" consciousness takes precedence over, yet includes, the physical, mental, emotional, and social aspects of his life.

The video producer who is sincere and committed to making programs that are effective, whatever the purpose, needs to be aware of his or her own qualification and to work on expanding consciousness because, ultimately, that's where maximum creative effectiveness lies. I'm simply suggesting that the more we can see and encompass, the better we can create because we can see (understand) better and farther. Even if this just amounts to seeing the topic of a program from a larger perspective, the benefit to a program is enormous. Audiences want substance. Their expectation and hope in watching a video is that it will lift them above their current understanding. You can meet that expectation only if your own thinking is advanced.

A commonplace viewpoint can take on fresh meaning and excitement when it is presented from the place in us that is true to ourselves. One of my teachers put it this way: "It's not enough to know how to produce programs; you also have to understand something about people and the world." When I asked the best way to do that, she said, "First, find out who you are, where you are, and where you want to go. Then everything else will fall into place naturally."

Historically the ocean has symbolized consciousness. At the bottom, there is stillness. As one approaches the surface, there is increased turbulence until, at the top, there is a great deal of activity. The water on top tosses and turns, creating waves and foam. Our daily lives are spent mostly on the surface with life's distractions, activity, and frenzy, but deep beneath all this is a stillness that is a vast resource—our own inner knowing.

When we dive into this stillness, becoming alone and in touch with who we uniquely are, an expansion occurs. We are able to see ourselves, our interests, and the world more broadly, as if from a high place. Substance and creativity come from this expanded perspective. This is not the kind of creativity that relates to technique but the dynamic ideas and inspirations that come in the night, the "aha's," the insights born of intuition, the fresh and unique perception. Programming that results from such consciousness is effective, compelling, and powerful no matter what the format or subject matter. It has substance. To read more about this, see the writings of Jung.

Let's shift gears now. Here's an opportunity for you to make such a dive right now:

Exercise I

Sit quietly. Put a notepad in front of you. Read each upcoming paragraph in full, then close your eyes and focus your mind on the italicized word for one minute. Just think about that word and nothing else. Then open your eyes and read the question only once more. Write the first responses that come into your mind. Repeat the process for each question.

- *Question 1: In what are you most consistently interested?* Base your answer not on what you would like to think you are interested in but on what you actually spend the most time thinking about. Be rigorously honest with yourself. List five in order. (***INTEREST***)
- *Question 2:* Why *do you do whatever you do?* To maintain a standard of living? To serve your community? To do something creatively fulfilling? To build a better world? To grow professionally? To have fun? To maintain your family? To gain fame, fortune, power? List three reasons in order of priority. (***MOTIVE***)
- *Question 3: What are your gifts?* List five talents that you have already identified and developed. (***GIFTS***)

Now examine your list and notice:

- Your answers to Question 1 reflect your *qualification* at this time (it's likely to change as time goes by). This is where your consciousness dwells at the moment. How do you feel about that? Now indicate five items that reflect what you would *prefer* to claim as your mental priorities. Then compare them and ask yourself how the shift can be made (if they are different).
- Your response to Question 2 is your *motivation*. How is your motivation qualified? Is your response what you would like it to be? Why or why not? What motivation would you prefer?
- Question 3 shows your personal, *unique resources*, which are always your starting point. Build on what you already have to create what you want.

Exercise II

Read the following and then put the book down and do what it says. This will take fifteen minutes.

Get into a space where there is as little stimulation as possible—perhaps a darkened room—and sit upright in a chair with a pad and pencil on your lap. Make sure that you will not be interrupted for ten to fifteen minutes. (You may recognize that this is the same requirement for practicing meditation, but this is not meditation which focuses on stilling the mind. This technique is "contemplation"— intensive thinking in a focused manner about a particular subject.)

We all know more than we think we do about both ourselves and the world around us. Our conscious mind knows what it has done in response to past experience. But our unconscious and superconscious are even greater resources because they are not limited by our experience or by time.

Follow this procedure to tap into your unconscious mind:

1. In whatever way you feel you can, deeply relax all the muscles of your body. One way to do this is to close your eyes and visualize each muscle group, name them in order, and state that they are fully relaxed.

2. Affirm that deep within you are *all* the answers to your questions. You might say something like this: "The answers to all my questions are in me now, available for my use at this time."

3. Mentally ask your unconscious a question about any project you have in mind: "I intend to produce a program on (_____). What is its purpose?" After asking the question, sit quietly and listen to your own voice coming up with the answer. Without opening your eyes, write it down. Don't disturb your concentration. Also ask:

   What is most important to communicate and to whom?

   Should I produce this program? Is it right for me?

   Who should the audience be?

   How will I get the money and other resources to do it?

   Who else should I work with?

   (And anything else that comes to mind.)

4. Continue this question-and-answer process as long as you like. Don't evaluate any response—don't even think about it at all. Just be receptive. Ask other questions that relate in any way. Be specific. Be direct. Write it down without opening your eyes. Your unconscious will respond. Listen patiently, then move on to another question.

Open your eyes and review your list. Appreciate your unconscious and especially your discovery of how to enlist its power to assist you in your project.

This exercise is very practical. Many notable people use it regularly as a way to access their unconscious potential. You can expect results the first time you apply it because there's no magic or skill required; it's just a matter of taking the time to be quietly alone with yourself at a deeper than normal level. Remember the analogy of the different levels of the ocean. Then, when you want to explore the depths of your consciousness, take a dive.

Summary

The consciousness of the producer is the basis of every project. It determines the outcome. Whether from one individual or a close-knit team, the finished program will reflect the consciousness. That's why most producers want to maximize their personal effectiveness—to become creatively and technically competent—not only to make a quality-looking program but, more important, to make one that communicates. "Quality in–quality out" applies equally to program content and its expression.

Self-knowledge is the foundation for the communication edifice. The more we know about ourselves (perceptions, values, preferences), the more we have to build upon. From our uniqueness comes our viewpoint, which determines our creative expression. Most accomplished and dedicated artists have strong opinions on things. They know who they are and where they stand, and this enables them to express themselves with purpose and confidence.

If self-knowledge is the foundation, subject knowledge is the superstructure that is supported by it. Obviously, the more we know about the program topic, the better we can express it. All of this deals with *what* we see as a result of who we are.

On top of this comes our attitude toward our experience, or *how* we see. The producer's attitude sets the tone. Team members should be selected not only for their competence and integrity but also for their positive attitude. This ensures that there are no weak "links" in the production chain, enabling the social system to function smoothly.

Synergy is a quality of interaction among team members such that the product of their work is greater than they could have accomplished had they merely cooperated. It's a step above cooperation, based on genuine caring about the outcome of the project.

Resonance is an even higher level of functioning requiring that team members are aligned to a common purpose that is more deeply rooted than most goals. This can be vocation, spiritual growth, social service, global peace—any value that invites genuine commitment. Resonance is based on attuned consciousness and is sustained by commitment to a common purpose, open communication, honesty, cooperation, trust, flexibility, and group harmony.

Consciousness expands because human beings learn. It expands from a narrow focus (self) to ever-increasing levels of awareness and relationship. This begins with physical qualification and expands out to spiritual qualification—the term *qualify* referring to the kinds of issues the mind focuses on most frequently. Qualification is our reference frame. It is also a useful way to view the characters we put on the screen—to ensure that their motives are consistent throughout the program. You can even analyze audiences in terms of their qualification of consciousness.

Exploring consciousness involves diving deep into our subconscious and superconscious, where the substance relating to self, relationships, and even program content resides.

Your consciousness communicates.

Notes

1. Christopher Meyer, "Leadership Can't Be Taught—Only Learned," in *Transforming Leadership,* ed. John D. Adams (Alexandria, VA: Miles River Press, 1986), 261.
2. *Webster's Ninth New Collegiate Dictionary.*
3. Michael Doctoroff, *Synergistic Management: Creating the Climate for Superior Performance* (New York: American Management Association, 1977), 36.

4. Barbara Marx Hubbard, *Manual for Co-Creators of the Quantum Leap* (Eastsound, WA: Island Pacific N.W., 1989).
5. R. Buckminster Fuller, "Our Spiritual Experience," a video interview (Cincinnati: Xavier University, 1984).

Suggested Readings

Adams, John D., ed. *Transforming Work.* Alexandria, VA: Miles River Press, 1984.

Bateson, Gregory. *Steps to an Ecology of Mind.* San Francisco: Ballantine Paperback, 1972.

Bennis, Warren. "The 4 Competencies of Leadership." *Training & Development Journal,* August 1984, 15–19.

Buckley, Karen Wilhelm, and Joan Steffy. "The Invisible Side of Leadership." In *Transforming Leadership: From Vision to Results,* edited by John D. Adams. Alexandria, VA: Miles River Press, 1986.

Cattell, R. "Concepts and Methods in the Measurement of Group Syntality." *Psychological Review* 55 (1948): 48–53.

Doctoroff, Michael. *Synergistic Management: Creating the Climate for Superior Performance.* New York: American Management Association, 1977.

Durst, G. Michael. *Management by Responsibility.* Evanston, IL: Center for the Art of Living, 1982.

Gaffney, Rachel. "Systems Thinking in Business: An Interview with Peter Senge." *Revision* 7 (2 1984–85).

Grove, Andrew S. *High Output Management.* New York: Random House, 1983.

Harman, Willis, and Howard Rheingold. *Higher Creativity: Liberating the Unconscious for Breakthrough Insights.* Los Angeles: Jeremy Tarcher, 1984.

Kanter, Rosabeth Moss. *The Change Masters.* New York: Simon & Schuster, 1983.

Lee, Philip, and Robert Ornstein. *Symposium on Consciousness.* New York: Viking, 1976.

Maiden, A. H. "Resonance." *Gala Newsletter* 11 (2 1980).

McWaters, Barry. *Conscious Evolution: Personal and Planetary Transformation.* San Francisco: Evolutionary Press, 1982.

Mushashi, Miyamoto. *A Book of Five Rings: A Guide to Strategy,* translated by Victor Harris. Woodstock, NY: Overlook Press, 1974.

Peters, Thomas J., and Nancy Austin. *A Passion for Excellence: The Leadership Difference.* New York: Random House, 1985.

Pinchot, Gifford. *Intrapreneuring.* New York: Harper & Row, 1984.

Russell, Peter. *The Global Brain.* Los Angeles: Jeremy Tarcher, 1983.

Torbert, William. *Learning from Experience: Toward Consciousness.* New York: Columbia University Press, 1972.

PART II

PLANNING THE PROJECT

· ·

No one has a guaranteed formula for designing a successful media project. I stress to my students that the *best* way to learn how to produce video and television is to *do* it. But I also see many early attempts at planning that are so far off base that no amount of experience can fill in the blanks. You have to learn some things from the experiences of others.

Because I am writing from my perspective, I offer *one* way to plan a project, design content, and organize a production. There are others. In the next three chapters, we'll look at the key issues involved in the planning of

a video project. I specify *project* here to distinguish the overall goal from that of a production, which, as we saw earlier, is a process of creating and combining elements into a program. A project is a larger concept, including within it the production

process, but it has other aspects as well, including how the program will be used, how it will be financed, how it will be evaluated, and so on.

In Chapter 4, we'll examine the nature of video, specifically as a matter of choosing the right medium for accomplishing a project's goals. Too many videos would have been better if they had been radio programs instead. Video is appropriate for some kinds of communication and expression but not all.

Once we've selected video for the right reasons, we then need to know how it works, how it structurally facilitates communication. So, in Chapter 5, we'll investigate the dynamics of the video medium to create projects that best use its strengths.

Then, in Chapter 6, we'll use a project needs analysis to lay out a project plan. We will then be in a good position to focus on designing the message (in Part III—what the program will contain and ways to organize its content).

In practice, you will often deal with audience issues before deciding on the medium—who the audience is, where they can be found, and which medium best suits these conditions. So we can focus on the critical relationship between the audience and message design, the chapter on audience issues will come later. You

should realize, however, that audience issues are primary at every stage of the process. In this section, we'll learn the importance of, and criteria for, choosing the best medium for the job at hand, how video works as a communication tool, and how to plan a video project.

CHAPTER 4

Choosing Video

· ·

With the arrival of electronic technology, man extended, or set outside himself, a live model of the central nervous system itself.

—*Marshall McLuhan*

C an you, in one minute, give an explanation for terrorism in the Middle East based on what you've seen on television? We've seen the pictures often enough, but what's the deeper story behind these events? We often can't answer questions like this because most TV news only gives us the surface of events. We miss either the context, the historical background, or the reasons events happen. Television doesn't handle depth or details well because there's not enough time (given the time spent on commercials).

How often do tears come to your eyes as you watch a movie on television? As often as at the movie theater? How emotional are the training videos you've seen? Do they make you sad? Happy? Do they elicit any emotion at all?

Your response to these questions suggests that each medium has strengths and weaknesses, and, consequently, each should be selected for a specific purpose—not just because it happens to be available or looks high-tech. You don't use a hammer to open a can of soup, and you probably don't use an electric mixer to stir the sugar in your coffee.

Just so, a medium extends us or our potential in a specific way. Sometimes electronic media are overkill, just like the mixer. To select the wrong medium is as disastrous to communication as using that medium poorly.

In this chapter, we'll look at the characteristics of various media in relation to video. You wouldn't be reading this book if you had not already decided to use video, but it's essential to understand that it is *not* the best medium for all situations. It's easy to get trapped into using video automatically. We'd rather set up a camera than methodically think through what the outcome should be and how *best* to accomplish it. Instead of the medium forcing the communication, the more effective route is for the communication to provide the basis for the medium and how it is used.

Effective communication requires the medium to be appropriate to the audience and how they perceive things. In this chapter we'll first consider some media conventions: what audiences have come to expect from media—their unique "grammar and language." Then we'll consider the broadcast and nonbroadcast environments where television and video are used so we can develop a sense of various audience contexts. For every media project you must consider how and where the audience will experience the program.

I've dedicated an entire chapter to selecting the most appropriate medium because it's better to choose wisely at the outset than to produce a boring or otherwise ineffective program.

Media Characteristics

. . . .

Every media expression has a technological component involving left brain activities such as reasoning, analytical thinking, organization, testing, and logic. Our minds follow a time-bound, linear pathway as information is organized for expression.

Additionally, every medium has its unique aesthetic or creative aspect, challenging our right brains to come up with fresh ways of seeing relationships and organizing space. Media use integrates these.

If we're going to use any medium effectively, we need to be aware of its unique characteristics and how they relate to the audience. An artist accustomed to working in acrylics can shift to watercolor, but it requires learning about the new medium and how it behaves. She also needs to know what people see and appreciate in watercolor. The same is true for video.

In a way video is similar to filmmaking; some elements of radio and photography apply; a knowledge of graphic design helps; and video uses an organizational process much like that for writing a book—but none of these alone is adequate preparation for using video successfully.

First, let's compare video's unique qualities with some of the other more commonly used media. You might feel you already know these things, but they are elaborated here primarily to emphasize the contextual relationship of video and other media. We shouldn't jump to the conclusion that a video is needed when another medium might serve the purpose better and perhaps less expensively.

Print

I once helped a nonprofit organization produce a two-hour video as a way to communicate to their constituency ideas and perspectives that were presented by panelists at their annual conference. The program was boring and scattered with poor and uneven sound, fluorescent lighting, and unsteady cameras. The speakers were not fluent and the editing made it even choppier in some places and too long in others. In addition to poorly communicating the views of the participants, the tape served to project an impression about the sponsoring organization that was not positive, and, as a result, the tape was never distributed to the membership. Had they done audio interviews with a roving reporter, then edited the material into a printed mail-out piece, they would have saved money and accomplished their communication purpose better.

Printing on paper, cardboard, plastic, and other surfaces is ideal for extending ideas and speech in words. It can also convey pictures and other images, but these are limited to still impressions. An important advantage of print is that tremendous amounts of information can be packaged easily. Printed matter can be readily mass-produced, distributed, and sold as a product.

The print medium does require that its producers and consumers are literate. The strength of print lies in its ability to convey complex and abstract thoughts in great detail.

Radio

How many one-on-one video interview shows have you seen where the picture of the people talking was really necessary? Frequently it's not. In many instances, the communication would have had more impact as a radio show or audiocassette tape because the listener's imagination would be stimulated better. Radio is ideal for extending voice and music. As with print, it delivers information in a linear, fixed-pace sequence—the rate of the human voice. It conveys personality very well and is immediate. Radio can be produced on location or in a studio. It can be segmented easily, and these segments can be sold to advertisers as products in themselves (airtime). This medium's audience is self-selective; that is, listeners decide whether to receive the signal. Programming can be prerecorded and sent through the mail as audiotapes, transmitted over airwaves, or beamed long distances via satellite. The audience must be able to hear in order to receive this medium.

Radio's greatest strength is perhaps in stimulating the listener's imagination. Costs associated with radio advertising are relatively affordable. Radio's limitations include its fragmented, special interest audience and the fact that listeners are constantly tuning in and out.

Audiocassette Tapes

One time, we were moving some production equipment onto a construction site for a shoot. A worker there had a headset on and one of our production assistants asked him what he was listening to. The worker, dusty and dirty from head to foot, took a drag on his cigarette and said, "Oh, it's just a self-improvement course."

Program producers often forget that the audiotape business is extensive. Although its largest application is in prerecorded music, special interest cassettes are also widely produced and distributed. Whenever speech and music can carry the communication alone (that is, when pictures aren't necessary), audiotapes should be seriously considered. Currently they are much more portable than video because of personal audiocassette players (like Walkman), automobile tape players, and other field appliances. CEOs speak to their employees with them. They're used to document conferences and workshops. And the playback is internationally standardized (as opposed to video). Also, of the media that contain speech, audiotapes are the least expensive medium to produce and mass distribute.

Slide-Tape Presentations

A slide-tape presentation involves showing 35 mm slides sequentially with a person's live narration or a specially prepared and timed audio recording. Presentations can be as simple as using one slide projector with a person reading or spontaneously speaking, or as elaborate as having multiple projectors controlled and synchronized by a computer along with a tightly edited original music and speech mixed track.

Slides alone can be boring, as we've learned from watching the neighbor's trip pictures. Why do you think slide presentations sometimes put people to sleep? Is it projector noise? The pictures themselves? The narrator? The easy chair? What can be done to prevent that from happening?

Taking professional communication a step further, "multimedia" shows integrate various media including slide projectors, film, audio, video, and live performance. The experience can be outstanding and communication can be very effective.

For large audiences, the strong advantage of slides is their projectability and excellent resolution. A thousand or more people in an auditorium can experience top-quality images no matter where they sit in relation to the screen. This is not yet true of video. For small audiences, the advantage of slides is low production cost because the materials are inexpensive and readily available. Slides are also easy to duplicate so that "sets" of programs can be sent to other cities for replay. You can rent projectors in almost every major city in the world. For conference sessions, slides, often combined with projected overhead transparencies and/or a projected computer screen, are used extensively.

The disadvantage of slides—lack of movement within a frame—is balanced considerably by the apparent motion that can be created using two or more projectors. Sometimes you can give a presentation the feel of a professional production just by using transitional movement (dissolves). At the high end of this medium, you can project a large number of slides quickly to create the feeling of a motion picture— but that's very expensive. If the audience is large, the need for image quality is great, and the image doesn't necessarily have to move, slide-tape can be an excellent medium.

Film

Film combines sight, sound, and motion to expand our potential for sharing images, emotions, and experiences. Movies are usually expensive and complex to produce, involving large numbers of people. Exceptions include small-scale animation and some "art" films. The medium is highly empathic—viewers live the screen characters' experiences through identification with them.

Large numbers of people can experience a particular film over time, but each showing of a film is limited to viewing by up to 800 people. And presentation to these audiences requires a specially designed theater as well as ongoing promotion and published show times. There are almost no limitations, such as literacy, on audiences. Although some people think movies do not appeal to blind people, others disagree.

Successful movies are highly profitable. The distribution of films for home video rental and sales can offset high production costs. Video distribution has become a primary industry in itself, another source of major revenues for film production companies. In some instances, revenues from the home video release of movies are even greater than those from the theatrical release.

In schools and other institutions, video tape players, which are more portable and easier to use, not to mention quieter and less expensive, have made 16 mm film projectors largely obsolete. For this reason, more and more educational, aesthetic, and training-type film releases are becoming available on video.

Movies and films are strong in their simulation of emotional realities with which audiences can identify. If the communication objective is to provide an experience of a message that audiences will *feel*, then film can be a powerful means of accomplishing it.

Television

Television is a public medium. It combines sight, sound, and motion within either a real-time or delayed sequence time frame. Film always displays past events. Television can display events as they happen, and, because of this, television programming feels more immediate, even when it's not. Television also creates empathy, but less so than film because generally it's viewed in a lighted room, often with other distractions. It's presented on a small, low-resolution screen, and the receiver usually has a poor-quality sound system.

Because most Americans own TV sets, the entire nation, or a large segment of it, potentially can experience messages or other program elements simultaneously. And although it is as yet impractical to have a global network, the potential is gradually being developed. Conceivably, every nation on earth could simultaneously watch an event unfold given ideal circumstances.

Some owners of TV sets choose, for one reason or another, at different times, not to turn the set on or not to watch it. So, like radio, television has a self-selecting audience (although less selective than for film). Television is generally viewed in the privacy of the home. There are few limitations on the audience—even those with sight or sound impairment can still appreciate the medium.

Although television suggests prestige and glamour through its association with celebrities, it is also widely criticized for shallow content (game shows, soap operas, sitcoms), a preoccupation with violence (movies) and sex (commercials), and predominantly negative programming patterns ("trash" talk shows, news). Although these broad generalizations may not hold up under scrutiny, public opinion polls show that people share these perceptions. The same polls indicate, however, that audiences enjoy watching television and feel that program providers are making an effort to upgrade their offerings.

Television is a powerful medium because it presents various interpretations of events including their live coverage. Because of this, it is colorful, fast-paced, and intrinsically interesting. But perhaps its greatest power results from the combination of its liveliness and the fact that more people use it than any other medium. As we watch we are aware that we're sharing the experience with many other people. Television use has become so pervasive that many of us habitually and casually tune into its fantasy world—and frequently tune out the outside, daily world.

From a producer's perspective, television is a very expensive medium to use. It uses highly sophisticated technologies, which in turn require trained technicians to operate and maintain. And, in the United States, its dependence on commercials to support programming severely limits the kind and quality of programming available, especially in terms of variety.

Its messages are usually confined to short time spans; therefore, commercial television does not convey details, elaborations, or abstract thinking very well. Viewing conventions have created an American television reality in which messages must have a high level of entertainment value in order to compete with the messages on other channels. So the medium is used primarily to entertain and only secondarily to inform. And television informs the public in a sketchy and narrow manner. Most Americans receive their news of the world from television, even though television news is only composed of the major daily headlines salted with tidbits of information. In some countries, such as Germany, France, England, and Canada, the greater proportion of programming is informational. In the United States, however, television is increasingly used to promote consumer needs and values (for example, MTV, shopping channels, program-length commercials, character dolls and toys, movie reviews).

Video

As it's used today the term *video* usually refers to any nonbroadcast, private use of video tape recordings. Video essentially is portable, affordable, and time-flexible because the equipment to produce and receive it is substantially smaller than for broadcast television. Because of the many formats for production, users in corporations, institutions, and homes can create programming of various qualities. The tapes people create can easily be shipped, handed to friends, sold, rented, or cable cast. Messages having the attributes and appearance of television can now be traded between children as easily as those shared by executives who need to reach thousands of employees at separate locations.

Video's advantages include its relative ease of production and distribution and, primarily, its portability. Additionally, and as a result of these factors, video has become the medium of choice for businesses and special interest groups who would otherwise not have the opportunity to use television in the same way.

The disadvantages of video include some of the same considerations that relate to television but on a smaller scale: expense and access to production equipment, the need for talent and technical knowledge, expense of tape duplication and distribution, the requirement that the receiver own or have access to a video tape player and television.

Computer

Computers extend our ideas through words, data, and images. Digital computers arrived in the 1950s; the PC (personal computer or miniprocessor), in 1978. These devices allow extensive editing and manipulation of information. They perform advanced calculations in seconds and can transfer information over great distances rapidly when coupled with telecommunication (satellite) technology. The computer is humanity's latest technological attempt to extend the human brain itself, primarily as a point-to-point communication medium like the postal service or the telephone.

The computer medium requires sophisticated, often expensive equipment for sending and receiving as well as software—various logical programs that provide a template or menu of information-handling options. The computer is most often used in conjunction with other media—printing (word processing, layout, graphics, typesetting, and so on), radio, automated programming, and video (for graphics). It's a component and integration medium.

Computers' advantage is primarily the rapid movement and manipulation of vast amounts of information and the ability to store and later retrieve that information. Further, the data and images can be handled and packaged in a variety of ways (printed hard copy, floppy disk, tape).

Computers handle automatically many of the more mundane activities that have in the past occupied large numbers of people. They provide services involving repetition, memory, and speed to replace people performing comparable acts. And, as opposed to print, radio, television, or video, computers are easily adapted for two-way communication.

The computer's disadvantage is that it is impersonal. It requires high-tech, often expensive equipment to send and receive. And people must take time to learn how to operate each of the programs involved. Computing is decidedly a left brain activity with a very low capability for expressing feelings or emotions. Instead of empathy, computer technology emphasizes logic, reason, accuracy, calculation, and memory.

Media Conventions

Each medium and its associated technology has a development history. From the time of its discovery, each medium evolves and matures depending on a variety of factors including costs, ease of use, ease of manufacture, distances involved, and other physical and economic factors. Over time, certain patterns are established through repetitious use of the medium, and the public becomes accustomed to thinking of its use in specific ways.

For instance, people primarily think of television as an entertainment medium. Efforts to use it to replace the classroom teacher have almost completely failed, not because the medium was not suited to education but because administrators did not know how to use it appropriately. Now television is used extensively in the classroom as a supplement to the teacher. Likewise, people perceive radio mostly as a provider of music and information, even though it also carries entertainment programs. Not too many people sit down after a hard day and prop their feet up in front of the radio, although they used to.

We call these customs and behaviors "conventions." Audiences develop a sense about what a medium is like by using it. When messages are presented in alignment with these conventions, the receiver feels comfortable. If conventions are disregarded or misused, however, there may be discomfort with the message, a lack of ease with regard to how the medium is being used.

Conventions can be broken, of course, and over time they change, but these changes are usually quite gradual. For instance, now that old movies are being colorized, and because some producers choose to use black and white film, we're replacing the convention of black and white film necessarily being "old."

Television, and consequently video, emerged from developments in radio and the movies. So many of their production and viewing/listening conventions carried over. The "grammar" and "language" of video and television production is filled with carryovers from the movies. The term *speed,* used to indicate that the mechanical parts of the camera have reached the sync point, is sometimes used (erroneously) for video, but it is virtually meaningless because VTRs reach sync speed almost instantly. Directors still standardize on the shot sequence convention of wide to medium to close up. Another carryover is "convergence cutting," where two or more activities in separate time/space frames are shown individually and then brought together.

These conventions are what audiences expect. The serious producer must be aware of these conventions because they are part of the message, cuing audiences to feel comfortable with the way the medium is being used. Later on we'll see that the grammar and language of each medium have tremendous implications for communication effectiveness. For instance, an advertiser needs to know the preferences of the target audience in order to produce a presentation that will appeal to them. If the commercial is at odds with the audience's expectations or perceptions, the message will be either rejected or otherwise ineffective.

People who rent or receive a video from someone have certain expectations. According to the nature of the material, they have different quality expectations. The tape produced by the local school principal is not expected to be up to the quality standards of a professional producer. If it matches, so much the better, but that is not the audience's expectation. Nonetheless, the audience might hope that the video will be somewhat amusing, if not entertaining, because the convention is that video is an entertaining medium—even when its purpose is otherwise. If the tape turns out to be totally devoid of amusing or entertaining elements, the audience will notice or even be disappointed. They might say, "That wasn't a very good video." And so the overall communication in it would be less effective.

Let's compare some film and television conventions in more detail because film is still widely used for certain broadcast applications including commercials, sitcoms, and movies. These conventions will illustrate some of the factors involved in any producer's decision to use either medium.

Making a movie can be very expensive. It takes lots of time, lots of people, and enormous energy. The film experience has been carefully *planned* and executed. This is the convention.

When we go to a movie, we are seated in the dark involved in a social event. Other people tell us when they think things are funny or sad. The big screen enlarges life; everything on it seems grander. It's the center of our attention and the movie's sound surrounds us. There are almost no distractions, and so we are compelled to become deeply absorbed in what is happening on the screen.

The television convention is very different. The screen is small and it sits in our homes where there is at least the possibility of constant interruption. The room's ambient light is one more potential for distraction, or we might be distracted when we see a newspaper or magazine and read the headline. Commercials are purposeful interruptions that require us to redirect our attention. The sound comes out of a speaker system that's probably poorer in quality than the system in most automobiles, although, with the advent of stereo television, that's becoming less true. Still, the sound is usually turned down enough that others walking through the room can be heard.

Television's immediacy is another of its conventions. In the early days, the networks covered live events. The *Today Show* was shot through a department store window, presenting New York passers-by to the rest of America. And when cameras became more portable, the electronic news gathering (ENG) industry flourished. Video was "doable" in the street, in the office, in the school, or on the battlefield.

Because we became accustomed to watching real-life events on television, a live context was created. Even today people say they feel television events are actually happening, even when they know they were previously recorded. The electronic quality of the image itself cues viewers that the event is immediate, even when the picture was shot a year or more before.

It's noticeable when inappropriate matching of medium to conventional context occurs. One evening I walked through our viewing room as a commercial was on TV. I asked my daughter what she was watching. "I don't know, I think it's a new sitcom," was her reply. I took a look and agreed. There was a family interacting at the kitchen table. But where were the one-liners and the applause track? Then the tag appeared, and we realized it was a commercial—it just didn't feel like one. It felt more like a sitcom because it was originally shot on video whereas most commercials are originally shot on film. The electronic quality of the picture communicated an erroneous message.

A very high percentage of network-level commercials are originally shot on 35 mm film. They have a film quality and a film look, even though they may have been edited on videotape. Film conveys to the viewer that the product is "worth" expensive and elaborate treatment.

In the above example, my daughter and I, making a judgment based on image quality rather than content, thought it was too "live" looking to be a commercial.

Many sitcoms are shot on tape and so it was easy to deduce it was one of those. It's interesting that many if not most situation comedies that are major hits were originally shot on film. Can you imagine what *M*A*S*H* would have been like if it had been shot on videotape? It would have been awful because the context of the program, the early 1950s, was the Korean War. Because film was all that was available until relatively recently, its use is much more identified with historical subjects. Historical subjects done on video do not usually invite the viewer to identify with the characters.

When video is your medium of choice, design the program elements with these conventions in mind. Make sure that your program and its presentation use the conventions in its favor. Or break them if you like, but as always, when going against convention, do so for a reason that your audience will appreciate.

The following guidelines will help you determine which medium is appropriate for your purposes. Use *film* as the camera original:

- When the content involves the past (history, flashback, regression) with character identification.
- When the message should also convey a context of great importance. "This subject is so important that it required lots of time, money, and energy to bring it to the screen."
- When texture is important, such as imagery, expressing beauty, sensitivity, atmospheric effects, and majestic scenery (the large screen makes life seem bigger).
- When it's desirable to increase the viewer's involvement (identification) with characters.
- When emotion is a strong part of a program.

Use *videotape* as the camera original:

- When the content should feel live (happening now).
- When keeping costs down is a priority.
- When presenting "talky" informational, educational, and training-oriented subjects.
- When what is said is more significant than how it is said.
- When there are production time constraints.
- When information is primary.

Another convention of these media is audience size. Television programs are usually produced so that millions of people can experience them at one time, which frequently happens. The Academy Awards ceremony each year attracts a global audience.

A film may also reach millions of viewers over time, but only if it's a blockbuster like *E.T.* or *Gone with the Wind.* Films usually attract smaller overall audiences (in a given year) than television. Most large theaters potentially hold 200–800 people at each showing. This is clearly not the medium to use to try to sell toothpaste or any other product having a near-term marketing objective. Nor would television or video be the best way to achieve strong character identification due to its distracting viewing conditions.

These factors certainly can and should be modified appropriately for any production. Context and convention are tools to help the program designer think about the various media options in order to increase communication effectiveness.

Video Environments

. . . .

One of video's prime attributes is its suitability for many different environments. It can be broadcast, cable cast, mailed, or handed from person to person or group to group. Each of these methods of delivery relates directly to how video is used, where it will be used, and under what conditions it will be used. These use determinations often come first because they respond to a specific need. But sometimes the context of a program's use is not determined until after the subject matter and audience have been clarified. Different conditions require different approaches.

If video is the medium of choice, the context within which it will be shown is important because it will influence the design of the project. Sometimes the reason for a video's failure is that too little attention was given to how it would finally be used. Experienced producers require the client to specify the tape's use at the outset of a project because too many programs have ended up on the shelf unused.

It's not unusual for a video manager to sit through program design meetings where the administrators haven't given any thought whatsoever to what they'll actually do with a tape once it's produced. Most professionals simply will not undertake a new production until and unless the program use factor is in place and *fully warrants* the investment of time and energy.

The most common *broadcast* environments are the national networks, their local affiliates, and independent television stations. *Cable* environments (technically speaking, these are not broadcasting entities—their signal is carried via cable instead of using the public airwave frequencies) include the national cable networks and local cable companies, most of which offer public access channels for public use. *Nonbroadcast* video refers to those entities that produce programming not intended for mass distribution; its audience can be immense but is most often of a private or special interest nature. Corporations, small businesses, and other institutions frequently use video for projecting their positive image, the promotion of products and services, sales, training and personnel development, research, documentation of meetings and other events, and so on. In recent years "corporate video" has enjoyed a tremendous growth rate and provides the bulk of video employment opportunities. Other applications of nonbroadcast video include religious, legal, educational, self-improvement, hotel and convention center, home video, aesthetic (video art), and personal video (home movies). And this list is expanding.

Because where and how a video program will be used influence the project design, let's look at the different implications of some of these environments.

Broadcast/Independent Television

Since the introduction of cable television and home video, the broadcast industry has undergone substantial changes. Audiences have significantly eroded from the national networks, and, at the local level, station managers have had to keep their bottom line in the black by making cuts both in personnel and in services.

The only way a producer could get a program on broadcast television used to be by working for a network or local station or buying the time—there were no other options. Now, TV stations rarely do their own productions, commercial or otherwise, in house. Almost everything except the news is contracted out to local producers. Even graphic artwork, which was always done in house, is often "farmed out." It's less costly for TV stations to contract for work than it is to have specialized employees on the payroll year-round.

This provides a major opening for independent producers and other program developers. Many stations are contracting for entire programs, specials that focus on community interests, documentaries, and even feature stories for the news. This market demands top quality, of course, and so prime considerations for a producer are budget and access to broadcast-quality production facilities and/or remote equipment. In some instances stations will provide the budget and access to their facility and equipment, with the producer providing everything else. Producing for broadcast requires high-level creativity and excellent technical quality. The finished program must look thoroughly professional; the content must appeal to a broad public audience; the production must have some entertainment value; the technical quality must meet rigid standards; broadcast industry editing conventions must be adhered to; and appropriate copyrights must be secured for visual and music elements.

Programming for this audience should have a general rather than specific appeal. If your program is about the joy and beauty of sailing, program managers in the Midwest will probably reject it simply because it would not appeal to the largest segment of their audience. But programmers for a station located in a sailing community might feel entirely different. The kind of programming that works for broadcast usually involves local people in local issues. It's upbeat, interesting, and informative.

Even if these criteria are met, there is no guarantee that a station will air the program. Program managers strongly consider whether the program will attract viewers away from whatever happens to be airing on the competing channels.

Cable Networks

Most programming shown on cable networks is produced by independent production companies. CNN produces its own newscasts and feature stories. All of the religious channels produce some of their own programming, usually in their own studios. And most of the other networks do a sprinkling of program production—mostly segments rather than entire programs—to give a unique look to the channel. Whole programs (movies, sitcoms, specials) are usually acquired from distributors and syndicators. HBO and TNT are notable exceptions because they also produce some features.

Segments and entire programs are increasingly being produced under contract. Each of the cable networks has a highly targeted audience in mind and each looks for programming that will appeal to its audience. By studying the program schedules of these networks, one can begin to discern the audiences they are working to attract. You can submit program proposals, treatments, and scripts and make presentations to their program managers—especially if your program fits their market and quality standards.

As the cable industry evolves, some existing channels will die and others will be created, all in the interest of appealing to specific segments of the population. These cable channels will work to narrow their focus, rather than broaden it, because advertisers are tending toward "positioning" their commercials as much as possible. Why spend $300,000 for a thirty-second broadcast spot to reach millions of people of whom only a small percentage are really interested in the product? On a cost-per-thousand basis, for many products it makes more sense to air commercials on a cable channel where most of the audience is already interested in the product category. Someone advertising automobile tires is throwing money away when the commercial on broadcast television also reaches millions of women and kids because, statistically, more men purchase tires. But on a cable channel that features sports and male-oriented activities, the same commercial will do a much better job, even though it may reach fewer people.

Public Access Cable Channels

Most cities have a cable station that offers one or more public access channels. These channels were created for public use—as the name indicates—offering any citizen the opportunity to produce and show her presentation to the wider community. Public access channels' early uses have been small group and personal communications including church meetings, community discussions, the eighth-grade variety show, and similar features. After consistently seeing boring programs lacking production values, the public has learned to pay little attention to them, thereby creating the convention that public access is "junk" TV. Nonetheless, public access provides a very useful service. As an introduction to the TV medium, it can be an excellent way to learn that there is much more to video communication than lights, cameras, and glamour.

Over these same channels, individuals and special interest groups attempt to sincerely express important issues, ideas, and concerns. They want to share something they feel is important or interesting with the wider community. Too often even these efforts "turn off" average viewers because of the producer's inability to create a proper context and follow through with the necessary production values to convince viewers that the content is worth their time and attention.

Several technical or production-related factors have to be taken into consideration when using public access:

- Public access audience sizes are consistently very small indeed. The larger the city is, however, the greater will be the chance for more viewers.
- Videos submitted to public access channels must meet a set of criteria: All program audio must be on only one channel of the tape. Cue tones are added so the tape will start and stop at the appropriate points. Copyrights must be obtained in writing for any borrowed content (consult your local public access coordinator for their specific guidelines). Content must not contain material of a commercial or promotional nature.

Although it still suffers from an image problem, in my opinion public access has great potential. When we scan the TV channels with our remote controls, we indiscriminately push buttons as we watch the screen. Rarely do we look at the channel call letters or numbers unless we are searching for a specific channel. This "grazing" factor has television programmers very concerned. We graze from channel to channel because we want to see if something appeals to us along the way. In the process we may encounter Sally's birthday party right next to a network movie. Most of us would keep on grazing but note that the access channel was one of our possible choices. We did, in fact, sample it even if for a second. And what if, in that time, there was something that caught our attention? What if its appearance quality was much like the professional channels? We would probably stay with it for at least a few more seconds.

When video is used in the proper context, is used for a good reason, and is well executed, we can expect that it will make an impact and even attract an audience. Viewers don't care what the channel is. When it comes to programming, the public wants quality, interesting shows. So what if they happen to be on an access channel?

At an out-of-town conference I once struck up a conversation with someone after noticing that we were from the same city. He had attended the conference specifically to try to meet one of the keynote speakers, who had had a profound effect on his life. It turned out to be someone I knew, and he went on to tell me how he had first heard this woman speak on television and that he had subsequently read her books. The irony was that I was the producer of the program he saw, and I had placed it on a public access channel merely to keep the program in circulation. Even if there had been only a few people watching that program, one of them had had a significant experience. He remarked that he thought he had tuned to public television and decided to give it a try. Had he sensed public access quality, chances are that he would have switched channels automatically.

Although public access has its downside, the upside is the potential for your video to be shown to the community. If you're going to consider using it, carefully weigh the costs and benefits against the purpose of your program.

Corporate/Industrial Video

Due to the availability of high- and low-end industrial-grade equipment, and their associated lower costs, video has moved out of the realm of the privileged few and into the hands of the many. Although the word *industrial* brings to mind images of blast furnaces and assembly lines, the term as applied here includes every application that is outside amateur or broadcast: corporate training and development programs, information tapes, sales and marketing tapes, documentation of seminars and conferences, corporate image tapes, resume tapes, video curricula, instructional video, video art, music video, educational video, video magazines, video newsletters, video inventories, legal and real estate video, and management tapes.

In the context of corporate or industrial video, the program will most likely be shown to relatively small (not mass) audiences, and viewers are likely already to have an interest in the subject matter. The tape will be either ¾ in. or ½ in. VHS no matter what the original may have been, because these formats are most commonly available in American institutional environments. And you can easily send the tape(s) around to different locations within a building or across the country so viewers can watch them at their convenience.

Some corporations create libraries of orientation and training tapes that are required viewing for all new employees. Other companies have arranged with their unions to pay their members an additional hourly fee if they view a series of videos and then pass a written test on what they learned. Corporate/industrial-type programs can be produced in house or out, and, because the technology is less complex and expensive than broadcast, the technical skill level of technicians can be somewhat lower than that found in broadcast environments. Most technical repairs are handled by outside businesses that specialize in this area. Nonetheless, writing, program design, and production require professional levels of communication and creativity and are usually handled in house.

Home Video

"Home video," as the name implies, refers to tapes that are used in the home. We are most familiar with movies available for rent at the local video store, but increasingly there are other opportunities in this distribution area. The home video market has grown tremendously in the past decade and is expected to continue as a primary source of family entertainment and enrichment.

The home video market presents a challenge and opportunity for the producer. The challenge is that the public primarily identifies home videos with movies, supplemented with a variety of exercise tapes. The opportunity is in what the industry refers to as "special interest" tapes. As yet, these kinds of videos have not been dynamic sellers in the video stores because it takes a lot of marketing energy and money to promote them. For the most part, these kinds of tapes derive their appeal from a notable host or hostess who leads viewers into the subject matter.

There are thousands of special interest tapes available on a full range of subjects. The market for these kinds of videos has developed slowly but is expected to grow in the near future. Michael Wiese, in *Home Video: Producing for the Home Market*, says,

The good news for producers is that more than two-thirds of the films in studio vaults have already been released [by 1986]. Consequently, the hunger for new product will be difficult to feed without new programming of all kinds. There is still plenty of time for innovative producers and programmers to develop and produce the future hits of tomorrow.[1]

Home videos are relatively inexpensive to produce but require a significant amount of time and energy devoted to marketing and promotion. Producing a program so that video stores will carry it is a prime concern. The future holds more innovative solutions to this challenge, but in the meantime small video distribution companies have appeared. They pay a producer a percentage of their net profit, incurring the costs associated with duplication. These distributors publish a catalogue of their offerings and send it to their client list or to a purchased listing of members of an audience they have targeted. The tapes are regarded as "sell through" items; that is, they are offered for sale with no rental involved. Special interest video sales have been slow, especially because few customers are willing to spend $30 and up for a video they haven't seen. They must already have a high level of interest either in the subject matter or in the on-camera presenter or both.

Bookstores and other specialty stores are selling videotapes. This trend will likely increase substantially as tapes become more affordable and as the public begins to use video as an information and enrichment tool in addition to one that provides entertainment. These are all opportunities for nonbroadcast producers.

Because the American public is most familiar with the kind of quality and production values that are exhibited by the major TV networks, the convention requires producers of home videos to at least approach that same level of quality. When it's missing, we feel either cheated or that the producers lacked a genuine interest in the subject matter—and these kinds of tapes simply do not sell or rent. So, although home video production budgets may be smaller, you must still pay attention to production quality as well as to distribution and promotion. Nonbroadcast video is primarily a marketing challenge.

Summary

Video has become the medium of choice for those who want to communicate to larger (but not mass) audiences. It has not replaced other media such as slide or multimedia presentations. But it is a medium that combines several positive features including cost, immediacy, manageability, and portability.

An intelligent approach to any mediated communication is to match the message to the medium that best meets the needs of the communicator and the audience—with the audience having the higher priority. Because whether the communication is successful depends on how the audience receives it, the audience should be understood before you decide on the medium. In this book we will consider the audience (as a subject) after selecting the medium in order to structure our study systematically. In practice, however, audience considerations help determine the medium.

Each medium has its own set of conventions that have been established over time. These often subtle factors help a producer to use each medium wisely by carefully structuring the program context, format, and message in ways that are already comfortable to the audience. Doing otherwise can generate questions of doubt, uncertainty, or confusion in the mind of the receiver. For a message to get through clearly and powerfully, it cannot be cluttered with this other kind of negative baggage or psychological "noise" in the system.

Since Sony Corporation introduced the portable video recorder in 1975, video has blossomed into a medium with many applications. The serious video producer must be familiar with all these and be open to future innovations.

Each medium represents an opportunity for reaching audiences in a particular way. And each carries with it specific costs, benefits, conventions, and requirements that, well managed, can lead to effective presentation.

The medium you choose communicates.

Notes

1. Michael Wiese, *Home Video: Producing for the Home Market* (Westport, CT: Michael Wiese Film/Video and Focal Press, 1986), 7.

Suggested Readings

Barnouw, Erik. *The Image Empire: A History of Broadcasting in the United States from 1953*. New York: Oxford University Press, 1970.

Cherry, Colin. *On Human Communication*. New York: Science Editions, John Wiley, 1957.

Degen, Clara, ed. *Understanding and Using Video: A Guide for the Organizational Communicator*. White Plains, NY: Longman, 1985.

Eastman, Susan Tyler, Sydney W. Head, and Lewis Klein. *Broadcast/Cable Programming,* 3rd ed. Belmont, CA: Wadsworth, 1989.

Esslin, Martin. *The Age of Television*. San Francisco: W. H. Freeman, 1982.

Gross, Lynne Schafer. *Telecommunication: An Introduction to Electronic Media*. Dubuque, IA: Wm. C. Brown, 1988.

Heibert, Ray Eldon, Donald Ungurait, and Thomas W. Bohn. *Mass Media III: An Introduction to Modern Communication*. New York: Longman, 1982.

Lazer, Ellen, ed. *Guide to Videotape Publishing*. White Plains, NY: Knowledge Industry Publications, 1985.

McLuhan, Marshall. *Understanding Media*. New York: McGraw-Hill, 1964.

Noam, Eli M., ed. *Video Media Competition Regulation, Economics, and Technology*. New York: Columbia University Press, 1985.

Presentation Consultants. *Home Video Publishing: The Distribution of Videocassettes, 1986–1990*. White Plains, NY: Knowledge Industry Publications, 1986.

Schwartz, Tony. *The Responsive Chord*. Garden City, NY: Anchor Doubleday, 1973.

Shanks, Bob. *The Cool Fire.* New York: Norton, 1976.

Shanks, Bob. *The Primal Screen.* New York: Fawcett Columbine, 1986.

Singleton, Lox A. *Telecommunications in the Information Age.* Cambridge, MA: Ballinger, 1986.

Wiese, Michael. *Home Video: Producing for the Home Market.* Westport, CT: Michael Wiese Film/Video and Focal Press, 1986.

CHAPTER 5

Video as a Communication Tool

· ·

When television is used with the effectiveness inherent in the medium, no other teaching medium can perform as well or as flexibly in making the world of information, imagination, and reality accessible to the thought processes of a learner—or a million learners.

—Bernard Friedlander

Now that we've decided to use video because it's the medium *best* suited to carry our expression to an audience, we want to consider the dynamics of the medium. I don't mean how it works technically. I'm talking about using video to communicate, maximizing its unique characteristics. This chapter is about communicating. We will discuss video techniques in other chapters.

Communicating effectively means our expression accomplishes something we want in those with whom we interact. Each medium has unique qualities the user can manipulate. They are the communicator's tools.

The tools we'll need for our video communication begin with our interactive model of communication and include the following: an understanding of what activates an audience; an understanding of audience identity—who they are and how they perceive others; empathy and sympathy, which are the structural basis of video communication; and an understanding of viewer choice, to structure communication so viewers' choice(s) are consistent with our communication objective. These tools are the source of video's power.

Interactive Process

Let's immediately acknowledge that video doesn't communicate—people do! Someone has consciously created everything we experience on a television screen. Video often seems impersonal because there is so much of it. But it's highly personal—you just don't usually see the senders of the messages. You see their representatives, such as narrators and actors. None of the messages on your TV screen originated with a machine—the thought came first, then the mechanics brought it into form.

Further, the television and video experience does not contain immediate feedback from the viewer, that is, video is most often *one-way.* As we saw earlier, the audience *seems* to be passive. We might feel we experience the ideas, images, stories, and interactions these invisible people send us without them knowing how we feel about them.

In the first chapter we identified communication as a *process* of human interaction where the receiver continuously provides feedback to the sender, thereby influencing the communication. We also saw that the interaction of participants is *complex;* that is, although the audience might seem to be passive, they're actually constantly responding, questioning, identifying, relating, and making other decisions. While we (as viewers) more often do not provide feedback to the sender, we nonetheless influence the communication not only by writing or calling the station but, more important, by *selecting* and *deciding,* both of which influence the process over time.

We can approve of program content, placement, or style; we can select another channel or another medium; we can choose not to purchase an advertised product. So we must replace our perception of television and video as one-way and passive. It is much more useful, from the producer's perspective, to regard the viewing situation as an *interactive process.*

Two-way video communication (in more conventional terms) does exist. Training programs in business and industry use interactive video, especially videodisk technology. The shopping channels have perhaps led the way in broadcast interactivity, and there are other excursions into two-way video, especially with the advent of fiber optics. These innovations are just an expansion of the technological system—the communication fundamentals remain the same. Now there is simply greater availability of immediate interactivity. Although *more* communication is desirable, *better* communication should be the video producer's primary objective.

Active-Passive

Most television critics still regard television viewing as a passive, spectator sport. Others, most notably writers and producers of children's programming, national commercials, and industrial videos, argue that viewing can be a more responsive—even active—experience. We're all familiar with the stereotypical image of the "couch-potato" viewer, the person who sits for hours in front of the tube, munching snacks, oblivious to anything else that may be happening in the room. Statistics show that Americans spend an inordinate amount of time watching television. In 1989, the figure was seven hours, forty-eight minutes, per day for the average household.[1] Patterns of viewing are difficult to describe because the mass audience is diverse, but we can easily see that most television viewing seems passive, that is, we sit and watch what is offered.

On the other hand, many programs and videos are more involving. Research indicates that children sing along with *Sesame Street.* They recite the alphabet and other program elements that are often repeated.[2] Adult viewers are even active to the extent that they *respond* to what is on the screen. In my household we sometimes sing along with the program—especially the opening themes of well-known programs—sometimes just to clown around or because we really like the tune. We also criticize, talk back to the announcer, agree, mock, and otherwise evaluate what we are viewing.

Ask children to sing the theme song of their favorite shows or commercials and they usually can. This shows that, as we watch, we not only absorb something, we often respond and repeat, and that response is participation in the "field," the dynamic of what is expressed on the screen. Sometimes the response is immediate. We jump out of our chairs because the experience is "outstanding," "weird," "outrageous," or "stupid." We might exercise to videos and learn how to paint and cook and dance. As the host demonstrates, we follow along.

Sometimes the viewer's response is delayed. We'll listen to gardening hints and not act on them until the appropriate time, perhaps when the weather is better. When the *Superman* movie is over, the eight-year-old will do as I and millions of other kids did when we first saw it—jump off high places with a homemade cape of some kind. But sometimes there's little or no response because we tune out. The response (reaction) that usually occurs is less physical than emotional. That's simply because the bulk of programming on TV and in videos is oriented toward cerebral and emotional experiences—another reason viewing appears to be passive. All this causes the producer to ask: Do we want our content to be received passively? Or should it provoke some response? We have that choice, and not to exercise it consciously is to diffuse our power. The answer to the question will be found in our project's communication objective.

Here is information that all producers should have in their consciousness. Research conducted by Clark Leavitt, sponsored by the American Marketing Association, indicates three points about human behavior that illuminate the operative factors in communication:

1. Stimulation is biologically positive. That is, *human beings need and therefore seek stimulation.*

2. *The essence of stimulation is change, unexpectedness, novelty, inconsistency* [and] *uncertainty.*

3. *People spontaneously seek out and explore areas of uncertainty* with the result that what is originally uncertain becomes *meaningful.*[3]

Applying this to video, we can see that audiences want to be stimulated. They want *experiences* (not just words) to help them explore life's uncertainties so they can resolve them and in the process create meaning.

If we intend to create a video experience that stimulates—provokes a response—we need to provide visual and aural experiences of change, uncertainty, inconsistency, and/or novelty. There are many television programs (and videos) that do this regularly, but let's use *Sesame Street* as an example because it's a common reference and its audience has a short attention span.

In Gerald S. Lesser's book, *Children and Television: Lessons from Sesame Street,* an entire chapter is devoted to program design and the techniques used to catch, hold, and direct children's attention.[4] These techniques activate the three factors discussed above. Bert and Ernie, the Cookie Monster, and Big Bird don't simply perform for the viewer's amusement. They *command* attention and a response. Kids who watch cannot help but sing and dance along and talk back to the screen when somebody's doing something that's obviously wrong—like misspelling a word or putting a round block with a bunch of square ones.

Let's use a specific example, the *Sesame Street Christmas Show* that airs every December, to see how they employed the three points. The plot revolves around *uncertainty* about how Santa Claus can get down the chimney. Big Bird seeks answers (*meaning*) from the program's other characters. He stirs up their curiosity and other feelings with *inconsistent* theories about how Santa accomplishes his entries. Finally, of course, Big Bird, much to the concern of his friends, who think he is lost in a snow storm, spends the night waiting for Santa.

The audience is poised, eager, expectant for the resolution of this conflict. And then, to the consternation of all, Santa comes to the rooftop when Big Bird is asleep. This is almost more than a kid can handle. Every element supports the suspense. The music, especially the theme song, is used as background throughout the program to create a memory of it. Then at the end the theme brings the show to an emotional high when Big Bird comes down to a room full of presents and a beautiful tree.

Special effects provide *novelty* to show us what Big Bird didn't see, how Santa comes down the chimney by transforming himself and his troop into a burst of light. Finally, the audience resolves their uncertainty and feels good about the spirit of Christmas and what it means.

My daughter has watched that program every year since she was about six years old and even now, as a college student, she's compelled to sing the songs, talk to Big Bird, and complain about his bungling. The catharsis—her emotional response at the end of the program—is always the same. What a feeling, to have grave uncertainty resolved through the experience of novelty, change, and the unexpected. It gives us hope that life, like the story, is meaningful.

No matter how diverse the audience, the technique for making a video experience more of an active (rather than a passive) one is to present situations that establish uncertainty or inconsistencies using novelty and/or change to bring resolutions that allow the audience to feel comfortable or satisfied. In the end, they "get" it. They accept it as having a meaning they understand—it makes sense and the conflict is resolved.

Writers, producers, and other storytellers purposefully seek out and often create uncertainty and inconsistency—often called "conflict"—because, without it, there's nothing to resolve. And the greater the conflict, the greater the satisfaction at its resolution because order and meaning are restored. Without conflict, a story is bland. What does the fact that human beings need conflict in order to enjoy a story say about us? Just that people are challenged by life experiences, so much so that it's a relief—often allowing learning—to know we're not alone in our problems and that they can be resolved. Our joy at seeing a screen character overcome obstacles is not only personal, we also see that certain values, attitudes, and actions (as displayed) can overcome our collective dark forces. It gives us hope.

To stimulate and involve your audience then, your video can create feelings of uncertainty, inconsistency, novelty, and unexpectedness.

Creating Uncertainty

The following suggestions can help you incorporate elements of uncertainty when designing your video presentation:

- Setting up information, circumstances, or questions that do not have an easy or obvious answer.
- Using a format that opens with a problem, challenge, or situation that calls for resolution.
- Using sequencing that unveils only one part of a process or technique at a time.
- Establishing a context that contains more questions than answers, more problems than solutions.
- Showing how things are done the wrong way.
- Using simulations or role-play to demonstrate a problem or situation without giving the resolution.
- Creating a failing character who is stumbling, bungling, or otherwise making a mess out of his pursuit of meaning.
- Using counterpoint—that is, the audio does not match the video; the visual communication is in some way opposite to the verbal or musical communication.
- Showing the resolution first (as in *Columbo*, where we see who did it) and then showing the process; present the ending first, then the logical steps that led to it.
- Juxtaposing two elements (ideas, objects, attitudes, people, values) that do not go together, allowing a conflict to ensue. Remember that conflict is the heart of drama.

Creating Inconsistency

You can include inconsistency by using these techniques:

- Using body language that conflicts with verbal language.
- Using counterpoint, where elements of the content or production are at variance with one another.
- Creating a character whose behavior takes a different direction from what his or her personality would normally suggest. This can be danger-

ous because, taken too far, the character can lose credibility with the viewer.

- Using an actor or even an announcer who takes a position and later acts out a different one, diametrically opposed to the first. One minute you say "Yes!" and the next minute you're saying "No!"—so which is it?
- Using the "bait and switch" technique. An offer or suggestion is made that something will happen if . . . , then, when the offer is accepted, something else (or nothing) happens.
- Using humor, where the comedian laughs about a circumstance and then says, "but seriously folks" and takes a different view. *The Cosby Show* uses a lot of this kind of verbal inconsistency to get laughs.

Creating Novelty

Incorporate elements of novelty into your video using the following techniques:

- Showing anything on the screen that is different or unusual, including the use of unusual sounds or music.
- Having a character do something strange—out of character or out of the ordinary.
- Using special effects visuals; showing images that have not been seen before (especially by using computer graphics).
- Showing talent or performers doing things that have not been done before. Chinese dance and acrobatic troops do this regularly and frequently amaze Western and other audiences.
- Using animation and other techniques that allow animals to sing and dance. The "California Raisins" Claymation is an example.
- Using unique imagery. The *Nova* series has taken viewers on adventures into space, under water, and into the human body. These images are intrinsically compelling because of their novelty alone. At the same time, they appeal to our quest for meaning.
- Employing techniques that present a new and better, more innovative, way of doing things. Sometimes an idea is so simple that it escapes attention and then, when it's presented, viewers are amazed at how "novel" it is.
- Creatively combining objects, elements, or pacing so the result is highly unique. Video art almost always involves novelty.

Creating Unexpectedness

The following techniques can help you achieve a sense of the unexpected for your audience:

- Using sound to provide an emotion that is then suddenly changed. Horror and suspense formats use this technique.
- Using images, sounds, or movements that are unanticipated.
- Creating characters whose behavior can be predicted but then who take

a different turn. The soft-voiced, mild-mannered woman who goes off-stage and screams at her kids; the physically handicapped person who gets up and dances; Wile E. Coyote in the *Road Runner* who always gets the unexpected (from his perspective) "in the end."

- Developing the underdog, who wins.
- Showing the trainer who can't get things to work when his student can.
- Using sight gags: slow motion, fast motion, chopped motion (Pixillation).
- Using missed cues: the ringing of a doorbell with the sound coming late. The *Carol Burnett Show* was loaded with these devices. Carol would pull a cord to ring for the butler and a gunshot would be heard, or a gun would be fired and the shot not heard until the actor looked offstage to find out why.
- Using spectacle, which is best kept secret until the last moment. Slow music is placed under a sensitive narrator's voice until there is a cue, at which point the music abruptly cuts to loud and fast tempo as fog enters the screen and laser lights move to the beat.
- Using subtlety. An interviewer might be discussing a topic and then bring on an item for demonstration or a model that illustrates her point.
- Using sudden gestures that create unexpected movement on the screen.

Creating Change

It's been said that "the only constant is change" and, "if you don't like the way things are, wait a minute because change is on its way." Change is essential for life. Optometrists know that one reason our vision degrades is that we don't use our eye muscles enough—we stare too often at a fixed point or into space. The muscles don't get enough exercise (change) to stay strong and flexible, so we develop near- or farsightedness. The lesson we can learn from this is to keep program elements changing on the screen.

What I call the "fatigue factor" sets in after about ten seconds. If nothing on the screen has changed in some way, the viewer begins to get tired of looking at it. Internal questions crop up: What's next? Is there something wrong? Why am I being shown this image for so long? And after about twenty seconds, fatigue begins to promote discomfort or boredom. At the thirty-second point, I've lost them. If I want to keep the viewer's attention on the screen, I know that something involving the image or audio has to change, if even slightly—such as a gesture—approximately every ten seconds.

Madison Avenue's response to this phenomenon has been to speed up the pacing of images and edits in commercials. Other producers have followed in this practice, but it has been overdone. While it's advisable to change some program element within ten to twenty seconds, audiences quickly become desensitized and distracted by images that fly by too fast. Certainly we must maintain a balance between keeping an audience's interest and bombarding them with too much content too fast. My parents say they don't watch television because "everything happens too fast." I've also heard this expressed by people of various ages from coast to coast. As producers, we need to know our audience well enough to be able to find the balance. Audiences can be lost as much from overstimulation as they can from understimulation.

You can create *change* in these ways:

- Keeping on-camera persons in an active mode if possible. Have them move around in the frame or at least gesture if they are stationary. Don't use squirming or other movements that would be disturbing, but human beings should appear fluid, not bored or stiff.
- Moving the camera if the subject doesn't move and, even better yet, moving the talent and the camera simultaneously. The generic open to *L.A. Law* displays this technique to perfection. The camera, talent, and cutting pace are choreographed well and the net effect is very compelling.
- Changing the shot itself. Certainly there will be exceptions, but frequent scene changes cue viewers that something else is coming while setting a pace.
- Using audio and music to cue that a change in the story line, pacing, or other program content is imminent. Alternate between slow- and fast-paced music.
- Using rapid or quick cuts, which are compelling simply by virtue of the change of pace. Use this judiciously. Studies have shown that cuts that are too rapid can cause discomfort and confusion, especially if the audience is young or elderly.

Prompting

I would add one other technique to Leavitt's list because I have seen it work so well in programs for children (including *Sesame Street*) and in other types of programs as well. It is what I call "prompting." To prompt a viewer to action (immediately or later), you make an outright request and then provide sufficient cognitive or emotional stimulation (motivation) for follow-through. We can ask our viewers to exercise, get a pad and pencil, make a phone call (à la 800 or 900 numbers), write a letter, or practically anything else. Because we have their attention, we can at least make the request. Often it pays off. The home shopping channels owe most of their effectiveness to this technique.

I remember that when I was a child there was a program that asked us to put our hand on the TV screen. The performer also did this so we could draw a line around our hands with a crayon. Primitive but, nonetheless, thousands of kids had their sticky little hands on their TV screens making crayon marks. It was fun and involving—we felt connected to the program host.

Do you remember the famous scene from the movie *Network,* where the crazed anchorman asks everyone to go to their window and yell out, "I'm mad as hell, and I'm not going to take it anymore!"? Go to your local video store and rent this movie and, while you're there, get a copy of *Scrooged* with Bill Murray—especially if it's near Christmastime. This movie uses the prompt very effectively in the end credits, but watch the whole thing so you can *feel* how you are set up. Invite some friends over for a "prompting" party.

The power of direct eye contact with the viewer (lens) has, I think, been under-estimated. Whether such prompting is subtle or overt, this—and the other communication tools we've examined—can definitely transform viewing from a passive to a more active and involving experience. The possibilities are only bound by our consciousness and creativity.

A word of caution here: The results of a ten-year government-sponsored study released in 1982 suggest that we (as producers) should temper these approaches in circumstances involving children and learning:

The rapid form of presentation characterizing American television in which novelty piles upon novelty in short sequences may be counterproductive for organized and effective learning sequences. The young child who has not yet developed strategies for tuning out irrelevancies may be especially vulnerable in this respect; even programs that seek to be informative as well as entertaining may miss the mark because they allow too little time for reflection. . . . Extremely rapid-paced material, presenting novelty along with high levels of sound and fast movement, may generate surprise and confusion in the viewer whose anticipatory strategies or well-established scheme are not yet prepared for coping with this material. Foreigners, for example, who are accustomed to a much slower pace of television say that they are almost physically pained when they first watch American commercial television.[5]

As responsible producers we have to consider our audience and use techniques that will be effective with them. Applying techniques for their own sake, or simply because the techniques are appealing to us creatively, can seriously threaten the effectiveness of our communication objective. Balance should be the rule.

Identity
. . . .

In observing the world around us, directly or through the media, we subconsciously, and sometimes consciously, look at who we are with respect to everyone else. To gain more information about where we fit into the scheme of our own reality, we construct responses to the question: "Who am I?" This is perhaps one of the more central and ongoing questions in our lives. Identity is directly related to the meaning we give to things. If my life is to be meaningful, I have to know who I am in relation to everyone else.

By observing the seemingly endless personalities in our lives and on our TV screens (and in other media), we pursue issues that relate directly to the formation of our identities. We want to "fit in"—most of us do anyway. Choosing whether to fit in requires some experience with the world outside ourselves. Are other people having experiences that I am not but would like to have? Are others getting a bigger or better portion of the "good" than I? Am I "normal" compared with most other people? Am I "cool"? Am I "in"? Do I present myself to others in ways that are acceptable? How does what I like or think compare with what everybody else likes or thinks? What's the standard? What's the norm?

At some level—especially in young people—these questions concerning personal identity come up all the time. The media—especially advertisers—use this obsession in very specific ways to motivate, sell, persuade, and convince. We're aware of this as viewers because it's relatively easy to see through the glitz and hype to the true agenda of advertisers—to get money out of our pockets and into theirs. Politicians want our votes so they can have more power; entertainers want our approval and attention. As producers, we need to observe the identity process from the viewers' perspective.

We can use this process to our advantage when creating media messages and experiences. If this sounds like audience manipulation, it is, and there is nothing wrong with it. Civilization is built on people convincing one another of various values and motivating others to take action. Manipulation, like anything, can be used for good or ill. We'll assume here that the power to motivate, to form and transform using the media, will be used morally with a keen appreciation of the ethics involved.

When you use identity as a communication insight, and tool, there are two primary viewpoints—self and other.

Self (Viewer)

Each "self" has a unique identity that sees "the world" from its own perspective. To illustrate, think about how your entire reality could be taken away from you in an instant if somehow you were rendered unconscious. Instantly you would be in another world. Your waking reality would be gone from you and from everyone else. Further consider that your reality and worldview move with you, and you alone. Today I'm seeing the world from the perspective of the university campus. Tomorrow I will be experiencing it from a theater stage where I'll be shooting on location. And next weekend my reality will be that of giving a talk at a conference. While I'm seeing the world from these perspectives, there are other people whose reality includes being shot at, being hungry, or making million-dollar deals. I am not experiencing Africa or a coal mine or the barnyard—they aren't even close to my reality. Yet these are everyday realities for others.

If I intend to communicate effectively with others, I have to understand or at least have some appreciation of their reality and perspectives. We can at least hope to find some element(s) of commonality between us because this allows communication to happen more easily.

In interpersonal communication we first meet the other on common ground, talking about what we already agree on, our common perceptions, where our realities coincide. Then we can move into areas where our references may differ. We work with the known and gradually move into the unknown.

We do the same with video. Present the personalities, images, ideas, or experiences that are already part of the audience's accepted reality and then move into areas that may be an expansion of this reality or completely new material. In this way the producer does not violate the identity of others, which would cause them to reject the experience or message. In essence we respect the identity and perspective of our viewers, acknowledging that their reality is at least in part the same as ours in order to present our material. Doing otherwise threatens the communication process because we can be seen as imposing our reality on theirs. We are open to the person who says, "Believe this because it relates to what you already believe," but we're closed to the message, "Believe this because I say it's so irrespective of what you think." This is what it means to empathize with viewers, trying to look at the message they will be receiving from their vantage point. As we'll see in the chapter on audience issues, this is the secret to "positioning"—the way advertisers gain access to the consumer's mind. The Dale Carnegie course in effective speaking stresses the importance of "speaking in terms of the other person's interest." Being sensitive to the receiver's identity keeps him or her open to what you have to say.

Other (Screen Characters)

Examining the self (as viewer) took us into considerations of what our audience already knows, thinks, feels, and sees. We now want to see the screen characters *as the viewers will experience them*. Will members of our target audience encounter characters who are sympathetic to their concerns? Will the characters be credible? Will the screen presenters (seen or not) have the same interests or values as the audience? Or will they offer material or views that are opposed?

It's often desirable or even necessary to present material contrary to the accepted interests and values of the audience—this might even be the communication objective. An example is a video produced by a labor union trying to convince company administrators of the value of its latest benefit proposal. Another example is a video that lays out the specifics of a plan for a corporate takeover. We want to focus not so much on the appropriateness of agreement or disagreement but on how best to structure a video presentation so that, when viewed, the audience (self) will be able to attend to it and accept the views of the other (presenter).

As discussed in the chapter on consciousness, if we know something about ourselves and about how our audience views the world, especially in the area of the program's subject matter, we can do a much better job of designing the communication.

For instance, let's consider a hypothetical coal mine (a subject totally out of the range of my reality). If the mine's administrators invited me in as an independent producer to consult on and eventually produce a video to help promote mine safety, my first advice would be that they try to find a producer or writer who knows something about mine safety or at least mining operations. As someone with no experience at all in mining environments, I have not earned the right to communicate on mine safety to the people who work there. I would not be credible in that situation.

But let's say the company owner has seen and likes my previous work and insists that I'm the producer for the job. (In the video production business, we're commonly asked to produce in areas totally unfamiliar to us.) Then it becomes my responsibility and challenge to create a team with some expertise in that environment and to design program elements that will be accepted by the miners.

I would not, for example, use an omniscient narrator (VO) with a polished voice, which is probably not a voice the miners would listen to with much belief. I wouldn't use a female voice for the same reason. Nor would I have a person employed by the mine do the narration because the miners have strong unions and they might consider the administrators to be the "bad guys." From the perspective of the miners (our audience), we have to find a presenter they will respect—probably the voices of highly experienced miners, men who have learned safety the hard way.

I could take the company's list of safety concerns and then find miners (from within the same company or other companies) and have these men speak on the appropriate issues and potential solutions. It would be good to have these experienced miners choose which of the safety issues they wanted to present, because the expression would be closer to each man's actual experience. Then the program would have greater relevance, integrity, and spontaneity. We want the self (viewer) to identify with and respect the voice and perspectives of our presenter (other), thereby making acceptance of the message easier and more comfortable.

Whether the format is comedy, documentary, drama, commercial, or instructional, it's important to spend time in the shoes of the target audience to become familiar with their reality. Examine their self-images and the perceptions they hold about the subject matter and its presenters. By integrating and blending these perspectives, the message can be presented in a more palatable manner, thereby contributing to, rather than detracting from, the communication objective.

Empathy/Sympathy

. . . .

Empathy is "the imaginative projection of a subjective state into an object so that the object appears to be infused with it."[6] This means trying to experience what someone else is experiencing. When I sit in the waiting room of the dentist's office and hear the sound of the drill, I get chills and attempt to shift my attention elsewhere. Although I'm not in the other person's situation, the sound alone may be enough to trigger an emotional response.

We might empathize with (feel with) the patient partly because we have a memory of what she is undergoing—we imagine what she must be feeling and, as a result, also experience something. We don't feel her pain, but we respond to the memory of our own. In other instances, we project ourselves into unknown situations where we imagine what the feeling must be like.

Most of us have not had hundreds of snakes writhing at our feet, but when we watch Indiana Jones in *Raiders of the Lost Ark,* we put ourselves in his boots and quiver. But we never completely lose sight of the fact that "this is only a movie." Empathy is a moderated emotional response to a situation triggered by memory and/or imagination. We can't feel exactly the same as Indy, but we do feel something and, whatever it is, it's stimulating.

Returning to the dentist's office, the sound of the drill not only stimulates our emotions through memory and imagination, it also triggers our feelings *for* the person undergoing the procedure. These feelings for another are called **sympathy:** "Oh, that poor woman." "Poor Indiana Jones, he's walking into a trap." We sympathize with Indiana Jones because we see the trap coming and he doesn't. When the danger is over, we experience relief (we knew he'd get through it—after all, it's only a story), but we also experience the thrill of it.

Television and video are highly empathic and sympathetic media. We watch the screen in part because we want to be stimulated as a result of what the screen characters are doing and feeling. Frequently empathy and sympathy are the mechanisms that draw us into a program and then extend our emotional range of experience. Through electronic media we can have a greater emotional range of experience and more frequent experiences. They also take us mentally away from our current concerns, problems, and feelings and from our mundane and everyday experiences.

A major source of the power of television and video to communicate effectively is their stimulation and extension of our experience and emotions through *empathy* and *sympathy*. Once we know that, to varying degrees, viewers experience what the screen characters experience, we can work backward. If we want the viewer to feel joy, then we need to show joy on the screen. If we want her to feel excitement, then that has to occur on the screen. Whatever we want the viewer to feel must be the experience of the screen situation and/or characters. A full spectrum of emotional experiences can thus be evoked.

To be effective, programs should trigger some *emotional* response in the viewer. If you aren't interested in emotional responses, use a different medium. Even informational and instructional programs can be made more compelling by evoking some emotional response. Much of television is boring because producers don't go to the trouble of using empathy and sympathy.

At the beginning of every project, you should make a decision on which emotion(s) the viewer should experience as he views the program. Marketing research suggests we especially consider the feeling the viewer will be left with when the program is over, because that is the impression that will last if anything lasts.

Let's get very specific here, because empathy/sympathy is one of the most important tools the producer has. They can directly contribute to program effectiveness when skillfully applied. The design (thought) process would proceed in this manner:

1. Consider the final emotional state. What single *feeling* or impression do we want the viewer to be left with when the program is over?

2. Consider the emotional flow of the program. Knowing what the final feeling will be, how should the content progress toward that conclusion? Create emotional peaks and valleys throughout that naturally lead to the final feeling experience. (Plot it out on Figure 14.1, p. 328.)

The following four examples show how empathy and sympathy work.

EXAMPLE 1

A video that asks viewers to take some specific action.

Communication Objective

To show the "Meals on Wheels" program and its positive effect in the community and to motivate more people to volunteer their time (so more needy people can be served).

Strategy

The objective itself suggests the direction of the design. Because it is an emotional one rather than an informational one, we would choose a personal presentation. We would use "real" people (instead of actors) to make our appeal. Because we want the viewer to take action (volunteer), we stress the problem at the outset. The intensity of a person's thirst relates to a prior experience of dryness. So we can show the social and personal circumstances—the elderly and others who cannot either cook or get out for meals—and then emphasize the urgency of the problem. The viewer can then better empathize with their plight.

Then we show how the problem is being eased—by volunteers delivering meals—and indicate that there are not enough volunteers. The viewer would be led emotionally through the content areas that allow for empathy and sympathy, finally arriving at a *feeling* (not an idea) that the contribution of his time is needed and will be greatly appreciated.

To the extent that the viewer actually does empathize with the plight of the screen characters, he will want to volunteer. That doesn't mean he will. There may be reasons why the viewer couldn't even if he wanted to, but for those who can, the communication will be a strong influence.

EXAMPLE 2

A video that seeks an emotional response from the audience.

Communication Objective

This program on subject X will move the viewer to tears of compassion.

Strategy

Even without creating a hypothetical subject, we can build an emotional structure for such a program. Again, taking our lead from the objective, the video should contain the following elements:

- *A central character:* He or she can be the empathic focus. We might want this character to closely match the characteristics of the target audience in gender, age, and values. We would not use a narrator voice-over format or a documentary format because these are more conducive to informational purposes. We want the character to be easy to empathize with.

- *A character who is believable:* Our character must be true to the experience of the viewer or at least within the realm of believability. If the character is too far removed, our viewer will dismiss the experience as an anomaly and reduce his level of empathy. Although *Night Court* provokes laughter, due to the characterizations, we do not feel *with* or *for* the characters because they are outrageously outside our ability to believe them.

- *A character with whom we can strongly identify:* The more the viewer identifies with the main character and his or her circumstances the better. We can facilitate this by creating situations for the character that are common to the audience's experience, especially those of a more universal nature. We all know what it feels like to be put down by our peers. We all know the feelings surrounding the need to perform our work better. These common feelings help us to "get into the character." The stronger the identity, the more powerful the potential is for emotional responses. Movies are perhaps the most powerful application of the identity factor because the large screen commands our attention and it's easier to identify with the character. Because of ambient distractions, the same story shown on television would require the viewer to work much harder for empathy. However, television can also absorb us and allow us to feel compassion, especially through the use of facial close-ups.

EXAMPLE 3

A corporate video that seeks viewer training and goodwill.

Communication Objective

This program will provide new employees with the *information* they need to understand the responsibilities of their jobs. We want to build loyalty by making them *feel proud* to be part of the company and *excited* about being members of the team.

Although the primary objective is to provide information, an emotional component has also been specified. If a video only communicates information, it will probably be dull. The department head or company officer may want to communicate information, but if you use video to do it, there should also be some kind of emotional appeal or viewers will become easily bored with it. Video "shows" in order to support "telling." You can use it strictly to tell, but that is not the most intelligent or effective use of the medium.

Strategy

Provide the information: Do this in a manner that is visually interesting. Instead of a manager talking to the camera, use his or her voice-over and show the action. You can heighten even something as dull as moving papers from desk to desk by using the unexpected. For instance, you could create a story by using extreme close-ups cut to up-tempo music or machine noises and having an animal take papers off one desk and put them onto another. Make it beautiful, or anything else, to breathe life into it. Try to command attention like *Sesame Street* does rather than simply presenting content. The likelihood that the information will be remembered will be improved. We've covered the informational part of the objective; now let's address the emotional requirements.

Analyze what it means to feel proud and excited: Recall the times you had those feelings. Analyze the components, the environment, the context, the words, the expressions that contributed to your feelings. Then put those elements together again, this time on video. (Remember, produce what you know.) Perhaps you could put the character of the new employee into situations so the viewer can identify with her. Or describe the teamwork or product. Use historical references, if appropriate. Build loyalty by showing company commitment to the team goal, to excellence, or to their employees.

Use up-tempo images and audio: Fast-paced audio and picture editing are warranted in this case to stimulate excitement. Because we want the new employees to feel excited about being members of the team, we should use visual and aural excitement in context—show the team interaction, the team clowning around, the results the team has accomplished, how members of the team regard each other after as well as during business hours. And show their vision and goals.

But what about the video that needs to be very serious?

EXAMPLE 4

A video that seeks to inform.

Communication Objective

This six-minute video will provide the board of trustees with the *information* they need to make a decision regarding X. It will leave them feeling *capable* of making a sound decision.

Isolated facts and figures are cold and open to interpretation. Sometimes providing information is the prime objective, but when it is, you might consider using a different medium. Video would not be the best choice. On the other hand, if the information reflects something meaningful to the sender and the receiver, or if the information is to be offered with a viewpoint, video can be an excellent choice. Video gets its power from its ability to present *people* and their many expressions—so if the content must be informational, tie it to the people involved. Make it personal or person-presenting. If it needs to be impersonal, use a different medium, such as a handout or computer disk.

Strategy

Use the viewpoint as a personal context for the information:

Give viewers the facts and figures but in the framework of a personal perspective. Especially at the beginning, use images to set the stage. Show the oil wells in action, the sweat of the hardworking crew, the cresting waves of the sea against the platform. Show the kids who are undernourished, not just the numbers. Show the housewife's frustration with the old way of doing things. Show the graph of a stock to indicate its trend, but animate it over a montage of images that remind viewers that the company serves *people*. Who are the end-users of this product or service? Build the story around them.

Make visual comparisons using a split screen. Use artwork with voiceovers to tell a short story, or use anecdotes. When there is a viewpoint, assert it powerfully and directly rather than hoping the audience will somehow subliminally extract it. Produce a skit. Project informational messages with confidence, openness, and visual strength so viewers will respect the point of view and gain information in the process.

Analyze the emotional component of the objective: Feeling "capable" involves knowing that the information available is both good (trustworthy) and comprehensive. You should ensure that all the relevant data are presented and that they are accurate. Executives will feel capable of making a decision if they have confidence in the information. The video can contribute to this confidence by showing high-level specialists interacting, the high-tech equipment involved, sights and sounds of computers, the videophone, the teleconference session, reams of data, trend charts, the legal library, and the happy customers. These elements speak to a certain audience of the investment, research, intelligence, and effort that have gone into the presentation of the information they are being offered.

These background elements should not be center stage in the video; rather, the information presentation needs to be primary. But the information, by association with these elements, is enhanced, thereby increasing the board's confidence. When the video ends, the board members should be ready to vote because they are now more enthusiastic about making a decision.

These four examples illustrate some of the ways to incorporate emotion in lecture-type videos by taking advantage of empathy and sympathy. Videos that contain an emotional component have increased potency and viability. Each situation calls for a unique approach, however, so different levels of emotional content are required depending on the specific objectives involved. When emotion is part of the communication objective, you should remember that empathy and sympathy are the operative mechanisms and design your video accordingly.

Choices

. . . .

Every program invites the viewer to make choices. The skilled producer creates a program and context where the choices that viewers make are in alignment with the communication objective. We'll examine some of these choices to get a sense of the complexity involved and then focus on how to structure content.

Watch/Don't Watch

The viewer's first critical choice is whether to watch a program. Sometimes we can be handed a video and, simply based on the jacket information or the title, we can make this decision. So we want to make sure that the title and packaging contribute to moving the viewer in the direction of accepting the program in the first place. Then, once he is watching the program, we want to keep the presentation as interesting as possible in order to hold his attention throughout. Whether he likes or dislikes the program might help the next potential viewer make the same decision. Systemically, every element of the program can be seen as contributing to, or detracting from, the viewer's decision to watch.

Program Length

How long is this program? The viewer has another choice—to watch just the opening, or stop it somewhere in the middle, or view the whole piece. For television producers this is a major concern because at any moment the viewer can "zap" the program. The program length principle in television and video is "the shorter the better." Shorter programs are easier to promote and easier and less costly to produce. All around the advantages of short programs outweigh the disadvantages. Resume tapes (videos produced by job-hunters) are usually five minutes long because employers don't want to spend more time than that. They just need to catch the flavor of the applicant's experience, the quality of the material, and the production values involved. A workable approach is to consider that your audience is too busy to spend *any* time watching your program; therefore, you should use only the material that is absolutely necessary to accomplish your communication objective. People sometimes decide not to watch a program simply because it's too long. Keep it brief!

Content Acceptance

Based on what we present and the way it's presented, we're offering our content for consideration. The viewer can accept or reject it, and her decision is based on so many variables that it's counterproductive to attempt to enumerate them. Psychological research, particularly in advertising, has had great difficulty reaching definitive conclusions on media influence. Human beings are complex and our behaviors and choices are inconsistent over time. But that's no reason not to face the issue. What can we do, given our subject matter, medium, and audience, to contribute to the acceptance of our message?

Most of this book concerns this question, so let's discuss it thoroughly here. First, let's look at just a sampling of some of the typical content choices our programs present to our viewers.

The viewer might have to decide to

buy a product or service

write a letter

take notes on the program content

buy a product rather than save money

recommend the program to others

tape the program for later playback

vote a certain way

buy one product instead of another

improve performance at work

apply the information or ideas provided

write the producer

Structuring Viewer Choices

· ·

Below we'll see some of the ways a producer can treat content to provide viewers with an experience that may eventually lead to the fulfillment of the producer's objective.

Describing

Content is usually described in a manner that builds sequentially from simple to complex, from past to present, from the few to the many. Description supported by appropriate organization and logic helps viewers determine if the content fits their perception, gestalt (worldview), or prior knowledge. It provides an impression or experience of the subject matter to expose the audience to it and give them the opportunity to accept or reject it. Description's power is in its good organization and faultless logic, qualities that make a presentation attractive and easy to accept.

Formats that use description include documentaries, instructional programs, news features, training and development programs, simulations, and demonstrations.

Comparing and Contrasting

We can present both sides of an issue, demonstrate two or more ways of approaching a problem, offer evidence for opposing views, and compare products by weighing costs and benefits. By comparing two subjects or entities (tangible or intangible), the producer can explore areas and issues that may or may not be resolvable. Frequently, good arguments can be made both ways on a topic, each seeming to be equally valid. The viewer will use her natural propensity to create meaning and order to reach her own conclusions, or search further.

We're probably all familiar with the advertising strategy in which various brands criticize their competition, especially in evidence lately because of relaxed broadcast regulations. The mere suggestion that "we invite comparison" implies the advertiser's open-mindedness and confidence in the product.

Comparison and contrast is best used when the objective is to allow the viewer the opportunity to make up his own mind after hearing or seeing different perspectives. Examples of formats that use comparison and contrast include *Nightline, Meet the Press, The Oprah Winfrey Show, 60 Minutes* ("Point–Counterpoint"), CNN's *Crossfire,* commercials, sitcoms, and training programs that compare the old with the new or the right versus the wrong way of doing things. Comparison and contrast is one of the most heavily used structures on television because differences can be *seen.*

Cause-Effect

An assumption underlying most commercial advertising is that you (the consumer) have problems: You're too fat; you smell bad; your clothes aren't clean; your back hurts; you're going to get cavities in your teeth; your diet doesn't work; you need a change of pace; your life-style is boring; you don't know the right people; and so on. Of course the proposed solution to all your problems is the purchase and use of a product.

"If you use our product . . ." begins a statement of cause. Take the recommended action and it will result in a solution—the effect. The cause-and-effect communication strategy is applicable in almost all television and video formats. It's used heavily because it relies on logic. Sure, if you own a cat and Fluffy seems listless, trying "Zipalong" cat food may make sense; or Fluffy may just be lazy. Nonetheless, if you buy the cat food, the appeal worked. It created the desire for a solution (which amounts to claiming the problem). The same is true of ideas, values, and other messages that suggest you (the viewer) will be better off (effect) by accepting the message (cause). The cause-and-effect strategy is a valid and important communication tool. Let ethics be your guide when using this strategy.

Testimonials

Testimonials are perhaps one of the most effective selling techniques. When considering something new, a product, service, or even ideas, we feel much more comfortable if we are able to get an honest opinion from others who have already sampled and accepted it. A testimonial shows people on the screen offering their personal and honest opinions about how they like the product or idea. We often choose our movies, restaurants, and TV programs because we have heard about them from someone else.

The strength of a video testimonial derives from the credibility of the source. The more we respect the opinion of the person giving the testimony, the more likely we are to believe that person and take action on what he recommends. Because we want to create order and meaning in our lives—including spending our time and hard-earned money wisely—we want to make good decisions. And the advice or recommendation of others we respect is some insurance against making rash or bad decisions.

Commercial television has elevated the testimonial to high levels of effectiveness. It bombards the public with experts—professional models usually but sometimes celebrities we've come to regard as "friends." They are enthusiastic about bathroom tissue, automobiles, or jeans.

Advertisers learned early on that showing the product gets you nowhere. As shown by their purchase decisions, people are less interested in the product and more responsive to suggestions on life-style and image. So advertisers create a personal style, an atmosphere, an ambience, for the kind of person who uses their product. "All my men wear English Leather or they wear nothing at all." "For those who think young." "When you care enough to send the very best." These slogans are saying, respectively: English Leather cologne is for sexy men who know what they want. Coke is for young people, even if you're only young at heart. And giving a Hallmark card communicates that you, the sender of the card, are a loving person who values quality. The real products are sex, youth, and good taste.

Testimonials can be very subtle. Turn on the radio, pick up any printed matter, talk to a friend, turn on the TV—people are giving their opinions about something. We look for meaning by comparing ourselves with others. This is one of the best reasons for using testimonials in any mediated communication. And testimonials are relatively easy to do from a cost and time perspective because they're not very complex to shoot and edit. Formats that use testimonials include commercials, documentaries, promotional videos, corporate image programs, training tapes, and how-to and self-help videos.

Storytelling

Everyone loves a good story told well. From our beginning people have sat around the campfire sharing tales of the hunt and gossiping about neighbors. Although this image may seem remote and primitive now, storytelling is still one of the most powerful communication tools ever devised. People kill other people because of stories. Presidents, most recently Ronald Reagan, are made because they can tell stories well. And some wars are fought as a result of conflicting stories or conflicting perceptions about the same story.

We hold stories dear because they are our direct link with the past, with what we interpret as real now, and with our deepest values. So it *does* matter how a story is told, what it contains, and how it is interpreted when retold.

Storytelling derives some of its power from our need for *meaning*. Stories provide us with the opportunity to make the most direct connection with "truth" (as we see it) because they contain characters, conflicts, and resolutions with which we can identify. Stories connect us with everyone else in our species.

Further, people use stories to organize events, hypothetical or real, into a sequence (beginning, middle, end) that makes sense (plot) and reveals a theme (moral). When people repeat a story often, it enters the culture as a myth, the basis for collective truth and wisdom.

Because storytelling is important to video communication, there is an entire chapter on it in this book. Above all, video and television producers must be adept at telling stories visually. A story format is best used when the communication objective centers on the expression of values, ideas, and life events—subjects that have an emotional component. Formats that incorporate storytelling include dramas, sitcoms, docudramas, role-plays, interviews (anecdotes), news, historical videos, commercials, and documentaries.

Finally, psychologists claim that we use storytelling to transmit our values and cultural heritage to new generations. It's significant that television (not school) now tells most of the stories to our children.

Informing

Throughout our lives we want to make "informed choices." Whether we're deciding what to buy or on a career, everything we do requires information. Gregory

Bateson defined **information** as "a difference that makes a difference."[7] Information consists of the data that affect our lives.

Without a person to examine and interpret it, information is just inert data. Human observation and interpretation transform data into information, making a "difference" within us.

We inform best by providing information that can make a difference to others. People get redundant information, that is, information they have already been exposed to. A smaller percentage of information is considered new. But old or new, information is a potential that dwells in our consciousness until we decide to activate it. A good way for a producer to think about information is as potential to stimulate the audience.

It's been said that, in our era, "information is power." Those with more information essentially have more potential than those with less. Because human beings are not constructed like computers, we can only absorb, store, and retrieve so much information at the conscious level. And, like currency, information only has real value when it moves, when it is shared.

As more information becomes available, and as our lives speed up, we have to prioritize carefully. We want to know about what directly concerns us and our future. If information is not perceived to have relevance for us now, or at least soon, we are likely not to seek it out or even to reject it if it comes our way or postpone its reception by simply remembering where it can be acquired should we develop a need for it later on. My friend Marty dislikes libraries simply because they overload his desire to know.

So much information is presented in videos and on television that many people decide not to watch. As producers we need to carefully consider when and in what context it's appropriate to provide information. And we have to be careful not to overload our programs with it. Whenever possible, a program that informs should also have a strong visual component so we can overcome the tendency of viewers to "turn off" their mental computers when they sense the information is redundant or not directly relevant to their lives.

I experienced this when taping a conference of chemical engineers. While the crew was totally bored with the highly informational content, the audience was genuinely interested. They were alert to the speakers and eager to absorb all they could while the six of us had to struggle to pay attention. But after the program was edited, including an abundance of illustrative visuals and a few entertaining sequences, the content began to make sense to us too.

Formats that use an informational approach include news, talk, interview, forum, how-to, demonstration, documentary, training and development, promotion, marketing, commercial, educational, and sales programs.

Modeling

In this context *modeling* refers to presenting characters, behaviors, or other expressions to help viewers form an impression and thereby make decisions. The woman whose laundry is "whiter than white," the man who gets his car muffler installed to his satisfaction, and the girl driving the sleek sports car—all these individuals model experiences advertisers think the audience would also like to have. The modeling technique is excellent in circumstances where the target audience is narrowly defined (well known) because we can create a screen character who closely resembles a typical audience member. By increasing the identification factor, we make it easier for viewers to relate, and therefore accept the message.

In modeling a person "stands in" for our interests, values, ideals, dreams, or desires. The technique's power is in the identification factor. We see ourselves a certain way, and the person on the screen reinforces that image. Advertisers present an image of the way they think we would like to be and suggest that we can become like the model by accepting the message, buying the product, or otherwise choosing the same style or behavior. The modeling technique is especially useful in programs that call for identification with the way others are, what they have, or what makes them happy. It's also used to promote values, ways of thinking, attitudes, and beliefs by putting persons (role models) on the screen who express these qualities. Examples include role-play, interview, talk, training, religious, drama, and commercial programs.

Summary

Video is a communication tool. It helps us accomplish our objectives. It does this through certain qualities intrinsic to the medium itself. Whether our purpose is concrete—to sell a product or an idea—or whether it's abstract—to share beauty, to empower others to realize their potential—as communicators we will not only draw on our creativity and skill, we will also need to use the tool (video) skillfully.

Although watching television or a video may seem to be passive, much more is, or could be, happening, depending on the context of the program and the viewing situation. Sometimes we want viewers simply to absorb our program. At other times we want to stimulate them sufficiently to become responsive to what they experience on the screen, perhaps even activating them to perform a specific task we have in mind.

Viewers are observers of themselves and the world. We all continuously explore other human beings and their behavior, thoughts, and decisions in a variety of ways. By doing this, at least initially, we come to know ourselves better, especially how and where we "fit" with respect to everyone else. The sensitive producer will stand in the viewers' shoes to see what they see, the way they see it. Although this attempt probably won't be completely successful, it nonetheless ensures that the message we send and the way we send it will have some relevance (meaning) and interest for the receiver.

We also need to understand how our audience will perceive the characters we put on the screen. Characters should appeal to our viewers if we expect the content to be accepted or at least appreciated.

Empathy and its relative, sympathy, also make video a potent communication tool. To provide emotional stimulation, a producer depicts the feeling the viewer should have. When viewers identify strongly with any screen character, their inclination will be to follow that character's emotions. When the character cries, the viewer will likely feel like crying. When he laughs, the viewer does the same, often internally. Viewers mirror the emotions they see on the screen, as long as they believe the context is genuine.

In their role as receivers of our video expression, viewers constantly make choices. They'll watch this and not that. Should they accept this character's behavior or not? Will they agree with the interviewee or not? Will they consider buying the product? Does the message make sense logically?

We want to present and package our videos in formats and through expressions that the viewers are already comfortable with so they are not jarred or conflicted by them. No one wants to feel he or she is under pressure or being coerced in some way. The packaging tools presented here include describing, comparing and contrasting, the testimonial, cause and effect, storytelling, information offering, and modeling.

What and how communication tools are used communicate.

Notes

1. Klain, Jane, ed., *International Television and Video Almanac,* 33rd ed. (New York: Quigley, 1988).
2. Schramm, Wilbur, ed., *Quality in Instructional Television* (Honolulu: East-West Book Center, 1972), 142.
3. Leavitt, Clark, "The Communication Response," in *Psychology in Media Strategy: Proceedings of a Symposium Sponsored by the Media Research Committee of the American Marketing Association,* ed. Leo Bogart (Chicago: American Marketing Association, 1966), 27.
4. Lesser, Gerald S., *Children and Television: Lessons from Sesame Street* (New York: Vintage Books, 1974), 102.
5. Pearl, D., L. Bouthilet, and J. Lazar, *Television and Behavior: Ten Years of Scientific Progress and Implications for the Eighties,* Vol. 1 (Washington, DC: U.S. Government Printing Office, 1982), 20.
6. *Webster's Ninth New Collegiate Dictionary.*
7. Bateson, Gregory, *Steps to an Ecology of Mind* (New York: Ballantine Books, 1982), 315.

Suggested Readings

Baldwin, Huntley. *Creating Effective TV Commercials.* Chicago: Crain Books, 1982.

Beattie, Geoffrey. *Talk: An Analysis of Speech and Non-Verbal Behavior in Conversation.* Milton Keynes, England: Open University Press, 1983.

Morgan, John, and Peter Welton. *See What I Mean: An Introduction to Visual Communication.* Baltimore: Edward Arnold, 1986.

Polsky, Richard M. *Getting to Sesame Street: Origins of the Children's Television Workshop.* New York: Praeger, 1974.

Randhawa, Bikkar, and William Coffman. *Visual Learning, Thinking and Communication.* New York: Academic Press, 1978.

Ries, Al, and Jack Trout. *Positioning: The Battle for Your Mind.* New York: McGraw-Hill, 1982.

Schramm, Wilbur. "What the Research Says." In *Quality in Instructional Television,* edited by W. Schramm. Honolulu: University Press of Hawaii, 1972.

Tannenbaum, Percy H., ed. *The Entertainment Function of Television.* Hillsdale, NJ: Lawrence Erlbaum, 1980.

Veith, Richard. *Talk-Back TV: Two Way Cable Television.* Blue Ridge Summit, PA: TAB Books, 1976.

Zuber-Skerritt, Ortrun. *Video in Higher Education.* New York: Nichols, 1984.

CHAPTER 6

Planning the Project

· ·

[A plan's] value is as an assemblage of thoughts, not constraints. The process of developing it is close to 100 percent of its value—or perhaps more than 100 percent of its value.

—Tom Peters[1]

 Here is a typical scenario. Someone who wants to produce a video and has never done it before calls. He's looking for guidance and expertise because the project is important and exciting, and he wants to know if I would be interested in consulting and even producing the video. Let's find out.

The potential client comes to the office and quickly demonstrates that he is not prepared to produce a video. He has an idea for a video or series that is so good he thinks the whole world will like it, but his description is scattered. I like to encourage enthusiasm and dreaming but not at the expense of substantial, practical thinking and follow-through. We must consider many factors when planning a video, and each one needs careful attention.

After the initial enthusiasm, we are asked the inevitable question: "How much will such a program cost? Can you give me a ballpark estimate?" At this point I explain to the potential client that the complexities of video communication require a systematic thought process. Before I can provide even a rough cost estimate, I need to know some specifics about the project. Then I lead him through a series of questions so he can begin to see what's involved. Usually the client has given so little thought to the substantials that only the roughest of cost estimates can be given and he must begin to answer critical questions we've raised.

This chapter deals with this planning process, which consists of addressing thirteen questions. The first seven of these constitute step 1—a **program needs analysis.** This information is needed to produce a treatment (see Chapter 2). The remaining six questions (step 2) make up a **production needs analysis.** Taken together, steps 1 and 2 constitute a project plan. The steps used in this planning process can easily be applied to most other kinds of media productions.

Some of the questions—for instance, those on program content and audience concerns—require such detailed and in-depth examination that they are examined more fully in other chapters. We will also briefly mention them here to show them in the natural order of the project plan.

Step 1: Program Needs Analysis

A program needs analysis requires that the needs of the program be addressed from the perspective of the person who wants the program to be produced. This can be yourself, a client, or someone else, but this person must be the one who has a communication need that video can fulfill.

Purpose

Question 1: What's your purpose? Why make this program? This is the most important question to address at the beginning of a project because everything else flows from it. Write out your purpose statement in one or two sentences, but not more than a paragraph, to keep it focused.

The purpose statement should be concise and accurate because the answers to the questions that follow relate directly to fulfilling the purpose. If the purpose is unclear or scattered, work with it until it's accurate. It's counterproductive even to move to the next question without having a purpose statement that feels right. Take time with it. Share it with others so you can get some feedback, especially from those who may be involved closely with the project.

We can often write the purpose statement "off the top of our heads," but this step is so crucial that your response also needs to be critically examined over time to determine if it really is an accurate purpose or merely a personal desire, wish, or expectation.

The purpose statement should always be written as a clear, concise conclusion to the statement, "I (we) want to make this video because . . ."

Some possible answers follow:

"I need to make some money fast."

"I want to share this material because it was so meaningful to me."

"I want to start up a production company and it's the best program I can think of with which to begin."

"I want everyone to understand and appreciate this critical issue that is important to me."

"We're making this program because the client wants it."

These are all poor purpose statements because the purpose only tangentially relates to communicating something. These purposes are acceptable, but consider carefully whether video is the proper vehicle to accomplish them. There might be other, more direct ways. Now let's look at some examples of purpose statements that are more viable because video is a good medium for accomplishing the intended purpose.

We (I) want to make this video because

"We need to *demonstrate* how this product or process works."

"We want to *provide information* to our audience in a way that also makes them feel good about us."

"I want to *entertain* . . ."

"I want to *express myself* using imaginative visuals."

"We want to *motivate* an audience to buy our product."

"We want to *provide training* for our employees without causing our training personnel to do repetitious instruction."

"We want to *show examples* of innovation and success in our field."

"I want to *promote* my vision to a wider audience."

"We want to *share* a surgical procedure with other physicians."

"We want to *illustrate* a better way of thinking or doing by showing people who have successfully used our techniques."

"We want to *motivate* our employees to . . . [stop smoking or the like]."

In each of these instances, the purpose is to use video specifically because of its attributes (sound-imagery-motion) as a communication medium. The earlier statements reflected what the designer hoped would happen as a result of making a video. They were the "effects." But we need a purpose statement that responds to a communications need. Although making money and spreading "the word" may be genuine needs, they are not very useful as purpose statements because they express personal needs to be fulfilled by the program rather than addressing the needs of an audience. Video is most often intended to be shown to *others*. Therefore, the purpose statement, your reason for producing the video, should be a statement that is other-directed.

Audience

Question 2: Who is the target audience? Because the audience question is central to all mediated communication, it should be addressed immediately after the purpose is known. Once you know why you want to produce a program, ask for whom it will be produced. The more that can be known about those who will receive the communication, the greater the likelihood the communication will be received and effective.

Because audience issues are vital and complex, there's not enough space to do them justice here. Nonetheless, this is the point in the program needs analysis where you normally would deal with the audience. If you're currently planning a project and using this section as a checklist, see Chapter 7 before going further.

Communication Objective

Question 3: What is your communication objective? Once we know *why* we want to produce a particular video, and to whom it will be addressed, the next task is to understand the communication objective. *What* specifically do you want to communicate or express?

We can easily become confused about the objectives involved in a production because there are often several outcomes we would like. Here we are specifically discussing the **communication objective,** not the content objective, the production objective, the sales objective, the distribution objective, or the personal objectives of the producer. Rather, what will the finished piece (program, segment, tape) *communicate* to those who see it?

This is a necessary consideration from a systems perspective because the communication objective determines the program's content.

If a system (program) has multiple purposes and goals, and they are not placed in clear priority and commonly known by all components of the system or sub-systems, conflict among them will ensue.[2]

In the past two decades many corporations have shifted from a product to a marketing orientation. They have learned that producing a stockpile of a product is useless, even if it's good, unless there are customers who want to buy it. These marketing-oriented companies have learned that customers drive the business. Therefore, the key to good business is to know what the customer will purchase and then provide it at a reasonable cost. The video communicator should also identify the customer (audience) and decide what content will work for them.

When I deal with clients who want to produce commercials, the first question I ask is "What do you want this spot to communicate?" I usually listen to five or more objectives before interrupting, and then I explain that, within a thirty- to sixty-second commercial or public service announcement (PSA), the producer gets only one choice. A good habit is to assume that a video program can communicate fewer messages better than many. It can, in fact, accomplish several objectives, but each time an objective is added, the potency of each one is decreased. If you have more than three objectives, consider a separate video for them, perhaps a series. I apply this rule to all programs, irrespective of length. Of course, many subjects can be covered in a full-length program, but only what the viewer takes away from it counts and that requires *focus.* Fulfill one primary objective and let others be secondary.

We usually select only one communication objective because viewers quickly forget the subject matter of programs. Even though we are intent on watching a program, few of us retain its content until even the next day unless we have a passion for the subject or are directly involved with it in some significant way.

Television, however, leaves us with an *impression* of the subject matter. Some of the content and imagery is retained, but mostly we come away with an impression of what the experience was like as a whole. The relevance and quality of the experience cue us whether to remember the details of the program. If we as viewers took some action or were changed in some way (as the program directed), then the program was effective. It accomplished its communication objective.

Don't confuse the purpose with the objective. The reason you produce a program is different from what you want to communicate. The former is your other-directed motivation to communicate. The latter is the primary and secondary messages you want to share (and leave) with your audience.

Consider what you want to communicate and then decide what the viewers' final impression, or a more active outcome, should be when the program is over. The ideal is to translate this final impression into observable behavior or attitudes that can be *measured* later on. For programs of any length or format, you can later determine whether your program is successful and to what degree only if your communication objectives are measurable.

Once the communication objective statement has been refined to its briefest and most essential expression, type it along with the purpose statement, provide a copy to every member of the team, and discuss it. This then becomes the standard against which all decisions will be measured. On one project the producer required us to memorize the objective statement so whenever the public asked us what we were doing, our response would be consistent and exact. It worked to create consistency, and it was good promotion for the program.

Examples of *clear, concise,* and *measurable* communication objectives are

- to educate viewers on meditation techniques they can use
- to stimulate an appreciation for the symphony orchestra, thereby increasing season ticket sales
- to create empathy for patients undergoing therapy so that viewers will financially support a new outpatient therapy program
- to move viewers to write or call for further information
- to persuade management to adopt a specific plan of action
- to expand the viewers' aesthetic appreciation of art glass, thereby increasing contributions to the museum's glass collection
- to inform viewers on the positive happenings in a community so they will join a particular organization
- to document a workshop so it can be replicated in other cities, by other groups

Avoid the following types of objectives because they are too general and have little to do with communicating:

- to get as many people as possible to watch the program
- to win video award competitions
- to impress an employer or employees
- to break into "show biz"

- to get a good grade on a video assignment
- to help out an organization, which would benefit from having a video
- to give clients the impression that one's firm is high-tech

Again, in these instances there is nothing to communicate. Identify the purpose, audience, and communication objective and specify them clearly; then other project questions can be answered more easily. Every time a content decision comes up, you can ask: Does this element support the communication objective? Remember that *content* relates to and derives from the communication objective.

When each person involved in the project knows the communication objective, there is a better focus on details. Creative work also becomes easier because there is a reference for content decision making.

At times confusion arises because of unspecified or confused objectives; the producer may have a slightly different objective from the talent or the writer or the funding source. If communication is to be truly effective, however, the objective must be commonly agreed upon by the principal parties. This is also an issue around which you can build synergy, which we discussed earlier.

Program Content

Question 4: What is the subject matter? Some people like to organize what goes into a program by including both the message and the way it is to be expressed (format, pacing, sensibility, organization). I prefer to handle expression and information separately. In this book, *program content* refers to the subject matter alone. If the objective is to train employees on the proper use of a computer program, the content will include the computer, the details of the program, and any other items and tasks relevant to its uses. The content will not include such things as the look of the video, its format, or its sound.

In this part of the program needs analysis, we describe the subject matter in some detail—not just with a heading such as "photography," "whales," or "increased product knowledge." We specify which areas relating to these topics will be considered, doing so with the targeted audience clearly in mind.

Again, because content is an important topic, we'll merely indicate that it should be dealt with at this point in the program needs analysis and move on. Chapters 8 through 12 deal with content specifically.

Program Format

Question 5: What is the most appropriate format for this program? Program format is essentially the structure within which content elements are organized and presented. The subject matter often suggests a format just because it's informational or emotional in nature. So you often have an immediate sense of what format is appropriate. But as the purpose and communication objective statements become clearer and better defined, the format, which will fulfill these objectives for the target audience, will become more specific.

Now we'll look at some of the general industry conventions surrounding format, which audiences have come to associate with different types of content. Some format names are even the same as the technique they employ, such as "animation" and "talk."

The following is a list of some of the more common formats and their applications:

DOCUMENTARY

Record event(s) for later editing. Present a point of view in context with "real" people instead of actors.

Function:

- convey information
- convey ideas
- convey history
- describe a subject
- describe and develop issues

CINEMA VERITÉ

Record event(s) as they occur with minimum influence from a director. Camera is often used in subjective mode, where the camera becomes the eyes of the subject, putting the audience directly into the experience.

Function:

- convey experience(s)
- describe issues
- observe personalities
- observe consciousness (attempt to convey people's thoughts)
- observe circumstances

EVENT COVERAGE

Record event(s) with minimal editing. Similar to documentary but instead of creating meaning, the purpose is simply to document or show the event. The video may or may not have a viewpoint.

Function:

- show an event: sports, conferences, entertainment, or other

PROFILE

Examine or present a person or organization so viewers can see elements of the environment, thinking, activities, and other experiences. Profiles give a brief sampling of the subject matter, whereas a documentary is a more in-depth presentation with a point of view.

Function:

- describe a person
- describe an organization/institution
- describe a process, activity, function

DEMONSTRATION

Provide a demonstration as a person speaks (on or off camera) about a subject.

Function:

- show an operation or procedure
- provide training
- provide examples of functioning

INTERVIEW

Observe one person (host) asking another (guest) questions to which he or she responds.

Function:

- elicit a point of view, opinions, values, attitudes, suggestions, ideas
- provide concrete thinking against which viewers measure their own thinking
- introduce a person and his or her perspective

DISCUSSION

Observe people (usually three or more) discussing a topic.

Function:

- examine personal perspectives
- compare and contrast viewpoints

INSTRUCTION

Offer instruction from one or more persons using visuals to illustrate. Instruction usually moves from the simple to the complex.

Function:

- teach, lecture
- present data, information

COMMERCIAL

Use a wide variety of techniques to sell a product or service. Commercial formats are usually brief.

Function:

- sell, motivate sales

MAGAZINE

Use a variety of techniques with segmentation to separate content into stories or other features. Each segment in a magazine format is brief but may be as long as fifteen minutes if the story is especially relevant or powerful.

Function:

- treat a broad subject having many aspects or dimensions that can be handled separately
- treat several disparate subjects

NEWSCAST

Observe persons on camera deliver news stories in rapid succession with cutaways to illustrate the stories.

Function:

- present several news stories

NEWS STORY

Observe one person reporting on a single story using visuals to illustrate it.

Function:

- tell one news story

IMAGE

Show the most salient features of a company, group, product, or service using a highly edited piece with strong visuals and music.

Function:

- present corporate, institutional image
- present brand (product) image
- present political image

ANIMATION

Move images of artwork or inanimate objects.

Function:

- cartoons
- feature stories
- commercials
- video art

AESTHETIC

Use unusual visual and sound combinations and treatments to stimulate the aesthetic senses.

Function:

- video art
- transitional pieces
- exhibition works

MUSIC VIDEO

Use highly imaginative, unusual, or stylized images to enhance a musical performance.

Function:

- provide entertainment
- sell media products

MEDITATION

Provide images and sounds to assist the viewer in achieving a meditative state or simple relaxation.

Function:

- demonstrate relaxation
- show integration of body, mind, spirit
- maximize individual potential

ANIMATICS

Use artwork or still photographs to create characters or objects to tell a story. Camera and editing provide movement; picture elements do not move. There is cutting between the art cards or photographs.

Function:

- children's stories
- commercials
- employee training

PIXILLATION

Record one frame at a time using stop motion camerawork. When edited together and played back, the effect is choppy like that seen in the Keystone Cops silent movies.

Function:

- children's stories
- commercials
- music videos

INTERACTIVE

Combine television with computer so the viewer can make decisions relating to the subject matter as the program progresses.

Function:

- training
- instruction
- entertainment
- information or sales

DRAMA

Observe actors performing lines to create characters that interact with other characters in front of the camera. Drama usually involves a story within which the characters encounter and overcome conflict on their way to some goal.

Function:

- entertainment
- commercials
- children's programming
- corporate training
- education

COMEDY

Elicit a response to humor using any kind of screen experience.

Function:

- stand-up comedian
- entertainment
- commercials
- corporate training
- education
- situation comedy (sitcoms)

TALK

Observe a host talk with several invited guests who may talk, perform, or do anything else that relates to their reason for being on the show.

Function:

- entertainment
- corporate training and development
- education

VARIETY

Observe entertainers singing, dancing, or performing in other ways. As the term implies, there are a variety of entertainment experiences.

Function:

- entertainment, promotion

GAME

Observe people play a game, often for prizes and further opportunity to play at higher stakes.

Function:

- entertainment, amusement

STREAM OF CONSCIOUSNESS

Provide a loosely structured dramatic presentation that does not clearly clue the audience to the beginning, middle, or end or use other typical story structure devices. Often in these presentations nothing seems to "happen" beyond the commonplace. The commonplace is, in essence, the subject and focus.

Function:

- entertainment
- aesthetic/symbolic/realism experience

Although this list is not exhaustive, it presents the more commonly used formats for television and video. Sometimes you should strictly adhere to the format selected. In other cases the subject matter may require a combination of two or more formats. The magazine format has a structure that can potentially contain examples of all the others. For instance, within the context of a magazine program, there could be segments that use profile, animation, documentary, demonstration, and so on.

When considering format, look at the preferences of the target audience. Do they prefer informational, humorous, or emotional presentations? Would they prefer the opinions of authority figures over an omniscient narrator's voice? Would they rather see staged or actual events? Whom do they respect? Should the message come from a celebrity, a skilled announcer, or a person more directly involved in the subject matter? What will they regard as credible? Which format can best carry your communication objective?

Other factors involved in the format decision include budget, available technology, promotion, distribution, and the production time frame. The subject matter especially will affect the format you choose. For instance, we normally wouldn't use humor for a serious subject, and we normally wouldn't use talk if our objective was to entertain.

Format gives structure to the program. It's the framework for the content. Viewers want to know how things relate; they want to feel they are on a logically planned trajectory that purposefully leads somewhere. A strong format has consistency. The subject matter is tied to it in such a way that viewers return to the structure itself for a feeling of security. They sense the logic within the presentation as long as each program element relates in some way to the format structure. Think of the program's format as a skeleton that supports and structures the content.

Program Elements

Question 6: What are the program elements? Program elements deliver the content. They include such things as interviews, music, sound effects, narration (voice-over or on camera), cutaways, performance, "B roll" (illustrative pictures), actors, special effects, character generated words and other devices, people, or items that directly relate to the presentation of the subject matter.

Soon after the format is determined it becomes apparent that certain elements will "clothe" the skeleton better than others. These format elements should express the content and meet the communication objective(s). The elements naturally flow from the requirements of the format and the demand of the content as it relates to the target audience.

The following examples show how program elements are derived from format. We'll use one hypothetical subject but a different format for each program.

EXAMPLE 1

A *documentary* on river boats

Program elements:

- notable narrator (kindly, older, male, good storyteller, easy smile)
- riverboats (that we can shoot)
- interviews (with riverboat captains and deckhands to be used on camera and with voice-over)
- old paintings and photographs (from the peak period of riverboating)
- sound effects of riverboats (paddlewheel, water over the bow, dance music of the period, engine room, calliope playing)
- two young boys (to stage in profile along the river bank to open and close—à la Huck Finn and Tom Sawyer)
- theme music (to be originally composed and recorded)
- interim music (upbeat, medium, and slow variations on the theme to be used throughout as needed)

EXAMPLE 2

A *profile* of a riverboat captain

Program elements:

- a riverboat captain (to be the focus of the program: an older man with lots of experiences, good storyteller, should look the part; he will tell his own story, on camera and with voice-over)
- the captain's home
- the captain's family album, other memorabilia
- interviews with the captain and his family
- interviews with former employees, coworkers, and other captains that can enrich or validate his story
- the captain's favorite riverboat music
- glamour shots of the boat in operation

EXAMPLE 3

A *drama* about a riverboat race

Program elements:

- two riverboat captains (played by actors)
- a woman (the love interest: she loves them both but can't decide)

- a staged race between the boats (to help her decide)
- a cast of 200 (passengers, in costume, for both boats)
- a shore location to stage the fight scene
- explosion aboard one of the boats
- originally composed and performed music

It's easy to get a sense of the scale of a project when preparing an element list like these. Each program element should contribute to the communication objective or be eliminated. Don't add items just because they might be cute, fun, or interesting. Each element should be justified by carrying a substantial piece of the communication objective. Otherwise, confusion will creep in and the focus will be lost, thereby jeopardizing the purpose. An effective way to ascertain element relevance is to ask: Can we eliminate this element and still accomplish the communication objective for this audience? If not, you will know that it's an essential part of the program.

Program Use

Question 7: How/where will this program be used? At the outset it's essential to determine, plan for, or otherwise ensure that the program will be used. Nobody wants to produce a program that just collects dust on a shelf. Because this question is as important as the audience question, we'll look at several considerations.

Audience location   *Where* is the target audience? Where do they view the programs they select—in the home, at work, or on cable or broadcast television? In a church, business, hospital, or other institutional setting? Do they view alone or with others? What in your tape will make them want to see it? Once these parameters are determined, one can begin to imagine the necessary steps to get the program into the proper environment.

Playback portability   What type of equipment will be available in the viewing situation? The most common formats for tapes sent through the mail or passed from hand to hand are VHS (home) and ¾ in. (industrial) videotape. Other formats may be appropriate in other circumstances.

Most programs are originally shot using tape sizes other than that used for distribution. You should consider the cost of duplication from one format to another and the sacrifice of technical quality due to generation loss. Most duplication houses accept masters in any of the standard formats including 1 in. (broadcast quality), ¾ in. (low- to midrange industrial quality), M-2, Super VHS, and Hi-8. Producers usually ask duplicators to make dubs onto VHS. In the United States VHS is the most commonly used because of the substantial number of playback machines available in homes, schools, hospitals, and businesses. Tapes must be converted to the proper standard when sent out of this country. Ask the duplicator about these issues and the associated transfer costs, which are high.

Any of the broadcast quality formats are appropriate for tapes that will be offered to cable or broadcast television. Many TV stations will not accept VHS for playback, but some cable stations do—especially as the technology improves.

Distribution If a video is not intended for cable or broadcast, the job of the distributor—or, in the case of corporate environments, the marketing or promotion department—is to get the program into the hands of potential viewers. The producer or producing entity can handle distribution independently. But self-distribution requires a serious commitment of personnel time and expense, so it may be more cost-effective to contract with an established distributor for this service.

A program that involves notable personalities and is intended for mass distribution may be offered to an established distribution company. These companies, referred to as "the majors," look for highly marketable programs. They usually distribute shows with high production and entertainment values. Other video distribution companies range from large book publishers who also distribute videos to small business specialty houses that publish an annual catalogue of their select video offerings.

The distribution objective is to get the program—or information about it—to as many members of the target audience as possible. Independent producers often enter into contractual arrangements with video or program distributors to do this or they may handle distribution themselves. In the case of videos intended for mail-order distribution, most duplication houses will handle "fulfillment" of the videos they duplicate. This means that, for an additional fee, the company will duplicate the video from the supplied master, generate and apply a label to each tape, and then send it to addresses that are supplied by the producer or distributor. If the video box needs a special label or cover, it's the producer's responsibility to have it printed. And fulfillment does not include video promotion, which is a promotion or marketing role best performed by those who have some tangible commitment to the program.

Positioning When companies launch a new product, they have carefully assessed how the product will best fit within the context of other products of the same type. The new product must have something about it that is uniquely attractive to compete with similar products on the market. Each product, to be a success, should occupy a clear and distinct position in the mind of the consumer, or the audience, in our case.

Think about the positioning of your video program, even if there's no strong competition from other videos, because the audience may not be interested enough to view it in the first place or may not be motivated to continue viewing it once it has begun. People always have some resistance to program viewing because of inertia and competition from other types of entertainment. So whether or not you consider your video or TV program to be a "product," positioning should still be a primary consideration.

Positioning was developed and elaborated as an advertising concept by Al Ries and Jack Trout in a book called *Positioning: The Battle for Your Mind:*

Positioning is not what you do with a product. Positioning is what you do to the mind of the prospect. That is, you position the product in the mind of the prospect.[3]

You must pay attention to how your target audience will perceive your video. What does the audience value in this kind of program? Should it be "the latest," "the newest," the "most comprehensive," the "first," the most "informative," the "only one of its kind," the most "interesting"? Or does it feature something that uniquely identifies it? Why would anyone want to watch this tape? The reason could be anything from a "name" presenter to unusual computer graphics—anything that arouses interest and brings attention to the program or its subject matter.

You can tell whether positioning is working by observing how people talk to others about the program after seeing it. Do they recommend it to other members of the target audience who have not yet seen it? Do they recommend it to people outside the target audience? It is ideal if they recommend it to both. But if you have positioned the program well, the traits the viewers pass on to others will be precisely those traits you predetermined as the identifying (positioning) elements. Again, ideally, these should relate to your communication objective.

Some of the specific elements involved in positioning a video include packaging, promotion, and presence.

Packaging If the program has been designed to be put into the hands of the audience, its container and labeling should communicate that the program

- Is an interesting subject that is well presented.
- Is an excellent experience of the subject matter.
- Has elements that make it attractive.
- Was produced for a particular audience.

Promotion We can't expect our target audience to watch a program they don't know exists. Most programs require at least some promotion, and a good way to approach it is to examine your response to the question: Where does my target audience usually find out about the programs that interest them? Do they subscribe to newspapers, magazines, or newsletters? Do they get information from friends or other sources? Do they read company newsletters? What specialty stores do they frequent? What other media do they regularly use? With what informational or social networks do they have contacts? Once you know the answer to these questions, an approach to promoting your program will be apparent.

In terms of positioning, promotion must relate to what is already in the mind of the potential viewer. You need to create an immediate and memorable impression about the program so that, when the title is heard, a mental connection is made with what already exists in the viewer's mind. We can oversimplify the point of the program in promotional materials by creating a title that quickly tells prospects the benefit of watching the program, distinguishes the tape from all others in some way, or relates the content to what viewers know about it. When the target hears about your program, they should have immediate interest.

We'll return to positioning later on because it also applies to using content to persuade.

Presence   Presence is closely related to positioning. We can only experience the media that we encounter. People buy products they see on the shelves—if a product isn't there, they can't buy it. The more frequently we encounter a product (program), or references to it, the more powerful the impression of it becomes.

Most advertising operates in this manner. Instead of directly motivating a person to buy a product, the continuous appearance of a brand name increases the number of people who are likely to encounter it, thereby creating an *impression* that the product is a commonly accepted and highly regarded component of the culture. If you (the consumer) want to be part of the culture, you will buy the product. The Coke and Pepsi wars are an excellent example. The "war" itself is a way of keeping the products in the minds of consumers, so neither Coke nor Pepsi suffers any substantial loss from the other's onslaught. Both gain in the long run because they reinforce their product's cultural significance.

Consider this: "On a typical day, the average American is exposed to 560 advertising messages but notices only 76 of them. Of these 76, only 12 will be remembered."[4] This is why "brand consciousness" has become so important. Items that are the most available generate the most sales. Likewise, the most available videos and television programs are the ones most often watched, talked about, and sold—further increasing the demand for them.

Maintaining a presence requires persistence. Producers, program designers, and directors are often more interested in the creative aspects of the production than in promotion and distribution. But some person or mechanism must be in place to ensure that the finished program attains a presence in the minds of its targeted audience. This can be the responsibility of a marketing department in a corporate setting, or a public relations or public information office, but it is usually handled by a private (public relations, advertising, marketing) agency or distributor.

Step 2: Production Needs Analysis

. . . .

The first seven questions formed the program needs analysis. Now let's look at the six questions that constitute the production needs analysis.

Financial Matters

Question 8: What are the financial considerations? There are some excellent texts on this subject listed at the end of Chapter 2, where budgeting issues were discussed. Refer to these books for the details of preparing a budget and other financial concerns. Also see Appendix B for a complete sample budget. In the planning stage, we are interested in identifying, without too much detail, the primary financial factors involved in the production.

How much will it cost to produce this program?   A producer typically arrives at a "ballpark" estimate by assessing the cost factors relative to the scale of the project. Sometimes a formula based on local standards (such as $2,000 per minute) can be used. With this framework, you can begin to get a sense of how expensive the program might be. But to make a valid assessment, you should research the specific costs involved once the personnel needs, scheduling, and program elements are known.

Scripts are rarely available in the planning stage, so instead of being able to create a detailed budget using a script "breakdown sheet," make a preliminary estimate of your production needs. With the systems approach, begin by making a list of every anticipated expense by "walking through" the four phases of the project. Estimate as closely as possible, but it is better to err on the side of over-budgeting. Allow a 10% contingency on top of the grand total. This will give you a sense of the finances needed for your project.

Various formats for budget analysis (in addition to the one in Appendix B) are shown in some of the books I've recommended. Consult the budget lists in these books to see the various expense categories that are likely to occur. They can help you think of items you may not have anticipated.

What will be the source(s) of production funds?   If the answer to this question does not readily come to mind, it's helpful to know what sources are possible. These include

- grants from foundations that have some interest in or association with your content area
- grants from corporations and businesses that support program production
- grants from the state or federal government
- grants from private interest groups
- investors (private individuals attracted to the subject matter and/or the potential for profit)
- limited partnership (you and some friends pool your money in exchange for shares in the profit or loss)
- gifts from friends, relatives, corporations
- creative fund-raising events
- the local TV or cable station (in exchange for air rights to the finished program)
- a distribution entity
- loans (which are not a very realistic source unless you have substantial collateral)

Who will have a financial role and what will be the arrangements between these participants? This question pertains to "above-the-line" administrators and others whose compensation is negotiable as well as to employees who will receive "below-the-line" fixed-rate compensation.

Who will share the burden of risk and the benefit of profit? Who will be paid wages? To avoid losing potential friends, these issues should be discussed in detail and agreed to *in writing* as soon as possible, including an indication of the time frame involved. (See Chapter 2.)

Who will market/distribute the program and at what cost to whom? Who will be responsible for managing the production budget, paying bills, compensating personnel, and other matters? Who will handle the distribution and be responsible for the bookkeeping? In the promotion and distribution stage, who will handle the day-to-day operation of sending and receiving tapes? Who will handle duplication and mailing (fulfillment)?

Technology

Question 9: What equipment and facilities will be used? What material will be used as the camera original? Film? Video? What film format: 16 mm, 35 mm, or larger? What video format: D-2, 1 in., M-2, Beta, ¾ in., VHS, S-VHS, or Hi-8?

You might use equipment because it happens to be available, which frequently occurs in corporate, educational, and other institutional settings. But some productions will require specialized equipment.

There's no shortage of rental houses to provide services and equipment for a fee. Video industry magazines, the telephone directory, and local video organizations can provide you with information on what equipment and facilities are available in your area. Trade groups, such as the International Television Association (ITVA), in most major cities publish directories of creative and technical services. You'll find these resources especially useful when you're mounting a production that will require several outside services.

People who rent equipment, studio space, or postproduction facilities to producers are eager to give prices over the phone for an amount under $1,000. If the amount is higher, you should visit them in person. While you're there, and if they don't offer, ask to tour the facility. Don't be too shy to ask questions or to take their time. The proprietor will sometimes "cut you a deal," especially if you are a first-time customer, in order to establish the relationship. They naturally want repeat business.

Locations

Question 10: What locations will be involved in the production? All you need to do in the planning stage is indicate how many locations there will be, where they are, and when you expect to use them. Location expenses can be a large part of the budget;

the more there are or the farther away the location, the higher the cost. You should also think of the type of transportation needed to get to the locations.

When I designed *The Evolving Earth,* a PBS special, I allocated six weeks of location shooting in the Southwest desert and on the West Coast. We did not approach our celebrity, on-camera host until the last minute, however, because we were nervous. We should have done it first! I flew to New York for a series of conversations with his agent, at our expense, and was finally informed that Orson Welles would be delighted to host our program.

Unfortunately, he would have required a helicopter to fly him from location to location. Because of this significant added expense, we had to consider a different narrator, after we had worked so hard to secure him. Should we change the number of locations? Change the distance between the shooting sites and the nearest helicopter service? Unfortunately, while we deliberated alternatives, our prospective narrator became ill and was not able to schedule work.

In this situation, locations were extremely important, which we didn't realize until we were well into the project. (See Chapter 2 for site-survey questions.)

Personnel

Question 11: Who will be involved in the production? Generally a production has four stages: design, preproduction, production, and postproduction. (Distribution is not considered part of the production process.) As few as two or hundreds of people can be involved in each stage. In the design (planning) stage, the producer begins to identify the roles required—director, camera operator, sound technician, announcer, talent, and so on.

You usually make personnel assignments when preparing the preliminary budget or when breaking the script down into its components. You often specify roles rather than names, but, as soon as possible—and to make the project plan complete and accurate for submission for grants—you should add names for each stage. The executive producer, producer, director, camera person, and audio technician are usually involved throughout the production but not always. Some shows, for instance, use a separate director for talent (shooting) and another for editing. This depends on the complexity of the production, skill levels, and personal preferences.

In the early stages of a production, the producer needs to find and then meet with the principal design and production team members. Because of the systemic significance of your personnel, you naturally want the most talented, creative, and responsible people, who are not always easy to find.

I spent weeks looking for a writer for *The Evolving Earth.* I finally found a program on public television that matched the kind of writing style our program required. I phoned the local TV station to get the name of the writer. They had to play back the titles of the show in order to find the name of the production company, which I then contacted to get the writer's number. I called his home in Los Angeles, we met, and he was hired. This proved to be an excellent decision and a good way to find talented people.

Scheduling

Question 12: When will the production occur and be completed? My standard method for estimating time needed is to total the time I expect each element of the production process to take and then multiply it by four. One hour translates into four hours, and a week translates into four weeks. Although this seems extreme, it takes technological and human entropy considerations into account. I'm always surprised by how long it actually takes to complete a project, and in spite of the fourfold increase, I still often underestimate.

Certain tasks require even more time, for instance, editing. If I were realistically to assess my estimated time against actual time spent editing, the multiple would be closer to six. Every producer I've known agrees. All we can do is factor in additional time.

You should develop a detailed time line in the preproduction stage. Every team member, especially those responsible for scheduling and coordination, needs to know how to prepare for upcoming events well in advance. In the planning stage it's sufficient to have a rough idea of the time involved for each of the four production stages. We just want to be able to determine approximately the time frame of the production so we can look at personnel, location, and equipment availabilities and also estimate when the finished program will be available. But when the project goes into preproduction, or if the project plan is part of a grant proposal, a more detailed assessment is needed.

Figure 6.1 presents a standard format for a production time line. This kind of chart allows personnel the opportunity to see the time period in which their services will be needed. Although it indicates time in weeks, it's more common to put in the actual dates of the production period.

Evaluation

Question 13: How will the success of the program be measured? What criteria will be used? To judge whether a program is effective, you must determine whether, and to what extent, the communication objective was achieved. Earlier, when discussing the construction of the communication objective statement, we noted that items should if possible be expressed in measurable terms. From a systems perspective, evaluation of the program's success often provides the most important feedback because it can determine how much the program will continue to be used. In corporate environments, a good evaluation may provide justification for producing even more programs and perhaps even expanded yearly budget allocations.

Determine what methods you'll use to assess the effectiveness of your program up front, in the planning stage, so that you can anticipate the evaluation criteria. When you as producer know how the success or failure of your program will be measured, you have a constant reminder of what the viewer must experience. It helps in the daily decision-making process, because you know that what happens (or does not) to the target audience is what counts. Evaluation plans are so important that most granting organizations—especially state and federal government programs—require one as part of a proposal.

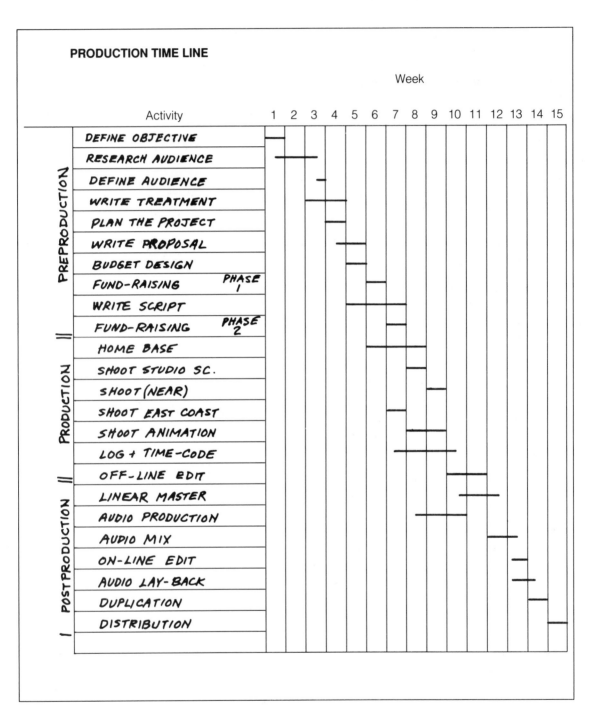

FIGURE 6.1
Production Time Line

This is a standard Gantt chart, which displays various steps in the production process against the time allotted. It is more common to enter dates across the top instead of numbers, as in this example of a fifteen-week production.

The evaluation's purpose is to judge whether the communication objective was met. Did the program actually accomplish its objectives with the target audience? Ask yourself how you can most directly measure the program's effectiveness. If your objective statement contains measurable elements, it's a simple matter of conducting a test. Another technique is to conduct a focus group with members of the target audience. After viewing the program, ask them specific questions relating to the objective. The program's success will quickly become apparent. The session should ideally be conducted by someone other than yourself, and it's advisable to audio record the comments and discussion so you can examine the outcome in greater detail later. Comments obtained in this manner are almost always genuine and valuable and can lead to improvements in the program. A simpler technique is to have members of the target audience fill out a questionnaire after viewing the tape.

Naturally, the best time to conduct the evaluation is immediately after production but before duplication or distribution. This allows time to rework the program if necessary, and it usually is.

Another way to test the effectiveness of a program is to submit it to authorities in the content area for review. Does it work for them? Does it fulfill the objective? Although these people may not always be "right," their opinions and feedback are often very helpful. I usually submit a program to content experts first, make any changes I feel need to be made, and then obtain evaluations from the target audience.

In a more elaborate manner, quantitative testing (surveys or interviews) can be done among members (a representative sampling) of the target audience to statistically determine whether the objective was met. Out of the total number of people who viewed the video, what percentage "got" the message? How many did not? And especially important: What did they get? How closely does that relate to your objective statement? Frequently the objective is A-B-C and the target audience actually perceives A or A-C or C or even D from the program.

Whatever approach one takes, time spent evaluating the finished program is well invested because it provides essential feedback and completes the project loop. Like a company launching a market-tested new product, you will *know,* before it's released, that the program will achieve its communication objective and, therefore, your purpose.

Summary

In this chapter we've examined thirteen questions that, when answered, constitute a project plan, including both a program and a production needs analysis. You can answer the questions briefly at first, to make an initial test of the feasibility of a video or television project. But once you are certain you are going to produce a video, each question, preferably in the order presented, requires serious attention. You may need to do research, do legwork, talk with friends and associates, do interviews with the target audience, and make phone calls—perhaps even more—to gather the answers. But the failure of most programs probably results from these issues being given insufficient attention at the outset of the projects.

To summarize the discussion, and to use as a checklist for your projects, the questions are repeated below.

1. What's your purpose? Why make this program?

2. Who is the target audience?

3. What is your communication objective?

4. What is the subject matter?

5. What is the most appropriate format for this program?

6. What are the program elements?

7. How/where will this program be used?

8. What are the financial considerations?

9. What equipment and facilities will be used?

10. What locations will be involved in the production?

11. Who will be involved in the production?

12. When will the production occur and be completed?

13. How will the success of the program be measured?

How you design a project communicates.

Notes

1. Peters, Tom, *Thriving on Chaos: Handbook for a Management Revolution* (New York: Harper & Row, 1987), 616.
2. Miller, James Grier, *Living Systems* (New York: McGraw-Hill, 1978), 108.
3. Ries, Al, and Jack Trout, *Positioning: The Battle for Your Mind* (New York: McGraw-Hill, 1981), 2.
4. Cortes, Carlos E., "Ads Still Portray All-White Society." *Media & Values* 37 (Fall 1986): 21.

Suggested Readings

Klain, Jane, ed. *International Television and Video Almanac*, 33rd ed. New York: Quigley, 1988.

Ries, Al, and Jack Trout. *Positioning: The Battle for Your Mind.*
New York: McGraw-Hill, 1981.

Strong, William S. *The Copyright Book: A Practical Guide.* Cambridge, MA: MIT Press, 1981.

Wiese, Michael. *The Independent Film & Videomaker's Guide.*
Westport, CT: Michael Wiese Film Productions and Focal
Press, 1984.

PART III

DESIGNING PROGRAM CONTENT

· ·

What do we want to say and to whom? And how do we develop and organize it? We'll begin our study of program content by starting with its most important consideration, the audience. We create programs to show to someone so that something (that the producer values) will happen as a result. Without an audience there's no need for a program. In Chapter 7 we focus on how to identify and analyze *the audience* relative to the subject matter of the program. Chapter 8 examines the process of *developing content,* technically and creatively. Then Chapter 9 provides the ground rules for *content organization,* showing how the subject matter should be structured to maximize its impact on the target audience.

I have organized these three chapters with audience considerations first to emphasize the importance of the audience from the project's first day. Sometimes we have identified the audience before the content, as in training and development programs, where a specific audience need warrants the production. In other instances we know the content before we know the audience, for example, when a lecturer wants to produce a tape as a way to

more broadly disseminate his or her viewpoint. Another example is performers developing a program to be a vehicle for their creative expression and career enhancement.

Whatever appears first, the program idea, the content, the talent, the money, the camera operator, or the vision, always identify and analyze the audience *before or as* you develop and organize the program content. Not doing so is a strategy for failure.

CHAPTER 7

The Audience

· ·

Another [turning point] came to me—at about 30—as a broadcaster, that my first allegiance was to the person tuned in, not to the client, the agency, the network or the station, but to the viewer.

—Hugh Downs

Every program should be directed to a specific audience. If our communications will be received and have an effect, we need to know something—hopefully, a lot—about the persons to whom we are directing the program. Experience has shown, and research has verified, that the more we know about the receiver of a message, the better equipped we will be to design and produce a presentation he or she will accept.

Let's clarify a few terms. An **audience** is the primary group of people at whom a message is aimed. A **target audience** is made up of people whose characteristics have been identified and studied, a particular group of viewers or one "persona" that typifies them. **Secondary audiences** are people outside the target audience who may also view, rent, or purchase the program. A video on eye-hand coordination for day-care children is an example. The audience is children. The target audience is boys and girls two to four years old attending a certain day-care center. The secondary audience is visitors to the center. Let's use this example to illustrate another term. A **market** (as opposed to an audience) is the people who will buy the tape, including day-care operators, other schools, therapists, and perhaps some parents.

The first challenge is to *identify* the audience as specifically as possible. Depending on the situation, we ask: "Who *will* the audience be?" Or, if that's not obvious, "Who *should* the audience be?" If our viewers will be senior citizens, we need to use language, images, and music that will appeal to them and avoid elements that will annoy or distract them. If our program is intended to reduce drug abuse, the audience could be those who do or are inclined to use drugs, or enforcement networks, or legislators. In this manner audience identification and analysis influence not only the content itself, and how it is handled, but also the format and other program elements.

Second, once we've identified who the audience is, we need to *analyze* what they are like. What are their characteristics? What do we need to know about them to make the presentation of our topic more appealing and acceptable? The more we know, the better are our chances of being effective.

In this chapter we'll look at two primary ways of answering these questions, including *demographic* and *psychographic* approaches to defining an audience. Both were rigorously developed and are frequently used by the mass media and marketing and advertising industries, but they're also relevant and applicable to small- to medium-sized nonbroadcast audiences. After examining these approaches, we'll turn to the practical matter of how this information is obtained on a more modest scale. This chapter provides the tools, practices, and procedures for relating a program to its target audience.

Who Is (or Should Be) the Audience?

If we're producing a sales or promotional video, our audience will be the known and/or potential buyers of the product or service. Commercials, for instance, are always made for a specific audience defined by the manufacturer or an agency. If the program is for employee training, the audience is the employees. If the tape is for education, the audience will be students involved in that subject area. And if the piece is a documentation of a workshop or other speaking event, the audience will be those who participated and those with an interest in the subject who could not attend. When a program is produced for a known audience, the "who" question is halfway complete.

If, however, the program content is known and the audience is not, there's preliminary work to do. This is the case in the following example:

Purpose Statement

Executives of XYZ Corporation want a video they can use to present a historical background of the company, its founders, their vision and philosophy, the company's steady growth in personnel and facilities, and its current record of achievement including satisfied customers. They want the video to (1) make

the company more visible, *(2)* promote a positive image, *and*
(3) thereby increase sales.

Communication Objective

We want this video to demonstrate *our company history and val-*
ues (founded on sound principles that have led to continual
growth and expansion: quality of service is excellent and service is
reasonably priced; employee and customer satisfaction is our first
priority). Viewers will be informed *and* impressed *with the*
company.

I've presented the purpose and objective statements to distinguish what the
video will do (why make this tape?) from what it will say (what's the message?).
The distinction is significant, as this principle indicates: *Audience relates to purpose;*
content relates to objective.

Answer audience questions in relation to the purpose, but answer content questions in relation to the objective. So, in the previous example, we look at the purpose statement and ask which audience can deliver 1, 2, and 3. Because the desired outcome is a widely spread positive image and increased sales, *where are the*
people who are potential buyers of XYZ's services? Do they attend trade conferences,
workshops, or other meetings? Are they on XYZ's mailing list or any other obtain-
able list? Are they former clients? Are they people or companies who have a *need*
for XYZ's services? How do we locate them? Where are they geographically?

Let's look at a few more examples of purpose statements:

Purpose: *To present the latest in our line of computer imaging*
technologies.

Audience approach: *Who cares? Who's interested in imaging tech-*
nologies—students, researchers, business and industry? Who
stands to gain from such information?

Purpose: *To encapsulate and present the ideas of noted author*
and visionary, Ms. Jones.

Audience approach: *Who would appreciate these ideas, her vision?*
Where can these people be found? Who can be helped or supported
by these ideas? Where are ideas such as these discussed, evaluated,
and applied? Where is her current audience?

Purpose: *To provide others with our model of marketing success.*

Audience approach: *What others? Who would benefit by the model?*
Who is not having success with different models? Who is working
in this field? Where are they?

With this type of questioning, we begin to understand *who* the audience is generally. As the project continues, we will get more specific information about the audience by inquiring into its characteristics.

Defining/Targeting the Audience

. . . .

To define or *target* an audience, we will give it descriptive characteristics that distinguish it from other groups of people. The labels and categories we use to describe the audience limit the group by excluding all those outside its description. "Males, 19–35" does not include females, males younger than 19, or males older than 35. Producers use targeting as a way to ensure program effectiveness, but we can also hope for a secondary audience outside our definition.

The first of the two primary approaches to **audience definition, demographics,** is quantitative. It uses numerical data concerning gender, education, geographic location, and audience size. It uses descriptors (words, categories, or phrases that distinguish one group from another) to express the relative size of a specific group in relation to a variety of parameters. The qualitative approach, **psychographics,** uses descriptors to indicate an audience's preferences, perceptions, habits, values, and life-styles. Marketing companies use both—separately and combined—depending on the circumstances. The broadcast industry relies almost exclusively on demographics; magazine advertising relies almost exclusively on psychographics; and many agencies, especially television advertising, integrate them.

Because of our predominantly nonbroadcast orientation, we'll select some of the more useful descriptors from both approaches and use them a bit differently. This will be our most serious departure from the way business is done by broadcasters. Our grounded and simplified approach, in addition to being less expensive, is also easier and much less time-consuming. Unlike the television networks, who look back to see how many viewers watched their programs, we, as producers, look forward to try to anticipate and understand the nature of who our audiences should or could be. It makes sense to use the same audience terms and descriptions, as they have proven effective in looking backward; we'll just borrow them to help us look forward.

Demographic Approach

Audience descriptors that help narrow (or target) the audience are the most useful aspect of demographics for the nonbroadcast producer. Let's look at the most often used categories.

What is the primary sex of the audience—male or female? What is the percentage of each? The sex of the audience is significant because we would use many production elements, including music, transition styles, narrator, and lighting, differently for males and females. Our judgments about men's, as opposed to women's, preferences are highly subjective (influenced by stereotypes, trends, and cultural norms), but we must all make our own assumptions about how the different sexes will respond to program content and expression.

What is the age range of the audience?   Age is an important audience factor because people's interest in subjects, as in presentational styles, changes over time. Music and clothing styles, editing pace, and even color preferences vary widely across age groups. Arbitron, one of the primary broadcast ratings services, uses the following age categories:

Women	Men
18–49	18–49
12–24	18–34
18–34	25–49
25–49	25–54
25–54	

Research tells them that these age ranges represent purchasing potential in relation to programming interests among these groups. Networks sell commercial airtime with audience descriptions such as

> Primary target audience: Women 25–49
>
> Secondary target audience: Women 18–34

Financial decisions, such as buying and bartering for programs to broadcast, are often based on descriptions as simple as this.

   In nonbroadcast applications, the gender-age demographic is commonly used as the simplest way to define an audience. It can be too simple and not as useful as some other ways to characterize age groups:

Preschoolers	Middle-aged adults, 35–55
Children, 6–10	Older adults, 55–65
Adolescents	Elderly, 65 and over
Teens	
Young adults	
Adults, 21–40	

What is the amount of formal education of the audience?   Education information helps us decide what level of language and type of message to use in our videos.

Didn't finish high school
High school graduate
Some college
College graduate
Postgraduate

Our presentation, whether its purpose is to entertain or inform, must be able to be understood by the target audience. These descriptions help us keep the content within the limits of the education of the group indicated, especially in terms of vocabulary, memory, and critical analysis capabilities.

What are the racial characteristics of the audience? Viewing preferences and habits also vary according to race. Commercials and other messages are frequently designed to appeal to a specific racial group because of the nature of the product or because of the intent to express pride or achievement among the group's members. The typical categories used demographically include Black, Brown, Red, Caucasian, Hispanic, and Asian.

What is the average household income of the audience? If your purpose is to produce a video for disadvantaged children in the inner city, perhaps to educate them on the consequences of smoking, don't use a narrator who looks wealthy. Don't show kids in the program who look like they attend upper-income schools. Your audience should be able to identify with the people in the program. Given your message, which people in the following income groups can afford to act on it?

Less than $12,000	$46,000–55,000
$12,000–20,000	$56,000–70,000
$21,000–30,000	$71,000–100,000
$31,000–45,000	Over $100,000

Another way to express socioeconomic status is to use the following class designations instead of specific numerical ranges:

Poor	Lower middle	Lower upper
Lower	Middle	Upper
Upper low	Upper middle	Upper upper

What is the location of the audience? The audience's location not only provides the producer with information about delivering the program to where it will be seen, it also provides content cues. For instance, people associate both positively and negatively (depending on circumstance and reference) with regional dialects, values, life-styles, and stereotypes. You should make sure that the provided cues contribute to the project's purpose; those that don't should be excluded. What appeals to New Yorkers may very well not appeal to people from Idaho and vice versa. Decorum and language proper for factory workers may not be acceptable to church groups. Remember our earlier example of the safety video for coal miners. We can characterize location either by region or by environment:

Geographic Region	Environment
Urban or rural	Corporate
North, South, East, West	Church

Northeast	Community
Northwest	School
Mideast	Factory/plant
Midwest	Hospital
Southeast	Library
Southwest	Court room
North central	
South central	
Mountain	

What is the marital status of the audience? Are they single, married, or divorced? Our life experiences qualify us differently, as we saw in our discussion of consciousness. Remember to put yourself in the audience's shoes and see how your content "fits" with the audience's typical marital situation.

What is the average household size of the audience? People who grow up in a family of nine have substantially different experiences from those who grow up in a family of three. Economics, space perception, roles, relationships, the sense of responsibility, and even the sense of time may all be affected. A producer should be sensitive to these areas to ensure that content cues are properly aligned.

What is the religious preference of the audience? Some messages may be appropriate for people who practice certain religions but not for others. Fundamentalists in all religions, for instance, derive meaning from literal interpretation of their scriptures. They may not be receptive to ideas or arguments that are in conflict with these teachings. The producer must know this, respect these approaches to consciousness (perception, belief), and present content that seeks agreement before moving into areas of disagreement.

You can certainly disagree with existing viewpoints, but if you want to accomplish your purpose with that audience, you must create a climate of openness and friendliness first and then gradually introduce controversy. Don't scare off the audience or immediately discredit your message. Religious descriptors include

Protestant	Hindu	
Catholic	Moslem	
Jew	Buddhist	_____

What is the ethnic heritage of the audience? Different cultures have different traditions and customs. If your target audience includes members of a specific cultural group, you should probably do some research. Cultural descriptors include

North American	East Indian	Canadian
Central American	Chinese	Russian
Mexican	Vietnamese	Australian
American Indian	African	European
South American	Japanese	Polynesian

What is the occupational classification of the audience? *White collar* and *blue collar* are terms often used to distinguish between professional positions and support jobs. The U.S. Census Bureau defines *blue-collar workers* as people "employed in precision production, crafts and repair occupations. They comprised 13.5% of full time employed adults or 13.313 million [American] consumers"[1] in 1988. Common terms used to characterize occupational status include

Professional/technical	Sales
Managerial	Retired
Clerical	Unemployed
Service	Part-time _____

We typically provide a blank line so people can fill in their own occupations.

Let's use these key demographic questions to see how the producer can relate the *purpose statement* to the demographics to arrive at an *audience definition*. We want to know who the audience will be so we can design content and production techniques that will be effective with them. We'll use the XYZ Corporation, putting them in the business of offering computer inventory design services for hardware (tools, lumber, electrical, plumbing) suppliers. For a fee, XYZ will design, set up, and maintain a computer inventory program for a hardware store. XYZ can provide the computers, but their main "product" is a unique-to-your-needs computer program to provide both data and graphic entries so you can see the product, know everything about it, and know how many units are in your store or warehouse at the touch of a button.

XYZ CORPORATION

Purpose Statement

Our purpose in making this video is to (1) make the company more visible, (2) promote a positive image, and (3) increase sales.

To use the targeting approach, list the appropriate audience descriptors as follows:

Audience Definition:

Males and females (equally)—Customers can be men or women, so let's design the video program for both sexes equally.

(Age) 25–35—XYZ knows that the people in a position to acquire their services are mostly young people.

Some college—People who value computers and know how to operate them usually have some college training or education.

(Race)—Not applicable.

Middle income—Our client list reveals them to be middle to upper-middle income.

West Coast—XYZ is well established in the East and is looking for new markets in the West.

(Marital status, household size, religion, ethnic heritage)—None is applicable.

Managerial—All XYZ's clients are owners or managers of hardware stores.

The producer has a much better idea of how to frame and design the program content with this demographic information. Every program element under consideration can be evaluated in terms of how well or how poorly it appeals to this audience based on its defining characteristics. Elements that won't appeal to the audience should be eliminated.

Psychographic Approach

The demographic approach gives producers a basic sense of who members of the audience are and how large the audience might be, but it doesn't tell us about lifestyle, values, beliefs, habits, and perceptions. The psychographic approach provides this further refinement. More often than not, combining demographic and psychographic descriptors is even more helpful.

What follows is a sampling of psychographic descriptions of market segments used by major marketing firms. These firms have designed, researched, and verified these segments, and we can take advantage of the results. We'll see how the segments are relevant for the nonbroadcast producer. Then we'll see how this information can be obtained on a smaller (than national) scale.

A major source for psychographic market analysis is the VALS™ (Values & Lifestyle) typology developed by SRI International (formerly the Stanford Research Institute) in 1987. Although VALS is used by media producers and advertisers to define "markets," the specific segments can also be applied to nonbroadcast, medium- to low-scale productions. According to a VALS 2 publication:

Consumers pursue and acquire products, services and experiences that provide satisfaction and give shape, substance and character to their identities. They are motivated by one of three powerful self-orientations—principle, status or action. Principle-oriented *consumers are guided in their choices by their beliefs or principles, rather than by feelings, events or desire for approval.* Status-oriented *consumers are heavily influenced by the actions, approval and opinions of others.* Action-oriented *consumers are guided by a desire for social or physical activity, variety and risk-taking. Each VALS 2 segment has distinctive attitudes, lifestyles and life goals according to its members' self-orientation.*[2]

The VALS 2 typology relates these three types of consumers to eight primary population segments, as can be seen in Figure 7.1.

THE VALS™ 2 NETWORK

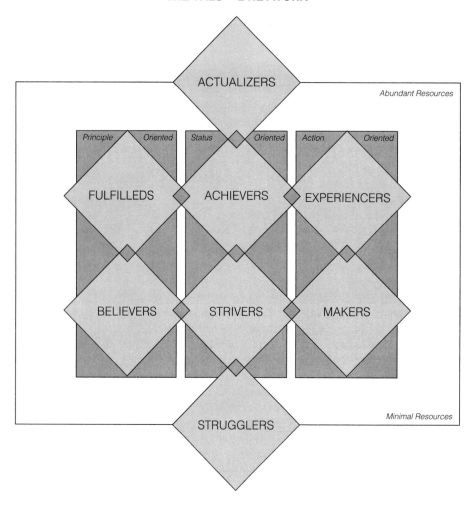

**FIGURE 7.1
The VALS 2
Network**
*This diagram
shows how prin-
ciple-, status-, and
action-oriented
consumers relate to
the eight VALS 2
typologies.
(Courtesy of SRI
International.)*

We'll briefly discuss the segments here. For the complete VALS's descriptions, see Appendix E.

- *Actualizers* are successful, sophisticated, active, "take-charge" people with high self-esteem and abundant resources. They are interested in growth and seek to develop, explore, and express themselves in a variety of ways. They are guided by principles and want to make a difference. They seek to make their consuming behavior consistent with their views of how the world is or should be.
- *Fulfilleds* are mature, satisfied, comfortable, reflective people who value order, knowledge, and responsibility. They are well educated. They are practical consumers who look for functionality, value, and durability.
- *Believers* are conservative, conventional people with concrete beliefs

based on traditional, established codes in relation to family, church, community, and the nation. Their education is modest but sufficient to meet their needs. They favor American products and established brands.

- *Achievers* are successful career- and work-oriented people who like to, and generally do, feel in control of their lives. They value structure, predictability, and stability over risk, intimacy, and self-discovery. Image is important to them. They are committed to work and family. They favor established products and services that demonstrate their success to their peers.
- *Strivers* seek motivation, self-definition, and approval from the world around them. They strive for security, are low on economic, social, and psychological resources, but are concerned about the opinions and approval of others. They think money defines success. They strive to be stylish.
- *Experiencers* are young, vital, enthusiastic, impulsive, and rebellious. They seek variety and excitement, savoring the new, the offbeat, and the risky. They are avid consumers and spend much of their income on clothing, fast food, music, movies, and video.
- *Makers* are practical people who have constructive skills and value self-sufficiency. They live in a traditional context of family, practical work, and physical recreation and have little interest in what lies outside that context. They are politically conservative, suspicious of new ideas, and unimpressed by goods having other than practical or functional purposes.
- *Strugglers* are people whose lives are constricted. They are chronically poor, ill educated, low skilled, without strong social bonds, aging, concerned about health, often despairing, and passive. They are focused on meeting the security and safety needs of the moment. They are generally loyal to favorite brands.

Advertising agencies use the VALS 2 typology extensively to talk about and study various market segments. The design of a commercial, for instance, begins with identification of the appropriate segment(s) (which do overlap) and then analysis of what media reach this segment and how to make messages appealing given its characteristics. The charts in Appendix F show how SRI International has associated each of these eight segments with life-style, psychological, and consumer characteristics. Figure 7.2 shows a 1987 survey to indicate how the VALS segments relate to the national population.

Other marketing organizations use different descriptors. (See Appendix G for a description of the Prizm™ System.) Mediamark Research Incorporated (MRI)[3] is a multifaceted consumer research service that uses a combination of demographics, psychographics, and other techniques including "geodemographics" (audience segmented by geography) and "volumetrics" (segmenting by volume of product purchased). Some of the MRI segments (descriptors) include

- *Outdoor energetics:* High-energy enthusiasts of both sexes who enjoy sailing, skiing, jogging, tennis

FIGURE 7.2
Attributes of the VALS 2 Segments

This chart shows how Americans rank according to the eight VALS 2 segments. Source: 1987 Leading Edge Survey. (Courtesy of SRI International.)

ATTRIBUTES OF THE VALS™ 2 SEGMENTS

Segment	Percentage of Population %	Sex (M) %	Median Age	Median Income $	Education (Some College) %	Occupation (White Collar) %	Married %
Actualizer	8	59	43	58,000	95	68	72
Fulfilled	11	47	48	38,000	81	50	73
Believer	16	46	58	21,000	6	11	70
Achiever	13	39	36	50,000	77	43	73
Striver	13	41	34	25,000	23	19	60
Experiencer	12	53	26	19,000	41	21	34
Maker	13	61	30	23,000	24	19	65
Struggler	14	37	61	9,000	3	2	47

- *On your toes:* Mostly young, affluent females who love dancing, skating, aerobics, health clubs
- *Surf and turf:* Hunters and fishermen
- *The cerebral:* Chess, checkers, and backgammon players
- *The creatives:* Painters, photographers, woodworkers
- *Home and hearth:* Couples who entertain at home and enjoy all that goes with it
- *The gentle pursuits:* Slightly older men and women who enjoy gardening, bird watching, flower arranging

Market analysts use these labels to *measure*—usually afterward—how many viewers (readers, purchasers) there were (demographic) for a particular showing and what their characteristics were (psychographic). In this way they determine how to position their future product (program) development and program strategies.

The producer can also utilize the same descriptors as a way to design content and expression criteria. To illustrate how content can flow from these audience descriptions, we'll once again employ some hypothetical purpose statements. (Keep in mind that we would normally also include the appropriate demographic data.)

EXAMPLE 1

A *sales* video for art supplies

Purpose

To introduce a new line of watercolor supplies (video to be shown in art supply store windows)

Audience

- *Creatives* (people who value creative expression)
- *Achievers* (people who value self-discovery and want to make an impression on their peers)

Content suggestions:

- show a person using the supplies creatively
- use voice-over to indicate the artist's thoughts as we watch the work in progress (introspection)
- show the artist feeling pride in her success as visitors greet her at a gallery showing
- incorporate sensitive electronic music (artistic) to catch the interest of passersby—include exquisite imagery and camera movement (also to catch people's attention)

EXAMPLE 2

A *training* video on managing a branch office

Purpose

To help managers vitalize their branch offices

Audience

Strivers (people who are striving to find a secure place in the world, easily bored, lots of problems, unsure)

Content suggestions:

- use a confident presenter, someone the viewer will feel has solved many problems similar to his or her own
- provide information based on *real* success stories
- show how the techniques can work for the viewer
- use a strong, moving, interesting presentation
- give the viewer hope that success is realizable
- offer follow-up resources

EXAMPLE 3

A *promotional* travel video

Purpose

To motivate people, especially fishermen, to visit a refurbished Canadian resort (to be shown on cable and in travel agency offices)

Audience

- *Outdoor energetics* (people who like the outdoors)
- *Experiencers* (people who are vital and offbeat, take risks, and seek excitement and fun)

Content suggestions:

- upbeat music and editing tempo
- fast-cut outdoor imagery (beautiful and exotic)
- people having fishing success, sharing risks
- a place to be alone in nature or to have fun with others
- narrator's voice full of vitality, experience
- good food (fish?), comfort in rustic setting

EXAMPLE 4

A *perspective* video on solutions to world hunger

Purpose

To show that hunger is not necessary, that a change in thinking and values is needed (to be shown on cable and offered to churches)

Audience

Actualizers (people who are educated and want to make a difference)

Content suggestions:

- appeal to higher ideals, values, principles
- provide accurate data on background of the issues
- assess the current situation regionally
- address serious issues (past failures)
- present visionaries with realistic ideas
- include beautiful music and images

To define an audience you'll need to gather information from whatever sources are available to assess who the viewers are and what they are like. The categories and terminology of demographics and psychographics are helpful for audience definition, and they have already been widely tested and applied with success in a variety of industries.

We've seen the importance of audience considerations and have discussed two approaches to describing the audience. Now we need to understand the needs of the audience.

Audience Needs Analysis

An **audience needs analysis** seeks to understand the real or perceived needs of the target audience. Such needs are derived from the purpose *and* the audience's perceptions relative to it. Although the manager or client (who hired you to produce a video) may want to increase production on the assembly line, the target audience (workers) may have strong conflicts with that purpose. The time for analysis of audience needs and perceptions is *before* the content is designed, and not after.

When you know who the audience is, you can use the information-gathering procedures following this section as a way to determine their needs relative to the purpose of the video. When you don't know who the audience is, the needs analysis begins with the preliminary step of identifying them, after which you can seek information about their needs.

A needs analysis includes a determination of specific program objectives. For instance, learning objectives are involved in a training video. What should the audience learn? What appeals to them? What will motivate them? In a sales program, what should the audience know about the product or service—availability, quantities, pricing? The analysis may also include attitude objectives. How does the target audience feel about what they might learn or experience from the video? How will their attitudes be changed? Why? Behavior objectives might also be involved. What should viewers do as a result of the program? Take a test? Make a phone call? Write a letter? Retreat? Buy something? Vote a certain way? The producer needs to know as much as possible about the audience's needs as they relate to the program's subject matter.

Be Specific

. . . .

With your demographic and psychographic descriptions at hand, describe one member of the audience. Distill the primary characteristics of the audience into the identity of a single representative and then design your communication as if you were going to appeal to that person. This is known as a **persona.** You can then keep him or her in mind throughout what can sometimes be a long production schedule. Visualize that person frequently. See him or her watching your presentation and try to become sensitive to his or her viewpoint. It helps if you know a similar person. Ask what the person likes and what he or she doesn't like. Also, try to develop a sense of what the person would need in order to complete your program evaluation questions if he or she were to fill it out. Anticipate the responses if you can. The following is a description of a persona:

Purpose

To demonstrate the horrible results of driving drunk so viewers will think twice.

Persona

John is 24 years old. He drives an older car, his first. He has a full-time job, low self-esteem, and a girlfriend he is trying to impress. He drinks because his friends do. He is not a problem drinker but a social drinker. For the first time he is in control of his life and enjoying the freedom of not living with his parents. He is most likely to watch television late at night (that is why this is a television public service announcement). He refers to himself as a "party animal."

Now it's easy both to see John and to design pictures, words, and music that will grab his attention and hold it. If, instead, we only had some demographic information—such as male, 18–25 years old, high school education, $18,000 annual

AUDIENCE ANALYSIS

YOGA FOR BUSY WOMEN

VIEWING LOCATION: The home.

VIEWING CONTEXT: Tape played by individuals once a day (morning).

DEMOGRAPHIC

Women

18-40 years old (primary)

40-50 years old (secondary)

Some college

Middle to upper-middle income

Urban (USA) E & W coasts

Working women

Married with children

PSYCHOGRAPHIC

Principle and action oriented

Actualizers

Achievers

Strivers

"On your toes"

Self-improvement orientation

Need help with discipline (video)

Frequent bookstores/video stores

Opinion leader

Self-motivated

PERSONA

"KATHY" is 26, married, employed, and has one child. She is a college graduate with a demanding job. Between balancing her family and professional activities, she takes time for herself. She values personal (mind, body, spirit) growth, nutrition, and feeling good about herself. Her approach is balanced — she's not a fanatic. Her social life suffers due to her focused commitment to family and job. She's average in appearance but perceives herself as overweight. She has tried and been disappointed by aerobics videos. She wants a low-impact approach that she can use daily. She wants to know and do more with yoga because she heard it has a spiritual component. Her husband is supportive.

Prepared: 8-13-88 By: D. Smith   Method: Brainstorm/Interviews

FIGURE 7.3
Audience Analysis

income, occasional social drinker—we would have much less with which to work. It's not easy to visualize or relate to statistics; that's why creating a persona is helpful.

When a message is designed to appeal to a large group, there is a greater chance that the message will miss many who make up that group. Being specific about an audience means the message will probably be effective for a particular part of the group, but it is also likely that others might be receptive.

We like to be treated as persons rather than as a part of a group. So messages designed with a personal appeal reach us more powerfully than those that lump us into a group. The persona you create is, in fact, representative of the larger audience. Yet it's counterproductive to create a persona who is so unique as to be unusual. We want as many people as possible for our audience. A complete audience analysis is shown in Figure 7.3.

Gathering the Information

. . . .

Whether you use the demographic, the psychographic, or a combined approach, there are relatively few methods to use to find out about audiences. Of course, SRI International, MRI, and the others undertake complex and costly studies. For non-broadcast applications, we don't have to do that. But we still need to investigate our intended audience. By using the same terms as those used by the "majors," we have the advantage of measurable descriptions and tested reliability. The challenge is to obtain the needed information from our actual or as yet intended audience. The techniques discussed here can help to refine our definition when the audience is known and specify it when it is not. They are also valid when we want to enlarge the audience so that an existing program will be more widely used.

Personal Interviews

Look through your address book. Make some calls to your friends. Find people you think might be interested in your topic. If the audience is known (as in a corporate setting), select a representative sample and approach each one in person or by phone, and ask if you can have ten minutes of their time to help you with a project. Tell them what the topic is and don't waste anyone's time if they're not interested in it.

If the audience is not known, interview people who you think might be interested in the topic. First, find out where these people are, then plan how to approach them for an interview. If the topic deals with mass transportation, ride the buses and trains and talk to anybody who'll listen. When we did our research for *A New Wrinkle,* a program to dispel myths about aging, we went to senior centers, hospitals, universities, shopping centers, and retirement communities to talk to older people. Not only did we find out about our audience, we learned a lot about the subject matter that broadened the program. Our audience turned out

AUDIENCE RESEARCH QUESTIONNAIRE

Name (optional):_____ Age: _____ City: _____

Educational level: _____ Race (optional): _____

Socioeconomic status: Low   Middle   Upper (income)

Marital Status: _____ Religion: _____

Occupation: _____

Number of hours spent watching television per week: _____

Do you rent videos?   Frequently   Occasionally   Rarely   Never

Have you ever purchased a video?   Yes   No   How many? _____

How do you find out about videos you want to see? _____
_____

What do you think makes a video good? _____

What are your favorite kinds of videos? _____

(Regarding the topic of the proposed video:)

Are you familiar with the topic?   Yes   No   Somewhat   Very

What is your opinion about it?_____

Have you had direct experience with it? What?_____

Where/how did you learn about it? _____

What, if anything, concerns you about this subject?_____

What should a video on this subject contain? _____
_____

How important is this topic to you?_____

Do you think such a video would find a wide audience?   Yes   No

Would you prefer a man or woman presenter for this subject?   M   W

Which would you prefer?   To be informed _____   To be entertained _____

Whom do you regard as an authority on this topic? _____

Would you watch such a program: Yes   No   Depends on _____

What advice/recommendations would you give the producers?_____

Where do you fit in these descriptions? (Check those that apply.)

_____ Actualizer	_____ Fulfilled	_____ Believer	_____ Achiever
_____ Striver	_____ Experiencer	_____ Creative	_____ Struggler
_____ Introvert	_____ Extrovert	_____ Inner Directed	_____ Outer Directed

FIGURE 7.4
Audience Research Questionnaire

to be one of our best research resources as well, and some of these people even appeared in the program.

Ask the demographic questions first to get the interview started on a personal note. Then move into the topic and presentational questions. Because the psychographic information will, for the most part, relate to your topic, it's necessary to have your questions in front of you. Although you will gain insights from spontaneous interaction, the interviewees will be more confident and respectful of your agenda if they see you are well prepared with written questions.

Figure 7.4 shows a sample audience research questionnaire. I prefer using the questionnaire as a guide for interviewing rather than asking people to complete a handout. You can get more from an interview because you can ask for clarification or elaboration if necessary. Interviews with ten well-selected members of your target audience should be sufficient. But make sure your sample is representative. Interview quantity isn't as important as sample representativeness.

You'll need to make a new list of questions for every program so the questions will relate to the details of your topic.

Focus Groups

If the audience is known, a small group session, conducted by someone other than the producer, can be very effective, providing useful information. Sometimes we'll show the group a mock-up of the video jacket or show part of a tape that's similar in format and content. People are eager to offer their opinions and perspectives. Have them fill out a prepared questionnaire that handles the demographic questions, then interview them as a group.

The benefit of a small group is that more ideas are sparked through interaction, and enthusiasm for or against various ideas or issues can demonstrate decisively what to do with the content. One can quickly discern from such a group whether it is the appropriate audience. Some in the group will respond and others won't. And you'll want to find out why.

Discussions

Situation: A newly formed jazz group wants to produce a music video. *Question:* Who should the audience be? Begin by answering the preliminary question: "What do you want the video *to do*—what's the purpose?" The pianist wants a tape to show other musicians. The drummer wants the tape to air on MTV. The bass player wants to build the group's following. And the manager wants to use the tape to get more "gigs." *Solution:* Get together to discuss and agree on the best (or top-priority) purpose for the tape. Identify which audience can fulfill that purpose. Don't shoot anything until the purpose-audience combination is clear.

Situation: A plant manager wants to produce a series of videos for all employees in the chemical mixing department to see as a way to standardize the variables involved in several processes. The audience is *employees in the chem-mix department,* which is roughly sixty people plus new employees, with no two alike in terms of demographics or psychographics. *Question:* How do we define this audience?

Solution: Because we know who these people are, and many by name, the issue shifts from *who* they are (because they're part of the same audience) to *what* they want in the video. How do we find that out? By getting them involved in the project. Facilitate a discussion in which you ask what the video should be like. What would appeal to as well as inform them? Audio tape their responses and use them in the program design. You will have sampled the collective consciousness of the audience, made friends, obtained content and presentation ideas, created anticipation for the production, and come to know your audience even better. They will respect you, and the effort, because their input made a difference. When the tape comes out, they'll be eager for it because they had some input. Put some of their names in the credits if they helped substantially.

Surveys

As a way to earn money as a kid I did survey work. I went door to door and, after introducing myself as a TV survey taker, I asked the resident a series of questions about what he or she watched the previous night. If the set was on then, I asked what channel it was usually tuned to, his or her favorite shows, and so on. I made a check in a box for most questions and wrote in names of shows. It took five minutes. I must have done thousands of these and I was seldom refused. People were eager to give someone information about what kind of television they watched. It gave them some input into the process.

Surveys are still fairly easy to do, but they are time-consuming. They can, however, be very helpful because the data tend to be unbiased, fairly accurate, and representative of the consumer's actual perception. Consumer perceptions are especially valuable if your program will be shown or distributed to a broad segment of the public (as in public access or other cable applications).

Situation: Your group wants to define the audience for a community access program on waste management, focusing on recycling. You want this information not only to know how to better design the program but also to aid in the design of a promotional effort to get people to watch and participate in a live, call-in program. You have public access facilities as well as a small grant from a local business and prospects for more grants.

Solution: Do a survey that is small but *representative* of your community. Randomly select homes that receive cable (you can see the wires)—perhaps five homes in five different neighborhoods. Your survey should include these kinds of questions: If such and such a program were scheduled on public access, what would motivate you (the interviewee) to watch it? What would it take for you to participate? What would be the best time? How would you find out about it?

Ask your cable station for a brief letter of introduction (on their stationery) to show the people you'll survey. When I did surveys, we were given an ID card. Now, simply identifying myself with the production company is enough, but people like to see some credentials up front.

Obviously, surveys can be conducted at any scale—small group or global. It is important that the respondents are randomly selected and representative of the wider population that will receive the program.

Questionnaires and Tests

Situation: You want to produce a video documentary of an event happening this year to promote it so next year's attendance will be even better.

Solution: Prepare a questionnaire to be handed out to participants. Ask leading questions about how the video could be used. What should it contain? How could the event be improved or better promoted? We also want to know whether participants would help promote the event by showing our video to other groups. Even as the documentary is being shot, feedback from these forms can suggest directions to take, ways of putting the material together, program length, interviews, and other elements.

We did this at a health conference and had an excellent response. People were eager to have some input into what the "camera crew" was doing—and the excitement served as promotion for the tape when it was completed. But remember that conference attendees are much more likely to purchase a tape if it is available during the conference. If you wait to try to sell tapes after the conference, the sales rate drops by as much as 90%.

Summary

When it comes to designing a program, the audience comes first. Do you have an idea for a show? If so, you should immediately identify the audience. Do you have a client who wants to produce a video? Does he or she already have an audience in mind? If so, find out who they are, where they are, how they will encounter your program, what they are like, what they need to know, and what they already know and feel about your topic and how valid it is.

The first task in program design is to study the relationship between the audience and the project's purpose. If this relationship is clear and workable, proceed. If not, work with the purpose statement to discover who the audience should be because *every* decision made thereafter will be based on this fundamental relationship. Once the target audience has been identified, you should analyze it to understand its unique characteristics and needs, focusing on those that can influence the program design.

To define or target an audience, use descriptors to distinguish one group of people from another. These can be borrowed from the major marketing firms who have developed them. We can also make up our own descriptors. Some of the established terms are demographic, relating to a person's vital statistics. Other terms are psychographic, describing a person's life-style, beliefs, values, perceptions, and habits. To the program designer, both kinds of description are useful to target an audience.

The methods used by the major production studios to gather this kind of information are extensive and complex. The nonbroadcast producer can use some of the same methods but on a much more reasonable and modest scale. These include interviews, focus group sessions, discussions, surveys, and questionnaires and tests.

From this information we can derive a complete picture of our audience—their identity, location, characteristics, and needs—relative to the program we intend to produce. With this analysis before us, we are well prepared to develop the program's content.

The audience we select communicates.

Notes

1. Pamphlet, "Niche Marketing: Identifying Opportunity Markets with Syndicated Consumer Research" (New York: Mediamark Research Inc., 1988), 14.
2. Pamphlet, "The VALS™ 2 Typology" (Menlo Park, CA: SRI International, 1988).
3. Pamphlet, "Niche Marketing: Identifying Opportunity Markets with Syndicated Consumer Research" (New York: Mediamark Research Inc., 1988), 14.

Suggested Readings

Beville, Hugh Malcom, Jr. *Audience Ratings: Radio, Television and Cable.* Hillsdale, NJ: Lawrence Erlbaum Associates, 1988.

Bogart, Leo. *Strategy in Advertising: Matching Media and Messages to Markets and Motivation,* 2nd ed. Chicago: Crain Books, 1984.

Bower, Robert T. *The Changing Television Audience in America.* New York: Columbia University Press, 1985.

Hanan, Mach. *Life-Styled Marketing: How to Position Products for Premium Profits.* New York: American Marketing Association, 1980.

Meyers, William. *The Image-Makers: Power and Persuasion on Madison Avenue.* New York: Times Books, 1984.

Wells, William D. *Life Style and Psychographics.* New York: American Marketing Association, 1974.

CHAPTER 8

Developing Program Content

· ·

Concept dictates procedure.

—Ansel Adams

When an experienced Hollywood screenwriter was in town, I invited him to speak to one of my classes about the "(un)real world" of moviemaking. He commented that script readers are overwhelmed with material. But out of the hundreds of scripts circulating at any one time, roughly 1% are "worthy" and fewer than that get produced.

This chapter is about the substance and the quality of the message itself. What do we have to say to our viewers? And, if we know what to say, how do we say it so that our purpose is realized? Will they respect what we say? Will they accept our message? Will they enjoy our expression of it? Will they remember it? Will it change them? Will it change us?

To answer these questions in the affirmative, we need to understand our content options and the context of those options. Although some options may be familiar, they're intended to provide fresh insight and stimulate creative thinking. We'll address certain issues such as clarity and usefulness that ensure our credibility and effectiveness as communicators. We'll learn some techniques to grab, hold, and move the viewer's attention. We'll revisit the need to position our content with respect to the target's preconceived ideas and perceptions. We'll examine the power of language because a video's message is often conveyed in words. We'll delve into the creative process itself and, finally, explore some specific techniques for developing content.

My guest also said that the reason the vast majority of scripts are rejected by the time the reader gets to page ten is that the writers haven't done their "homework." This book is a guide to doing just that.

Content and Context

. . . .

The **content** of a program can be considered to be everything contained within it, but for our present purposes the content is the message system, what the producer has to say. Because a message begins as thoughts—rather than the words, images, and sounds that convey it—our tendency is to focus on presentation over substance. It's one thing to compose a shot according to aesthetic conventions; it's another to compose it for a particular communication need. Sometimes these coincide, and sometimes they don't. Our focus now is the translation of the thought to the program and from there to the audience.

The **context** of a program is the frame of reference within which the content is situated. Because nothing happens in isolation, viewers pick up certain cues from the program's content and presentation that inform them about various related factors. Audiences constantly seek out these cues and use them to create meaning, because they want to know more than simply what the producer has to say. Who is the producer? What are her values? Why did she show us this and not that? Why did she produce this program? What's in it for her? Who paid for this program? How much did it cost? Who's responsible? As viewers experience the context, they acquire more information to help them determine to what extent they will appreciate and accept the program's content (message).

Content cannot occur without a context (unless the content is meaningless), so it's important to match our consideration of content with attention to context as well. To begin, we'll consider some of the more common content options along with their contexts. A program can use any of them independently or they can be combined to provide variety. Try to look at these familiar words from a new direction—see them as ways of giving form to thought as a producer does.

Information

Information is content that informs. Information can come from pictures and movement as well as from speech, other sounds, or their combination. Do you remember the way Walter Cronkite ended his newscasts? "And that's the way it is, December 14th, 1982." This communicated the context, that the news of the day is information and not entertainment.

Because the producer is making a statement about how things are, her or his information must be supported by some evidence, reasoning, or other justification. It's not usually enough to offer information in a program. One must explain or imply along with it why it's offered, why it's important, where it came from, what it means (if known), how it relates, of what use it might be, and so on. This takes time and is, therefore, one of the reasons newspapers and magazines are much more "informative" than television. And television will stay less informative as long as its primary mission is commercial advertising. Noncommercial (uninterrupted) videos have a decided advantage.

The challenge of using an informative approach is first to make sure that the viewer accepts the credibility of the information source. Without it, the information loses validity. For information to be useful, it has to be true or at least based on some truth. Second, is the information relevant to the viewer? Does it make a difference?

The period at the end of this sentence is visual information. It makes a difference in your life because it makes you pause. However, if I were to give you facts relating to its size, color, shape, density, and chemical composition, you would probably be bored. As meaning-seeking beings we thrive on information; we can't live without it. However, the "information age" has overwhelmed many of us, making it necessary to prioritize our exposure to information. Sometimes watching a video can even be an escape from information. Again, it's critically important to know your audience and how they will respond to more information.

Description

Description is content that gives form to the qualities and characteristics of a subject so that the viewer can understand and appreciate it. The form can be visual or verbal, and the subject described can include other than physical things, for instance, a dream, feeling, vision, or experience. Description doesn't require verification by others to be valid for the describer. But if the describer wants others to accept the description, he or she should try to place the unusual in a context with which they can identify.

Description is a way of sharing our world with others. We often describe things simply to verify that others see the way we do. This creates a bond. If we are alone in our perceptions, we run the risk of being isolated or considered "abnormal." Consider the people who describe UFO or near-death experiences in great detail. They're free to describe what they saw but the audience is also free to reject it. The producer is "on solid ground" only as long as the description matches the perception of the target audience. When it does not, the "ground" gets shaky; credibility is jeopardized unless the same experience can be provided for the viewer as well.

Description is at its best when it's specific. The more detailed and concrete the expression the better. *Rose* is more descriptive than *flower*. A close-up shot is more descriptive of a horse than a wide shot showing it in the distance. When you think of descriptive words or shots, notice that there are many variables. For instance, if the scene calls for a car, is it a family car or a race car? What color? What size? What manufacturer? Foreign or domestic? Old or new? Unless you leave these interpretations completely up to the director's insight, the shooting script should describe these items precisely.

Narration

Narration is content that tells a story. It is perhaps the most powerful means of communicating content. That's why we will devote an entire chapter to storytelling (see Chapter 11).

Don't confuse the term *narrator* with *narration.* The former is a person who tells a story. But stories can be told without a narrator, as seen in many commercials. For instance, the Michael J. Fox Pepsi commercial in which he and his girlfriend inadvertently trap a dog inside their truck—with the ignition keys in its mouth—is not narrated. The story is told by an anonymous narrator—the writer or producer.

Narration, as story, has a beginning, middle, and end. It always involves a series of events and characters who move, in spite of (sometimes increasing) conflict, toward a goal. This includes real-life and fictional situations.

Documentaries are stories that are often "narrated" (told) by a person on or off camera who has some relationship to the subject, even if the association is peripheral. Corporate image programs tell the story of the business. Sales and promotional videos tell the story of the product or service. Training tapes tell the story of how the company gets things done properly. Although all these formats could communicate their content in other ways, the story motif makes the content more interesting and memorable.

Question

The *question* is content that seeks some (usually cognitive) answer or resolution. It creates a mystery, a mental challenge or problem that moves viewers. Because the mind seeks order and meaning, anything that creates chaos, confusion, or nonsense causes it to go searching for an answer. Detective and crime stories are powerful because they raise questions and then resolve them. Audiences want resolution because it helps them feel that everything is under control—things are as they should be. As a content device, framing content as a question is an excellent tool when the objective in some way relates to the audience feeling satisfied, in control, self-assured.

The challenge of the scriptwriter is to generate questions in the viewer's mind without implying the answer too soon. The scriptwriter tries to keep the audience "hanging." As long as there is no resolution, viewers will keep looking for one, and paying attention.

Conversation

Conversation as content allows the viewer to observe an interaction between two or more people. It distances the viewer somewhat but conversation nonetheless is a very strong device for communicating relationships, for increasing identity with dramatic characters, and for allowing the audience an opportunity to oversee a situation or observe an interaction. Conversation is a primary element in situation comedies, soap operas, and talk-show formats, to mention a few. Because good relationships and personnel interaction are highly valued by business and industry, training and development programs stress conversation as well. We're all familiar with the role-play situation where viewers are assumed to identify with the characters involved. If we don't, it's probably because the conversation doesn't seem "real." Viewers need some level of identification for the interaction to seem genuine.

In the context of conversation as a content device, the producer or writer says to the audience, Look at what's going on between these people. Conversation can be quiet, dull, bright, interesting, even noisy or disturbing—depending on what is being conveyed. Part of the power of conversation is in its ability to communicate *relationship* to the audience. Although what the characters say may be interesting or even important, the audience is also privy to how well or poorly the participants relate to one another. This provides more cues to perceive the meaning of the situation and what is exchanged.

Performance

Performance, as a content device, puts the message into an experience that is fun, interesting, and possibly exciting. Many television commercials show the product or its representative(s) (screen characters) singing, dancing, doing tricks, and so on. They perform for us because they don't want us to be bored with their message.

When a station manager threw a major party for a retiring CEO, I made a twenty-minute video retrospective using photographs from old movies for background and pasting snapshots (photocopies from the CEO's family album) over the heads of the lead actors. We recopied and edited the mock-up photos, added a music and sound effects track, and the result was a comic newsreel. Hundreds of people attended the banquet and the video was a hit. What could have been a sober event turned out to be great fun.

When you want to leave the audience feeling happy, having had a good time, performance is a reliable way. Although performance may seem unsophisticated, most major corporations with video departments rely on it. Managers who want their board, stockholders, employees, and customers to *feel* good about the company can't achieve that result as well with other devices.

Message Presentation

William Wells, in a chapter on audience responses to television commercials, makes a distinction between the two primary modes of media presentation. He says that every commercial is made of two basic ingredients, lecture and drama. Lecture refers to a direct message to the viewer—when the screen presenter speaks to the audience. Drama is an interaction between screen characters who are seemingly unaware of the audience. Drama puts the viewer in the position of observer, looking in on an interaction. In addition to being the major component of commercials, drama and lecture constitute the bulk of what we see in television programs and in video. Each mode exerts its influence in a different manner:

Lectures *present facts intended to be believed. The presenter displays the product, demonstrates it, and talks about the benefits it can provide. . . . Faced with a lecture coming at them through the television screen, viewers occupy their minds with other matters, discount part or all the evidence, derogate the source, or counter-argue every point. So, lectures present argument and evidence, broadly defined. Members of the audience process that informa-tion at arm's length and use the outcome to help them think about how to behave.*

Dramas exert influence in an entirely different way. Like fairy tales, movies, novels, parables, and myths, television commercials (and other) dramas are stories about how the world works. View-ers learn from dramas by *inferring [emphasis added] lessons from them and by applying those lessons to the circumstances they en-counter in the conduct of their lives. From the viewer's point of view, conclusions drawn from dramas are "mine," while conclu-sions urged in lectures are "ideas that other people are trying to impose on me."*[1]

How do you decide whether to use drama or lecture or a combination of both? Look at the program content—is it weighted toward information? Is the informa-tion best conveyed in a speech? Or can it be inferred from watching performers act out a story? Look at the audience definition—would this group of viewers prefer someone talking to them about what to do or think? Or would the group respond better to watching a story unfold? How much time do they have to watch your program? Stories often take longer than lectures, but not in all cases. (Commer-cials can tell a story in thirty or sixty seconds.) In a drama the viewer can ex-perience some of the emotions portrayed by the actors. Lectures can be less expensive and time consuming to produce because they can present a great deal of information in a shorter time. Many producers use the lecture format because they assume that simply telling the facts on a TV screen is persuasive, although this is not necessarily true. Finally, consider which method will accomplish the communi-cation objective—audience as witness (drama) or audience as student (lecture).

Content Structural Devices

Content structural devices are ways to structure content. We have seen how to give ideas form, or structure; now we'll give that form a purpose and have it do some specific work. These devices also become part of the content.

Prologue

The **prologue** is a brief section of images and/or sounds that precedes the title of the program. It can introduce the subject matter by "setting up" the audience, giving them a feel for the setting, time, and characters involved. A prologue is more often used in programs of longer length, that is, twenty minutes or more, because there is time for it.

Used in nonbroadcast programs, the prologue sets the tone of the program, establishes the subject matter, and gently moves viewers into the media experience. For instance, in a training video on packaging, the prologue might begin with the packages arriving at the consumer's home, to the delight of the receiver. Titles would appear over the final section of the prologue and then the program open might begin with a manager talking to employees in the packaging department.

The Hook

The **hook** consists of images and/or sounds designed to grab the viewer's attention and hold it. The prologue can also be a hook if it's used to secure attention. Although the prologue is most often used in longer programs, the hook is frequently used in shorter pieces because there is little time available. The producer wants to grab the viewer's attention immediately. For this reason the hook usually contains the best visual material, even if it will be repeated later on.

The hook is commonly used in news stories, profiles, commercials, documentaries, and sales and promotional pieces. If we're profiling the circus coming to town, the hook will be a series of amazing performances. If we're documenting a conference, the hook will be selected, brief one-liners from the key speakers. If the program is a narrative, the hook can be some of the heightened action scenes cut together as a **montage** (a sequence of shots relating to the same theme).

The Background

The background is content devoted to presenting a historical, causal, or formative context to provide a perspective for the audience. It orients the viewer by communicating preliminary information that will be the basis of the primary content. HBO comedy specials frequently present a background profile of the featured comedian. The coverage of the Olympic Games shows the background of selected competitors.

Backgrounds are not always historical or based in the past. They can also provide the basis for cognitive or abstract content. For instance, in an educational program on DNA, or genetic codes, the background material might be a perspective on nature's diversity and interconnectedness. A department store's role-play video on friendly customer interaction may initially describe why lessons on the subject are needed. A discussion program, or public forum such as the kind Ted Koppel mediates, can background the topic under consideration by showing current events. To determine whether backgrounding is needed, ask yourself if there is any content the viewer might need to know to understand the communication message (or objective).

The Focus

The focus content is the primary content, or communication objective. The term *focus* presents the producer not only with a sense of what is primary but also with a reminder that that's where the audience's attention consistently belongs.

We often see programs that go off on tangents, such as in some television wildlife programs. The content jumps from the bird to the tiger to the monkey to the wasp to the sea lion and so forth. It's better to focus on a particular animal or at least a species, a set of behaviors certain animals have in common, or the delicate balance of an ecosystem—anything to bring the subject into focus.

Every program should have a variety of elements but it is crucial to constantly bring the audience back to the focus. Otherwise, you are randomly directing their attention. Instead, you should lead the audience purposefully from one essential point to the next essential point (you must justify everything) and finally bring them to your destination. The director's ability to move an audience's attention is the basis of electronic media's power. The communication objective equals the focal point.

The Action

Action is intrinsic to video. The action content is where people (or other elements) on the screen are doing something. You don't have to have a chase scene in your training program but I advise showing people involved in some activity. This could be moving objects from one place to another, following a process, or having the speakers or other participants move. Keep the frame active.

If what's in front of the camera is not moving, consider moving the camera, or at least vary its perspective by shooting from other angles and distances. Network documentaries use dollies to move along with the narrator, thereby changing the background reference. Industrial programs sometimes incorporate aerial footage. Music videos follow talent through myriad environments.

Although content is most often expressed verbally, the message is often revealed by action—or inaction. Let those in front of the camera demonstrate the content by their actions, in addition to or even instead of just talking about it.

The Repeat

A **repeat** is a recurring piece of content, which can be humorous, that cues the audience to content importance because it shows up again and again. One form of repeat is the "running gag," where humor is created because a funny phrase or action keeps returning.

With frame-store and motion control technology now commonplace in video production centers, the repeat is being used with great frequency. Music videos, video art, entertainment shows, animation formats, even kids' shows repeat selected scenes in rapid succession. This emphasizes the image. Sounds can also be repeated.

Because repeats can be sequenced very rapidly or can be spread out, they can be used to establish continuity within a sequence or throughout a program. Every year, on certain anniversaries of national significance, television networks repeat images of historical importance (the Kennedy assassinations, the moon landing). These are also a type of repeat.

The Setup

As the name implies, the **setup** involves content that prepares the viewer for a new direction. It can be a soft shift or a hard, emotional shift depending on the producer's purpose for that content area. Most programs include a variety of sub-topics that relate to the main theme. The setup occurs at the beginning of these subtopics and serves the same purpose as a topic sentence in paragraph writing. It introduces the new angle or direction and specifies how it relates to the program focus. An example is the magazine show format where the on-camera host sets up the context for the coming story. *20/20* and the others do this on every program. A nonbroadcast example is the discussion group or panel presentation where the moderator makes a transition from one subject to another, which requires some setup or explanation. These illustrate the soft approach.

A skillful dramatic director uses sights, sounds, and movement to set the audience up for a coming emotional experience in the hard approach. Horror and fright movies depend on the setup to provide contrast for the upcoming experience. Seeing the monster as the girl backs into it is not nearly as scary as watching her back up and not seeing the monster. Music, lighting, and acting combine to create anticipation (which is always more dramatic than knowing). When the director has the monster's hand creep around the girl's legs, the effect is highly charged.

The Reveal

The **reveal** allows only part of the content to unfold at a time. For instance, in a promotional video for a new-model car with design features never seen before, we're given small but exciting glimpses of the fender lines and the spinning wheel cover with a close-up of the leather upholstery stitching and the digital stereo. The producer reveals this a bit at a time (also using the setup) and then—crash cut— music up, the cover is pulled, the crowd gasps, the engine roars, the tires screech, and cut to the interior of the car with a beautiful woman wearing leather gloves and a flowing chiffon scarf.

A content reveal works best when it hides something. As with the setup, the producer strives to create *anticipation*—we want the viewer to want more. This kind of material makes television compelling because if you look away you might miss something. Of course, if you rely heavily on the reveal, there has to be a good reason to create audience expectation. You don't want to let the audience down. Ask yourself: Is there something about this content that can be revealed gradually that leads to a payoff?

The Payoff

The payoff is what the audience has been waiting for—the question is answered; success is achieved; the boy gets the girl; the sale is made; the jury's verdict is positive; the problem is solved; the conflict is over. It's the resolution of the setup. The payoff is always related to the problem or question that was set up earlier.

Although this implies that the payoff is toward the end of the program, we can also use it in the body of the program. For instance, we can set up viewers to anticipate a boring speech and then crash cut to a payoff—an exciting, tightly edited montage presenting a visual analogy of the points being made by the speaker.

An effective technique is to relate the video payoff to a "real-world" payoff. After screening the program, hand out T-shirts with the logo or design that was seen in the video. One company I've worked with has developed this technique into an art form. Their umbrellas, pens, flashlights, and other **promotional gifts** (to employees and clients) display the company logo. Their programming ties it all together into a major public relations effort. This is a gimmick, but people like it and tend to remember the video far beyond its play date.

The Transition

The **transition** moves the viewer's attention from one content area to another. We're all familiar with the way news anchor teams use clever verbal transitions to tie unrelated stories together. "And so the *search* goes on for more victims of the Alaskan avalanche—John." "Right Carol, and the *search* is on in Washington today, for the vacant seat in the Senate." Within ten seconds we've shifted attention from images of tragedy to ones of political opportunity. Although I use this as an example, I don't encourage this type of transition. It calls attention to itself and distracts attention from the focus—in this case, the stories. A more graceful transition would simply be a pause, then a cut to the other person, who begins his story. Another is to change the pictures on the screen and thereby cue the upcoming speaker.

Transitional content connects two scenes, segments, or stories, and it should, if possible, *relate* them. It serves as a bridge and should do so gracefully without calling attention to the shift in attention. Transitions work best when they maintain a steady flow of energy from A to B and show how the two relate. The audience should know they are at point B but should have little awareness of how they got there.

Certain transitional words and phrases can help:

Additionally	Again	Also	And then
Besides	Finally	Likewise	After all
Furthermore	Above all	In fact	That is
For this reason	Especially	However	Next

The Interlude

An **interlude** is a clean break, a pause, or a departure from the basic content to a different but related expression of it, including expectation of returning to it. Because video can be an entertainment medium, information and lecture-type programs often have some kind of entertainment content as a break from the serious, left-brain experience. The viewer's senses are refreshed, and he or she is then ready to focus again on words and/or numbers.

As a young filmmaker I observed a friend who made documentaries and was very skilled at interludes. In every program, no matter what the topic, he would have a talented local performer write and perform a song that illustrated the sequences of his program. I noticed the effectiveness of this device. On most projects I now carefully consider what entertainment value is possible within the program, realizing that the audience needs a break—especially if the program is twenty minutes or longer.

We've talked about just one kind of interlude but many others are possible—and they don't have to entertain. They just have to be a change of pace from the basic content.

The Flashback or Flashforward

A **flashback** consists of scenes or sequences of content that refer the viewer to a time in the past with respect to the present time of the program. We've seen this device so frequently there's no need to belabor it here. Just remember that the audience can get confused easily if the cues to the flashback or **flashforward** (fog, diffusion, different location) are not clear and consistent.

Language

A major aspect of program content is the spoken word. Language, as a symbol of our thoughts, is actually the way we first give our content form. Language is so common in our experience that we take it for granted. We pick up others' meanings so quickly that we tend to ignore what was actually said. But in video, where what is said is evaluated and remembered, you should use language accurately and clearly.

Although the subject of language is too vast to elaborate upon here, we should look at a few practical aspects to increase our awareness of language as a primary provider of stimulation and meaning. With every communication tool, the more we understand it, the better we can use it.

Specificity

"Street" vocabulary contains words that are overused and abused—"wow," "terrific," "cool," "great," "all right," for example—that don't carry meaning very well. In a structured program the verbal expression needs to *say something* with focus. Potent conversations come from direct and specific comments and replies, not a lot of stylistic verbiage. Reporters use language that is specific to describe an event or tell a story. Screenwriters emphasize directness and specificity as a way to promote focus, clarity, and emotional expression.

Statistics

Statistics provide a concrete expression of some quantifiable relationship. Many training and promotional videos use statistics seemingly just to impress people.

Consider this from a university admissions video: ". . . tuition increase over the previous year of 16%." But we ask: 16% of how much? They gave us only half the relationship. And how does that compare over a five-year period? If they don't want to give out their tuition cost, they shouldn't use the statistic. Always look for the relationship that is involved or implied when you use statistics.

Numbers can be manipulated, so if you choose to use them, show the entire relationship. And express it visually as well as verbally by showing numbers, graphs, or charts on the screen. Give viewers time to derive as much meaning from the information as possible. And then, when you know they've got it, cut to the next issue. Fatigue with statistics sets in quickly. Show the relationship(s) involved, convey the meaning (sometimes allowing audience interpretation), and move on.

The Spoken Word

We often see screen characters in conversation. When directing people to converse in front of a camera, or when writing the script, keep the audience in mind. If the conversation is dull, the audience will feel dull. If it's lively, witty, sarcastic, interesting, adversarial, or whatever, the viewers will empathically receive its emotion. Such dynamics are also very important in conversations in formats other than drama, especially where "real people" are in front of the camera, such as in training tapes, documentaries, and lectures.

The following maxims are from H. P. Grice's[2] *Logic and Conversation.* They are helpful directions to the nonprofessional talent when deciding what will be said on camera.

> Say no less than is necessary.
>
> Say no more than is necessary.
>
> Don't say what you don't believe.
>
> Don't speak without evidence.
>
> Be relevant.
>
> Don't be obscure.

These apply equally to dialogue and monologue situations, and I would add one more:

> Express the appropriate energy of the scene.

The *way* something is said is as if not more important than *what* is said. In drama, actors need to know their characters' attitude and motivation. But this also applies to nondramatic formats and in-house talent. Audiences pick up the screen character's attitude, temperament, and character. We even sense a speaker's hidden agenda. Audiences pick up a speaker's attitude not only from the words used but also from behavior and subtle nonverbal cues.

I once videotaped a corporate vice president who wanted to congratulate his managers on a job well done. The man had a "deadpan" personality and said everything with the same level (and lack) of enthusiasm. He said, "Great job," but he communicated "not bad."

After several retakes, we took a break. The director noticed the executive's golf bag in the corner and they got into a putting match on the carpet. We reset the shot as they played and, with the tape rolling, we got a shot of the vice president exclaiming "All right!" as he sank a ball in the cup. When cut into the final scene, this emotional expression played naturally. The words weren't what the script called for, but the message was.

Content Issues

· ·

As you are forming content ideas in your mind, you should address some key issues either before or as you begin to express your content ideas on paper.

Is This Content *Positioned?*

Positioning, as we noted earlier, ensures that what you have to say fits the pre-existing mind-set of the target audience so that there is either an easy acceptance of it or a positive association with it. For example, if we're using video to teach dog owners to train their pets, the target audience is dog owners. The communication objective is to teach these owners five basic techniques to discipline their dogs in order to promote the sale of a "sonic" leash (which makes a sound only dogs can hear). Every content element must deliver at least a portion of that objective.

We have many positioning questions. For example, what does the target audience already think about dog training? What image do they have of the training, especially the use of choker leashes? Does the practice look harsh? Does it seem like it's painful for the animal? Do they wish there was a better way? The content can then be structured to communicate that the method is comfortable for the dog, requiring no harsh treatment, and that the ultra-high frequency is a harmless cue to the dog.

Should we do a montage showing how the sonic leash is manufactured? Would that work in this context? Does it relieve the owner's concern? Does it help sell the leashes? Perhaps, but I would exclude it because the audience's interest is primarily in the dog and how it will learn and not in the craftsmanship of the device. They want to know whether the device works, how it works, why it's better, how long the batteries will last, and whether it's been successfully tested.

Positioning relates to what Dale Carnegie said: "Speak in terms of the other person's interest."

Is the Content *True?*

Whenever you read a script, after each statement, stop and ask whether it's true. From my understanding, is this statement an accurate expression? This relates to the validity of the content.

Another aspect of truth concerns the validity of the presentation. Is the edited juxtaposition of scenes an accurate representation of a relationship? When it comes to dramatic material, is this character true to his or her circumstances? Do the characters live up to the viewer's standard of what is appropriate? Does what they say ring true? Advertising researchers refer to this as **"verisimilitude,"** an essential quality of "rightness." We're familiar with the injunction "To thine own self be true." For the video producer we might well add, "And don't violate your audience's truth in the process."

What's the *Evidence* and *Reasoning?*

When you make assertions, they must be supported by evidence. Reasoning—in particular, the accuracy, validity, and relevance of the supporting arguments—goes a long way toward effecting genuine attitude change, especially with audiences that have a higher intelligence level.[3] Ask yourself *what* makes the message true. What is the basis for its truth? Is it because you happen to believe it to be true or because most of the people in your field believe it? Or is your message based on research or personal experience? And does the message follow logically from the evidence?

In English classes we learn that reasoning is a process of offering major and minor support for a position. If the support relates well, is logically presented, and indicates a powerful causal relationship, then a case is well made. Because video and television attempt to condense messages into smaller time frames, fallacious reasoning can easily creep in.

Here we'll describe some types of unacceptable forms of argument including **false analogy, circular arguments,** and **equivocation.**

False analogy   The **analogy** offers a superficial or accidental similarity between the items being compared: "If Sally can paint this well after three lessons, so can you." Not necessarily: Sally may be more mature or may have other skills that enabled her to learn quickly. The evidence that one can paint merely by taking three lessons is insufficient and fallacious.

Circular argument   The evidence is based on the validity of other evidence, based on the validity of other evidence, and so on. "We know this technique works because our field reps report that their clients say it does." So where does it end? More reasonable evidence would be reports from users of the product or service, citing them by name or presenting them on camera in an unprompted testimonial.

Equivocation   This false reasoning is based on a loose or ambiguous definition of terms. "I use this product at home and I can tell you, it lasts a long time." How long is long? How did you use it at home? If you want to make statements like these, define the terms, make the usage specific: "I used this product to paint and seal my basement floor four years ago and the floor hasn't cracked or peeled in that time. We use the basement a lot and it still looks like new."

"What is" and "what ought"   This reasoning suggests that something is right simply because it exists. "Sales of contraceptives in the past two years have increased X%, and our product has led the way." An increase in sales in itself is not a good reason for using contraceptives. Nor is it a good reason to buy that particular product. Just because more people bought it is no reason to believe that everyone should.

Assuming the whole to be like the parts or vice versa   What is true for one person may not be true for all and, conversely, what is true of the group may not be true of the individual. This kind of fallacy has been the basis for much racial misunderstanding. "When you need people to work in high places, you should find some American Indians. The TV stations in our area had their towers erected by a family of Indians. They did a great job." In fact, many TV towers were erected by Indians who specialize in that field. But that in no way argues for the validity that this is work any Indian can or would do, much less be good at. Other ethnic groups, and people with no particular ethnic identity, can also do this kind of work. People are individuals first. To attribute their work preferences to their ethnic heritage is unjustified.

Is the Content *Balanced?*

A message that presents a singular viewpoint is one-sided; it stands alone. A balanced message, however, is two-sided; it presents both sides of a message. Balance is especially relevant for presentations involving issues, ideas, and perspectives—presentations likely to be in a lecture-type format. Research results show that the one-sided approach works better for audiences who already agree with the message.[4] The balanced, two-sided approach is more effective in instances where the audience does not already agree with the message or where there is uncertainty about their agreement.

   This same relationship holds for advertisers. One-sided commercials work well when the target market already widely accepts the product. But if the competition is equally strong, or the product is not firmly established, then a more balanced approach is suggested.[5] For other formats, such as documentaries, producers may also decide that, within the program, certain parts of the content deserve balance while others do not. And in dramas, the story line may involve elements that require balance as the plot unfolds in order for the audience to understand or better appreciate a character.

What's the *Context?*

One of the most significant questions that producers increasingly ignore is the program's context. Every expression, message, and communication has a context, a framework that explains *why* the source is communicating and what's behind the expression. The context itself communicates. To hide this information from the audience is a serious mistake because their trust is heavily based on the perception of the source's motive for communicating in the first place.

The context is not always, and doesn't need to be, overtly expressed. The context of every political commercial is to sell a candidate to the voters. But look closely at the context behind the ad. Some producers choose to show flag waving, brass bands, large crowds, and celebrity endorsements. The message is that the candidate is a proud citizen and an outgoing person who is not afraid to deal with people. Ads that more modestly show the candidate in community meetings, factory settings, and community planning sessions express a different context. The context communicates that this person is on the side of the common person; she or he understands the problems of the constituency and listens to their needs. These contexts indicate the values of the communicators and how they see the role (and strength) of the candidate. The visual and aural images these producers use to communicate point directly to the context they have created, one they believe the audience will accept.

We've all seen programs that didn't work because the context was out of sync with our own thinking. When the context is not clear, the audience will assume one, so don't risk an incorrect assumption.

Context also relates to the audience's processing of meaning. The target audience will perceive your subject matter in relation to the available contextual framework or background in order to determine just how important your message is. "The meaning of anything depends on its surroundings."[6] The weekday news anchor is perceived to have more status, for instance, than the weekend anchor. The actor who is on the screen the most is perceived to be the one with whom to identify. The first news story is perceived to be the most important happening of the day, and so on. Through these contextual relationships, we come to terms with how message elements relate to one another, and we derive sense from them.

I like to use the example of Barbra Streisand's hour-long HBO special *One Voice* to illustrate contextualizing. Every element related to and supported the context of world peace. The songs she selected, their words, and her unique styling took on new meanings as a result of the context. The "live" audience and viewers at home seemed to see that the content and the context were in perfect accord. Her motive was not only *clear* but *appreciated*. I believe that this is the secret to gaining access to the viewer's heart and mind.

Is the Message *Clear?*

Clarity aids understanding. As noted earlier, clarity comes from being very specific (not general), showing and/or telling with accuracy, and, if possible, obtaining feedback from the source in order to clarify even further. Advertisers say that "specifics outsell generalities" and "statistics don't sell."

You can't be too clear. Never fear that, because you're being clear, the receivers will judge you to be simplistic. But if they did, they would nonetheless have gotten your message. A good rule of thumb is to design programs so your parents would get the message. Not that your parents are naive, they simply often have a more practical viewpoint as well as some distance from your project.

Who *Benefits?*

People view programs for some personal benefit. We often forget this and design content for our own benefit, as I did with *The Tender Clay.* It's fun to use computer graphics and other effects, but if they don't really contribute to the benefit of the viewer, the effort and expense are wasted. The content may or may not overtly communicate what benefit the audience will get by their acceptance of your message, but you should try to make sure that they feel they have benefited. If they feel their time was well spent, they may recommend the experience to others.

Is It *Visual?*

Video means "I see." If you want your viewers to see what you mean, show them, don't just tell them. Otherwise, use radio or print.

Is It *Memorable?*

Extensive research by psychologists and advertisers has been done on this simple question: What factors make a message more memorable? The following is a sampling of some of the findings:

- Learning is best recalled in the environment or conditions under which it occurred: Things learned under water are best recalled under water;[7] things learned while happy are better recalled when happy;[8] and things learned in a particular room are better recalled in that room[9] (that is, if possible, study in the room where you'll take an exam).
- For recall of products advertised in commercials, emotional approaches showed significantly better results than informational approaches. And the stronger the emotion, the greater the effects on memory.[10]
- "When exposed to material, people are likely, without prompting, to organize it and remember it according to how it makes them feel, especially if it makes them feel good."[11]
- "A cogent message [pertinent, relevant] is easier to encode [take in] and later recall than a garbled, ambiguous message."[12]
- Message repetition (as opposed to a single presentation) leads to better learning and retention.[13]
- "Attitudes persist because people remember the substance of the conclusion of the message, or perhaps their own thoughts about the message, rather than the specific arguments that are contained in the message."[14]
- "Nonsense materials—words that don't mean anything—are most quickly forgotten. Meaningful materials, especially facts and concepts related to a person's previous structure of knowledge and values, are least forgotten."[15]

The Creative Process

Where does content really come from? How do we get ideas for programs? What makes one idea much more expressive than another? And how do we generate these ideas? All these questions involve creativity.

In our product-oriented society, we tend to see creativity as something to pursue or acquire. But it's not something we have or do, it's what we *are* by virtue of being human. Whether or not we choose to apply it, *everyone* is endowed with creative potential. Some just choose to exercise it more by finding opportunities to be expressive. The more opportunity, the more creativity will be expressed—and the opposite is true.

Before offering two techniques for you to express your innate creativity, here is an analogy I first heard from my friend and colleague Stan Grindstaff, a producer who also lectures on creativity and professional self-presentation.

Creativity: A Natural Process Model

Consider a project, such as a video production, as having seasons, stages it will go through that display different climates. To illustrate the characteristics of each stage, we'll use symbolic terms: the water cycle, when the project is very fluid and stillness prevails; the air cycle, when the idea or concept is born but as yet up in the air; the earth cycle, when the content is solidified—the time for action; and the fire cycle, when the results emerge and are released.

Figure 8.1 shows that, with respect to any undertaking, the creative process begins with no particular idea. This is the cool, *winter* stage. *Water* is its symbol. Like icebergs, things move slowly, ideas are not yet formed, there is uncertainty but nonetheless a gathering of factors. This is the time to *listen,* the time to be *still,* the time to *conceive* by being open and receptive to ideas, directions, or perspectives relating to the possibility of a program and/or its content. The winter part of the cycle requires introspection, intuition, and evaluation (right-brain functioning). If you don't know what to do, don't do anything—just be grateful for what shows up. If [and when] you know what to do, if you sense a flow, go with it.

When the idea shows up fully formed, you have entered the *spring* season, symbolized by *air.* The climate is warmer; frozen processes begin to thaw because the idea has germinated. One moves from stillness to making connections with others, seeking agreement with them, enlisting them, building synergy or even perhaps resonance. Related ideas flow more quickly; the direction becomes clear as gestation occurs. Imagine and visualize what it will be like when it works. Move with the flow, gathering agreement as you go.

The gathering of ideas, agreement, and resources throughout the spring leads to the season of expression, the *summer.* Its symbol is the *earth,* where ideas and content become solidified and grounded in concrete expression. The form appears; the expression is born. This is the time for action, the preproduction and production phases in which creativity is fully brought to bear on the task. This is the time to build the presentation, which requires achievement, analytical thinking, and conscious attention to detail. Do the obvious; make it happen.

WINTER	SPRING	SUMMER	FALL
WATER	AIR	EARTH	FIRE
WATER/AIR/EARTH/FIRE	WATER/AIR/EARTH/FIRE	WATER/AIR/EARTH/FIRE	WATER/AIR/EARTH/FIRE
STILLNESS GATHER FACTORS (SETTING)	CONTACT KNOW AGREEMENT (MIND & HEART)	PROACT DO THE OBVIOUS (MOVE, SPEAK, SHOOT)	CREATION RESULTS (SHARE & RELEASE)
NO IDEA?	IDEA!	EXPRESSION!!	CELEBRATION!!!
COOL ➡ WARM ➡ HOT			
LISTEN	IMAGINE	PRESENT	PAUSE
CONCEPTION	GESTATION	BIRTH	GROWTH
TRUTH	LIFE	FORM	LOVE
BEING		ACHIEVING	
RIGHT BRAIN		LEFT BRAIN	
INTUITIVE		ANALYTICAL	
SUBCONSCIOUS		CONSCIOUS	

FIGURE 8.1
The Natural Process Model of Creativity
(Used by permission of Stan Grindstaff.)

The final season is the *fall,* symbolized by *fire,* when the project is finished. The program is ready for release to its intended audience. There is celebration in its completion and quality. This is not a time of completion as might be expected, but rather a time for assimilating growth that results from having moved through a process. Share, celebrate, and release the good work.

This model has been very helpful to me because it puts certain activities into a time frame to orient the progress of a project. It helps maintain perspective and reduce frustration and impatience when things don't seem to be working out. These cycles also help me balance several projects at the same time. I always know which project requires action and which requires contemplation or planning.

Techniques for Creating Content

There are lots of ways to stimulate creative thinking and exercise our creative potential. (See the recommended reading list at the end of the chapter.) I've found a few techniques to be especially useful in the context of designing program content.

Previsualization   This refers to the practice of mentally seeing the program and its elements before its production. **Visualization** is the skill required to do this. We all have the capability, but some have developed it more than others simply by virtue of frequent practice. A simple exercise that helps us begin visualizing is to close your eyes and hold out your hand. Then, imagine an apple in your hand and get as specific as you can when seeing its size, shape, color, and other visual characteristics. Do this with several objects. Then take the next step—imagine a watermelon in front of you in the same way, and then go inside the melon and see what it looks like from that perspective. How many seeds are there? How big are they? What is the texture like? What colors are present? Finally, do this with a more complex object such as a typewriter, computer, or airplane. With your eyes closed, go inside the object to see and describe what it's like. You don't have to be accurate about what's inside—it's perfectly legitimate to see a candle inside your computer if you want to—the challenge is to form as clear a mental image as possible of whatever you choose to visualize.

Be sure to do this exercise in a space and during a time when you won't be distracted. Relaxed concentration is necessary, which can only happen when you are still, comfortable, and undistracted.

Now, how do we visualize an entire program? See its parts, in order. What if you don't have any idea of what the elements are? Trust that your creative imagination will spontaneously create these elements *as you visualize* them. When we turn our attention to something internally, our imagination turns on automatically to begin creating meanings. The mind does this because we think in images. If meanings don't come from external stimuli, we switch over to the internal source and get stimulation from the imagination. Even the words we speak trigger pictures first. When I say *round,* for instance, you may not see the letters r-o-u-n-d, but you may begin seeing round things.

To continue the exercise: Become quiet, close your eyes (preferably in a darkened room), with a pad and pencil in front of you. Write the title of the program at the top of the page. Imagine yourself sitting alone in a beautifully appointed Hollywood screening room. See the lights go down. Then let your imagination fade into the first scene, either the opening or the prologue.

Your mind quickly presents scene after scene, sometimes faster than they could possibly appear in any program. Just watch and let it flow—don't evaluate or criticize—and as you can, write "bullet" words in outline form on your notepad to describe what you're seeing. Don't pay attention to details unless they seem important. For now, just put down on paper what you see, in sequence. Attend mostly to the imagery and sounds.

We all have an internal meter to tell us whether something is working. It's called *emotion.* As our imagination presents us with material, we become emotional. If we don't like what we see, it's a sign that this particular direction is probably not working. Stop. Draw a line under the notes you have just taken. Begin again with a fresh fade up and your imagination will put on a different "reel" for your consideration. When the material works, you'll know it because you'll get excited. When that happens, keep going. Alternate between these decisions to stop, restart, and move forward until the entire program lays itself out on your pad in outline form.

When we close our eyes for a long time, however, our minds get the message that it's time to go to sleep. This frequently happens when the imaginary program is dull. When I sit down I decide whether to do just the program opening or additional sections. If I find I keep drawing stop lines, I'll stop and forget it for a while so I can come back to it fresh.

I can often stay awake and keep the visualization going longer by deciding ahead of time that I'm going to imagine the best material I can. By getting excited in advance, I find my will challenges my imagination to pull out its best material.

Brainstorming   This is a technique done with a group for the purpose of generating a *quantity* of ideas. **Brainstorming** has five primary rules: (1) make no comments as ideas come up, (2) get as many ideas as possible, (3) stay with ideas only, (4) build on ideas already given, and (5) at the end, choose the best.

After presenting the rules to the participants and encouraging the free flow of ideas, offer a "seed" question relating to the content: What are ways to express the communication objective? Then let everyone just say their ideas as they come. No idea is too weird or ridiculous at this point; you'll evaluate later on. Encourage "piggybacking," where ideas pick up on previous ones. Have fun with it. Spontaneity balances equifinality, and brainstorming encourages spontaneity.

Overcoming inertia   *Inertia* is the tendency of a body at rest to stay at rest. How can we get motivated to express our creativity in the first place? The other side of this principle is that a body in motion stays in motion. If you can begin an activity—anything that gets your blood circulating faster than normal—you will have a tendency to continue doing it. (This is also a way of overcoming depression.) The hard part is the discipline to take that first step but, once taken, each future step is easier because there's momentum. This is the mechanics of motivation.

In terms of the psychology of motivation, it's essential to have a *reason* for wanting to move (or create) in the first place. The stronger that reason, the more willpower behind it, the greater the motivation. Here is a helpful electrical principle: "Energy moves along the path of least resistance." So move your energy in a direction of positive and creative performance.

One powerful technique involves thinking about your personal purpose, how you are contributing to the world, what you are here to do. Again, in a quiet state, make an inventory of your unique gifts. What talents, abilities, and special skills do you have? List them. Then mentally scan whatever corporate, community, or world problems you think are the most important and list these. Focus on the level where you would most like to make a difference. Your mind will automatically begin making relationships between what needs to be done and what you can bring to the situation.

In his book *Higher Creativity,* on stimulating breakthrough insights, Willis Harman states that

at the most fundamental level, the basic problem of modern society is a crisis of meaning. . . . One of mankind's most powerful needs is for life to have meaning, to make sense.[16]

Summary

In this chapter we have addressed several issues relative to the development of program content. The first was understanding some of the more common types of content including information, description, narration, question, conversation, and performance. Each of these is appropriate to different communication objectives, and each carries a different context, which we also discussed.

Second, we examined several content structural devices— parts of a program that, by their placement, determine how specific content is used. The "hook" grabs the audience's attention. The "background" gives appropriate reference. The "focus" centers the viewer's attention on the most important theme or issue. The "action" expresses content in other than verbal ways, showing viewers rather than telling them. The "repeat" reinforces specific content by virtue of its occasional, repeated appearance. The "setup" gets the audience ready for something. And the "payoff" is the resolution or other satisfying experience for which the audience was set up. The "transition" moves viewers gracefully from one sensibility to another without calling attention to the process. The "interlude" provides a break in the experience to give freshness and a change of pace. And the "flashback" takes the audience back to a past event or situation in order to establish content relevant to the present. Because so much content is expressed verbally, we also looked at the need to be specific, the use of statistics, and observations about the spoken word.

We then considered certain content issues that contribute to effective presentation. Is the content positioned so it blends with preexisting audience perceptions? Is it true? Are the words and their meanings accurate? And in the sense of verisimilitude: Does the content ring true, have an air of rightness about it? What is the evidence and reasoning involved to support statements, perspectives, or arguments? Is the content balanced or does it express a one-sided perspective? What's the context—why is the producer communicating about this message? Is the message clearly expressed? Who benefits from its acceptance—the producer, the audience, or both? Is the content a visual as well as aural experience? Finally, is the content memorable? Will the communication objective be retained after the showing?

We concluded with an examination of the creative process—the generation of content ideas and images. We discussed an analogy to the seasons of nature—winter, spring, summer, and fall—to show how every project has its phases and appropriate times for quiet and activity.

To conclude, we examined three techniques for developing creativity. Visualization, most often an individual technique, requires going inside oneself, diving into the depths of one's subconscious and superconscious to bring up possible images. A group activity, "brainstorming," pools mental resources to generate a volume of ideas so the best among them can be selected. Finally, we discussed the technique of taking a "gifts inventory" to overcome psychological inertia. This involves a comparison of one's personal gifts (talents, abilities, skills) with perceived needs in one's organization, community, nation, or world. Seeing how much we are needed is a strong motivation to act.

The content we choose and how we use it communicate.

Notes

1. Wells, William D., "Lectures and Dramas," in *Cognitive and Affective Responses to Advertising,* ed. Patricia Cafferata and Alice M. Tybout (Lexington, MA: Lexington Books, 1989), 13. Used by permission of publisher.
2. Grice, H. P., "Logic and Conversation," in *Syntax and Semantics III: Speech Acts,* ed. P. Cole and J. L. Morgan (New York: Academic Press, 1975), 41–58.
3. Kline, J. A., "Interaction of Evidence and Reader's Intelligence on the Effects of Short Messages." *Quarterly Journal of Speech* 55 (1969): 407–413.
4. Lumsdaine, A. A., and I. L. Janis, "Resistance to 'Counterpropaganda' Produced by One-Sided and Two-Sided 'Propaganda' Presentations." *Public Opinion Quarterly* 17 (1953): 311–318.
5. Faison, E. W. J., "Affectiveness of One-Sided and Two-Sided Mass Communications and Advertising." *Public Opinion Quarterly* 25 (1961): 468–469.
6. Lerbinger, Otto, *Designs for Persuasive Communication* (Englewood Cliffs, NJ: Prentice-Hall, 1972), 23.
7. Godden, D. R., and A. D. Baddley, "Context-Dependent Memory in Two Natural Environments: On Land and Underwater." *British Journal of Psychology* 66 (1975): 325–332.
8. Bower, G. H., and P. R. Cohen, "Emotional Influences in Memory and Thinking: Data and Theory," in *Affect and Cognition,* ed. M. S. Clarke and S. T. Fiske (Hillsdale, NJ: Lawrence Erlbaum, 1982), 291–332.
9. Smith, S. M., A. Glenberg, and R. A. Bjork, "Environmental Context and Human Memory." *Memory and Cognition* 6 (1978): 342–353.
10. Thorson, Esther, and Marian Friestad, "The Effects of Emotion on Episodic Memory for Television Commercials," in *Cognitive and Affective Responses to Advertising,* ed. Patricia

Cafferata and Alice M. Tybout (Lexington, MA: Lexington Books, 1989), 314.

11. Isen, Alice M., "Some Ways in Which Affect Influences Cognitive Processes: Implications for Advertising and Consumer Behavior," in *Cognitive and Affective Responses to Advertising,* ed. Patricia Cafferata and Alice M. Tybout (Lexington, MA: Lexington Books, 1989), 110.

12. Anderson, J. R., *Cognitive Psychology and Its Implications* (San Francisco: W. H. Freeman, 1980), 310.

13. Wilson, W., and H. Miller, "Repetition, Order of Presentation, and Timing of Arguments and Measures as Determinants of Opinion Change." *Journal of Personality and Social Psychology* 9 (1968): 184–188.

14. Petty, R. E., and J. T. Cacioppo, "Issue Involvement Can Increase or Decrease Persuasion by Enhancing Message-Relevant Cognitive Responses." *Journal of Personality and Social Psychology* 37 (1979): 1915–1926.

15. Lerbinger, Otto, *Designs for Persuasive Communication* (Englewood Cliffs, NJ: Prentice-Hall, 1972), 132.

16. Harman, Willis, and Howard Rheingold, *Higher Creativity: Liberating the Unconscious for Breakthrough Insights* (New York: Jeremy Tarcher, 1984), 183.

Suggested Readings

Bogart, Leo. *Strategy in Advertising: Matching Media and Messages to Markets and Motivations,* 2nd ed. Lincolnwood, IL: NTC Business Books, 1986.

Gawain, Shakti. *Creative Visualization.* New York: Bantam Books, 1982.

Marsh, Patrick. *Messages That Work: A Guide to Communication Design.* Englewood Cliffs, NJ: Educational Technology Publications, 1983.

McKim, Robert H. *Experiences in Visual Thinking,* 2nd ed. Pacific Grove, CA: Brooks/Cole, 1980.

Osborne, Alex. *Applied Imagination.* New York: Charles Scribner's, 1953.

Samuels, Mike. *Seeing with the Mind's Eye.* New York: Random House and the Bookworks, 1980.

CHAPTER 9

Content Organization

· ·

Organization is not only a binding force holding all of the various parts and aspects together, but it is a relating force as well, for the structure and patterns of organization relate the diversity of elements and constituents together in meaningful ways.[1]

ur systems approach suggests that organization is a major factor in managing technologies, but it's even more significant for developing content because it is the pathway of the viewer's attention.

Content organization leads viewers through a series of experiences, directing their minds and emotions to the intended destination, calling attention to this detail and that overview. When the organization "carries" the message along well, viewers are more likely to "get" (and accept) the communication objective because they have been brought to it logically. The journey makes sense.

In Chapter 2, "The Production Process," we saw how a production moves forward through the various stages of concept, outline, treatment, and script. As the design and preproduction phases progress, more information comes in, ideas become solidified, options and possibilities become clearer, and our picture of the program begins to fill out. Content organization is intensive in these phases, but it doesn't stop there; it's not a one-time activity.

It's a creative *skill* used constantly, well beyond the writing of the script. So the issues discussed in this chapter apply to all stages, even to the production and postproduction phases (because editing is mostly content organization). This is why the chapter topics in this book are not arranged according to the sequential steps of a project. Instead, we focus on a variety of communication, perceptual, critical thinking, organization, and technical skills that are needed to use video effectively overall.

A writer puts content into the script in a certain pattern. The director may interpret that script differently and change the order. The camera operator may suggest to the director that, instead of a wide shot, the sequence should open on a series of close-in pans, resulting in another order. And when the producer gets to the editing console, an entirely different decision may be made as a result of seeing an even better way to arrange the scenes. The approach to becoming an effective producer is not to segment the organizational process into discrete activities but to *develop the skills mentioned above* so that, whenever one is in the process, the quality of one's consciousness and creativity will make the difference between mediocrity and excellence.

In this chapter we'll look at principles of organization, some of which you may recognize from high school English, literature, or writing classes. These conventions are intended only as guidelines—there is plenty of room for creative experimentation and combinations. Sometimes breaking the rules is appropriate, but if you do, you should have a good reason.

Putting Things in Order

. . . .

The producer-director's (or writer's) power to direct the viewer's attention is through content organization. We lead the viewer from point A to point Z, manipulating his or her attention using images and sounds. Video can also employ the Socratic method (directed questioning), which guides viewers step by step to a destination (communication objective) by asking and eventually resolving a series of logical questions.

In a murder mystery, for example, viewers get clues selectively, to pique their interest, some of which lead to erroneous judgments and dead ends. The producer wants to direct, or misdirect, us so the ending will be a surprise. Is it more fun getting there (the unfolding of the story) or finding out who did it (the climax)? In the end, all the questions are answered and meaning and order are restored. Audiences experience an "aha," from satisfaction that the resolution logically fits the questions.

The producer takes viewers down a specific thought-content path (through the program's organization) to most effectively provide a logical and emotional experience. And viewers seem to arrive at the destination on their own. As before, the more that is known about those being led (the audience), the easier it is to design a path that effectively gets them to your destination.

I was at a meeting where the director plotted out an emotional flowchart, a graphic representation of what viewers would feel as the program progressed, for the production team. This producer intended to create empathy by putting on the screen what he wanted the audience to feel. He presented a format for a half-hour fashion/entertainment program that was full of emotional peaks and valleys, all for the purpose of creating the final "high" to leave the audience with the feeling related to the communication objective (to get viewers to shop at a certain department store). The technique worked, and I have used this emotional flowchart since I first saw it (see Chapter 14).

Alfred Hitchcock was a master of this technique. He meticulously plotted the audience's emotional state throughout every sequence of every film he made.

Content organization has four primary components: unity, development, organization, and continuity.

Unity

· ·

Unity means that elements work together to support one major theme, idea, or experience. It means that a subject is treated consistently throughout the entire program. The piece then has "integrity" and is true to the central idea—the communication objective.

To achieve unity, stick to the main idea. Each sequence, or scene, can have its own direction, but it should still be related to the primary theme, and the relationship should be clear. Often it's good to have the actor or narrator simply state the objective directly. At other times it may be more appropriate to submerge the objective into a monologue, song, or interview response.

Unity is also related to the experience of the program as a whole. Remember, the viewer will retain an overall impression, not the details, facts, and statistics. Therefore, most special interest and commercial producers work hard to leave audiences with one *memorable* impression.

Journalist Bill Moyers's many works provide an excellent example of unity. Typically, at the beginning of his programs, he presents some music and fast-paced images of the subject matter (the hook), and then he comes on screen (called a "stand-up," even when he is sitting down). He tells viewers why the subject is of interest by giving them a brief, often illustrated, background. Then he provides details that relate to the theme, usually in historical or chronological order.

In his series *The Power of Myth,* with Joseph Campbell, Moyers organized the content by the complexity of the ideas. The simplest ideas come first, then the more complex, with each step built on the language and concepts already presented. Each program's theme relates to the series as a whole. Usually at the beginning and at the end of each program he reminds viewers how that particular program is related to the whole series by using a generic open and close. Then at the end of each program, Mr. Moyers does a final stand-up (a framing device) and summarizes to "set" the impression of the objective in our minds. The visuals and other material throughout the body of the program build an impression. This impression is made very explicit at the end, in case someone missed it. He achieves unity in that every element of the program relates to the theme, the theme is clear, and a lasting impression is firmly established.

At a very practical level, unity of program content requires unity of purpose among the producers and crew. As we discussed earlier, one of the primary purposes of having a script or storyboard of a program is so everyone involved can see the program as a whole. Professional script readers want to see the unity in a piece in the first ten pages. The opening must establish a context, introduce the primary character(s), set the situation in time and space, create the conflict, and suggest the theme of the story. And frequently investors make financing or funding decisions based on a reading of the script or treatment, so the vision must be apparent throughout.

Because video is a social medium and production occurs over an extended period of time, you should frequently remind everyone (including yourself) of the focus. This becomes challenging when someone else comes up with a focus that everyone likes better or when an interview moves off into a more interesting area (than was your intention). At the outset of a production, be sure that you and another key person are firmly committed to the communication objective. To shift objectives in midproduction is to diffuse, confuse, and potentially destroy the purpose.

Further, when a project does not have adequate funding, there are other threats. If people are compensated poorly or not at all, they may have difficulty staying attuned to the objective over an extended period of time. They will have other interests and obligations. Commitment to the objective is vital. In major productions the budget and production scale create high intensity over a brief period of time so people are either on the same track or off the production.

A focus that's too broad can also weaken unity. When the content is very general, or covers too large a topic, unity suffers. To maintain unity, *limit the subject and sharpen the focus*. It must be clear to viewers that what they are watching is a program about X and not X, Y, and Z. Clarity in the communication objective is helpful for limiting and focusing.

Subject:

Music (too broad)

Rock music (still too broad)

Rock music of the 1980s (better)

Female rock musicians of the 1980s (even better)

Focus:

It's enjoyable (too broad)

Has had an effect (still too broad)

Made an impact on teens (better)

Clear objective:

To show the impact on teens of female rock musicians of the 1980s

Examples of weak focus:

Air pollution *is a big problem.*

Marketing *is important.*

David Copperfield *is a great magician.*

Crystals *can be effective tools for healing.*

Nutrition *is a serious subject.*

The elderly *have many problems.*

To turn these into themes having greater unity, we must limit the subject and sharpen the focus:

To demonstrate that air pollution in Los Angeles takes many forms.

To show how higher profits are created by shifting from product to market orientations.

To show how David Copperfield designs his own magic tricks.

To show how quartz crystals facilitate healing with the mind.

To offer current nutrition facts and tips for teens.

To prove that being over 70 doesn't mean you're too old to contribute to society.

These examples would not make good titles, but they are good examples of communication objectives because each holds together as one central idea, issue, or experience. Whether one's purpose is to entertain, inform, inspire, motivate, or sell, the process of limiting and sharpening the focus results in greater unity of the overall program.

Development

· ·

Development refers to the way the subject matter is handled throughout a program. A program progresses by clarifying, illustrating, and proving points that support the communication objective. Each point is made and then developed. In a documentary development contains informational elements (evidence, demonstration, testimonial) that support the subject. In a drama development includes identifying the characters, showing the situations in which they are involved, carrying out the conflict, and moving the story forward through action and events. In a training tape development gives details and instruction often by using examples, techniques, and role-playing. Development both elaborates and validates the communication objective.

Going back to the Socratic method of directed questioning, development contains proof of the ideas, concepts, and experiences provided. It supports the answers to the questions in the audience's mind. It proves that the theme has validity by showing why it works. It's not enough to make a claim; viewers also want evidence proving the claim to be true. If we want the audience to accept our communication objective, we must provide good development because this is how we state our case. It's the body of the program, usually occupying the most time.

General and Specific Treatments

Generalized content carries few details. It makes broad claims, provides an overview, and pulls things together in simplistic ways. A wide shot of race cars on a track denotes "racing," whereas a follow shot of one car on the track denotes "a specific racer," also generally suggesting a race. Since the early films, directors have organized scenes that begin with a wide shot to establish the environment, then a medium shot, which brings the situation closer, and then the close-up, which puts the audience into more personal contact with the subject.

This sequence of wide, medium, close-up, and extreme close-up shots is not only camera directions, it is also the technique directors use to move the audience's attention from the general to the particular. A scene that begins with a rapidly spinning and screeching tire exemplifies the particular. A scene that begins with a vehicle seen wide to show police shooting at it exemplifies the general. Personal preference dictates which you choose. As insurance, directors will often shoot several wide, medium, and close-up angles, providing the editor with as many cutting options as possible.

The established video convention is to move from the general to the particular. Open with a wide shot of the city to establish where the characters are; dissolve or cut to a medium shot to specify which part of the city or a particular place such as a restaurant; then dissolve or cut to a close-up to show the characters seated at a table. Use extreme close-ups (ECUs) to direct the viewer to a very specific object or area, thereby giving it importance. With people, use the ECU to move viewers into the actor's intimate space to emphasize expressions, especially when there is strong emotion in the eyes or in other facial features. Good camera operators instinctively zoom in (no matter what the program format) when the talent's emotion increases. As the emotion subsides, it's time to widen out.

This progression works because viewers want to know where the situation is in time and space; it orients them for the details to follow. They want to see the broad environment and circumstance before seeing the facts in their bare, more isolated form. Using words, images, or both, the technique of cutting fom the general to the particular is the **deductive** arrangement (from the Latin prefix *de,* meaning "away from," and the verb *ducere,* "to lead"). We lead the viewer's attention from one place to another for specific reasons.

Jazz music also follows a deductive arrangement. Someone begins a theme and then each player performs a variation on it, individually expressing it. Most sitcoms and made-for-television movies use this method because it works well for programs with time-ordered plots.

The opposite technique leads audiences from the specific to the general and is referred to as the **inductive** arrangement (Latin *in,* "into," plus *ducere,* "to lead"). It is not common in video but it is used occasionally in sequences in which the producer wants to direct the viewer's attention to details. For instance, in some documentaries the focus begins on one person and then becomes generalized from that person's situation.

We did a documentary on kidney transplants by opening the program with a woman eating a hamburger. The narration voice-over (with music) said, "Mrs. Peterson is eating salt on her hamburger today. For most of us, no big deal, but Mrs. Peterson has never had salt on her hamburger before. She was born with kidney disease. Two weeks ago Mrs. Peterson had a kidney transplant, and it has changed her life-style dramatically." We then went into the generic program open and commercials, coming back to trace Mrs. Peterson's steps toward surgery. The development showed her experiences and life-style, then gradually moved into the general—other people who suffer from kidney disorders. This worked well because people like to identify with an individual.

In this case, the specific was a symbol for the focus of our program. Had we used the deductive method, we would have begun the program with an exterior of the hospital and then followed Mrs. Peterson into surgery.

In many dramatic presentations the inductive mode has been used to good effect. Filmmakers show us long and laborious pans over the contents of a person's room, laboratory, or the like. From these items we learn something about the leading character. The opening of *To Kill a Mockingbird* is a classic example.

The inductive arrangement works well in situations where the development establishes a pattern, using the individual or a small element as a way to set it up. The following are context statements demonstrating some ways to think about deductive and inductive developments:

Deductive Development (general to particular)

- Ice skating (general) is both an art and a science and here are the reasons (particular) why . . .
- Company X (general) manufactures and distributes quality products (particular), which include . . .
- Child abuse (general) is a social problem with several interrelated causes (particular) including . . .

Inductive Development (particular to general)

- Robin Cousins (particular) is a master ice skater, who demonstrates that figure skating is both an art and a science (general).
- Product Y (particular) is a quality product, made by a quality company (general) . . .
- Joey Carter is an abused child (particular). His abuse, and that of many others his age (general), is caused by several interrelated factors.

Program organization often flows naturally from the statement of the communication objective. One of the first things the objective suggests is whether a deductive or an inductive arrangement would work better. Signs along the way may suggest different directions, but with the objective statement in your mind (and on paper), the production will reach its goal if you measure each decision against the most direct route to the destination.

The next step in the development process is to use techniques that support the objective.

Use Descriptive Details and Imagery

Describe the content by showing it, not just telling it (watch commercials to see description at its best). Use close-ups. Break up an action into its component visuals. For example, when someone is playing a guitar, there are at least three opportunities for close-ups: the left hand, the right hand, and the face. Any combination of these can be superimposed over the other. Use unusual and extreme angles; go for interesting or dramatic lighting; use slow motion and images or sounds to enhance the objective.

Use Factual Details

You can express factual evidence in images as well as words by showing images that support the action and/or words. Use graphics such as charts, graphs, or cartoons. More frequently, especially on television, directors use words and phrases to introduce visual expressions, which is effective because words are very specific.

Define Terms

Viewers need to understand and not just see or hear your message, so if you use terms that are not going to be familiar to your target audience, find a way to define them. Use your own definitions rather than those found in a dictionary or textbook. Viewers want to know how you apply the word or idea.

One nice technique is to use character generated (CG) pages cut to the beat of music or tempo of a sound effect. A sequence in an instructional program used the periodic crash of a pile driver as an opportunity to cut to a key word. CG pages can also be inserted as the narration flows, quick cutting to the page to fit the words or interrupting visuals in progress. The viewer focuses attention on the definition after seeing a quick cut to a CG page. A visual communication principle is *when there are words on the screen, viewers cannot resist reading them.* If the production is more aesthetic or entertaining than informational, use the context of the action to clarify any ideas, concepts, or words that need definition.

Use Illustrations

Illustrations can be created in a variety of forms including straight visuals, graphics (art card or computer), slides, CG material, images from books and magazines (be careful of copyright infringement), or anything creative you can think of to *show* the point(s) being made about the content. Anything at which you can point a camera is a possibility.

Images should usually clarify content. Avoid symbolism and subtlety, which television does not convey well. Use **visual analogies** to expand viewers' perception of the content. If your intent is to express how a business network functions, shoot the branches of a tree and how they relate to the trunk, perhaps as a superimposition. **Anecdotes** or short stories are also very useful. For interviews ask the interviewee if he or she has any brief stories to tell to illustrate the points. These anecdotes are often the most powerful material of an interview and in some cases can be photographed as "B" roll (or inserted) scenes over the interview.

Another technique is to use *hypothetical situations*. Create a situation or role-play to illustrate a point. If the narrator talks about littering, show your viewers what it would be like if people in their neighborhood regularly threw garbage into the street or show them what a mound of one year's waste would look like along-side the city skyline (for scale).

Simulations are often used in corporate training tapes and other presentations where some process, procedure, or technique is being taught or discussed. They are especially useful in situations involving interpersonal behavior and process interaction. To show viewers their preparedness for a major civil emergency, Mercy Hospital in Cincinnati staged a mock airplane disaster including dead and critically wounded victims, fake blood, hundreds of panicked onlookers, and the interaction of several other city services. Imagine the difference between this and a video of hospital staff members on a panel having a discussion.

Illustrations give viewers something concrete to see. They are also an excellent way to incorporate entertainment value into a program that might otherwise be dull.

Parody is another dynamic and entertaining technique used frequently in corporate programs. A presentation might mock a famous TV program or movie, using in-house people in the starring roles. Dialogue could incorporate company jargon and "in jokes" while using the style and format of the movie or TV show. *Star Trek, Cheers,* and *Star Wars* are easy formats to parody, but any program can work as long as the character types, language cues, and action are recognizable. Select the most vivid impressions the movie or TV show left in your memory to be content elements.

Organization/Logic

All that happens between the beginning and end of a program must be ordered. Audiences gain security and the feeling of order from seeing events in a sequence that has some reason. A poorly organized production can't be disguised. The resulting experience for viewers is confusion and dissatisfaction. Without order, the objective is confused or lost entirely.

Whether we look at a newscast with its clever verbal transitions that tie stories together, variety shows that place performers in order of audience appeal and up-beat following downbeat acts, or a training tape that describes a manufacturing process, organization is what holds these programs together.

Viewers take good program structure for granted because it's the norm on the national television networks. When it's not there, they might have a feeling of being adrift, floundering without a sense of where the program is going. They ask: "So what?" "What's going on?" or "What happened?" If these questions come up while you are producing a program, look at the content organization. There is probably material that does not belong there or that is out of sequence.

The organization of ideas, information, and creative expressions requires more than just general organization skills. If one approaches program content organization in the same way an office manager organizes an office, like things would be put together—files in the file, pencils in with all the writing tools, pads with paper supplies, and so on. One can find the items quickly. But using this style of organization to produce a program would create a video that is deadly boring.

Just as we tend to organize objects in neat rows or compartments, so we could structure content dealing with subject A first, then move to everything relating to subject B, and then place all the subject C elements together. But this does not work well for organizing an emotional experience on video.

When content is being incorporated into a video or film, *integration* and *contrast* are crucial. Mix things up in a way that makes sense. Viewers want to experience the unexpected; they crave change and uncertainty, as we saw earlier, because it's stimulating and challenging. An example of boring organization:

Open: Establish subject matter

Develop: Subject A

Develop: Subject B

Develop: Subject C

Close: Summary

An example of better ordering through *integrated* subject matter:

Open: Dynamic visual hook

Theme: Presentation of theme

Tease: Subjects A through C, just touching the surface of each so the whole can be seen

Develop: Details of subject A

Develop: Relationship of A to B as transition

Develop: Details of subject B
(Entertainment interlude)

Develop: Relationship of B to C (transition)

Develop: Details of subject C
(Entertainment interlude)

Develop: Relationship of C to A and B (transition)

Close: Overview (unification) of content (whole), with similar images and sound content to open the program so it ends as it began

Integration applies to the elements in a sequence or segment as well as in the entire program. It maximizes stimulation and provides variety. Instead of putting all the water shots together, all the crowd shots together, or everything relating to one idea together, place them throughout the material. Establish a topic and elaborate it, but don't dwell on it. If there's more to say about it, come back to it in another context. Use print media to elaborate ideas. Video is best at presenting ideas in an entertaining way.

Organizing the body of a presentation should be a process of letting the subject unfold naturally. There are several organizational patterns that can be suggested, but each subject and situation requires its own unique treatment.

Standard ordering of material:

- *Natural order:* A subject follows according to order of its relationship to the subject preceding it. (1) Time: First the seed is planted, it germinates, then it gets bigger, it branches out, then it flowers, then it is pollinated, and so on. (2) Space: An architecture video might begin at the entrance of a building and proceed through the space as pedestrians would normally tour it.
- *Chronological order:* Subjects are presented according to their relationships in time. Historical subjects, for instance, deal with the earliest events first, then progress to the most recent. Cooking requires a specific sequence of events; so does manufacturing, processing, and distributing products.
- *Logical order:* Subjects are presented according to deductive or inductive reasoning. (1) Deductive: Present general subjects first and then give specifics. Focus on a basketball team and then the individual players. (2) Inductive: Provide details first, then show how they relate to a broader subject. Focus on individual players and then the basketball team.

Less conventional ordering:

- *Aesthetic order:* Some images blend well from one to another but some do not. An apple can dissolve nicely into the earth from space but not very well into an automobile. *Like geometries are associated better than unlike ones.*
- *Technical order:* This order usually shows the steps involved in the ordering of a process or operation. A video on how to process color film at home takes the process step by step. A video on how to manage a fast-food restaurant also takes the instructions a step at a time based on a standard sequence.
- *Symmetrical order:* This type of order refers to the framing technique of ending the program with similar or the same elements as were involved at the beginning. This is a common ordering for electronic media because viewers are reminded of how the program began. It completes the cycle by unifying the content. It's a powerful way to create a lasting impression. Our documentary on Mrs. Peterson began and ended with her eating a hamburger. It served both as hook and as climax.
- *Intuitive order:* When your intuition suggests that subject C needs to follow subject Q, it may not be logical, it just feels right. This type of order involves risk, but you should always leave room for "happy accidents."

- *Problem/solution:* A series of problems is presented with a solution proposed immediately after the problem. For example, establish that the work on a production process is slow, then deal with possible solutions; show how the quality of workmanship is low, and then deal with solutions to improve it.

Presentational Order

The sequence and placement of material as well as its orderly presentation can affect the impact of your message.

Issue 1: Ordering presentations   Does it make a difference which speaker or issue is presented first or second? The determinant is the time delay (1) between two messages and (2) between the last presentation and when the audience effect change is measured. Although the researchers who investigated this issue dealt with longer time delays (of days), we can still postulate that the same results are probable given shorter delays.

If two presenters in the same video argue different viewpoints and present their opinions one after another, the first presenter will have a persuasive advantage, given that the measurement of the audience's attitude change is measured after a time delay. This is referred to as the **primacy** effect.[2] The opposite situation, called the **recency** effect, gives a persuasive advantage to the second presenter when there is a time delay between the presentations, so that the first message is forgotten but the second one is fresh in the audience's memory. The delay could be a shift of attention to almost anything, including an entertainment interlude. In this second instance the measurement of attitude change was taken immediately after the second presentation.

In practical terms this calls for an assessment of the timing of the audience's response or resulting action. Simplistically, just remember that you want the message that fulfills the communication objective to be as fresh in the audience's memory as possible and as close as possible to the time when you want the audience to act on it. This is why the ending of a program should always clearly and powerfully summarize or at least reemphasize the salient point(s) of the communication objective. It's also the reason political commercials are most powerful the day before the election, and why sales are advertised on television near the sales date.

Speech persuasion research indicates that the most important material should be placed last. This "climax" order clearly does not apply to video, where it is necessary to grab and hold the viewer's attention up front, but it does reinforce the importance of closing the program with the main point(s).

Research into the ordering of broadcast news stories by Annie Lang suggests that the way news stories are commonly structured (brief in length, emotional priorities, entertainment value) fosters "low levels of attention and, as a result, poor memory for the content presented." If you present what is new or different first, and then show what caused the change followed by the consequences of that change, viewers lose comprehension because they don't often have prior knowledge of the situation. The study suggests that a better ordering would be episodic, that is, to present the story "in chronological order with the causes first, the change next, and the consequences last."[3]

Finally, Cohen[4] found that attitudes are more effectively changed when the audience is first informed about *why a message is relevant* to them. Establish the relevancy of the material first and then present it. You'll recall the model Bill Moyers uses for his programs, described earlier, that does this consistently.

Issue 2: Order versus disorder   Orderliness itself communicates. What assumptions do you make and what message do you get when you walk into someone's room for the first time and see a total mess? What message do you get when you go to pick up your equipment at a rental studio and the gear is dirty and scattered everywhere? Are you confident about using it on a shoot? When we experience orderliness in others, it gives us a comfortable feeling, a level of confidence in what's happening. And when order is not present, the opposite occurs. Disorganization also leads to a reduction in persuasibility (attitude change).[5] And it interferes with an audience's retention of the message as well as their perception of the source. Organization is important to use and demonstrate.

Continuity
. . . .

Organization involves the ordering of program elements, but it also involves attention to how one element leads into another, commonly referred to as **continuity.** There is *shot continuity,* where each scene bears a relationship to the one before and after it; *subject continuity,* where one subject leads into another in a particular way; and *program continuity,* involving those elements and production techniques that unify the entire program.

To achieve continuity, some element of what came before should be carried over into the present. It can be an idea, word, image, or even part of an image— anything to maintain the relationship between the parts of the program. A paragraph becomes more than a string of words when the words carry some of the thought forward with the sentences building on one another. This literary synergy is what gives life to the written word. Continuity is essential to the successful use of any medium. It brings the audience from what is known to what is not yet known, from the familiar to the new, and in the process it unifies the elements of the whole program.

Continuity is also one of those attributes (we'll discuss others later) that identify a production as "professional." It's often subtle, but when the content "works," the overall effect suggests *integrity.* The program holds together well. It feels right.

You can create continuity using a variety of techniques including music, sound or sound effects, camera movement, lighting, talent mannerisms, dialect, and repeated lines or images. Begin organizing content by looking at possible transitions.

People often begin scenes with an element carried over from the preceding scene. The element could be a rolling ball that cuts or dissolves to a spinning gear, a weed growing through the pavement becoming a tree, or water pouring from a glass dissolving to a flowing river. The more closely the two images resemble each other, the better (motions need to match screen direction). Although I've used images to illustrate, planned transitions should also be constituted of audio and action elements. Think about making connections between content elements.

Transition techniques such as dissolves, wipes, or other switcher effects can be used to create continuity, but you should not overuse them.

Important images, sounds, or words can keep returning, especially those relating directly to the communication objective. *Jaws,* for instance, used the same undertone of music every time the shark was about to appear on the screen—but not when it was on camera—to clue the audience that it was about to make an appearance.

Good continuity calls attention to occasional relationships between scenes, between shots, or between content elements, but it does not call attention to itself by becoming obvious. It should always be secondary—it is not part of the content but the way the content moves forward.

The important continuity design question is this: What is/are the thread(s) that can be carried forward throughout the program to unify it?

Summary

We've seen that good content organization is necessary not only to structure material but also to direct the viewer's attention and consciousness along a stream of ideas, experiences, or feelings toward an objective. An effective video presentation establishes a context, a sense of the subject, and where the program will be going at the outset. It takes the audience step by step through an experience, allowing viewers to gradually move from where they are to where the producer wants them to be.

Strong, effective organization means that the elements are unified. That is, each one supports or contributes to the communication objective. Unity also requires that, throughout the program, elements must relate to the main issue or idea and the relationship has to be made clear. Otherwise, the audience may become confused and distracted.

Another aspect of unity involves presenting an experience that, as a whole, leaves a memorable impression. People watch a substantial number of videos and television programs. What will make yours stand out? If the elements of the program hold up as one focused experience, its energy will be more potent. This kind of focused energy occurs best when the production team is also focused, working together toward the fulfillment of the same goal. This task becomes more controllable when the communication objective is as specific as possible. Limit the subject and sharpen the focus.

Another essential component of organization includes the principles of content development, that is, how the body of the program is structured. This led us to consider where and when the content should move from the general to the specific and vice versa. We noted the importance of employing factual details to provide evidence and other support for the main points as well as the importance of defining terms and illustrating the content.

We examined ways to organize the content, beginning with a discussion of the importance to video of integrating content material rather than lumping like subjects together. We reviewed several of the more common methods of content ordering, including natural, chronological, logical, aesthetic, technical, symmetrical, intuitive, and problem/solution. Then we examined research on the ordering of presentations. Finally, we considered the necessity of providing some form of program continuity—ways to use program elements to extend the content and further unify it.

Although many programs are organized finally in the postproduction phase, good content organization requires attention up front and throughout the entire project. Unity, development, organization, and continuity should be built in—created beforehand—and not discovered along the way. Although there can be many "happy accidents" throughout the production process, good organization is never one of them.

How and whether a program is organized communicates.

Notes

1. *Upper Triad Journal* (number 233), "Commentaries on the Esoteric Philosophy" (Manassas, VA: Upper Triad Association, 1989).
2. Miller, N., and D. T. Campbell, "Recency and Primacy in Persuasion as a Function of the Timing of Speeches and Measurements." *Journal of Abnormal Psychology* 59 (1959): 1–9.
3. Lang, Annie, "Effects of Chronological Presentation of Information on Processing and Memory for Broadcast News." *Journal of Broadcasting & Electronic Media* 33 (Fall 1989): 441–452.
4. Rosnow, R. L., and E. J. Robinson, *Experiments in Persuasion* (New York: Academic Press, 1967), 135.
5. Jones, J. A., and G. R. Serlousky, "An Investigation of Listener Perception of Degrees of Speech Disorganization and the Effects on Attitude Change and Source Credibility." Paper presented at the ICA convention, Atlanta, Georgia, 1972.

Suggested Readings

Comstock, George A., et al. *Television and Human Behavior.* New York: Columbia University Press, 1978.

Lewis, Herschell Gordon. *On the Art of Writing Copy.* Englewood Cliffs, NJ: Prentice-Hall, 1988.

Lowery, Shearon A., and Melvin L. DeFleur. *Milestones in Mass Communication Research,* 2d ed. New York: Longman, 1988.

McCrimmon, James. *Writing with a Purpose,* 7th ed. Boston: Houghton Mifflin, 1980.

Williams, Joseph. *Style: Ten Lessons in Clarity and Grace,* 2d ed. Glenview, IL: Scott, Foresman, 1985.

PART **IV**

MAKING IT WORK

· ·

The topics we're about to consider can make the difference between a program that's mediocre and one that's excellent. Our coverage of content so far has emphasized a logical approach to designing a project: Know your audience well; consider carefully what you want to say to them; be fully aware of your context and language; unify the content throughout its development; ensure logical organization; and include continuity devices such as planned transitions. Now we'll turn from the technique (rules, procedures, formal structures) to the art of making a program and making its message work.

We'll examine two broad, significant areas in some detail: **persuasion,** which is the art of attitude change—convincing the audience to accept your communication objective. We'll look at persuasion first not because it's necessarily more important but because most formats include persuasion as a major component.

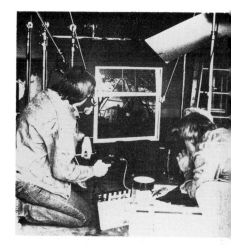

The second area is the art of *storytelling,* which is the foundation of video, television, and film. Storytelling is one of the most powerful human urges. Aside from being good at video production, I strongly recommend that you learn how to tell stories well. Every other technical skill should be subordinate to storytelling.

Master these two arts—persuasion and storytelling—combine them with systems organization, creative imagination, and technical skill (craftsmanship) and you have my formula for using video effectively.

CHAPTER 10

Persuasion

· ·

The truth is always the strongest argument.

—*Sophocles*

F requently a video's purpose is to persuade. Whether we hope to sell a product or service, invite the adoption of an idea, suggest a better way, or compel action, we approach our audience in a manner that will convince them to accept our message. Persuasion is pragmatic communication. We want something to happen as a result of the video experience.

This chapter focuses on certain persuasive practices and theories and also on certain "source" characteristics that influence persuasion. These theories are important because they help us explain *why* certain messages have an impact on their receivers. These explanations suggest specific techniques. Additionally, when we know the theory beneath the practice, we can use our tools more skillfully. For those who may want to go into more depth with the theories, see the references cited. Our emphasis here will be on the practice of persuading with video. Many of the examples are derived from broadcast television simply because it provides a common reference.

In the persuasion process using video, the source (producer) presents a **message** (program content) through a **medium** (video) to a **receiver** (viewer). As we saw, this "post office" model is limited, but it's useful as a framework for considering the dynamics of persuasion. Each of these four elements contains a multitude of variables that determine the success of the persuasive event. The interaction of these four elements is so complex that there will never be a formula that will guarantee consistent persuasive success.

Since Aristotle people have sought such a formula because of the potential persuasion holds. We have seen its power historically in our great leaders and sages. We have also seen the devastating results of the power of persuasion used destructively in the hands of tyrants such as Hitler. These leaders, knowingly or not, applied certain interpersonal and communication skills that worked, so those of us who seek increased effectiveness want to know how they did it.

Practice and Theory
. . . .

By far the bulk of the research relating to theories of persuasion relates to speech and interpersonal communication. Researchers clearly have emphasized the "word" rather than the "picture," much to the dismay of visual communicators. But because video and television utilize language communication so extensively, the theories are still relevant for our purposes.

Our approach will be to highlight a theory along with certain research findings where appropriate, and then show their application to video communication. There are more theories than the ones presented here, and our examination will not include the details of the specific studies (such as their development and elaboration). Neither will we address the research design, methodology, or follow-up studies (which in some cases are contradictory).

None of what follows can be described as fully tested, proven, or validated. The theories may or may not stand the test of time. Therefore, no rule applies every time for all people everywhere. This is why persuasion is not only a study in technique but an art involving every aspect of our ability to perceive and communicate. The theories presented here have been selected based on my own successful observation and application of them.

Learning Theory

Learning theory[1] is based on studies done on the nature of animal and human learning. As we saw earlier, humans thrive on meaning. As we learn, our attitudes, beliefs, perspectives, and values change, and psychologists study this change to understand why and how persuasion occurs. One of the primary results of learning is the creation and processing of meaning.

Elaborated by Carl Hoveland and colleagues at Yale University in the 1950s, learning theory suggests that source variables such as credibility, attractiveness, status, and intent (among others) provide incentives for us to adopt a new idea or attitude. We try a product; we don't like it. Learning occurs. We watch a program on the greenhouse effect; learning occurs. We watch a video on gardening; learning occurs.

Just because we learn something doesn't mean we'll adopt a new behavior or opinion. We may continue to buy a product simply because we need it and there's nothing else available where we shop. We may choose not to plant a garden this season, and so on.

The video producer must ensure the credibility of the screen characters and their presentation to keep viewers open and receptive to learning. How viewers use what they learn is their decision.

When covering a workshop, conference, or other event, the producer should be selective about the people he or she interviews. They need to be articulate, poised, and enthusiastic and have an appearance that doesn't detract from perceived credibility. The same applies to talent we hire or select for a part in a drama, documentary, or training or sales presentation.

There must, of course, be something to learn. The content should contain some fresh insights, information, or facts that contribute to the audience's knowledge or understanding of the subject. The keynote of these learning theories: *Teach the audience something new, give them positive associations, and make the content relevant.* The following three areas of learning theory are especially pertinent to persuading with video.

Classical Conditioning Theory

Classical conditioning theory[2] asserts that, if a certain neutral stimulus is frequently associated with a certain response, the stimulus itself will trigger the associated response. When the bell rings, kids line up in the school yard. When we see people eating popcorn at a movie, we get hungry for it. When an intense TV program is interrupted for a commercial break, we are cued to head for the bathroom or refrigerator.

The video communicator must decide how he or she wants the audience to respond and then in the video repeatedly show that response in association with the program content. If the communication objective is to create a positive image for a new product or service, show the screen characters or others having positive feelings and experiences using it. To create negative responses to drug use, for example, show the negative associations that go along with it.

As you watch commercials, observe how the leading characters experience exactly what the advertiser thinks the audience also wants to experience. Commercials don't sell the product so much as the benefits the viewer will experience by using the product. People don't really want objects as much as they want to feel good, lose weight, be healthy, be smart, have fun, and so on. The strategy is to show positive associations between the viewer and whatever you're "selling." The keynote of classical conditioning: *Use positive associations consistently.*

Operant Conditioning Theory

Operant conditioning theory[3] suggests that people seek to optimize the positive and eliminate the negative (consequences, feelings, ideas, values) in their lives. We like rewards and try to avoid punishment. We like to win; we don't like to lose. We seek to have more and better rather than less quality.

Parents use operant conditioning regularly by telling children that if they do something they will be rewarded. Each time they do what they're asked to, they get a reward. Likewise, the threat of punishment or harm is a strong reason to avoid the circumstances that may lead to it. The military hierarchy uses the threat of punishment or disgrace of the individual. The toothpaste commercial that shows the little girl at the dentist's office with no cavities demonstrates to all little girls (and their parents) that the toothpaste is desirable. Nobody wants cavities. Operant conditioning offers the video communicator the opportunity to use arguments, evidence, and images that clearly show the rewards or benefits of using the product or adopting the message.

Several studies have shown that it's more effective to present a message in positive terms even when the subject is negative. The commercial, instead of stating "Use brand X because it eliminates bad breath," would be more effective if it stated "Use brand X because it freshens your mouth." The difference may seem subtle but it's significant in terms of effectiveness. *Eliminates* is a negative word. So if your message sounds negative, transform it into a positive message.

Training videos can show the time saved by following a particular procedure, the increased product quality that results from a team effort, or the bonus that's given for higher-quality work, extra effort, or lack of sick days. Documentaries can present the positive implications of pollution control on health and the economy or the benefits of space technologies in terms relevant to the taxpayer. Demonstration tapes can reveal the before-and-after effects of using a product or following a process—positive evidence of the effectiveness or benefits. The keynote of operant conditioning: *Express the message in positive terms.*

Vicarious Conditioning Theory

The theory of vicarious conditioning[4] suggests that we respond positively or negatively to a stimulus based on our observation of how others respond. Video has power because of our identification with screen characters—we see their life-styles and might imagine ourselves in them. Our day-to-day realities might seem quite ordinary without these vicarious experiences that can lift us out of ourselves. Frequently we enjoy or identify with the experience so much that we buy into its trappings and paraphernalia. This is demonstrated by the enormous success of movie character dolls and other promotional materials.

Vicarious conditioning theory supports the strategy of presenting content in association with people enjoying or appreciating whatever you're trying to promote, whether an idea, a product, or a procedure. And it supports presenting the material in a manner that's outside the ordinary. If the audience sees the screen characters having positive experiences, or fulfilling a fantasy or dream, members of the audience are more likely to be persuaded to adopt products associated with these experiences. The "Learn to Ski" and other exercise videos are examples in the nonbroadcast area. These simultaneously promote the apparel and the activity. If people can't experience the activity, they might settle for the look.

These theories operate on the basis of association—a positive relationship between the content and those who are seen using or implementing it. The majority of American television commercials are based at least in part on these theories. The keynote of vicarious conditioning: *Make the message desirable.*

The theories we'll look at next depart from association and learning as the predominant modes of persuasion, focusing instead on the psychology of the persuasive situation.

Variable Perspective Theory

Variable perspective theory[5] acknowledges that people have preconceived viewpoints. It suggests that, to effect attitude change, you need to know what the existing perspectives are and whether there is any resistance to changing them. Studies consistently indicate that *audiences see what they want to see and hear what they want to hear.* One of the major propositions of this theory is that, as a result of people's preconceptions, audiences more easily accept ideas or suggestions that are closer to their own perceptions. The corollary is that they more easily reject those suggestions that are very different from their perceptions. The task then is to produce or frame messages so they either conform to or align with the perceptions of the target audience. This is the basis for positioning: If we know what the receiver thinks, it's much easier to structure a convincing message by appealing to what he or she already accepts.

Commercials often enlighten us: "Real butter has the same amount of cholesterol and calories as the leading brand of cooking oil." "You know our cars have class, but did you know they also have the best gas mileage in their class?"

Commercials lead the audience from what they already believe—their current perspective—to what the advertiser wants them to accept, which is often the same thing. But when it's not, begin with a common perceptual reference. Align with the audience's current perceptions before leading them into the new. The keynote for variable perspective theory: *Align (blend) with your audience.*

Cognitive Consistency Theory

Cognitive means "mental," and *consistency* means "continuous over time." People need to feel they can trust their perceptions and beliefs over time. This theory[6] suggests that our minds seek balance, stability, and familiarity as another way to establish meaning. When we hear something in agreement with our opinions, beliefs, values, or actions, the message or information reinforces that we are right and justified.

Audiences, therefore, appreciate programs that show both sides of an issue and then resolve the question in the direction of their own attitudes. As a result, they more easily accept the content. In fact, people select programs because they already agree with the perspective presented or are attracted to the subject matter. For instance, a video on neighborhood improvement projects won't appeal to people who don't care about the neighborhood.

Audiences resist content that threatens their preexisting attitudes. If they are somehow obliged to watch this content, they will criticize (to themselves or openly) the writers or producers as ignorant, biased, or otherwise lacking. A principle of selling as well as of interpersonal communication is that you never tell the other person he or she is wrong—even when you think he or she is. Find the agreement and move logically, a step at a time, until the receiver arrives at your position. Salespeople know that as long as they can keep the prospect saying "yes," there's a greater likelihood that a deal can be made. The keynote of cognitive consistency: *Know your audience and seek agreement with them.*

Cognitive Dissonance Theory

Cognitive dissonance theory[7] involves two conflicting values or choices. It's the flip side of cognitive consistency theory. You are going to buy a new car. Dissonance is created when you like some unique features of each auto and must choose which to buy. Buying in itself creates dissonance when you want to save your money but also want to buy a car. And dissonance shows up when we observe or listen to others. A person may say she doesn't like Michael Jackson's music yet go to his concerts anyway. Talk-show hosts sometimes express interest in subjects we know they regard as dull. And we've heard about business executives who say they are concerned about poor environmental conditions in their plants but do nothing about them. All these situations cause dissonance in our minds because there is a conflict. Something doesn't mesh.

To use this to persuasive advantage in video contexts, an ad might compare two products, neither of which makes as much sense as the third, which you advocate. Arby's does this in its attempt to suggest an alternative to Burger King's and McDonald's hamburgers. The persuasive communicator acknowledges the two elements in conflict and then helps move the viewer to some action or idea to reduce or resolve the dissonance. People don't want to be in conflict for very long, so it's relatively easy to get a third alternative accepted when the other choices present a conflict.

Because conflict is an essential element of good storytelling, you can be sure that, if there's dissonance in a situation, there's also a potential for producing a good story.

In training and educational programs, you should not place together perspectives that suggest different directions. If there is ambiguity, it's better to separate the two areas of content so as not to cause dissonance. Where it's appropriate to show a conflict, it's best to announce the conflict before presenting the material. Knowing that a conflict is coming takes some of the shock out of it. Or you could choose not to disclose it early, thereby increasing the shock value if that better supports the objective. The keynote of cognitive dissonance: *Present conflict and then help the audience resolve it.*

Impression Management Theory

Impression management theory[8] suggests that people present themselves in certain ways to achieve goals. Whenever we're going into a situation in which we want something, for instance, a job interview or a sales meeting, we dress the part. We attempt to put all the factors of our personal presentation into alignment with what we feel is expected. This may include what we wear and our hairstyle, speech, mannerisms, resume, and anything else that contributes to the image we want to project. We do this because we want something; we're hoping to persuade someone to our way of thinking.

The video producer needs to be sensitive to these personal presentational factors no matter who is on the screen. The message and its presentation must display cues the audience will recognize as being consistent with their perceptions. A typical video application of this kind of communication is the business promotional presentation, where the backgrounds, props, lighting, and characterizations must exhibit the proper corporate image.

There's probably a company in your town, like mine, where a dress code (whether formal or not) is in evidence. Most middle- and upper-management employees wear the same colored suit and the same style of shirt and shoes. This corporate "uniform" is rarely the result of a company requirement but a fashion statement that people interpret as having meaning (success, power, office with a view, limo privileges, and other perks).

Although we may smile at this seeming overattention to appearance, what's happening is quite important. Corporate image, audience perception, competition, dominance, territoriality, self-expression, and self-confidence are at stake. The video communicator should be sensitive to these elements and make sure screen characters exhibit the symbols appropriate to the perceptions of the target audience. The keynote of impression management theory: *Use screen characters and elements that make a good impression (the one intended) on the audience.*

Functional Theory

Functional theory[9] suggests that a person's attitudes are shaped by his or her perceived *needs* rather than from the imposition of outside sources' views. This is the basis for doing an audience needs analysis. If we know why a person has a particular attitude, we will be in a better position to persuade him or her. Daniel Katz, who elaborated this theory, suggests four *functions* attitudes perform:

1. *Instrumental, adjustive, or utilitarian function.* We hold favorable those things that we associate with satisfaction and pleasure. Content that gives us pleasure by its nature or presentation is more easily accepted.

2. *Ego-defensive function.* We protect ourselves from unacceptable truths that might hurt us. If content threatens our belief system or other perceptions, we tend to reject it. This suggests we should be sensitive to our target's ego needs.

3. *Value-expressive function.* We like to be able to express and realize our positive ideals and values. This helps us to see and be the kind of people we want to be. Images and ideas (content) that empower or otherwise assist the audience are eagerly welcomed.

4. *Knowledge function.* We look for understanding and meaning.

With increased awareness of and information about our target audience, we'll be able to see which of their needs, expressed as one or more of the above functions, are predominant so we can structure the content accordingly. For instance, a video for actors should be sensitive to their ego needs; a video for adolescents should show an awareness of their emotional and social needs. The keynote of functional theory: *Analyze and respond to audience needs.*

The Source

The communication *source,* in the context of this chapter, is the writer or producer of a video or television program—the person or persons with something to say. By virtue of the message itself and how it's presented, the audience can discern a lot about this source. They will also discern much about those we put on the screen to represent our message. How these characters are perceived makes a big difference in message acceptance.

We have all listened to someone tell us something incredible they heard from a third party not present. Someone responds, "Yeah, but consider the source." Whenever we experience another's performance (through the media or in person), we scrutinize the source to determine relative trustworthiness, expertise, reliability, and believability.

Knowing as much as possible about the source of a message is important to viewers. As producers we can make sure that the cues the audience receives are the ones we want—those that support the acceptance of our objective. The following are some of the source characteristics operative in various video situations.

Credibility

In *Rhetoric* Aristotle wrote that a credible presenter is one who exhibits intelligence, good character, and goodwill toward the audience. We would generally trust such a person and, therefore, accept what she has to say. But studies on attitude change reveal that, although this may be generally true, it's really more complex.

The following summary statements from speech communication literature indicate some of the factors involved in making a presenter credible. I've added a "keynote" at the end of each to indicate in practical terms the essential lesson for the video communicator.

- People tend to agree more with statements attributed to trusted sources than with the same statements attributed to nonrespected, nontrusted sources.[10] Keynote: *Build trust.*
- The source with the higher credibility has a substantially greater immediate impact on an audience over a source with lower credibility.[11] Keynote: *Use strong presenters near the time when you hope the audience will act on the communication objective.*
- Low credibility cues the audience to the fact that the conclusions cannot be trusted.[12] Keynote: *Never send low-credibility cues.*

- Three characteristics of TV newscasters suggest they are credible: reliable logical statements, showmanship, and trustworthiness.[13] Keynote: *Give evidence that the presenter is logical, professional, and honest.*

- The four qualities upon which audiences make judgments relating to credibility are *safety* (warm, gentle, ethical), *qualification* (experienced, informed, knowledgeable), *dynamism* (energetic, bold, assertive), and *sociability* (likable, cheerful).[14] Keynote: *Select talent that has or coach them to exhibit these qualities.*

- More important than these attributes themselves is how the audience perceives them.[15] Keynote: *Learn which of the above qualities matter most to the audience.*

- The effects of low credibility are reduced and sometimes eliminated by identifying the source after the presentation, not before.[16] Keynote: *If the presenter is weak or has weak credentials, identify him or her after the presentation.*

- When the source has high credibility, it's best to identify him or her early in the presentation.[17] Keynote: *If the presenter is strong and has good credentials, identify her or him before the presentation.*

- In some instances a less credible source will be more persuasive than a highly credible one, for instance, when the low-prestige source advocates a position opposed to his self-interest.[18] Keynote: *If the presenter has low prestige, he or she will do better by advocating a position that is not in his or her interest.*

- Trustworthy sources do even better when they are presented on television, where source characteristics (attributes of the presenter) are highlighted or promoted.[19] Keynote: *Promote the program to reach as large an audience as possible.*

- When a source perceived to be untrustworthy then demonstrates that he or she is trustworthy, effectiveness is substantially increased.[20] Keynote: *If the presenter has a bad reputation, find a way to prove it false.*

- As the subject matter becomes more personally relevant or important to the audience, the credibility of the source becomes a more important factor.[21] Keynote: *If the audience already has a high degree of interest in the subject, pay even closer attention to presenter credibility.*

- When there is foreknowledge that the intent of the source is to persuade or change attitudes, effectiveness is decreased.[22] Keynote: *Don't tell the audience your intent is to persuade.*

- A physically attractive source is more persuasive than a less attractive one.[23] Keynote: *Use physically attractive presenters.*

- The content of a message is remembered longer than the character of the source who presented it.[24] Keynote: *Pay more attention to what is said than to who says it.*

- Disorganized message presentations lower the credibility of the source, even if the credibility was originally high.[25] Well-organized presentations increase the credibility of a source, even those perceived to have only moderate credibility.[26] Keynote: *Always organize your presentations well.*

Identification with the Audience

You persuade a man only in as far as you can talk his language,
by speech, gesture, tonality, order, image, attitude, idea, identify-
ing your ways with his.

—Kenneth Burke

We touched on the importance of identity as a communication tool in Chapter 5. Because it relates so crucially to persuasion, it warrants further discussion here. Viewers can more easily relate to screen characters who are similar to themselves physically, psychologically, emotionally, and every other way. When the source exhibits characteristics that approximate our own, we tend to have more respect for what he or she has to say. We say we can "identify" with such sources because we perceive them as sharing something of our own identity or experience. This shared perception becomes an inclination to accept the message or at least maintain openness to consider it.

A program appeared recently on our cable access channel with a presenter on astrology who, although apparently knowledgeable in his field, looked like he walked in from a dirt-bike race. It was bad enough that he made his points by citing books he had read (instead of speaking from his own perspective), but the crowning blunder was his appearance. He lost credibility with the audience from the very first shot. Audiences expect intelligent people to *look* intelligent.

This is not to say that presenters who are similar to their audiences will always find agreement or that they will necessarily always have more persuasive impact than others who are less similar.[27] There are always exceptions. But for the discerning video communicator, creating similarity between the source (narrator, leading character, testimonial provider) and the audience is a good practice.

Similarity not only relates to the personal and visible aspects of the source but also to the perspective(s) being offered. We use similarity when we address our audience by saying such things as "We Americans are fond of . . . ," and "You and I well know the value of . . . ," and "Those of us who have experienced . . ." In these instances we make our commonality the foundation for what follows.

I occasionally see programs in which the screen representative suggests there are similarities but the context of the show indicates obvious disparities. This can happen on discussion programs when everyone gathered is supposed to know and like each other, until the moderator touches a sensitive area; then the similarities dissolve and conflict ensues. Sometimes this is entertaining, but is it effective communication?

Effective communication requires opening windows to meaning rather than building walls. When we think and act (on camera or off) in ways that distinguish ourselves as separate from others, as knowing more or being right, we're creating blocks to smooth (effective) communication. Blending with the other, and seeking and returning frequently to commonalities, encourages open exchange and an atmosphere of mutual receptivity.

Instead of criticizing the other's viewpoint, try to illuminate him or her regarding your perspective without alienating him or her. I once overheard someone say,

"Can't you talk to me without criticizing me at the same time?" The trick is to safeguard the receiver's openness and receptivity while leading him down the path of persuasion. The attitude that "I'm right and you're wrong" gets you nowhere. That of "let's explore together to find the truth" creates a partner and sustains the "field" of interactivity where genuine communication can occur.

Strategically, the content presenter (on or off camera) can appeal to what the audience already knows, feels, has experienced, or believes. He or she can align with them on precisely the points that describe and define them. This is the essence of positioning. We want the audience to "own" the message, as if it came from them initially. The producer can use the audience needs analysis to extrapolate from each item and incorporate program elements that relate directly to audience characteristics and needs.

However, sometimes the opposite of the usual positioning approach is required. For instance, if the audience for a video is males 25–40 attending prenatal classes in order to support their wives in the delivery room, the narrator of the video should probably be a woman because expertise and direct experience outweigh gender similarity in this situation. Nonetheless, if the audience is especially sensitive to sexist issues, a man might be selected. A man—especially one who has gone through the delivery process—might do as credible a job of presenting the subject. The criteria discussed here require careful analysis and discernment to arrive at the best mix of persuasive factors.

Status and Power

We clothe our screen characters in power. We put them in lab coats, give them medals, put their diplomas on the wall, raise them physically on platforms, use a low angle to exalt their position in the frame, and caution them to "speak" rather than "talk" as a demonstration of higher education.

Audiences do take more seriously messages presented by people having more status and power. *Status* is an expression of relative rank or position. Although the president of the United States may encourage us to stop smoking due to the risk of cancer, we are more likely to accept the message when it comes from the surgeon general. Although the president has more status politically, in terms of the topic the surgeon general has even greater status because he is immersed in research related to it. Status relates not only to position with respect to authority but to position with respect to the topic.

Although we give more credence to those with higher status, their status alone does not necessarily mean they have a greater ability to persuade.[28] Some members of the audience may not like the presenter for some reason; they may feel strongly about the issue and opposed to the presenter's views, or they may not like the presenter's affiliations, and so on.

In some cases we may want to indicate the status of the screen presenter, and in other instances we might choose to let it be implied. Voice cues[29] and language cues[30] (culture, dialect) disclose the status of a presenter, even when it's not known; so it's a mistake to disregard the presenter's status as a factor in any communication design. Again, the way status should be handled depends on how it might influence the communication objective. This is one of those areas where not to decide to handle status purposefully is a decision.

Power is also a relative term, expressing the ability of a person to cause a reward or punishment—a positive or negative experience for another. We speak of a powerful program, a powerful actor or narrator, a powerful presentation, to indicate that we (as audience members) were deeply moved. What moved us was an encounter or experience that brought us face to face with our potential for *change,* whether positive or negative. In every instance, however, the authority for the communicator's power is the audience, the public, the receiver—those who attend, comprehend, and respond to the "powerful" communicator.

We give our politicians, television networks, and rock stars power because we accept that they can (and therefore do) effect change in our lives. We perceive that these entities have resources (money, influential friends, access to technologies, the ability to punish) that we value or respect. How much power would the president have without these resources? With them, and the potential to utilize them, he is one of the most powerful men on earth.

Our power as video communicators derives from our audience's perception of us and of our program's potential to cause change in their lives. The moment I put something on their television screens, they begin making assumptions (according to their perceptions) about me, based on the decisions I have made. As long as my program reflects images, themes, messages, and experiences that are true to me, they are a reflection of me and my team.

As the program unfolds, the audience learns more about whether to trust me, whether to agree with me, whether to accept my message. My effectiveness (power) is in their hands as receivers, because they are always free to accept or reject whatever I'm offering. The best I can do is to provide presentation and content cues that are both consistent with my purpose and acceptable (and I hope attractive) to my audience.

If the characters on the screen and behind the camera all play their parts with excellence and integrity in pursuit of these objectives, the audience will probably accept the presentation and message. The next time they encounter another of our presentations, they will be more receptive, perhaps even eager to empower us again to offer them a perspective, vision, or experience.

In a study by J. W. McGuire,[31] not only must the powerful communicator be in a position to administer some reward or punishment, he or she must additionally convince the receiver(s) that such rewards or punishments will be used. The recipients must believe that the source will find out whether the receiver (audience) complies with the message. This is how power comes full circle; it's a process of human interaction and not simply a force one communicator has over another.

Summary

In this chapter we have sampled theories of persuasion, seeing how they apply to videos when the objective is to create an attitude change. Although no technique results in successful attitude change every time, the theories support practices (especially in the area of advertising, where most research has been conducted) and provide insight into making programs more potent.

The first three theories we discussed—classical conditioning, operant conditioning, and vicarious conditioning—suggest that association is a significant factor in persuasion. When we observe others experiencing a positive or pleasurable stimulus, we, by association, respond favorably to the source of their delight (the message or product). We repeat positive experiences and seek those we see others having.

The next group of theories—learning theory, variable perspective theory, and cognitive consistency and cognitive dissonance theories—relate broadly to attitude change as a result of the learning process. Life experience, input from others and the environment, perspectives we grew up with, and other learning qualify and condition our views.

A human being is not a "tabula rasa," a blank slate upon which others make their mark. We each have a unique processing strategy based on our life circumstances, and it changes as we live and learn more about ourselves, others, and the world. The effective communicator looks carefully at his or her audience to understand their meanings, values, experiences, life-style, and other perspectives to prepare and present a message as consistent with these as possible.

Impression management theory relates to learning theory, suggesting that we have learned how to present ourselves to others in various circumstances to get what we want. The video communicator's challenge is to create screen experiences that provide audience cues consistent with the already held impressions. This is another kind of positioning.

Finally, functional theory suggests that attitudes are changed in response to the receiver's perceived need fulfillment. Therefore, the effective communicator understands which needs "drive" his or her audience so the message can appropriately contribute to their satisfaction or realization—the reason for an audience needs analysis.

In the last part of the chapter, we considered the communication source in detail, sampling study results relating to the source's credibility, identification with the audience, status, and power. When our screen presenters, whether actors, on- or off-camera narrators, interviewers, or moderators, make assertions or otherwise present a message, the audience picks up certain cues to form their decisions whether to believe/accept the presenters.

The skillful producer also pays attention to the presenter's physical and psychological characteristics to maximize their positive potential for moving the audience.

How we persuade an audience communicates.

Notes

1. Hovland, C. I., I. L. Janis, and J. J. Kelley, *Communication and Persuasion* (New Haven, CT: Yale University Press, 1953).
2. Staats, A. W., and C. K. Staats, "Attitudes Established by Classical Conditioning." *Journal of Abnormal and Social Psychology* 57 (1958): 37–40.
3. Skinner, B. F., *The Behavior of Organisms: An Experimental Analysis* (New York: Appleton-Century-Crofts, 1938).
4. Berger, S. M., "Conditioning Through Vicarious Instigation." *Psychological Review* 69 (1962): 450–466.
5. Upshaw, H. S., "The Personal Reference Scale: An Approach to Social Judgment," in *Advances in Experimental Social Psychology,* Vol. 4, ed. L. Berkowitz (New York: Academic Press, 1969).
6. Rosenberg, M., and R. Abelson, "An Analysis of Cognitive Balancing," in *Attitude Organization and Change,* ed. C. Hovland and M. Rosenberg (New Haven, CT: Yale University Press, 1960), 112–163.
7. Festinger, L. A., *A Theory of Cognitive Dissonance* (Stanford, CA: Stanford University Press, 1957).
8. Goffman, E., *The Presentation of Self in Everyday Life* (New York: Doubleday, 1959).
9. Katz, Daniel, "The Functional Approach to the Study of Attitudes." *Public Opinion Quarterly* 24 (1960): 163–204.
10. Lorge, I., "Prestige, Suggestion, and Attitudes." *Journal of Social Psychology* 7 (1936): 386–402.
11. Hovland, Carl I., Irving L. Janis, and Harold H. Kelley, *Communication and Persuasion* (New Haven, CT: Yale University Press, 1953), 30.
12. Hovland, Carl I., and W. Weiss, "The Influence of Source Credibility on Communication Effectiveness." *Public Opinion Quarterly* 15 (1951): 635–650.
13. Markham, D., "The Dimensions of Source Credibility of Television Newscasters." *Journal of Communication* 18 (1968): 57–64.
14. Berlo, D. K., J. B. Lemert, and R. J. Mertz, "Dimensions for Evaluating the Acceptability of Message Sources." *Public Opinion Quarterly* 33 (1969): 563–576.
15. McCroskey, J. C., T. Jensen, and C. Todd, "The Generalizability of Source Credibility Scales for Public Figures." Paper presented at SCA convention, Chicago, December 1972.
16. Greenberg, B. S., and G. R. Miller, "The Effects of Low-Credible Sources on Message Acceptance." *Speech Monographs* 33 (1966): 127–136.
17. Greenberg, B. S., and P. H. Tannenbaum, "The Effects of Bylines on Attitude Change." *Journalism Quarterly* 38 (1961): 535–537.

18. Stone, V. A., and H. S. Eswara, "The Likability and Self-Interest of the Source in Attitude Change." *Journalism Quarterly* 46 (1969): 61–68.

19. Andreoli, V., and S. Worchel, "Effects of Media, Communicator, and Position of Message on Attitude Change." *Public Opinion Quarterly* 42 (1978): 59–70.

20. Walster, E., E. Aronson, and D. Abrahams, "On Increasing the Persuasiveness of a Low Prestige Communicator." *Journal of Experimental Social Psychology* 2 (1966): 325–342.

21. Choo, T., "Communicator Credibility and Communication Discrepancy as Determinants of Opinion Change." *Journal of Social Psychology* 64 (1964): 1–20.

22. Papageorgis, D., "Warning and Persuasion." *Psychological Bulletin* 70 (1968): 271–282.

23. Chaiken, S., "Communicator Physical Attractiveness and Persuasion." *Journal of Personality and Social Psychology* 3 (1979): 1387–1397.

24. Kelman, H. C., and C. I. Hovland, "Reinstatement of the Communicator in Delayed Measurement of Opinion Change." *Journal of Abnormal Social Psychology* 48 (1953): 327–335.

25. Sharp, H., and T. McClung, "Effects of Organization on the Speaker's Ethos." *Speech Monographs* 33 (1966): 182–183.

26. Baker, E. B., "The Immediate Effects of Perceived Speaker Disorganization on Speaker Credibility and Audience Attitude Change in Persuasive Speaking." *Western Speech* 29 (1965): 148–161.

27. Goethals, G. R., and R. E. Nelson, "Similarity in the Influence Process: The Belief-Value Distinction." *Journal of Personality and Social Psychology* 37 (1979): 1469–1476.

28. Bettinghaus, E. P., *Persuasive Communication* (New York: Holt, Rinehart & Winston, 1968).

29. Putnam, G. N., and E. M. O'Hern, "The Status Significance of an Isolated Urban Dialect." *Language* 31 (1955): 1–32.

30. Buck, J., "The Effects of Negro and White Dialectal Variations upon Attitudes of College Students." *Speech Monographs* 35 (1968): 181–186.

31. McGuire, J. W., "The Nature of Attitudes and Attitude Change," in *The Handbook of Social Psychology,* 2nd ed., Vol. 3, ed. G. Lindzey and E. Aronson (Reading, MA: Addison-Wesley, 1969).

Suggested Readings

Applbaum, Ronald, and Karl Anatol. *Strategies for Persuasive Communication.* Columbus, OH: Charles E. Merrill, 1974.

Bettinghaus, Erwin P. *Persuasive Communication,* 2nd ed. New York: Holt, Rinehart & Winston, 1973.

Cafferata, Patricia, and Alice M. Tybout. *Cognitive and Affective*

Responses to Advertising. Lexington, MA: Lexington Books, 1989.

Hovland, C., I. Janis, and H. Kelley. *Communication and Persuasion.* New Haven, CT: Yale University Press, 1953.

Jones, John Philip. *Does It Pay to Advertise? Cases Illustrating Successful Brand Advertising.* Lexington, MA: Lexington Books, 1989.

Lerbinger, Otto. *Designs for Persuasive Communication.* Englewood Cliffs, NJ: Prentice-Hall, 1972.

Petty, Richard, and John T. Cacioppo. *Attitudes and Persuasion: Classic and Contemporary Approaches.* Dubuque, IA: Wm. C. Brown, 1981.

CHAPTER 11

Storytelling

· ·

Those who tell stories hold the power in society. Today television tells most of the stories to most of the people, most of the time.

—*George Gerbner*

Most of what we see on the media is framed as stories. When I began working in television, people in the newsroom kept referring to their news items as "stories." This struck me as somewhat odd because I thought stories had to do with fiction and entertainment. But what the reporters were doing, in fact, was *telling* what had happened that day, what they felt was important or of interest to their viewers. Then I realized that whenever we tell something to someone else, if we want to make it interesting and more memorable, we frame it as a story.

Almost everything in the media involves storytelling in one form or another. Even live events such as a baseball game or the Olympics involve a storyteller or narrator for the "story" as it unfolds. After becoming aware of the pervasiveness of storytelling on television, I decided I should find out about the art of telling stories using video. This chapter presents these findings, which are the backbone of effective presentation.

We'll look into these question: Why is storytelling significant? What gives it its power? Where can we get story ideas? How can stories be told in various video formats? And what techniques can we use to strengthen a story?

The Significance of Story

Let's begin by examining the significance of the story and then looking at story-telling in the context of video production. This will help us design and produce stories with a better appreciation and understanding of the power we're wielding.

Every civilization that ever existed was built on a story. Every nation and religion is based on a story about its founders. Every corporation has its story—the myths about how it was formed and by whom. And everyone has a personal story, which he or she may enjoy telling. Through stories we share our common humanity and create meaning.

Anthropologists mark the discovery of fire as an evolutionary leap. Instead of going to sleep when it got dark, humans could expand the day by sitting around a bonfire gossiping and sharing stories of the hunt or of friends, kin, better ways of doing things, the events of the day. The campfire was the first social context for sharing news.

Those who told the best stories, and told them well, were revered. These early "anchorpersons" not only provided entertainment, they created the "glue" that held the society together. Those who share a common story are related in some way. This was the origin of the clan and tribe—individuals who share a common heritage and life orientation as a result of a common story. The story is repeated through the generations to perpetuate kinship bonds. Elaborate, often complex kinship rules provided for every imaginable situation. But the criteria for applying these rules were how the person was related.

For instance, among American Indians a young man whose biological relatives were dead was accepted as the son or brother of a man who took him in based on his personal characteristics being matched with the "spirit" of the clan. The relationship was as strong a bond as blood kinship. If the lad were aggressive and big, he would be welcomed by a member of the bear clan. If he were cunning and fast, someone in the fox clan would be more inclined to adopt him. The bonds were based on the mutual recognition of a relationship to the central stories of the clan. The story or myth represented and extended the characteristics of the group, which was known as its "spirit."

What happened around early campfires, and what happens now around our electronic campfires (the media), is still primarily entertainment, but it is also the building and binding of community. The media now tell most of our stories, and we respond to these stories selectively. Those of us with a common reference, for instance, those who decide to watch music videos, are perhaps members of the "music video clan"; others who know these people may understand how to relate to them through this membership. So it is with the "fundamentalist clan," the "Ivy League clan," the "rock 'n' roll clan," and so on. The labels "Christian," "academic," "executive," "Democrat," and "American" also refer to groups who share stories. When a story has meaning for us, it becomes a part of our identity.

In addition to identifying with others through our stories, we also come to terms with ourselves and the external world through them. Norma Livo and Sandra Rietz put it this way in *Storytelling: Process and Practice*:

"Story" is a universal mirror that shows us the "truth" about ourselves—who and why we are. When we look into this mirror, we see daily routine and mundane circumstance transformed into something profound. "Story" takes the ordinary and binds it into all of human existence, revealing the significance of the trivial. Through "story" we can transcend the experience of daily living and know ourselves as more enduring than the little occurrences that mark our individual existences. Inside "story" we can accept pain, find justice, and experience exaltation. Inside "story" we can recognize and understand our own motivations, because we are the people in the stories. When we enter into "story" we find the story inside ourselves. "Story" defines humanity.[1]

The Function of Story

The term *story* refers to a linguistic structure, a way of organizing an expression according to a pattern that has meaning. Story is quite different from description, illustration, instruction, or exposition, which simply provide ideas and information. The story's organization—with a beginning, middle, and end—contributes to increased coherence. The relationship of the parts makes it easier to remember what has been told.

Further, story makes the ideas or information personally relevant. When we see an athlete breaking a world record for speed, we may be somewhat interested. But if we have been shown a profile of the person in training from which we get the story of her intensive struggle and motivation, then we have an even better appreciation of her accomplishment. More important, the story provides a moral lesson in the consequences of *character* in specific situations.

Our response is heightened for two reasons. First, we can now relate to the athlete more personally. We've seen what she's been through, the competition she's facing, the dedication and discipline of her training, and her fears and concerns. When she wins we are glad because we can now identify with her. Second, her accomplishment is ours as well because what one human can do, others can do. Although we may not be runners, through her story we saw how qualities of character (thought, attitude, discipline, and practice) led to victory. By applying these qualities ourselves, we too might fulfill our goals.

In practical terms a storyteller takes a series of related pieces of information and organizes them into a story that "tells" well. One method to use is selective focus, or "telescoping," which allows us to show much more of life than is usually possible. One hundred years can be condensed into ten minutes by eliminating what isn't memorable, such as eating, waiting for a bus, irrelevant conversations, and so on.

Storied information is also larger than the facts. Systematically the story is a whole greater than the sum of its parts. This explains the problem with most nightly television newscasts. We get a stream of headlines that present the facts, but complete stories are too long to be told on television. Although we got the headline: "Person indicted on six counts of conspiracy," we didn't get what radio announcer Paul Harvey refers to as "the rest of the story," which is the causal background, history, motivation, and personal events leading up to the alleged crime. And we often don't get the outcome. For example, when we had a drought in my area, the news was full of reports on it. However, none of the local media marked the point when our aquifers were filled again.

Yet, to be satisfying and complete, every story must have a beginning, in which the situation is *set up;* a *confrontation,* in which the character faces the conflict or problem; and a *resolution,* in which order is restored. Subplots are developed to advance the plot and to add excitement, suspense, information, or novelty. We also continuously observe the characters' actions and speech to better identify with them. In the end, when the climax is reached, a character must have been changed in some way—must have learned something from the conflict. A classic example is the end of *The Wizard of Oz.* Dorothy says, "Oh, Aunty Em, there's no place like home."

In movie or television dramas we sometimes identify with the criminal. We rejoice at his escape because we know the whole story—we saw *why* he committed the crime. If we only had the facts, we might not be as sympathetic. Sometimes the abbreviated version of a story is adequate; more often it's not.

Audiences like stories partly because they provide a catharsis of positive or negative emotions, emotional relief through empathy. And during the story we can step outside our ordinary lives and live without limits.

Stories also extend the commonality of human experience. As children we grew up with Cinderella, Mickey Mouse, and Big Bird, characters whose stories point to common themes. The American Dream is built on the success stories of another group of "heroes" such as Thomas Jefferson, Thomas Edison, Amelia Earhart, Henry Ford, and John Wayne. Their stories involved a leap from obscurity to great wealth and/or fame. Their stories support the myths of our time and become commonly accepted.

Harrison Owen, writing about the function of corporate myths, says "when you know *The Story* [about the company's founding], and the story is yours, you are part of the group. If you don't know *The Story,* you just don't belong."[2] America, or any culture, is sustained as a unified whole by commonly held myths.

Finally, in other chapters we've noted that it's essential for the producer to create *order* and *meaning* to get a message across and to have it accepted. Without these a program fails. So "storying" the content, or breaking it up into smaller stories or anecdotes, is a good organizational device to create clarity and meaning.

Story Sources

Where do we find stories? The answer varies according to the situation, but certain perspectives can help us. Begin with yourself. What's your story? People are naturally drawn to other people's stories.

Beyond your own stories, what interests you might interest other people. For example, you're driving down the street and you see a new highrise where six months ago there was just a big hole in the ground. You're amazed at how fast it went up. You can't imagine how construction workers can accomplish so much in so little time. What kind of organization and coordination does that take? Here's your story—how highrise buildings are built or the construction process.

You're stopped by the police for speeding. After you settle down you wonder how the radar system worked so well, especially when your car was going in the opposite direction from the police car. Can radar "read" both directions? How does police radar work, anyway? Here's another story, which most people probably would welcome so they would know when to put on the brakes or how appropriate a radar detector might be for them.

If something interests you, if it reveals a mystery or a problem without a solution, and you can't get an easy answer by asking someone else, there's a story in it. By researching and producing the story, you will be performing a service for the rest of us who also wonder about the subject.

You don't have to have access to police radio bands or news wire services to know what's going on in the world. TV stations often get their news from newspapers and magazines, looking for angles to those stories that may be interesting to their viewers. Even smaller neighborhood newspapers can be sources of stories. And interesting people usually have interesting stories. When you hear about someone interesting, note the person for possible use as a resource later on.

Another approach is to fill a reporting gap. While the mainstream media choose to focus on the breakdowns, the tragedies, and the sensational, you might look for the breakthroughs, the innovations, the private initiatives, and the stories of people creating and exploring. Most of these "good news" stories aren't reported. But many people see a substantial market on the horizon for them, and more of this kind of programming is being seen on cable and even broadcast television all the time.

Because of the time constraints of commercial television, the video arena is wide open for people to take any story of the day and develop it into an entire program. If a newscast can't expand a story, maybe you can. One of the morning network shows interviewed a producer who did this successfully by creating an hour-long documentary on New York City street art. His idea came from seeing a one-minute news story on subway graffiti.

Another approach is to become sensitive to conflict by identifying where it is and analyzing its nature. Is it man versus man, man versus himself, woman versus the system, man versus fate, or woman versus nature? Whatever it is, you can find the drama of the story by focusing on why there is opposition and what sustains it. What is the result of it? What can be done or is being done to resolve it?

As we saw in Chapter 7, "The Audience," any story idea should relate directly to an audience need or interest. When you have an idea for a story, the first question must be: *Who* will watch the program? Who will buy or rent such a tape? If you can answer that question, even tentatively, it's appropriate to go further. If not, file the idea until an audience becomes apparent.

Story Context

Viewers of a video or television program want to know: Who is telling this story? Why is he telling it? This helps them orient themselves in relation to the topic because they get a sense of the consciousness and credibility behind the story as well as the producer's motive. The audience gives commercial messages a certain amount of attention knowing they are being sold something. But they give different attention to a documentary because the purpose is perhaps educational and the viewpoint is more fully developed. "Who" and "why" almost always make a difference to the message receiver.

Point of View (POV)

From whose perspective is the story being told? Who is the storyteller? The following are some of the options.

First person   The subject of the story tells his or her story to someone else, often an interviewer or host. This includes the "person on the street" interview, the casual profile in the subject's home (à la Barbara Walters's interviews), or a more formal studio conversation. Often the best material gained in interviews is anecdotes, the personal stories that give clarity and potency by example. Simply ask the interviewee for personal examples of the point she is making. The situation may even warrant using a *subjective camera* approach to illustrate the story she tells. In this way the viewer's experience comes entirely from a first-person perspective. When a person can tell her own story, there is maximum personal involvement and subjectivity.

Narrator   A narrated story is told by the one who has gathered the information to tell it, such as in the typical news-type presentation, whether a stand-up on location or a report from the anchor desk. Also included are all the industrial and special interest programs that use a presenter. The presenter on camera can speak to the audience directly or off camera as an "omniscient" voice over the pictures that illustrate the story. As we've seen in many commercials, even children can tell stories well. Narrators usually attempt to tell their stories as objectively as possible because their role is observer-reporter.

Authority   The story is told by one whom the audience respects as an authority on the subject. When the producer needs to lend credence to a point, it makes sense to have an authority make the point instead of the program host or narrator (unless she is the authority for that topic). An authority or expert has some personal investment in the stories he tells.

Producer   The story is told by the producer (or writer) of the program. We've seen this on *20/20,* where the "producer" sets up the piece and then cuts away to a prepackaged story. The format suggests that the presenter is the producer but that may not be true. When we see the credits we often learn that the producer was someone we never saw. Most programs are written by people the audience never sees. In some instances, depending on the context, the producer may wish to be seen on camera so the audience can directly experience the source of the story.

Another way to tell a story is without a presenter. Producers can tell the entire story using pictures and sound. By implication, viewers will understand that the storyteller is the producer. The cinema verité format is an example.

Outsider   The story is told by someone who has some connection to the story but is not its focus. This could be eyewitnesses, friends, business partners, family members, or neighbors. Each tells the portion of the story he or she knows. This can be used for stories within a story, but one would not base an entire program on this kind of storytelling because it's fragmented.

Producers often combine these methods to heighten interest in the program and create a sense of activity. Magazine and newscast formats sometimes utilize several storytellers within the same story. In addition to heightening interest by creating action, this also amplifies the apparent importance of the story. On the other hand, too many storytellers used just for effect can diffuse the overall impact.

Why Is the Story Being Told?

One of the most difficult questions every program writer or producer must answer is this: Who cares? We've already seen that *relevance* is critically important if messages are to be accepted and remembered. So we want to be clear about why—from the audience's viewpoint—the story is being told.

In newscasts, the reason for telling a story is usually implied. News writers learn that, for an event to be newsworthy, it should contain one or more of these elements: *timeliness, proximity* (happening close to home), *significance, conflict, prominence,* or *human interest.*

The reason for "good news" stories should be explained openly. People may not see why the producer considers it good: Is it good for the audience or the people in the story or both? The reason for commercials, however, is obvious—to sell. But in training tapes, documentaries, and other special interest programs, the reason may also need to be clarified. This has been done by some corporate sponsors of national television programs who, because they are committed to the values expressed in the program or series, tell the audience that the program "is being brought to you without commercial interruption due to the seriousness of the topic." Then, in the program open, we are told directly how the subject is relevant to the viewers.

Audiences can quickly discern whether a particular program is relevant or is even of passing interest to them. Early on, the producer must address the "why" question. It doesn't have to be explicitly stated as in the above example, but you must deal with it somehow. If your topic is intended for a narrow audience, you can ensure your target audience is watching by indicating the topic's relevance explicitly. People who are not interested will have switched channels, tuned out, or not selected the tape. If, however, the program is intended to attract as large an audience as possible, the "who cares" question can be approached indirectly, implied by the format (e.g., sitcom). There then would be a stronger likelihood of attracting a secondary audience.

For example, if you say the program is about learning to sail, you will attract those who want to learn. But if you want to attract a much larger audience, you would approach the subject more generally, incorporating more of the beauty of sailing, including entertaining segments, thereby cuing the audience that a story about sailing is being told in order to entertain. The general rule is that *if the audience is narrowly targeted, make the relevance explicit. If the audience is broadly defined, imply the relevance within the context of the program.*

Story Structure

We've looked at story structure generally, now let's look at the details. The structure must include a *beginning,* a *middle,* and an *end.* Even a thirty- or sixty-second commercial accomplishes this. Within this general structure other elements give story its unique character.

A story must have a *hero* with whom the audience can *identify* who has a **motive** they can understand. It must also have a *conflict,* a problem or obstacle standing in the hero's way. The conflict is often personified as a villain, or **nemesis,** who represents values in opposition to those of the hero. The **plot** is a series of events that provide the action, leading the hero through increasing conflict toward the goal. The **theme** is the core of meaning, often referred to as the *moral* of the story. The hero, attempting to overcome the conflict, displays some *virtue* (courage), which leads to the story's *climax* (where the goal is attained) and the lessons learned. Often the hero is different as a result of the experience. Finally, in the **denouement,** all elements are restored to order; there is balance and harmony.

Structuring Stories for the Screen

As a video communicator, you have two choices for telling stories: (1) *showing* the story and how it unfolds or (2) *telling* the story by putting a presenter in the position of storyteller. In the first, the audience identifies with the characters and oversees the plot's events. The experience is usually emotionally engaging and intense as a consequence of this identification and action orientation. In the second, you put the viewer in the position of listener, just as a child listens to a story. Listening to a storyteller is usually a less intense experience, but it can still be emotional because, instead of identifying with the characters through provided visuals, the audience uses their imagination. Supplementary images should be used, but the context remains one of listening to an illustrated story.

Which option is appropriate? Several factors apply. Should the audience derive the story's imagery from the screen or mostly from their own imagination? Should the audience *feel* the story or *know* it? Should the audience be left with an *experience* or *information?*

Practical concerns such as budget and time constraints often make the decision easy. If you use actors to show interaction through events, it is usually more expensive and time-intensive. But the other option runs the risk of placing too much burden on viewers' imaginations and attention and possibly losing their interest altogether. As we have already seen, radio and audiocassettes stimulate the imagination as well as and sometimes even better than TV or video.

Showing Stories

Full-length *drama* is, of course, the natural format for showing the interaction of characters and events. It's the backbone of television and film entertainment. But stories can be presented in training, sales, promotion, and documentary programs as well. *Docudrama* is another relatively expensive option, where historical (or other) characters play out the circumstances surrounding an event or illustrate a viewpoint. The BBC incorporates high standards using this technique. More financially feasible is the *miniplay,* where a skit is enacted for a brief section of a program. In a training tape about courtroom procedures, one could stage a mock trial or case reenactment.

One of Xavier University's promotion tapes begins with its founding and, instead of simply having the narrator talk about it, the producer staged a miniplay with costumed Jesuits arriving on the banks of the Ohio River at Cincinnati. Their canoes were met by townsfolk and Indians. This dramatized hook was ideal for an otherwise very talky program, and it provided entertainment throughout. The producer cut back to miniplay footage when appropriate to the progression of the subject matter, for instance, a scene in a log cabin classroom.

In another situation, when a local neighborhood was being demolished to make way for new construction, a television station produced a historical profile of the area using their news anchorpersons in various acting roles, restaging some historical events. Although this piece aired about ten years ago, I still remember it, especially an interaction between a present-day white reporter and a female black resident from the earlier era. In their nighttime, door-stoop conversation, the woman told her historical stories in present tense. These kinds of techniques bring content alive. *When there's a story to be told, consider staging it rather than merely having it read.*

To separate a skit or miniplay from other program elements, consider special effects to cue the audience to the shift between them (as with flashbacks). Sepia and fog filters work well by slightly tinting or diffusing light to distinguish the miniplay by giving it a different texture.

Telling Stories

When the producer, narrator, or any other person on or off camera is *telling* a story, the challenge is twofold: to employ visuals that enhance the telling and to incorporate action. Always ask interview guests to bring slides or color pictures with them. Film or video is preferred if they have it. (Avoid using video formats below the quality level of the main piece.) One can also create visuals using electronic tools, such as a character generator or computer or electronic paint system. If these are not available, take notes on conversations and shoot location footage to enhance what was said, or have an illustrator or artist prepare art cards, to bring the story to life.

Although video animation is expensive and requires highly specialized equipment, there are always ways to innovate using artwork. I've used art cards to create cartoon stories for kids. Nothing within the frame moved; all the action was due to cuts, dissolves, wipes, and different moves over the cards—a technique referred to as "animatics." With music and sound effects one was hardly aware that the piece was not animated. The story as told by a narrator was also performed, and not merely read, so this also made a big difference.

The second challenge—to create action in situations where a person is telling a story or offering an anecdote—is actually easier. Either the subject matter in front of the camera moves, or the camera itself moves, or both. That's not to say that something is moving all the time; we don't want this to be artificial or make viewers dizzy. But motion is still one of the best ways to make video compelling. This kind of camera movement should be skillfully coordinated with the subject matter so the audience is unaware of it. The movement should emphasize composition and grace, with no bumps, jerky motion, or false starts and no change of speed between a zoom-out and a pan right or zoom-in to zoom-in.

If someone is going to be on screen for more than five minutes, let's see them in different environments. Get him to come out from behind the desk to sit on the corner, then take him to the computer room for a "walk and talk" to the camera, and so on. (An interview situation is, of course, an exception, as is the newscast and a few other circumstances where it's appropriate for the talent to stay in one place.) Even if you're using only one camera, change the perspective on the talent to make him active in the frame. Without movement storytelling becomes tedious. Rely on what video can do best—move, change angles, and provide contrasts.

How the Story Is Told

Just like a good joke, it's not only the material itself but also the way the material is presented that is important. Why can some people tell stories better than others? They invest more of themselves in the telling, making things up as they go along, enhancing this, diminishing that, increasing and then lowering their volume. And certain techniques can enhance the telling of stories with video.

Begin Powerfully

For the hook, select scenes that most powerfully and quickly express the *sensibility* of the piece. You don't want to give away the climax or theme, but you can create a poignant question in the audience's mind by inference, suggestion, or implication. Get the audience's interest and pique their curiosity. You don't necessarily have to use an upbeat tempo to begin powerfully. Whatever the tempo, the images (audio as well as video) must be potent.

Immediately after the hook, if you haven't as yet established the main character (hero), do so, preparing to move directly into the conflict or problem. Think about using an unusual, attention-getting beginning. You might have a narrator, perhaps speaking in a flashback mode, tell the first part of the story with voice-over images of the place where the story will end (rather than begin). You might use video and natural sound only or music only. Another powerful technique for a program open is to have the storyteller speak for several seconds over a blank screen and then bring up the appropriate imagery. Further, you might open with the impact of the problem or conflict fully displayed, for instance, a mother finding out her daughter or son has decided to go to college 1,000 miles away.

Use the beginning as an opportunity to demand the audience's attention, even if the format is informational, for instance, in a lecture on particle physics. Instead of opening with a professor announcing the topic, make the first shot a slow motion close-up of an explosion of light (using artwork of deep space) with high-impact music. Then bring in a voice to tell the story of the "big bang" and how scientists believe our galaxy was formed. After this the professor can tell her story. Almost any information can be expressed visually, at least in part, within the context of a story. By beginning powerfully, you allow the audience to get into the story immediately and become hungry for more.

Unfold the Events

Think of one event leading into another and so on. The character should be revealed to us not so much by what he says, or with what the narrator says, but by his behavior. A story by definition requires a sequence of events, not descriptions or monologues.

To link events together the writer or producer should look at the hero's motivation. The hero wants something to happen and that *desire* determines the direction of events. To establish conflict, create situations to thwart the hero's progress. Ask yourself: What is the cause and effect of these events? Often you can present the effect first and the cause then becomes part of the enlarging question to be resolved at the end. Instead of having the characters ask the questions, you can simply show the behavioral action and let the question be generated in the viewer's mind.

The director's task is to stage action and events so the audience understands the story without words. One of the most common ways of doing this is with the close-up shot to reveal a character's emotion or eye contact with others. An event can be as simple and subtle as a person's facial response to someone else.

Many mainstream television producers have ignored this simple guideline. Sitcoms have often failed precisely because the characters are merely vehicles for presenting "one-liners" and sight gags. The writers have written jokes but no action. Audiences see through this, and these programs fall flat very fast. Look at the sitcoms that work to see well-developed characters working out conflicts through a series of events (not a string of jokes). Create interesting characters and then let the action carry the story forward. This applies to lecture-format presenters as well.

Focus on the Plot

Every scene should carry the story forward. It's usually better to resist the tendency to have the hero or other character state the purpose of the story or any other message you want the audience to get. Storytelling involves *showing* a message, a moral, a theme, or a lesson instead of preaching it. Make sure that your characters don't irritate the audience by "selling" your message overtly. This is the essential difference between storytelling and any other form of expression. Let the events carry the expression completely. When the audience is caught up in the experience of the story, there will be a greater likelihood that they will "own" the message when the story is finished.

Keep the Plot Simple

Use only the number of characters necessary to carry the storyline. Keep the plot as simple as possible to avoid confusion. For instance, if you're using a flashback technique, make sure that the scenes in the flashback are obvious. Use a color or diffusion filter, use the same location—but be sure the audience knows what is dream or in the past and what is not.

Avoid symbolism for the most part unless it's justified and to some extent made obvious. Video audiences don't generally expect symbolism. If part of your plot hangs on the audience's understanding of what happened as explained by a symbolic image, you can lose them quickly if the story doesn't cue a symbolic context.

This is especially true of visual content. My students often have to explain certain parts of their videos to the rest of the class, describing what they intended in a particular shot because the class didn't see it or interpreted the scene differently. Be aware that there is a big difference between *universal symbols* (a dove equals peace) and *personal symbols* that only the individual producer understands. To avoid misinterpretation, never assume that an audience will see things the same way you do. If you like, shoot a scene two ways—with and without a symbol—and ask for opinions when you get to the editing stage.

Highlight the Characters' Style

We remember characters who exhibit qualities we don't frequently encounter in our day-to-day lives. Screen heroes can get away with being outrageous, opinionated, or courageous. Their "style" uniquely carries some traits and helps the audience to identify with them. The audience may also value some element represented by the style or mannerism. It endears the character to the audience. This is why most characters in films and on TV have personalities that are unique. We can see ordinary people anywhere, so show the audience someone really different.

Modulate the Mood and Tempo

Just as we tire quickly of listening to a person speak in a monotone, we also get bored with the same mood. One reason for going to a movie, renting a video, or playing a tape is to change moods. Within the story, certain events should be upbeat, fast paced, and exciting. And these should alternate with others that are soft, slow, and delicate. The transition between the two can be interesting as well.

Public speakers learn that, if they want their listeners to pay attention, they should whisper or speak very softly and slowly before raising the volume. It heightens the audience's interest—they're afraid they might miss something. Have some characters talking softly, then have a loud percussive noise direct attention across the room. Crash cut to the enthusiasm of the main character interrupting. Or create a scene in which a board of directors is having its stuffy but noisy meeting in a wood-paneled room, with the CEO speaking loudly. Cut to a female board member who leans over to another member and whispers to him, "It'll never work."

Moving the emotions of the audience from event to event so they are on a roller coaster is much more interesting than maintaining an even pace throughout. Even lecture-format programs should contain some tempo changes to keep them interesting.

Highlight the Characters' Relationships

Video is a people-oriented medium. The main character of any story, even a news story, should not be presented in isolation. One of the best ways to get to know a character is by observing his or her interactions with others. Show these interactions directly; put the viewer in the position of overseer. Let the audience evaluate the character for themselves. An audience can tell whether an interaction is staged or artificial. Be careful to invest whatever is necessary to make these character interactions "real." Use talented actors and rehearse them well.

Make It Unpredictable

If the audience sees early on how the story will end, there is less excitement and perhaps less motivation to continue viewing. This is another reason for designing the ending of a program first: It becomes easier to work backward so viewers won't guess the ending. When the climax does occur, viewers should be at the peak of the catharsis, satisfied by the character's accomplishment and pleased with the outcome. A rule of good storytelling is to create audience anticipation for the ending but never let them know what it will be until it actually happens.

Summary

One of the most powerful forms of communication is the story. Storytelling is an essential part of human interaction, playing a central role in the maintenance and development of culture. In this chapter we have examined the story, beginning with its significance as a factor in early human communication.

Story is a particular kind of communication structure. It identifies characters within a context of time and place, moving them through a series of events toward a goal. These events display the difficulty in and process of attaining the goal through conflicts along the way. In the end the conflict is resolved; lessons are learned; the protagonist (hero) achieves the goal by overcoming the antagonist (villain or other obstacles); and order is restored.

The story structure *creates increased interest* because it involves the audience in situations they might not normally experience and it *promotes memory* for the experience so that the theme (or moral) is retained. And story can *create meaning* from a variety of life experiences. You can easily telescope time forward or backward, providing only the salient information. This is in contrast to "real" life, where we experience present time only, and much of our activity is mundane and seemingly unrelated to the themes of our lives.

Video stories can come from real-life observation of the events, relationships, and processes that pique our interest. They can be sparked by the imagination. And they come from seeing needs, alternatives, or innovations that others apparently don't see.

Every story has a context within which it is told. Who is telling the story? Why is it being told? The answers to these questions help the audience gain a sense of the perspective and credibility of the teller and his motivation. You can address the context either directly or subtly.

After looking briefly at the typical story structure involving the hero, conflict, theme, and other essential elements, we noted that the producer has two prime ways of structuring stories for the screen. You can *show* a story or *tell* a story (or both). The former uses actors to enact the story while the audience oversees the unfolding of the plot. The latter uses a storyteller, narrator, or other to present the story verbally, often with accompanying visuals and sounds. The one you choose will depend on several variables including audience preference, cost, available time, and the producer. Both structures can result in compelling video experiences.

We concluded our study of storytelling with an examination of several factors that relate to how to tell stories with video. These include beginning powerfully, focusing on the events of the story, developing characters and their relationships, keeping the plot simple, modulating the tempo, and keeping the ending hidden.

The stories we tell, and how we tell them, communicate.

Notes

1. Livo, Norma J., and Sandra A. Rietz, *Storytelling: Process and Practice* (Littleton, CO: Libraries Unlimited, 1986), 4. Used by permission of the author.

2. Owen, Harrison, "Leadership by Indirection," in *Transforming Leadership: From Vision to Results,* ed. John D. Adams (Alexandria, VA: Miles River Press, 1986), 117.

Suggested Readings

Egri, Lajos. *The Art of Dramatic Writing: Its Basis in the Creative Interpretation of Human Motives,* 3rd ed. New York: Simon & Schuster, 1960.

Livo, Norma J., and Sandra A. Rietz. *Storytelling: Process and Practice.* Littleton, CO: Libraries Unlimited, 1986.

PART V

MAKING IT GOOD

· · · · · · · · · · · · · · · · · · ·

A good program reflects quality work in every way. It looks professional. We have discussed how the presentation communicates about the producing team. Production values, or the lack of them, send definite cues to the audience about the intent, purpose, and competence of the producers. All of this affects program effectiveness directly and profoundly.

Production values directly result from a commitment to quality throughout all phases of production. Achieving quality in a video production requires a determination that, no matter what, nothing will go into the program until it is the *best* the team can accomplish. Nothing, including time constraints, budget constraints, or personnel or equipment problems, should allow us to accept

anything less than the best we can do.

Sometimes, however, we choose or accept limitations. Maybe the budget isn't enough to afford recording on 1-in. tape. Or maybe you can't afford to rent a dolly. You're worried about missing the deadline. Or your leading actor got the flu, and you're on location

with twenty extras, and it rained most of the day. A commitment to quality means that, in spite of breakdowns, the team will somehow compensate so the outcome is not negatively affected.

The audience doesn't care about your limitations, breakdowns, or circumstances. They probably assume that you are able to manage your life in a manner that will transcend circumstances to provide a video experience they can appreciate. Ask any dedicated athlete if there's an easy way to win. Every worthwhile endeavor requires commitment and dedication. Producing video is rarely glamorous. The mix of fun, hard work, occasional frustration, tediousness, and excitement makes video production both challenging and highly fulfilling, but the real excitement comes from working cooperatively and creatively with people you respect and enjoy and, later, from viewers' feedback when they got the message and enjoyed the experience.

Here's a quick example. A group of five students in my advanced TV production class recently came very close to winning a national video competition. Out of 2,000 entries, their project placed third. Their goal for the class was to produce a network-quality short story that could win a competition. At the beginning they detailed specific production values as their technical strategy to show the judges that they could produce "network quality." Their list included

- sound effects and ambience (recorded separately) wherever possible to be mixed with music
- camera moves that would appear to be gear driven
- visual economy (showing only what's necessary)
- a cutting pace that matches the emotional flow
- a visual "payoff" at the end that matches music cues

These were their technical guidelines for every shot and edit they made. And they accomplished their goal.

We have already talked about the viewer who **grazes** the channels with a remote control to find something to watch. Production values, before content, cue the audience whether or not to continue watching. These values, or their lack, immediately tell viewers about the competence, creativity, and consciousness of the production team.

In Chapter 12 we'll examine production values relating to the audio portion of a production. Chapter 13 will focus on video production values, and Chapter 14 on postproduction values. Keep in mind that "quality in" is required for every production element. In our systems approach, the smallest details are the ones that require the most constant attention.

Audio Production Values

What we are striving for is the creation of sounds that, when put together with an image, will seem appropriate to that image and to its emotional context. In many cases the sounds one hears are not the same as the sounds one would hear if actually present at that location, but they should be in character with the subject, expand upon the image, and feel realistic.

—Walter Murch

The phrase *production values* refers to specific techniques that give a program a unique style. These techniques can be anything from complex camera moves coordinated with talent movements to simple catch-lights in the talent's eyes. You can think about these techniques contributing to the effectiveness of the program as a positive value added. Each technique must display excellence in its execution, communicating contextually that the production team is competent.

Beginning producers may not manage their respective production systems well because they fail to pay close enough attention to the details involved. Or they may see techniques merely as established ways to make a program and give them insufficient time and attention.

In this chapter we'll examine some specific techniques to add value to the audio portion of a program, focusing on those that audiences notice most often. Many of these techniques—which are also commonly discussed in books on video and/or audio production—may be familiar from either prior experience in production or just from watching television. The difference between a technique and a production value is in the mastery of the craft and a commitment to excellence. We'll work on transforming ordinary audio techniques into positive values and positive attitudes. These audio elements will, by their very presence in a program, suggest a highly talented, organized, creative, and intelligent production team.

Developing an Ear

Videographers and cinematographers are said to have developed an "eye" only after years of experience composing subjects in the viewfinder. The same time and practice are also required for the audio technician and any producer who cares about quality sound. Just before an important shoot I close my eyes and imagine what the world would be like without sight or hearing. This exercise hypersensitizes my sight and hearing. It enables me to pick up sights and sounds that others don't because every point of light and sound seems special and worthy of consideration. Because light and sound compose our medium, we must develop a sensitivity to them in detail to use them fully.

Information theory, developed by Norbert Weiner and others in the field of **cybernetics,** regards information as every "bit" of input. In a silent environment, a tap, heard once, is one bit of information. Two taps are two pieces of information. When we hear two taps, we assume and look for a relationship between them. If the taps are identical we assume they came from the same source. If they are different we assume two sources are involved and that there is a connection between them. A third tap adds more information about the source (background) and the relationships involved (foreground).

Now, put this book down, close your eyes, and listen to the sounds of your present environment. Listen as if you were hearing impaired. Take one minute.

Answer the following questions after you have plugged both ears with your index fingers to shut out as much sound as possible. Don't look around; keep your eyes on this book.

- How many different sounds did you identify?
- What sound was farthest from you (background)? Name the source.
- What sound was closest to you (foreground)? Name the source.
- Did you hear any sound coming from yourself (such as breathing, heartbeat, or sniffling)?
- Is your sound environment simple (having few sounds) or complex?

Repeat this exercise in a variety of environments. You will increase the quality of your "ear" by developing a habit of discriminating (hearing different sounds) and discerning (paying attention to what different sounds are like). This will help you fashion sounds for your productions. When you listen to music, develop the habit of identifying as many instruments as you can. When you hear an air-conditioner or motor, discriminate among the various sounds that make up the drone. When you're part of a live audience, shift your listening attention from the speaker to the audience itself. Take every opportunity to develop your awareness and sensitivity to sound.

In the above questions, what's important is not the number of sounds you could discriminate but *how well* you could focus on each and *what information* you could derive from them. Do these exercises in unique environments such as old buildings, long hallways, and airport terminals. Try to increase your level of appreciation for each sound and what you can learn about the source as a result of the sound alone.

Audio Planning

There are three components to program audio: voice, music, and sound effects. These provide the information, emotion, and presence of the program, respectively. Through human speech we gain knowledge and understanding of content and context; music provides an undertone of emotional energy; and sound effects and/or natural sound draw us into the piece. These three elements can be tied together in an endless array of combinations, and none should be considered more or less important than the others. Even if sound effects are less evident than the voice or music, as program elements, they deserve attention.

Simplicity/Complexity

Every program you produce will have a unique mix of voice, music, and effects based on how the audio relates to the communication objective. A simple audio plan may involve speech only or music only, or speech and natural sound. Some very powerful public service announcements (PSAs) use natural sound exclusively. Simplicity's power can never be overestimated. A complex audio plan utilizes all three elements, interweaving them alternately to express the content, feelings, and proximity the producer orchestrates. We now turn to specific audio production values.

Voice Selection

Who should provide the spoken portion of the program? Should the voice be male or female? What age? What dialect? What personality style—high key or low? To answer we'll look at the communication objective and also at what I call the *sensibility of the piece.* Every program has a unique feel or texture, a quality related directly to the subject matter and the overall impression the audience should receive. This is the sensibility.

The on-camera narrator for a documentary on Shaker cooking should carry both the sound and the visual sensibility of the historic community—perhaps an older woman who reflects the Shaker way of life. She would be thin rather than stout and have gray hair rather than blond; her speech would be precise, lacking contemporary slang words. In contrast, the sensibility of a training tape on telephone pole wiring suggests the rugged and experienced voice of a male lineman. A training tape on computers, however, could use either a man or a woman because either could be perceived by the target audience as competent in that area. The sensibility in this case suggests a well-educated professional whose speech should include high-tech jargon and whose demeanor should reveal a well-organized mind. In a dramatic presentation the actor must be associated with the sensibility of her character to convince the audience they are the same.

In Chapter 10, "Persuasion," we stressed the importance of similarity between the content presenter and the audience to gain their interest and appeal to what they already perceive about the subject. Now we can add an additional criterion: The sensibility of the piece helps envelop the audience in the experience.

Should the voice we select be presented on camera or as voice-over? A common rule is to show the speaker on camera only when he or she is well known, liked, or respected by the target audience or brings to the screen some visual emphasis related to the sensibility of the piece. An exception to this rule is using authors on camera to present subjects with which they are most familiar—such as Jacob Bronowski's *The Ascent of Man* and Carl Sagan's *Cosmos* series. In these cases the presenters were not very well known to the public, but the programs, because they were nationally promoted, helped establish them as public figures. The same applies to sports figures who may want to be seen simply to increase their visibility. To create celebrity status for the presenter by showing him or her on camera, you need a person with a certain uniqueness of personal style. You'll recognize this uniqueness when you encounter such individuals.

When the choices you've made relating to the voice component of your program are in harmony with the sensibility of the piece, and at the same time communicate credibility to the audience, the value of this element will be apparent.

Music Selection

Music is a matter of taste. Every producer will have different preferences and approach music issues from different perspectives. Should music be used at all? Research suggests that messages with an emotional component are more effective and more memorable. Music, then, can augment and improve almost any program. A program's emotional content comes from both pictures and sounds, and their interaction, but music is a primary emotional source. It also carries an entertainment quality audiences appreciate. Music is transformed into a production value when it matches the sensibility of the piece in placement, tempo, color, and lyrics (if there are any)—when the sights and sounds augment one another.

Placement refers to where the music is used in the program. Pay attention to the way music is used on sitcoms as a bridge in addition to the open and closing theme. Notice the music placement in made-for-television movies and soap operas, where it strengthens the drama in the scenes. And notice how documentaries use music as transitions and to add emotion to diverse content areas. Music should always enhance but never overpower. As with every technique we'll discuss, the audience should never shift their attention away from the content to the music. When viewers are made aware of the music, they have been distracted from what it's there to express.

Tempo is often the most predominant musical quality of a program. Studies have shown there is a direct biological, cellular response to syncopation or rhythm.[1] You can easily select the right tempo for your video by determining whether its action is fast paced or slow. Are the ideas presented in rapid succession or slowly in a particular scene? Will the visuals be cut or dissolved? Should the audience be stirred up or lulled into a peaceful, sensitive state? Remember empathy and plan the tempo of the music so that it matches, creates, or contributes to the emotional response you are trying to achieve. Remember that an up tempo is exciting and a slow tempo is soothing.

Music also possesses a quality known as "color," derived from its ability to stimulate a spectrum of feelings. "Hot" jazz can conjure up images of flame and sizzle. The fullness of a symphony orchestra can expand us, can open our senses, and can cause us to take a deep breath. This is emotional manipulation at its best.

Should the music have lyrics? Again, if the words relate to the content in some way, for instance, by promoting meaning, then they are appropriate. Music and lyrics have a well-known power to create memory. The commercial jingle is perhaps the best example. In addition to creating a memory for the message, lyrics can convey specific thoughts and feelings to enhance meaning.

The voice can also be considered a musical instrument. I have just completed a home video program, *The Book of Co-Creation*, which has an original musical score. The composer and performer, Oman Ken, in addition to being a highly talented musician, is also skilled in the use of synthesizers and music computers. In a few pieces he used his and a female voice to provide a dimension just by singing sounds such as "ahhhhhhh" and "ouuuuuu." When reshaped and synthesized into the instrumental foreground, the voices created a feeling for the listeners of being lifted off the floor. As we edited the piece, those of us in the control room were astonished at what we felt—as if we were standing in the Lincoln Memorial experiencing the entire space filled with choral voices.

Sound Effects

Sound effects are appropriate when viewers should be drawn into a scene rather than standing outside it as observers. You can observe the different techniques on the nightly newscast. Watch for stories that cut to a location package where the journalist is talking voice-over with no natural sound—the viewer's feeling is of being in the speaker's space and not the location where the taping took place. Then notice the stories where natural sound is used behind the voice-over. You now have the feeling of being at the location you are watching. So natural sounds, and sound effects created to simulate them, bring viewers into the setting they are watching.

Can you imagine an Indiana Jones movie without sound effects? In this case, if the producers used only the natural sounds as recorded on location, the experience would be very flat compared with the sparkle of well-planned and balanced sound effects recorded separately. The decision to plan for sound effects and/or natural sound becomes a part of creating positive production value when sound is used with conscious intent to involve the viewer.

How close do you want the audience to be? Audio effects can create either distance or closeness. Which of these will promote greater effectiveness is a matter for each producer to decide.

Audio Recording

. . . .

Because production values relate more to qualitative (rather than basic) use of audio techniques, we'll leave it to other texts to describe the ordinary techniques of audio production. Our focus will be on those special areas that cue the audience about our competence as communicators and producers. To be an effective producer, you should view these considerations as fundamental.

Technical Considerations

These technical procedures will help you produce high-quality audio for your video.

Use virgin tape stock For all original rolls, do not use "one-pass" tape. With used tape you run the risk of having dirt and edge defects, which, although not immediately apparent, may retard the sound quality as the tape is replayed. Because tape quality directly influences the quality of the program, it makes sense to use the best. It's false economy to stage an elaborate shoot and then record it on questionable tape.

"Pack" the tape before recording **Packing** refers to putting a virgin tape into the machine that will be used as the recorder, fast-forwarding to the end of the tape, and then rewinding back to the head. Packing creates a wind tension on the cassette that is identical to the recording machine rather than to that of the factory machine. This ensures even unwind tension and reduces the likelihood of static attracting dust particles, which reduces the probability of dropouts, those flashes of white horizontal lines that interrupt the picture. This technique is especially valuable when using ¾-in. recorders in the field. Although this procedure is not absolutely necessary, professionals don't usually record anything important without packing the tape first.

Use the automatic gain control (AGC) and audio limiter switch purposefully These switches are found on most video tape recorders (VTRs). They serve two distinct purposes, but many students think they are the same thing. Know what you want before activating them. The AGC in the on position indicates that, when the volume level is below a certain point, the machine will automatically raise the level. With the AGC on, the background noise will be raised to a normal level during a speaker's pauses, and when she speaks the background noise will recede. You've probably heard this annoying effect because news videographers sometimes leave the AGC switch on constantly. This is a mistake. That switch should only be used in situations where there is no noise in the background.

The audio limiter switch is a volume compressor. It is intended to ensure that the audio does not distort if the sound source gets louder abruptly. Equipment designers put this control on some VTRs because they intend them to be used for electronic news gathering (ENG) work where the operator cannot watch and ride the volume units (VU) meter. The limiter should only be used when the sound source is erratic (up and down) and when the operator is unable to ride the level. Otherwise, keep the limiter off, especially when setting levels. In this way the compression will not interfere with the audio as it is recorded.

Create gradual audio level changes   Whenever you need to move a level up or down, do so gradually. The listener's attention should never be directed to a shift in levels.

Play back a portion of what you record   This simple feedback practice saves time and headaches when working on location. Play back the tape for every setup (even in the studio). A setup may involve one or several shots. Not every shot needs to be played back, but never move to another setup without sampling what you just recorded. Every time you think of the next setup, think of playing back the previous one. And don't forget to take a headset for this purpose when going on location. Think of a headset as a part of the VTR subsystem when you develop your equipment checklist. And make sure you have the right connector to plug it into the deck.

Attend to background sounds   You may or may not want them. Perhaps you'll even want to emphasize them at times, such as when a train is passing behind talent whom you want to have yelling above the noise (in a documentary on trains, for instance). But you must realize that *sound establishes direction;* it cues the viewer to direct his or her attention toward its source. Because you want to direct the viewer's attention purposefully, you must be sensitive to the relative levels of sound—foreground and background, right and left, above and below—to orchestrate them according to where you want the viewer's attention to move. We don't usually have sounds that distract from the focal point of what we are shooting.

People hear before they see. Infants turn in the direction of sounds to see what caused them. Sound signals existence; sight verifies it and makes it identifiable. A nice transition then is to introduce sounds from the incoming scene so that, when you cut to it, the audience will have already shifted their attention—just like the infant, searching for what's going to happen next.

Microphone Selection

Beginning producers sometimes assume that, to get good sound, all you have to do is point the microphone at the sound source. But recording sound as a production value involves a different assumption as well as practice. Every microphone is designed for a specific purpose. Many good books describe microphones and their specific pickup characteristics and patterns. Learn the characteristics of every mike you use. Although some of the material in these books may be more technical than you need, there are some simple usage principles that are critical for obtaining "clean" sound.

To select a microphone you must understand that sound is a vibration of air-waves emanating from a source. Clap your hands. Imagine a ripple of sound waves spreading out 360 degrees. Your ears pick the sound up quickly and qualitatively because they are close to the source. But the person across the hall hears the sound as it bounces off or is blocked by a variety of surfaces, each affecting the intensity and quality of what she hears. Her reception of the hand clap sound will also include some extraneous noises. So the *sound environment* makes as much difference to the quality of your recording as the kind of microphone used.

If we set up ten different microphones to record the air vibrations caused by your voice as you speak, and then played back each separately, we would be amazed at the difference. No two recordings would sound identical—even if the mikes were positioned in the same place for the recording. That's because microphone manufacturers design these instruments for different applications. The three major categories of mikes are named for the characteristics of their sensing (pickup) elements:

Dynamic microphones require no power and are the most rugged, for location use. They are mostly used with amateur equipment but their quality can be excellent.

Ribbon microphones are delicate and are, therefore, mostly used in studios where they are stabilized.

Condenser microphones require batteries or some other source. They are the most common type of mikes for video and film production fieldwork.

Manufacturers also designate microphones by their pickup pattern characteristics:

Omnidirectional microphones pick up sound equally in a 360-degree pattern. Use these mikes when environmental sound is to be included along with sound from the primary source. They pick up everything equally in all directions.

Bidirectional microphones pick up sound primarily at the 0- and 180-degree points relative to their position. This "figure-eight" pattern is useful when a mike will be stationary between two sound sources—as when two singers face each other.

Unidirectional microphones pick up sounds primarily in front of their positions. These include *cardioid* microphones, which have a heart-shaped field of sensitivity, that is, they pick up sounds best in front and on the sides but not in back. These mikes are used to minimize environmental sound directly in back of them. They are often used as "hand mikes" for this reason. At the other end of the unidirectional spectrum are the *shotgun* mikes that pick up in an extremely narrow field directly in front of them. These are used when ambient sounds on the sides and back need to be reduced. Many people also use them to gather sounds from a distance, but this is not their purpose and it stretches the quality of the signal according to the distance involved.

Using the right mike for the right purpose is essential to transform an ordinary technique into one with audio value added. For instance, a *lavaliere* (a small microphone worn around the neck), usually used for interviews, is not a good mike to use for recording music. Its frequency response is intended for voice, so it would seriously reduce the quality of the music. And it's inappropriate to use a shotgun mike to record sound effects simply because it can be placed some distance from the source or because it needs to be kept out of the shot. It can do these things, but these are not good reasons for using a shotgun. A better reason for using a shotgun mike is that its narrow pickup eliminates surrounding sounds or that its emphasis on high frequencies is needed.

Each time you need to use a microphone, select one based on these considerations: (1) the *frequency response* desired, (2) the *directionality* of the sound source, and (3) the sound *environment characteristics* (closeness or hollowness, sounds that may need to be blocked out). Mike selection should be based on qualitative concerns rather than on convenience or expediency. For details relating to microphone brands, models, frequency responses, and pickup characteristics, consult one of the books listed at the end of the chapter.

Microphone Placement

There are three factors involved in placing a microphone: the *distance* of the mike from the source, the *direction* of the sound from its source, and the mike's *appearance* if it will be seen on camera.

To work optimally, mikes should be within the manufacturer's design and pickup range, usually *as close as possible* to the sound source. You'll know when the mike is out of range as you move it away from the source because the pot (volume control) will need to be turned all the way up. This brings extraneous noises up as well, which is not good. The proper range should be approximately one-third to one-half its full capacity.

If the sound source is stationary, the direction of the sound will be constant. But if the source is moving, the mike will need either to move or generally to favor the predominant direction. Even on network television I often see people miked with a lavaliere on the far side of the lapel. When a person is speaking to that side, everything is fine, but when he turns in the other direction, he's off mike (Figures 12.1a and 12.1b).

Lavalieres are properly placed in the *center* of the speakers' body about the spread of five fingers from the throat and not near a shoulder. This distance is

a   b

**FIGURE 12.1
Guest Lavaliere
Placement: Incorrect and Correct**
*In photo **(a)** the mike is attached to the lapel opposite the direction he is speaking. Photo **(b)** shows the correct position.*

within the pickup pattern of the mike and it also provides some room so that, on a medium shot, the mike can be cropped out of the frame.

Another common placement problem is pointing a shotgun mike straight at a person whose head is turned, speaking perpendicular to the mike. Whichever mike you use, imagine a straight line emanating from the sound source and then place the microphone in the middle of that path.

Finally, and no less important, consider where the mike should be aesthetically. I use this rule: *The microphone should never be in the shot* unless there is a good reason for it to be there. For example, some performers like to hold on to a mike. Reporters like to hold or position a hand mike so the station ID on it can be displayed. And instruments (guitar, drum, piano) require close mike placement, which audiences have come to accept. But because we never want to do anything to attract the viewer's attention to technique, usually it is best not to show the mike.

The Sound Environment

We're familiar with the way light reflects off surfaces but perhaps less sensitive to the way sound waves bounce off the same surfaces. Experienced sound technicians, especially consultants who design sound studios, are acutely aware of this factor because it has a profound effect on sound quality.

Generally, audio quality for video requires that you deaden the environment to prevent the sound from ricocheting around the room, which creates a hollow sound like being in a large hall. When that kind of sound is desirable, you should place hard surfaces far from the sound source. But more often, voice and other sounds are improved when they have a rapid falloff, that is, a short distance to travel, and when they are partially absorbed rather than reflected. This is why most audio recording studios and announcer's booths have walls lined with sound-absorbent material.

Studios usually provide some way to modify the sound-reflecting characteristics of the space. Some studios have portable baffles; others lay out carpeting or pull a curtain around the subject. Even coats and other clothing items can be hung from light stands to create a more enclosed audio quality. It may look bad, but it'll sound great. Just make sure none of the mess is in the shot.

On location the challenge is greater. We recently produced a PSA for a cloistered order of Passionist nuns to attract potential novices to their order. We needed to record a narration by one of the sisters, but they never leave the convent. The only quiet place in their facility was a large chapel. So we set up a cardioid mike on a stand about six inches from her face, off to the side slightly so there wouldn't be popping "Ps" (audio distortion occurring when words beginning with "P" are pronounced), and then draped our coats in a semicircle in back of her and the mike so her speech wouldn't reach any of the distant walls and bounce back. Without the coats the audio sounded as if it had been recorded in the capital rotunda in Washington. But with them, it sounded like it was produced in a recording studio. Because we were just recording voice, the appearance of the environment made no difference. Then, when we recorded the sound of the entire community of sisters singing (to provide the music element), we let the sound bounce all around the chapel, giving it a natural echoing quality. We accomplished two distinctly different sound qualities using one environment and one mike.

When the sound environment also happens to be the visual environment (on camera), it's, of course, necessary to place any baffling materials outside the shot. On most location shoots the environment can be altered in advance to some extent. You can use carpeting, drapes, or anything porous.

As we discussed earlier, an audio plan is based on the sensibility of the piece. From this every audio element can be selected. If you need a hollow, castlelike sound, take your narrator into an open environment with hard surfaces and record the sound separately from the picture, especially if there is little or no lip sync involved. You will know when the audio needs to sound close in, having little or no reflection, and when it should be hollow, bouncing off surfaces that provide some echo effect, depending on the sensibility of the piece and the effect you're trying to create.

Echo, as a sound effect, refers to sounds that bounce off surfaces and return to the source, as in our chapel example. *Reverberation* is a different effect, which is accomplished electronically (within an audio system) to continue the pulsing of a sound . . . ound . . . und . . . nd . . . d. The echo effect sustains a sound by its reflection off various surfaces whereas the "reverb" effect sustains a sound by making it last longer. If you're simulating sounds in a cavern, you would choose echo. If you're creating a more ethereal sound for a singer, the reverb effect would be more appropriate. Most popular vocal recordings contain at least some reverb because it gives the voice a fuller quality.

Every environment has unique sound characteristics and, just as we scout a location to understand the lighting and electrical needs, we should also *listen* attentively to the space. Are there sounds present that should not be recorded? Are there sounds that need to be present that aren't there? How dead or active (reflective) is the space acoustically? When you understand the environmental characteristics, you can plan to prepare the environment properly well in advance of the shoot.

You can also change the sound of the environment altogether. One way is to record "presence" in an environment you prefer that is separate from the space where the foreground audio is recorded. I like to do this in natural settings because there is never a good forest sound when you want one. The mike always picks up too much air hiss, wind noise, and even distant traffic sounds. Or you can take your recorder into a dense forest early in the morning or late at night or use prerecorded sound effects from a library.

One time we needed to record people talking in a noisy factory. We recorded about fifteen minutes of the ambient factory sound—without voices—and then recorded the voices (on camera) when the factory machinery was shut down. Then in the audio mixing session we were able to control the level of the factory noise independently, keeping it reasonably under the voices. The speakers didn't have to yell to be heard, and the balance between background and foreground was perfect.

Lip Sync

When the talent speaks or sings, we usually want his lips to match the sounds he emits. Every year, despite warnings to the contrary, a student or two in my introductory class will attempt to include some lip-sync segments in a music video. The intent is fine, but this technique requires special **sync** player/recorders because no

FIGURE 12.2
A Synchronous
Audio Recorder
(Courtesy of Nagra
Magnetic Recorders,
Inc., New York.)

two amateur recorders run at exactly the same speed for an extended period of time, even the same model made by the same manufacturer.

What *does not* work is what seems to be the most expedient: taking an audio cassette recorder into the field, setting up the singer or speaker and having him pantomime to a prerecorded tape as you shoot video, then editing the two together. The sync will only last a few seconds. The difference in recording speeds then becomes pronounced, increasing with time.

The professional method of recording lip sync is to *use an audio sync recorder* as source and playback in the field. A few audio tape recorders, especially those designed for film production, are designed to maintain sync (Figure 12.2). They are expensive but can also be rented. These usually record ¼-in. magnetic tape and, after putting a beep (sync point) at the head of the scene, record a sync pulse on one track and the primary audio on another. Some models can also lay down a time-code track at the same time. If this type of audio recorder is used as the source for both the playback (for the performers) and for transfer to videotape, then sync can be perfectly maintained throughout.

Another professional method is to *use an audio synchronizer* in the postproduction stage. This device acts as an interface between audio recorders and video recorders, providing a SMPTE standard time-code track so that both the audio and the picture are always in sync. The purpose of these synchronizers is to keep audio tracks that were recorded separately in sync. In this case an ordinary cassette recorder is acceptable for the playback on location to provide a track for the performance. You can find audio synchronizers at most high-end postproduction houses and audio production studios that serve video producers.

There is another, nonprofessional method: *Use a VTR in the field* to play back the sounds the talent can then pantomime. This requires a second VTR to record the picture. Both should be of the same format and manufacture, if possible. The method works well, especially if the scenes are short. Be sure to bring along a monitor to play loud enough for the performer to hear. Shoot several takes. And it helps to slate the scene with both a visual and an aural cue such as a hand clap or a clap-stick as they do in the movies. This makes the editing job much easier when the time comes to transfer the video onto the tape containing the audio.

Rerecording

These same technologies are used for *rerecording,* known as "looping." Rerecording involves lip-synching most if not all of the speech or other vocal segments of a program. Most people aren't aware that much of television and film is rerecorded. On variety programs where the talent both sings and dances, the dancer usually pantomimes the song because it's difficult to sing and dance well simultaneously. Producers almost always rerecord rock musicians for their music videos.

Rerecording has tremendous potential as a production value when it's done well. Often sound recorded on location is noisy, full of hiss and unwanted sounds. It has that "tinny," man on the street interview quality. This is why most major motion pictures and TV dramas are completely rerecorded. This also substantially increases the options for controlling the quality of the sound and including other audio elements.

Another good application of rerecording is in long shots when the talent is walking or riding in the distance. As long as the talent's lip movement is visually unresolvable, the audio can be rerecorded in the studio later on and mixed with environmental sounds that add to the sensibility.

In rerecording, you must make sure (1) that the recording machine(s) are in sync and (2) that the lips match the sound. Although an operator can easily maintain sync, it requires trial and error for the talent to do a good job of matching his or her voice to the visuals. This is where another, newer technology comes in, the *audio dialogue replacement* (ADR) unit. It is a digitizing computer (that converts audio into numerical bits of information), which can make the talent's performance "fit" by compressing or expanding the audio to match the video.

Voice-Over

What transforms a voice-over from a simple technique to a production value is the quality of the recording. After you select the most appropriate voice for your piece, take the person into a high-quality audio studio where the environment and technologies can make the most of it. Too many producers record their voice-overs in environments that happen to be available or expedient (the shooting location). It's worth the cost and time to do voice-overs well because they carry the verbal energy of the presentation. Even the best narrator recorded anywhere but a sound studio will not sound quite as good.

When recording the voice-over, use the high- and low-frequency controls of the audio board, or an audio equalizer, to adjust the quality of the voice. Make a test to hear how it sounds, especially when recording directly onto videotape (as opposed to audiotape). To check the quality of audio on the videotape, listen to your playback through a TV monitor because that's what your audience will hear. Never record your final takes until you've tested the sound quality (that is, played it back). For location shoots be sure that the headsets you take along cover both ears entirely because you want to evaluate what you've recorded without extraneous noises.

Sound Effects

As we saw earlier in our discussion of audio planning, you draw the viewer into the screen experience with sound effects. The creaking steps, the squeaky door, the gunshot, the crackling of a campfire, the unseen footsteps, the crowd noises, the roar of a jet engine, the croaking of frogs—all these are sounds that bring the viewer into the scene. Like the music, the effects have a direct emotional effect and, therefore, should be used wherever appropriate based on the sensibility of the scene. Sound effects can be obtained by paying a needle-drop fee to the owner of a sound effects library, or the sounds you need can be recorded live, which is much more fun. Most radio stations and audio recording studios have both music and sound effects libraries. The skillful use of sound effects is one of the hallmarks of good audio production values.

Audio Sweetening

As we discussed in Chapter 2, "The Production Process," the manipulation of audio quality and placement has developed into a science (and art), referred to as "sweetening." A well-equipped audio studio can modify the quality or pace of any sound, enhance the sound, reduce distracting "artifacts," and add synthesized sounds. With digital recording and playback machines now becoming commonplace, the audio is completely manipulable, whether you wish to create special audio effects or clean up a track full of background or other noises. You can do all of this without generation loss.

In a sweetening session, the engineer first transfers all audio elements or tracks, using time-code synching, to a multitrack (16 or 24) audio tape recorder. A video tape recorder (usually ¾ in.) is "interlocked" (synched) with the multitrack audio recorder so the picture as well as the time-code numbers can be used as sync references. One shuttle control operates both machines. When the picture and sound are in perfect sync, the machine transfers each element onto its own dedicated section of the multitrack tape. When all of the audio (voice, music, effects) is on the multitrack tape in its proper position, each is then properly balanced in relation to the other tracks in terms of volume and equalized in terms of frequency response to maximize quality. Then, during the mix, all tracks are recorded onto a master audio track. The final step is the lay-back of the (mixed) master audio onto the master videotape. Everything stays in sync throughout because all tapes have been referenced by the same time-code numbers.

Although the sweetening service is billed on a per hour basis, a good audio engineer can work very quickly once he knows what needs to be done, thus keeping costs down. Audio sweetening, once a luxury, is becoming a necessary part of every production.

Audio Editing

The following comments relate primarily to off-line editing or putting together a rough cut. To produce the on-line "master," you build the program from start to finish by assembling and inserting scenes in the order of their position in the program. Rough-cutting more often involves the assembly of one complete track at a time to have maximum control over program length.

The Linear Master

To rough-cut a program that relies on verbal content, you usually cut the visuals to match the voice track. In these instances you will normally begin by editing a "voice" **linear master,** a tape that contains all the properly timed *audio* portions of the program in sequence. When that is done, any video to cover the existing pictures associated with the audio track is inserted. This results in the program rough-cut or *work print.* The editor builds the audio track first, providing an exactly timed voice linear master into which other visuals can be inserted.

When inserted in this manner, the visuals are referred to as **B roll,** a term derived from the film convention of using an **A roll,** which carries the voice, and a B roll, which carries the picture. In the film processing lab these two rolls, perfectly matched in sync according to their sprocket holes, are photographically printed onto another roll of film. This "print" or master is a composite of both **A and B rolls.** This is how dissolves are accomplished on film. The scenes to be dissolved alternate between the A and the B roll, so there is a fade-in/fade-out overlap. Because the B roll predominantly carried the pictures, television producers came to refer to video inserts that cover pictures already associated with audio as B roll. If you hear someone in video say they want to shoot some B roll, or if they ask if you have any B roll scenes, they're referring to cutaways or other visual inserts that will cover the picture currently associated with the audio.

An alternative rough-cutting procedure, when the picture is the predominant element, involves the preparation of a "picture" linear master. This is done, for instance, when visual interest supersedes the audio content or where the pacing of images is important. In this case the "picture" linear master would contain the total *visual* sequencing of scenes, allowing the audio to be appropriately matched to it later on.

Which element (audio or video) carries the heavier burden of *communication?* This then is likely to be the track that will determine the timing of the program and that tells you which track should be assembled first as the linear master.

Audio Pacing

Because the audio provides so much of the emotional experience of the program, the cutting pace should be directly related to the sensibility of the piece. Excitement should have a fast pace, and sensitivity a slow pace. Even the rate at which words are delivered enhances or detracts from the effect desired.

Beginning editors sometimes do not allow enough room for a breath, for instance, between the out-point and the in-point, and the edit, therefore, becomes noticeable. During rapid speech there will be less time left for the breath. In every case try to cut the audio so it seems that the speaker is continuing along at a regular pace—as if every sentence were connected. Professional narrators know when to pause to allow a split second for an edit. If you're working with in-house people who tend to ramble, stop to give a brief lesson on how to "punch" certain words and where to pause, especially at the end of paragraphs. Don't forget that the pace of the speaker will be the pace of the audience's sensibility, so determine how fast or slow *you* want them to go, and then structure the audio pace accordingly.

Audio Levels

The most blatant cue to the audience of poor audio production values is when the audio levels between edits do not match. This can easily happen if you don't check the levels at *every* edit, especially when starting a fresh session after the equipment was used by others.

Picking up where you left off requires going back to the levels already recorded and testing the next edit by playing back the transition. Be sensitive not only to the volume but also to the quality of the sound. Many editors will put a piece of tape on the controls to mark them so they can return to the same relative position. When using an audio *equalizer* (Figure 12.3), it's especially important to mark the posi-

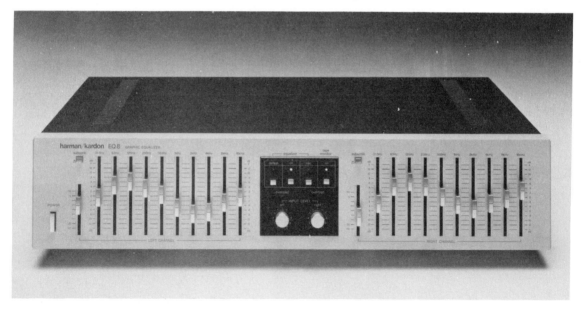

FIGURE 12.3
An Audio Equalizer
This piece of equipment allows discrete frequency response control over every part of the audio signal. (Courtesy of Harman Kardon.)

tions of the controls because each slider affects the high, midrange, and low frequencies, and it can be very difficult to find the proper positions once they have been changed.

Summary

Production techniques are the methods used to create a program, and they also provide cues to the audience about the credibility of the producer. These cues often determine whether the audience will watch the program in the first place or, if so, whether they will accept the message it presents. When an ordinary technique is done with a commitment to quality, it is transformed into a production "value."

In this chapter we examined some specific elements of the audio system. Before you can develop good audio technique, you must do two things: first, make the commitment to quality and get agreement from the team to do the same, and, second, develop an awareness of and sensitivity to sound. This requires some conscious effort because we tend to take sound for granted.

The chapter provided techniques for becoming more sensitive to sound. These should especially be practiced in the shooting environment—the places where sound will be recorded. While these spaces are being scouted for electrical and lighting considerations, also take the time to listen attentively to what the microphones will pick up.

Once we know what kinds of sounds are already present in the shooting environment, we can design an audio plan to incorporate them, eliminate them, or mix them with additional elements. The plan will detail the kind and quality of sounds to be used in the program and how best to record them. And you will need to make selections relating to the voice, music, sound effects, and appropriate equipment. The criterion for selecting each should be how well it contributes to the sensibility of the program. With the audio well thought out before the cameras "roll," you can be more confident that the recording session will go smoothly.

Technically, recording audio on videotape is a relatively simple technique, but too often we bypass some important considerations in the interest of expediency or cost. We examined some of the more common techniques that can make a difference in quality, such as using virgin stock, "packing" the tape, using the automatic gain control and limiter consciously, and others.

Certain aspects of sound recording are more specialized. We focused on those that particularly affect the quality of the sound. We often select microphones, for instance, based on convenience, but frequency response and range should be the primary considerations. Microphone placement makes a big difference as a quality cue both technically and aesthetically (mikes as a rule should not show unless there is a reason). So does the nature of the reflective surfaces and the area of the space where the recording takes place.

We examined ways of recording lip sync and rerecording (or looping) voice over the picture of lips moving. These techniques are especially important as audience cues because they can significantly improve the quality of the sound, thereby bringing viewers into closer involvement with the screen characters. But handled poorly, they can have the opposite effect.

We discussed the importance of recording voice-overs in a high-quality environment (studio) or modifying the existing environment so it has better acoustic qualities. And we looked at the use of sound effects to bring the viewer into the scene as well as to contribute to the sensibility of the content.

Finally we touched on editing the sound track, the procedures involved in preparing a linear master, the editing pace, and the importance of maintaining proper volume level and balance between scenes.

The sound of a program communicates.

Notes

1. McLaughlin, Terence, *Music and Communication* (New York: St. Martin's, 1970), 44.

Suggested Readings

Alten, Stanley R. *Audio in Media,* 3rd ed. Belmont, CA: Wadsworth, 1990.

Andrews, Donald Hatch. *The Symphony of Life.* Lee's Summit, MO: Unity Books, 1966.

McLaughlin, Terence. *Music and Communication.* New York: St. Martin's, 1970.

Nisbett, Alec. *The Technique of the Sound Studio.* Stoneham, MA: Butterworth, 1979.

Oringel, Robert S. *Audio Control Handbook: For Radio and Television Broadcasting,* 6th ed. Stoneham, MA: Butterworth, 1989.

Utz, Peter. *Today's Video: Equipment, Set Up, and Production.* Englewood Cliffs, NJ: Prentice-Hall, 1987.

CHAPTER 13

Video Production Values

· ·

In looking at an object we reach out for it. With an invisible finger we move through the space around us, go out to the distant places where things are found, touch them, catch them, scan their surfaces, trace their borders, explore their texture. It is an eminently active occupation.

—Rudolf Arnheim

I n the last chapter we established the difference between a simple technique and a production value in the audio portion of a program. We turn now to production values involving the video component. We will emphasize those areas that are often ignored or mishandled and learn how to transform simple techniques into *values* to enhance our communication.

This chapter addresses three primary areas in visual presentation: elements in front of the camera (including the subject matter), elements relating to the image-forming process (using the camera), and lighting. Entire books have been devoted to these subjects, but here we'll just focus on the communication cues that are most often neglected.

In Front of the Camera

· ·

What happens in front of the camera shapes experiences into program content. This is how the script comes alive and the vision becomes reality, so it is important to make something special, unique, or interesting happen.

To approach this subject systematically, we'll begin with the background. Begin by separating the background from the foreground elements. Give your attention first to the background and then move forward to the foreground. This makes the process methodical, which saves time and reduces the likelihood of elements being neglected.

You should know the foreground, or focus, of the scene—such as people talking, a car, an animal—in advance. The first step then is to understand the background in relation to the foreground (subject matter or focus area).

The Background

Just as program content should be organized to have unity, the relationship of foreground to background should also be unified. Decide what the background should be based on the subject matter, which will be in front of it. The background should pick up and extend the foreground elements and contribute to the sensibility of the scene. Often on broadcast and cable television the background clashes with what people are wearing in pattern, color, or style.

The background should provide an appropriate visual field against which characters or other subjects will be seen. It can also be a plane within which the talent can move and relate to a broader environment. Whatever happens in that space, it should enhance the subject or at least not interfere with it by attracting attention to itself. The director manipulates viewers' *attention* and directs it, moving their thoughts and feelings accordingly. Producers often abuse or neglect the simple guidelines that relate to the design and use of backgrounds. But these areas provide an excellent opportunity to create positive value.

Make the relationship genuine   Take your cue from the subject matter to create a background that has a direct relationship with the topic. Every aspect of the background, including size, color, texture, and shape of furnishings as well as props and lighting, should relate to the focus of the scene and the sensibility of the program overall. For instance, if the talent is an author, the background could contain bookshelves. If the subject is technical, display related equipment. Our background in the children's show *Max B. Nimble* was a toy store. This setting not only contributed visually, it also provided opportunities for various skits based on that context.

Keep it simple   As discussed in terms of information theory, every sound or visual element results in increased complexity. A stronger design can be achieved by keeping the number of elements in the background to a minimum. Unless they're necessary, eliminate lines, patterns, and colors that don't contribute. A busy background distracts from the foreground. The more visual information (i.e., clutter), the more opportunity for distraction.

Keep it still   Keep the background elements stationary because our eyes naturally gravitate to and follow anything in motion. Background motion is often appropriate and desirable. But movement, like complexity, needs to be justified. If there is no justification for it, eliminate the motion.

Use color harmony   What color is the person who is the center of attention wearing? Use background colors that relate to that portion of the color spectrum (as opposed to the opposite colors): that is, use warm colors with warm clothing and cool colors with cool clothing. Another possibility is to match the background color to the color tones of the talent's shirt, tie, or dress.

Light it properly   The background should usually be somewhat darker than the foreground or subject matter. When we discuss lighting you'll see that a dark background enhances separation and a brighter one distracts from the subject matter, with the possible exception of a pure white background.

Give it depth   A flat background looks flat. The video screen is two-dimensional, so anything we can do to create the illusion of depth helps to bring the image field perceptually into a third dimension. Whatever the shot or program format (talk, interview, news), some planes or objects should be delineated so there is at least an illusion of depth.

Many years ago the Cincinnati, Ohio, NBC affiliate, WLW-T, created an ingenious effect to increase the appearance of depth in their news studio. For their wide, establishing shot, they suspended over the camera a textured piece of cardboard (approximately poster-board size), cut on a bias (trapezoid shaped), with grid lines that tapered away from the camera. When angled into the shot from above, it created the illusion of a very believable ceiling. And it eliminated the studio lights from the shot. To viewers, the news set looked as if it were situated in a large room with a high, beautifully textured ceiling. And the studio was actually quite small.

Entertainment Tonight uses the same kind of effect, which is accomplished electronically and with much more creative abandon, showing sometimes as a floor and at other times as light corridors leading into the set.

Give it texture   The TV screen's surface is smooth and flat, which is boring. So we have to create as much texture as possible to help viewers "feel" the space. This is another area where lighting is important. When designing and constructing the background, use textures as well as depth. It's usually best to select plants, trees, textured walls, furniture, clothing, and wood surfaces for textural qualities as well as their relation to the subject matter.

Make it warm looking   Unless there is a good reason not to, create a background that feels natural, inviting, and conducive to whatever is happening in front of it. The background should envelop the subject matter without distracting from it. This will unify the background and foreground. Although blue shows up on the TV screen, it is cold and, therefore, not the best color to use in situations displaying personal warmth.

To create an inviting environment, don't leave open space with chairs formally placed; rather, arrange the seats so people will seem closer. Cameras normally create the illusion that spaces are bigger than they actually are, so darker-toned backgrounds, closely placed furnishings, warmer colors, and narrower pools of light contribute to a more intimate feeling. Lighter tones, open spaces, and broadly lit areas should be used when the sensibility requires an open and spacious feel.

The Set/Setting

As we move our attention from the background toward the camera, we next encounter the set, or setting, which is the space within which the subject matter is found. In the newsroom it is the news desk; in the interview show it's chairs on a platform; in a documentary it might be a desk and chair where the subject will be interviewed or a locker room; in a drama it's the space in which the actors move. Again, the furnishings, colors, materials, supports, and textures—whatever is involved—should be there for a reason, to enhance the sensibility of your program.

Backgrounding

Such programs as *Hill Street Blues* (Figure 13.1) and currently *L.A. Law* have made television history because the activity of the background substantially contributed to the believability of the environment. Our attention, by design, is shifted between foreground and background as we see the police take someone off to prison or colleagues interacting, their comments temporarily interfering with the story line. This kind of action backgrounding adds realism to the scene, creates tremendous depth, and enriches characterizations.

Some programs layer the background action. There may be three or more planes of activity in addition to the one in which the primary characters interact. This effect can sometimes be carried too far. When backgrounding becomes obvious, it will shift viewers' attention from the story to the technique.

FIGURE 13.1
Backgrounding
This photo from the Hill Street Blues set shows action in the background that runs parallel to the foreground action. (Courtesy of MTM Television Distribution Group.)

Talent

Actors need experience to perform well on camera. To direct someone on camera, you need personal sensitivity, the ability to observe people and details, and an awareness of what's being communicated on various levels. People communicate verbally, and they also communicate nonverbally through their gestures, dress, attitudes, and body language. A skilled director is aware of all these dimensions simultaneously, making certain that each is in sync with what needs to be communicated. This is especially true for directing nonskilled people who may not be aware of their own "hidden" messages. Attention to these details can add value in several areas:

Prompting   Carefully choose which method to use to prompt the talent. I've developed a hierarchy of preferences, which follow, in order:

- Talent delivers the material with no prompt. This creates the most spontaneity and naturalness but requires her to memorize or be very familiar with the material. This gives the best results.
- Talent reads from a TelePrompTer. If he does it well he can maintain naturalness. Although some spontaneity is lost, there can be good results.
- Talent divides attention between notes (which she holds) and the camera. People who have experience in front of large audiences can do this well. This provides satisfactory results.
- Talent reads cue cards held next to the camera. It's hard to keep the cards close to the camera and also keep them quiet as they are pulled. In addition, viewers can usually tell when cue cards are used because the talent's eyes shift between the camera and the cards or he continuously looks away from the lens. Cue cards should only be used as a last resort, when none of the other options can be used.

Talent movement   People on camera should appear natural in their movements. It seems artificial when someone sits in a chair and talks without moving. It's a good idea to vary the shots whenever possible (e.g., arrange in advance for the talent to stand up and walk over to another area). But the movement must have some motivation. In a one-on-one interview with a live audience, the talent can get up and go into the audience. Without an audience the host and guest can probably just sit, but viewers may get fidgety if they notice the talent doing so.

Perhaps a comically staged commercial skit, miniplay, song, or another guest can be introduced to break the tedium of watching people talk. Would you just sit and talk for an hour in your home without some kind of break or interruption? It helps to spend time designing and staging creative interruptions.

A news reporter in the field can stand in front of a camera and deliver a story. But in a documentary, profile, or story, the talent should move. In the **walk and talk** the camera follows the talent while panning the background, which gives some variety to the shot. Determine the starting and ending points of the walk in advance and rehearse it several times so the camera operator can coordinate the movement, pace, and picture composition with the talent. Some follow-focus may be required if the shot is medium or tight because you don't want the talent to walk out of focus.

Although videos usually begin with a wide shot, a "walk and talk" has more options because you can cut to a variety of other shots from different positions. Industrial programs and even commercials frequently have the talent walk and talk, giving viewers a tour of a facility or a sampling of several environments while maintaining continuity through speech. If you can use a crane or dolly-mounted camera for the walk and talk, the production value will be increased.

Verbal communication   A high percentage of program content is delivered verbally. Video, a people-oriented medium, requires that people on camera be fluent. The speaker should not use pauses unintentionally or phrases such as *you know* and *like*. Although some of this may contribute to a feeling of spontaneity, a pattern of unintentional interruptions communicates a lack of awareness or possibly a dull intellect—neither of which is acceptable in a media production. If necessary, the talent can use a TelePrompTer or notes. Or you can record several takes and edit the best ones together.

Nonverbal communication   Cable access programming in particular can give the impression that producers have not yet discovered the importance of nonverbal communication, especially in the areas of dress choice, proximity (the space between people on a set), and body language.

What a person wears communicates. It helps the audience decide whether they should trust what the person is saying. In *Nonverbal Communication,* Mark Hickson and Don Stacks cite several studies that indicate:

The type of clothing you wear has a significant effect on how others perceive your credibility and position. Furthermore, the type of clothing you wear also tells others something about your communication style.[1]

On-camera presenters' dress should reflect positively on their credibility and should convey something of the sensibility of the program. Discuss clothing and other personal matters before the shoot so the talent will be prepared. In particular discuss whether the talent should wear the type of clothing to which a lavaliere mike can be attached and its cord hidden, if one is to be used. Additionally, to keep clothing from interfering with the video signal, which results in banding and active **moiré patterns,** avoid stripes, dots, checks, and prints. Also avoid pure white or pure black because the camera does not resolve their textures very well. It's important to have a good reason for exceptions to these rules.

The space between people—or, more precisely, the distance people use to separate themselves from one another—also communicates. **Proxemics** is the study of people space, and it has much to offer the video communicator. For instance, if the distance between people is greater than conversational separation, we sense a lack of genuine engagement (Figures 13.2a–13.2d). In the figures, notice that one person standing suggests superiority over the person sitting. Would this be true if the woman were the one standing? What is the effect when they are both sitting? And what assumptions do you make when you see them closer or farther apart?

FIGURE 13.2
Proxemic Behavior

The distances people use to separate themselves have a communication effect. Each figure expresses a different context in terms of the actual or perceived relationship.

When people are closer to one another on screen, viewers sense engagement; sometimes there's too much engagement, which is also a message. The camera tends to make people look farther apart than they actually are, so you may need to compensate. Let the talent know why they are positioned as they are. Have the seats placed well in advance of the talents' stage call so you will have time to explain where each person will sit, why, and how close they should be to each other.

Proxemics involves more than just closeness or distance. For example, I produced an hour-long show featuring Buckminster Fuller and Barbara Marx Hubbard. The two did a walk-on entrance so the waiting audience of 600 could stand and applaud them. Fortunately we weren't broadcasting live, because we had to retake the opening. When Fuller came out and was shown by the host, Michael Toms, where to sit, he told Michael he was completely hard-of-hearing on that side and would not be able to hear Hubbard. So we had to shift his position and mike assignment while I explained the interruption to the audience. We could have avoided this embarrassment had we found out more about the hearing problem we knew Fuller had.

Academics have developed an extensive literature on the nature and meaning of body language. Although some of the specific interpretations are open to debate, research nonetheless indicates that body language is a powerful form of expression. For example, when we cross our arms or legs, slouch or sit erect, lean forward or back, we provide visual cues (Figures 13.3a–13.3e).

Many people we see on camera don't display an awareness of nonverbal communication cues, probably because people on television and in videos increasingly are nonactors, with little on-camera or other presentational experience. It's very important to give such people direction.

People usually want direction. They want to know what looks good, what to do, what to wear, how to sit, and other such information because they want to do the best job possible. Even criticism, if framed constructively, can be appropriate and is often welcomed. The talent is usually grateful later, after she's seen what a difference these pointers made. The more inexperienced the talent, the more direction he will need.

It's gratifying to direct experienced professionals (as I have Dinah Shore, Kirk Douglas, and Steve Allen). They delivered what I asked for even better than I expected, in the first take. This is the ideal, of course.

Eye contact   Where should the talent look? At the camera, host, or guest, at the other characters, or elsewhere? This decision is critical for a director. Dramas determine this issue for you—the characters should shift their eyes according to the action and the other actors. In a lecture-style format, however, you must decide whether eye contact should be made with the camera, with other on- or off-camera person(s), or with both.

The talent should be told where to look. We've all seen people speaking to the wrong camera. And then there are the guests who talk to the camera in response to the host's questions, signaling to the audience a greater interest in their appearance on TV than in the host.

This decision should be based on the *context* of the program. Who's talking to whom? And what is the relationship of the audience to those speaking? If the talent is to address the viewer, as in a newscast, eye contact with the camera is appropriate. But you need to make sure the talent can tell which camera is on her so she can shift her gaze accordingly. If the audience is in the role of overseer, then the speakers should ignore the camera entirely and converse among themselves, allowing the audience to observe their interaction. Where a live audience is present, speakers should not look directly at the camera because the interaction should be between the talent and the live audience. An occasional nod or reference to viewers (the camera) may be appropriate, as long as it is done purposefully. The context of the program should determine eye contact, and the eye contact should be consistent. The director and the talent should agree on this at the beginning of every taping session.

Makeup   Beginning producers often think the only purpose of makeup is to improve a person's appearance. In video makeup has other purposes. First, it gives the skin a smoother texture—a better surface for lighting. When a person is in the shot, skin surfaces must absorb the light so they don't produce shiny, specular

a

b

c

d

e

FIGURE 13.3
Body Language

(a) Crossed arms and legs suggest the communication is closed for the person on the right. The woman on the left, however, is open to interaction. *(b)* The woman who supports her head with her hand is communicating boredom or disinterest. *(c)* The woman who leans back in her chair creates more distance and disengages. Note that the smile contradicts the rest of the body message. *(d)* When we lean toward a person, the message is one of interest and engagement. Extending hands with fingers touching has been interpreted as a sign of self-importance. *(e)* When two people who don't know each other very well interact, they sometimes display mirroring, a body language message that one person seeks to be in agreement with the other.

(mirrorlike) highlights. Shiny noses, foreheads, and even legs are not only distracting, they are cues to the audience of an amateur production.

Makeup also provides consistent skin tone from face to face when more than one person is on camera. Video engineers painstakingly set color levels so different cameras' output will match during cutting. If the talents' faces have different tonal ranges and colors, the audience will notice it. Look at the makeup used by any nightly news team. For consistency, each person uses the same foundation. This is also done in dramatic productions, including most sitcoms.

Our studio makeup kit contains three different tones of foundation: light, medium, and dark. The director assesses which is appropriate for the group of people involved, and then everyone uses the same foundation. Over the foundation they can apply their personal preferences for eyeliner, blush, mascara, lipstick, and so on.

For the camera and lighting, the makeup base should be consistent from person to person when they're Caucasian, and the skin surface should be matt rather than glossy. Use makeup for people with black or brown skin in exactly the same way. The color of the makeup is not important, but there should be consistency of color between individuals in the same shot unless people of various skin colors appear on the same screen; then consistency is less important.

When people of dark skin are on camera, background and lighting decisions are more important than makeup color. Try to reduce the contrast between the flesh tone and the background by keeping the skin somewhat lighter than the background. Tonal separation is needed between the subject and the background so an illusion of depth can be created. If the subject and background match in luminance level, the effect will be flat and dull.

Makeup can also transform a person's street appearance into a more professional appearance, creating the context of an experienced performer. For some smaller-scale productions that involve only one person on the screen at a time, we don't use foundation but just brush on some powder. Makeup should rarely be eliminated altogether. Everyone looks better on camera when the skin surfaces are well groomed and soft.

Attention to Visual Details

While in a film class, I heard the statement attributed to Italian filmmaker Federico Fellini (*8½, La Strada*), that not one frame in any of his films contains anything superfluous. He chose to include, or decided not to remove, every tree, telephone pole, blade of grass, and bracelet. As a result of seeing its benefits I developed a working technique to eliminate the superfluous, which I call the "positive-negative criteria" (PNC—not to be confused with BNC, the video connector). I do a "PNC check" with every camera setup. When all the technical elements are in place (camera, lights, mikes, talent blocking), just before the camera rehearsal, I ask myself two questions.

First the negative question: *Is there anything in the shot that does not belong there?* I observe every detail. If an element doesn't in some way contribute to the sensibility of the piece or the expression of the communication objective, I remove it. I keep asking the question until I can say to myself, "Everything that's in front of the camera needs to be there."

Then I ask the positive question: *Is there anything not in the shot that ought to be there?* Is there anything that would make the shot better or more expressive? If so, I add it. Again, I base this decision on the sensibility of the piece and the communication objective. When I have answered the negative and positive questions, I am ready to rehearse the talent with the camera and shoot.

The following items should *not* be included in shots:

Mike cords should never show either on the floor or on the talent (Figures 13.4a–13.4d). The talent should be told in advance to wear clothing in which mike cords can be hidden. Ask them to wear clothing with lapels, layered clothing, or jackets so the cord can be tucked inside. Although microphones can be visible in some situations, the mike cord should never be seen. When clothing can't be discussed in advance (which is often the case for location documentaries), and the on-camera person turns out to be wearing a smooth dress, sweater, or turtleneck outfit, use a mike off-camera (such as a shotgun) instead of a lavaliere.

FIGURE 13.4 Mike Cords Should (Almost) Never Show

The talent is usually asked to thread the mike cord up underneath the clothing. In the top right photo, for example, the cord is tucked behind the man's tie. If the clothing doesn't accommodate the mike cord (bottom left), use a shotgun mike instead of a lavaliere. Any cords on the floor should also be completely hidden. Cords on mike stands should be taped to the backs. The idea is to eliminate any vectors that work against keeping attention where we want it.

sweater
unkempt

sleeves

background
seam

cords

mike
too
obvious

chair
too
light

floor and
background
seam

bad
shadows
(all over)

cords

FIGURE 13.5
Background Seams
Showing

Background seams
are vectors that
lead the attention
out of the frame on
both sides. They
also artificially
divide the compo-
sition into two
or more textures.
Arrows indicate
some other problem
areas: What's
wrong with this
picture?

Background seams should never show. It's important to pay attention to where the background meets the floor or riser (a horizontal line), where flats are joined, and where seamless paper overlaps. These lines create distracting vectors (more on vectors later) and divide the composition (Figure 13.5). Move the camera position, the set pieces, or whatever to keep visible lines out of the shot. If there is no practical way to move objects—as in a factory workspace or hotel lobby—change the camera angle or frame the shot to avoid them.

Chairs or other set pieces that may be in the background are also distracting. Even if not lit, they will interfere with the focal point. This "visual noise" should be eliminated. Eliminate *anything* that is not necessary to the communication of the scene.

Props that look like props should also be eliminated (e.g., plastic flower arrangements typically on end tables between hosts and guests on interview shows). Use props only if they relate to the sensibility of the piece or the content, but don't use them solely as set decorations or just to add color. If necessary, make the pattern of shots tighter so the set shows less. Remember that simplicity is powerful.

Subject Matter

When thinking about subject matter (what to put in front of the camera), keep in mind that certain subjects are intrinsically more interesting than others. We've already seen the importance of uncertainty, inconsistency, novelty, change, and unexpectedness as ways of heightening interest. Now we'll discuss specific visual subject matter and how it affects viewers.

Eyes   People often look first at other people's eyes. Research has shown that infants are primarily attracted to eyes. Studies done with monkeys positively established that eyes are compelling, even fake ones stuck onto inanimate objects. Have you noticed that all the Muppet characters have big eyes?

People   Television and video are people-oriented media. Because I have a strong attraction to nature imagery, I started out by making the natural world the focal point of some commercials and documentary work. I later learned that people in my audience are not as interested in nature, but everyone is interested in people. Even "impersonal" TV newscasts feature stories exclusively about people.

Animals   After people, audiences prefer animals. Watch viewers during a cute kitten or puppy commercial or when a horse or other animal is on the screen. Animals (and kids) can be used very effectively to get a message across, sell a product, or entertain.

Written words   When there are words on the screen, viewers are compelled to read them. Billboards and bumper stickers work on the same principle.

Geometry   Lines in space have power. Read about sacred geometric symbols[2] for a new perspective on visual communication.

All of the elements we put on the screen are intrinsically composed of geometric shapes and relationships. Individual shapes affect us as we perceive them and can change us. For instance, we can get a feeling of expansion and peace from seeing the interior geometry of a Gothic cathedral. Airport terminals can give us a feeling of either social confusion or self-importance depending on the shape and scale of the interior.

One theory suggests that geometric images combine to produce symbols (a circle equals unity; a line equals duality; a triangle equals trinity; a square equals nature), which directly affect the subconscious mind. Robert Lawlor has another perspective: "Our experience of the world is due to our organs of perception being sensitive to variations of the wave frequency patterns which surround and pervade our field of awareness."[3] In other words, when you smell a rose you respond not only to the chemical substances of the flower but also to the geometry of the molecules' construction. Scientists have identified 103 basic elements in the universe. What differentiates you from a flower or a gold ingot is the geometric organization of these basic elements.

The incorporation of strong geometric relationships in your programs can make a difference. Consider the way a shot is framed, whether the subject is centered, the placement of horizontals and verticals, and overall composition. Many film cameras have cross hairs, and some medium-format still cameras have grid lines, in the viewfinders. It is unfortunate that video camera viewfinders don't include these lines because they help us see the geometries in every image we compose. After you read about the principles of geometric harmony, try applying them.

The Camera

In this section we'll discuss some technical aspects of camera handling. However, we'll emphasize the aesthetic aspects of imaging because in this area substantial value can be added.

The Camera Support

Think of the camera as the eyes of your target audience. Your camera handling will provide their experience. Remember that a tripod is not simply something on which to mount the camera. Each support device has its own context and perspective.

Tripod A camera on a tripod puts the audience in a stationary position. As we pan, tilt, and zoom we direct their attention in different ways. We bring the action closer by zooming in or move it farther away by zooming out. This creates an impersonal quality, putting the viewer in the role of passive observer.

Hand-held camera A hand-held camera creates a more personal quality, as if you are saying: "Come with me. Look what's going on." The audience is in an active mode. They move along with the subject. If the camera is held steady, the audience can keep their balance and easily see what's going on.

On the other hand, if the camera operator is unsteady or purposefully creates erratic movements (as we occasionally see in commercials), the viewer's vision is distorted, which creates discomfort.

These movements attract attention, but the audience is cued either that the camera operator is doing a bad job or that the camera is being moved for effect. This technique should be used with caution. Even in cinema verité films or tapes, cameras that move to follow action are mounted on dollies or steady-cams. Without these supports, hand-holding is more often a negative cue to the audience, a convention in early news footage or home movies.

The dolly/crane With the camera mounted on a rolling device that moves smoothly up and down, forward and back, you are saying: "Look at what's happening from various perspectives." The steady-cam, used properly, can simulate a dolly or slight crane movement. These movements keep the background, and often also the foreground, in motion. The viewer's perspective shifts gradually. Because the movements are smooth, slow, and steady, the audience's attention is on the action and not on the camera technique, avoiding "camera awareness."

A major difference between film and video "grammars" is in the use of a dolly or a zoom lens. Both allow the viewer to get an increasingly closer view of the subject, but the effect is completely different. A dolly moves the viewer into the action, whereas a zoom brings the subject closer to the viewer through different framing. You see few zoom shots in a movie, and very few dolly shots in a TV program.

Before the zoom lens was invented, every shot in Hollywood was done using a tripod, dolly, or crane. To get in closer the cinematographer changed to a longer focal length lens called a **prime lens.** Years later, when news videographers had to get in close without taking time to change the lens and without trampling people, the zoom lens was invented and it replaced prime lenses in video. Today both prime and zoom lenses are used in film work, but only the most expensive video cameras can accommodate prime lenses. Zoom lenses are always less sharp (in terms of resolution) than prime lenses because they have more air surfaces and longer barrels, which create internal reflection artifacts.

Camera Movement

An audience needs to see only a simple pan or tilt to determine whether a production is of high quality. If the movement is unsteady, too fast, or otherwise erratic, we know that inexperienced people were behind the camera. And the producer—even if she's not the camera operator—is responsible for the decision to use such a shot. Never "jar" viewers' sensibility. Keep their attention on the subject.

Partly because cameras were extremely heavy, the film industry early on developed gear-driven camera heads. When handles were turned the gears very gradually panned or tilted the camera. Professionals still favor these heads today because of their steadiness. This is why movies consistently have camera movements that are almost perfectly smooth. But gear-driven heads are expensive and also very heavy, making them impractical for television stations and nonbroadcast video applications, especially in the field. However, a good fluid-filled camera head (or "fluid-head") can approximate the gearlike effect when used properly.

Finally, when you edit your shots, be very careful not to include the tail end of an unintentional or bad camera move as this will cue operator incompetence.

Filters

Video producers do not use filters as much as filmmakers and still photographers. Filters do add expense. But they can also easily add value to a production. You may have noticed that an orange filter (which has an orange top and a clear bottom) is quite popular among commercial producers as a way to add color to sky areas. This filter is often used in car and soft-drink commercials. See your local photo dealer for books on filters.

Filters for a video camera can be very expensive. So when a filter isn't available, you can substitute another technique. Use the white-balancing electronics of the video camera to fool the system. Instead of white-balancing on a white card, use a colored card or other surface. If you tell the system that what it is looking at is white, though it's not, it will automatically filter in the complementary (i.e., opposite) color. For instance, if you want the image to be blue overall, perhaps to create a nighttime effect, put a yellow card in front of the lens and press the white-balance button. Watch the monitor as it turns blue. The deeper the yellow target, the deeper the resulting blue; the paler the yellow, the paler the blue. You can also change the filter wheel to see whether the daylight (5,600 K) or the tungsten (3,200 K) setting gives you a better color. The effect can be the same as that from a filter but without either the expense or the additional optical surface, which degrades image quality slightly. However, you have little control over the color you get unless your kit is full of differently colored cards for white-balancing. All cameras respond differently, so you will want to experiment first.

Below are the complementary colors. Red is the opposite of cyan, yellow the opposite of blue, and magenta the opposite of green.

Red	(magenta + yellow)	Cyan
Green	(cyan + yellow)	Magenta
Blue	(cyan + magenta)	Yellow

Another filtering technique that adds value involves the use of a diffusion filter. These filters, which are available in grades, create subtle textures to hide blemishes and make bright objects glow.

Although plastic, gauze, aluminum screening, and nylon can be used instead, they are very difficult to control. If you or your organization decide to invest in filters, I recommend the diffusion set because you will probably use the subtler grades (i.e., 1, 2, or 3) more frequently and will have the most trouble substituting household items for them.

Imaging

Consider the video frame: a rectangle with an aspect ratio of 3:4, which encloses a certain space. What should you do within that space? How should the image elements be organized for maximum effect? What pictorial dynamics are involved in attracting and holding attention within that space? How do people respond to images? The study and practice of "composition" address these concerns. Now, in the "information age," our study must expand to include pictures that can be taken apart pixel by pixel, manipulated, and synthesized.

"Imaging science" is the technical field concerned with these areas. You can read more about its technical details in several trade magazines on the subject. Composition is our focus here, and better resources for aesthetics and composition can be found in art stores and art libraries. Author Rudolph Arnheim[4] has made a lifelong study of pictorial dynamics and I recommend his books. Our discussion of composition is in part based on his works as well as that of Herbert Zettl,[5] whose book *Sight, Sound, Motion* has become a standard for media aesthetics.

To increase my awareness of the dynamics of imagery, whether in content or in composition, I take *an energetic approach,* beginning by considering the screen as a field of energy. When you place bits of information in this field, the relationships between them develop and transform.

In terms of program content, energy can take infinite forms. It can be rough or smooth, sensitive or dynamic, angry or friendly, warm or cold, coarse or refined—and all the areas in between—depending on the sensibility of what you're creating. A soft-spoken person slouched in his or her chair creates energy different from that of the same person sitting up. A jet fighter exhibits energy different from that of a passenger plane. A touch-tone telephone has energy different from that of a dial phone. An actor's front has energy different from that of his back. Everything and everyone exhibits a distinct energy field, which, when seen in relation to other energies, creates a certain dynamic.

W. Barnett Pearce states: "We live *in* communication (rather than standing outside communication and using it for secondary purposes)."[6] Communication is not something that we do, it's something we are.

To make something happen in front of the camera, you must work with these energies, combining and shaping them into experiences to move viewers. As your tape records a scene, be sensitive to the "feel" of the energy on the screen. Try to sense the energy of those who are watching it with you because they are picking up these energies empathically.

Let's turn to compositional energy—the interactions of points, lines, shapes, textures, colors, and size relationships. In addition to seeing content—that is, a person, animal, spaceship, product, or whatever—try to see fields of energy in motion. You can manipulate this energy by changing the lighting, the relationships within an image, or the shot itself. Your challenge is to be attuned to the screen dynamics, working with them to affect the viewer's experience. Fortunately, the physiology of perception is fairly consistent within the human family, varying primarily with culture and interpretation. So, when you look at the screen, your feelings will be similar to those of others—if they have as much interest in the program as you do.

Dynamic center The **dynamic center**[7] of an image is not necessarily the center of the screen but the area of the screen where visual energy is focused. This area contains the essential information without which the image would lose its meaning. If a shot pans a horse and rider, the dynamic center moves around the screen with them. During a shot of a person speaking, the center is the face. For a shot of water being poured into a glass, it's the water streaming from the pitcher to the glass. The dynamic center on a video screen most often changes constantly as the subject, camera, or shot moves. You should try to keep the dynamic center in an appropriate relationship with the frame and the other elements within it. Because various TV receivers cut off more or less of the image, the dynamic center should always be somewhere within the **TV-safe** area (Figure 13.6).

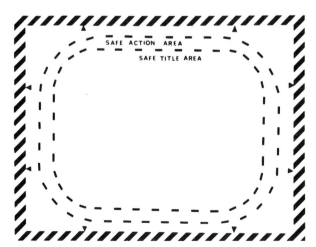

FIGURE 13.6
TV-Safe Area

Because every video screen (viewfinder, playback monitor, TV set) shows a different amount of the picture area, this imaginary field helps to ensure that the subject matter is well composed. All video screens include this area. (Copyright Society of Motion Picture and Television Engineers—SMPTE.)

Remember, the dynamic center is neither a point nor the center of the screen. It's a constantly changing (in size, shape, content) field of visual energy. From cut to cut it can jump from one side of the screen to another. It can even jump off the screen and back—such as when a girl runs out of the frame to pick up a baseball and then comes back into view. Was there a dynamic center to the image while she was off camera? There was not unless some other energy center attracted attention.

It is well established that *viewers are attracted to the brightest element(s) on the screen.* Even infants will turn toward a strong light. This is one more reason for keeping the background somewhat darker than the people in front of it. The dynamic center should usually be the brightest element in the space; but if it is not, no other element should be so bright that it detracts from it. If the subject is a product, for instance, a bottle, which should be lighter, the bubbly liquid in the bottle or the label? It depends on the communication objective. If it's brand recognition, make the label the brightest element in the scene. If it's to make viewers thirsty, highlight the bubbles more than the label. You can show both in the same image, but the viewer will primarily attend to whatever is brighter.

In Western culture we read from left to right and top to bottom—as you are doing now. We scan TV images in the same way. So in terms of placing elements on the screen, we need to understand the dynamics of viewing.

Our first encounter with an image happens in a split second. First we attend to the brightest area of the screen. Then our eyes go to the top left and scan across and down. We stop where there are either eyes, a face, areas of personal relevance, or other bright elements. We look at the bright spots first. Once we've completed a quick scan, we go back to survey the dark areas. Shadows and dark areas are mysterious. They hide things. So we spend a few milliseconds looking at what seems hidden. Then our eyes leave the screen from the bottom right corner, unless there is something to keep our attention within the frame. This entire scanning process takes place in seconds. Remember that fatigue begins in about ten seconds. If the energy becomes static, the viewer's attention goes elsewhere.

As producers we do things to counter this tendency to leave the screen. We've discussed some of the options in terms of editing pace and other image changes, but you can also do a great deal within an image to hold the viewer's attention. For example, you can compose the elements so that attention moves in a circular motion and stays within the frame. You can also move the dynamic center so attention will follow it or use interesting or unusual compositions.

Vectors Every visual line—whether short, long, straight, curved, or jagged—is an energy pathway along which the eye travels. These lines give direction and often lead to a destination. They are called **vectors:** "a force sent out like an arrow in a particular direction."[8] They can be as subtle as the line of a necktie, which moves energy both up and down, or a wire that leads to a microphone. Both directors and actors consciously use these vectors.

Vectors move energy forward in the direction of their movement, and the eye follows automatically. An actor will put her hands to her face in gesturing to move

FIGURE 13.7
Graphic Vectors
(continued)

the viewer's attention to her face. If she wants to move attention elsewhere, her arms will go in that direction. When someone points, our eyes follow. When someone looks up, we look up. He looks left; we look left.

One time, while I was directing a studio program, I wanted to get the talent to look left. But I was in the control room and couldn't talk to her, and I didn't want the floor manager to interrupt. So the floor manager positioned himself in front of her and did a very abrupt head turn—and, as planned, the talent turned to see what he was looking at. This technique worked so well that everyone in the control room broke out laughing.

Herbert Zettl, writing about vector "fields"[9] (that is, combinations of vectors within a frame), refers to three types: *graphic vectors* (Figures 13.7a–13.7c), which are stationary elements that lead our eyes in one direction, such as the direction in which a car is pointing or the converging lines of a building; *index vectors* (Figures 13.8a–13.8c), which point in one direction, such as someone's eye or hand movement or arrows; and *motion vectors* (Figure 13.9a–13.9c), elements in motion, such as an airplane in flight or railroad wheels coming toward the camera. Motion vectors determine *screen direction,* dictating in which direction the subject should be moving within the frame and between shots.

Because most images are composed of vector fields, our attention moves from element to element much like the rolling ball in a pinball machine. As we'll discuss

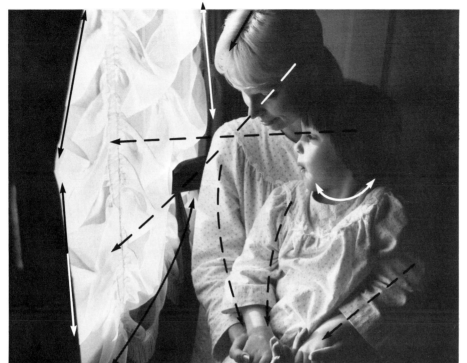

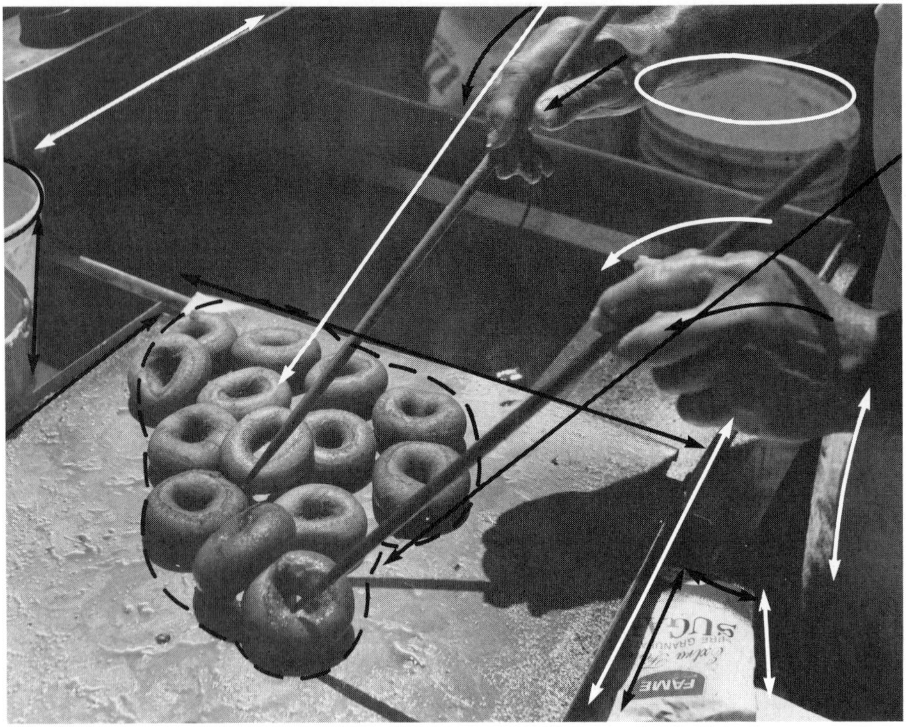

FIGURE 13.8
Index Vectors
(continued)

later, the light (or highlights) on the surface of the subject actually creates these vectors.

Because vectors are the route along which visual energy travels, a good director becomes so sensitive to them that it is almost impossible to watch a TV screen without noticing their use. Vectors are somewhat difficult to study on movie or TV screens because they move so fast. But you can use the shuttle on a video edit controller to slow the action down to examine these energies more carefully.

Much more could be said about composition, but we will have to leave it for further research. However, there are a few more areas of image management that we'll briefly discuss here because they are so often a major reason for image dullness, discomfort, or breakdown.

Headroom   Although some other writers and some video engineers disagree, I believe that, for the proper amount of **headroom,** you should have the top of the talent's head just under the top of the frame, touching the TV-safe line (Figures 13.10a–13.10b).

First, because the very center of the screen is static, anything placed there for any length of time is in an "energy dump." Eyes in particular do not belong there because, once you have seen them, there is nowhere to go in the frame except the ceiling, which has nothing to do with the dynamic center. Second, with more of the

FIGURE 13.9
Motion Vectors
(continued)

talent in the screen and less ceiling space, the screen is more interesting because the focal point is the person and not the environment. The center is not necessarily static—it can be just the opposite. However, using the center to frame people is dull and out of accord with the principles of good composition.

One rationale for putting the talent's eyes dead center in the screen is that, when you zoom in, you don't have to tilt at the same time, making the shot smoother. However, this is not a problem for most camera operators. And many camera persons at the major networks frame in the way that I criticize here. Based on your personal taste, you can decide for yourself.

Design Regarding *what* is seen on the screen, a good designer can make masterful images with the objects found in a broom closet. The subject matter isn't as important as what you do with it.

Media communicators rarely take courses in design, although they ought to. Design—the relationship of light to form, color to texture, and so on—is what transforms mere objects into an energy dynamic.

To find resources on design, begin in art museum bookstores and libraries as well as specialty art and photo stores. Better-quality magazines and large, hardcover books (the more expensive ones with higher paper quality) often feature design-oriented images.

a

b

FIGURE 13.10
Headroom

Figure (a) shows the proper positioning for "headroom" on a medium shot: The top of the head touches the top of the TV-safe area. Figure (b) shows the eyes placed in the center of the screen, which results in too much headroom.

Visual economy   Good design is a result of good seeing. It includes simple, uncluttered elements, with strong, definite, well-organized vectors, and excellent light quality. Strong designs utilize **visual economy** (showing only what's necessary), which promotes a sense of unity and cohesiveness. Purposeful tonal or value placement, strong vectors, bold geometries, unusual perspectives, an emphasis on textures, and color harmony—these are the characteristics of an image with strong design values.

Color usage   We all experience color differently, and the way you use it is a matter of taste. We are aware of music's emotional effect on us, and color also has an effect, but we are less conscious of it. Nonetheless, artists achieve emotional effects with color. Advertisers use it to sell products. And color therapists use it to heal. Because we have to use color anyway, we should put it to work for us purposefully, depending on what we're trying to accomplish in a scene.

Figure 13.11 shows how color correlates with various energies and musical tones.[10] I keep copies of this chart in my camera cases and production binder for easy reference. The ideal is to integrate all elements and put them to work to focus the communication.

HARMONICS OF COLOR AND SOUND

Color	Musical Note	Positive Qualities	Negative Qualities
Red	C	Power, strength, will, honor inspiration, initiative	Rage, anger, frustration, lust, revenge, destruction
Green	D	Hope, enthusiasm, growth, sharing, expansion	Envy, jealousy, disorder, greed, resistance
Blue	B	Love, wisdom, gentleness, trust, kindness, patience, sensitivity	Fear, self-pity, separateness, worry, anxiety, detachment
Yellow	E	Joy, sincerity, harmony, praise, discipline	Criticism, cynicism, selfishness, bitterness, laziness
Orange	G	Illumination, courage, analysis, loyalty, intellect, confidence	Sluggishness, ignorance, cruelty, procrastination, aggression
Purple	F	Mercy, devotion, loyalty, idealism, meditation, grace, wisdom	Obsession, injustice, moroseness, intolerance, retribution
Indigo	A	Synthesis, ritual, unity, inspiration, balance, world service	Pride, separateness, conceit, arrogance, deceit, rigidity

FIGURE 13.11 Harmonics of Color and Sound

To maximize the relationship between sound and picture, certain colors are used that enhance the energy dynamic of the piece. For instance, a scene that expresses sensitivity would incorporate the color blue and the note "B." This combination can be used when the sensibility of the scene is a negative, such as for anxiety.

Realize that the colors you select are not "in" the things you regard as subject matter but in the *light* reflected off their surfaces. You can modify these color qualities by gelling or otherwise controlling the light.

Select colors and sounds to harmonize with the kind of energy in your program. For example, in a studio interview with a sincere, well-organized intellectual, I try to incorporate yellow, which harmonizes with these qualities. The guest might wear yellow in her dress; we would select props including yellow (flowers); we could use a yellow background (or letters) for the character generated titles and credits; and so on. If I were designing music or sound effects for this energy field, I'd choose the sound A (Ah) to augment it.

Color harmony *Harmony* means "balance," a feeling of "rightness" when elements work well together. Systemically, every color on the screen is a different pictorial element. Many colors equal a complex image and lots of information. Few colors equal a simple image and focused information. Good color design focuses attention on a form rather than scattering attention around the frame. Both approaches can be appropriate at different times.

Color harmony is present when the image elements display one predominant **hue** (red, green, blue, yellow, orange). There can be other shades and variations of the same hue in the image in terms of **luminance** (brightness) and **saturation** (intensity of color), but they should all be within the same spectral range as the primary color. For example, a pink flower floats on the surface of a pink bowl sitting on a pink lace tablecloth.

You can include whites, blacks, and grays—neutrals—without interfering with color harmony. But when you introduce complementary hues—that is, colors opposite one another—you create less harmony and more discordance. Colors are "discordant" when different hues are randomly mixed or overlapped, especially when complementary colors exist within the same frame.

The principle: *Color harmony requires everything within the frame to be in the same relative area of the color spectrum.* The closer the colors are to the color of the subject matter, the more harmonious the image. The further they are, the less harmonious. This is not to say that colors should never be mixed or that complementary colors should never be situated within the same shot. Rather, when you want a strong, attention-getting, unusual image, apply the principle of color harmony. It strengthens any design by giving an image more power. However, discordant color use gives the viewer information and images that more closely approximate the world of color we daily experience. Color, as a production value, requires conscious and deliberate choice.

Camera angle On television and in videos, we commonly see the world from the perspective of tripod height, that is, five to six feet above the ground. This is usually acceptable, but don't forget to use the camera from other vantage points when appropriate.

Beginners often assume that they must look into the viewfinder in order to operate a video camera. The result is that their comfort level becomes the criterion for camera height. In fact, there's no need to use the camera's viewfinder at all. Use a monitor. It has a larger screen, and it usually shows the picture in color. And in some instances you can modify your viewing. For example, to shoot over the heads of a crowd, hold the camera at arm's length over your head with the viewfinder tilted down. Whether or not you can see into it, zoom out and aim the camera steadily at the subject by visualizing an imaginary laser light coming out of the camera lens and projecting onto the subject. News videographers frequently use this technique.

I've suspended a camera from an airplane on wires; thrown a camera in the air with it running in slow motion; tossed it back and forth between volleyball players; given it to ice skaters to dance with (i.e., for subjective camera); held it inches over the ground from the tailgate of a van; and strapped it on roller coasters as well as dune buggies. Cameras are expensive and delicate, so you must take appropriate precautions. But use the camera creatively; go for unusual perspectives and movements. Frame objects in the foreground out of focus to create depth. And, as always, have a good reason. Ask yourself whether it's justified.

Lighting

Lighting is one of the most respected and challenging production values. Every image ultimately is a result of the light that illuminates it. As with sound and color, we take light for granted and must make an effort to be aware of it.

I have found good books on lighting to be rare. Students can have difficulty getting experience with lighting, and to learn it you have to do it. So I recommend that you attend hands-on workshops, classes, or seminars on the subject. Because of its potential as a production value, we'll discuss a few relevant lighting topics here.

Light Awareness

Just as it's important to develop "an ear" for sound, so it's essential also to develop "an eye" for both composition and light. Watch television with the sound off. Pay attention exclusively to the light. Go into a natural place and close your eyes for a while; then open them as if you were a blind person seeing for the first time. Watch for exquisite light and try to understand what makes it so.

Begin to see light as something separate from the subject matter. Don't look at a desk. Look at what the light reveals about the wood surface. Don't look at a person. Look at what the light does to his skin surface, his eyes, his hair, his shoulders. Notice *surfaces* and the relative textures the light creates. Outstanding lighting can be seen regularly on *L.A. Law, Designing Women,* and *thirtysomething.*

Lighting Backgrounds

Lighting should begin with the background. What can be done with background lighting so it contributes to the sensibility of the scene or subject matter? What do you want the scene to communicate? You can use a venetian blind effect (an ellipsoidal light with an insert) or project shadows from plants or tree limbs. Create or enhance texture by strong sidelighting. Use wood textures to increase warmth. If the background must be a flat surface, use light to give it some differential form. "Cookie patterns," opaque materials with patterned holes in them, are commercially available or you can make your own out of posterboard or foam-core.

It's usually best to keep the brightest areas of the background somewhat less bright than the subject matter that will be in front of it. Fill in any dark areas to the point that some textured detail can be seen on camera. Bring down "hot spots" or highlights to a white that also reveals some texture. The best way to regulate these levels is to use a **light meter** on the set so you can see the relative luminance values and ensure desired evenness and/or use a **waveform monitor** to set the levels according to technical video standards. (Information pertaining to the use of light meters can be found in books on photography. Most video production books carry sections on how to read a waveform monitor.)

Think about color harmony between the background and the subject matter. I recently watched a crew set up for a studio interview. The director noticed that the host wore a blue tie so he changed the background gels to match. The effect he created was very pleasing.

When the background needs to be flat, place the foreground subjects some distance away so you can light the subject without casting distracting shadows on the wall. Background materials that merely provide ambience are best kept some distance away from the subject so they will be slightly out of focus.

Reflectors

Light reflecting off a white surface is essentially another light source, a highly diffused one. Some photographers use only two lights, a key light and a back light. They use a reflector for the fill. (The purpose of a fill light is to provide some texture in otherwise deep shadows.) You can also create a nice effect by photographing in window light using the sunlight as the key light and placing a reflector opposite the key to provide the fill. Duplicating this effect in the studio is not as easy as it seems. Instead of shining a spotlight through a window, position a large sheet of white foam-core near the window and reflect the light from it. This resembles daylight much better because daylight is more often diffused by clouds.

Most reflectors have both a shiny and a dull side to reflect with more or less diffusion. We wouldn't have been able to shoot *The Tender Clay* in a dark forest without reflectors. Because the light went in and out as the sun moved over the trees, we shot one sequence entirely with hand-held reflectors, some of which were placed sixty or more feet away. Especially with the shiny side of the reflector, sunlight can be bounced extremely far. We used four-foot square sheets of plywood covered with aluminum foil as reflectors, but large sheets of foam-core material are also excellent and weigh less.

One crucial detail pertaining to the use of reflectors: You must keep them still. When they move it's obvious, which is a negative cue to the audience. When reflectors must be moved to follow the talent, move them very gradually; also keep the subject away from the background, where shadows can be cast. Use the diffuse side to diminish reflector movement when the subject is close to the camera.

Specular/Diffused

An immediate, negative audience cue is shiny faces—forehead, nose, cheeks, and so on. Makeup, although important, cannot cover up poor lighting. Makeup only provides the lighting surface. Diffusion material—scrims, diffusion sheets, bounced lighting, foam-core reflectors, even bed sheets—prevents shiny faces and specular highlights. People should almost always be photographed in diffused light to soften the light reflecting off the skin by spreading the source light into a wider pattern.

However, you need specular light for strong points of light, for instance, on jewelry or glassware or for star bursts or reflections in liquids. The lighting director provides the full range of light control from specular to extremely diffused. The softer the sensibility of the scene, the more diffuse the light should be; the harsher the sensibility, the more specular the light.

Specular light also creates shadows that have hard edges. Diffuse light results in soft shadows. Wherever you are, hold your hand up with spread fingers so it casts a shadow on a nearby surface. You can determine the diffuseness or specularity of the light source (even without seeing it) by looking at how sharp the shadows are. Sharp shadows equal specular light. Soft shadows equal diffuse light. Specular light is used to enhance texture, for instance, a man's beard. It brings out every bit of detail by revealing hard shadows. Diffuse light is frequently used to light women because often we prefer a soft-skin effect. Diffused light minimizes shadow sharpness and, therefore, texture.

A diffusion filter can also be used to soften flesh tones, but too often it becomes obvious. Do you remember the shots of Maddy Hayes on *Moonlighting?* It's better to begin to establish softness with lighting and to reserve the use of diffusion for special effects. In that way the entire area has the same quality of light and actors moving through the space are not lighted differently. It's also easier to maintain consistency from shot to shot.

Contrast

In terms of lighting contrast for television, you can add positive value by making sure there is a full range of tones on the screen from pure white to pure black. There should not be massive areas of the image that are either white or black. Ideally most of the dark and light areas should have *texture,* with traces of pure white and black. This gives the most pleasing, normal contrast range. The image then is "crisp" and has "snap." The "normal" contrast range for television is 20:1. With high-end equipment it can be 30:1.

After you've set the lights for a scene based on aesthetic and technical needs, point a camera at the set (or location) on a wide shot and display the image on a nearby monitor; then adjust the monitor using the camera's color bars. Display the scene again, then turn off the color on the monitor completely. First, do you have any highlights that are totally washed out, with no detail? If so, reduce them either by changing the light or stopping down the iris (aperture) of the lens. Next look at the black areas. Make sure that, wherever desirable, the black areas have *some* detail—texture—in them. If viewers want to explore those areas, they should be able to find something. Finally, turn the color back on and see how the image looks overall; evaluate it again. Variations may be appropriate in some situations. You may want high or low contrast, or "high-key" lighting where the overall image tends to be very light or bright and "low-key" lighting where the image is mostly dark. Too often we see washed out highlights because the subject is overlit and the shadows are totally black. This prevents us from exploring the mystery of these spaces any further.

Color

We've already discussed the importance of color in another context. In terms of lighting, never take color for granted. Once you understand the sensibility of a scene, use color to enhance it. Notice that almost all television performers and producers use color purposefully. Actors and actresses frequently have red hair. Costumes usually maintain some semblance of color balance. Backlights are gelled, and blue seems to be the most common gel color. I sometimes use a gel over talent lights that is called "smoke." It warms skin tones just slightly and causes darker hair to display a more auburn color.

If the sensibility of the scene is cold and stark, or it's a night scene, use a slight blue gel to express this coldness. The picture need not look blue, necessarily, but it can have a subtle cold tint to augment the feeling. Do the opposite for a scene that is supposed to be warm.

Lighting the Space

Beginners usually learn the basic three-point lighting setup for placement of the key light, fill light, and back light. This technique is important to understand and is useful for shooting a single individual or a one-on-one interview. But often several people are on camera who need to move around the set (studio or location). In these situations it's best to light the space rather than the talent.

Look carefully at the set to understand where the light would be coming from (its directionality) if it were a real-world space (an office, a living room, a factory). When you see where the light would naturally come from, set up your lights accordingly. People commonly use "soft-boxes," large reflectors, bounced light, and "scoops" to illuminate large areas. If the space is properly lit, actors should be able to move around in it and always look well lit because there won't be any hot spots, cast shadows, or dark places that call attention to the lighting. The light will appear "natural" for the environment, which is the desired effect. But you must be able to model the light in certain areas while maintaining a proper exposure level. That's the purpose of lighting instruments, and here also light meters (or footcandle meters) are invaluable.

Summary

Our focus in this chapter has been on the image—what happens in front of, and behind, the camera so the video portion of the program will express positive presentational values in addition to communicating the content.

Our first concern was with what happens in front of the camera, and we began by considering the background. It should be simple and still; it should have depth, texture, and warmth; it should be properly lit; and, most important, it should have a genuine relationship with the subject matter.

Moving forward, we discussed the set, which provides an environment for the subject matter, which is often people. It too must have some relationship with the program theme or content. We discussed backgrounding, where actors purposely interact in the background area. This theatrical device cues the audience that the environment is more "real," as opposed to a studio setting, and it increases the dynamics of the drama by adding more elements of interest.

We considered some specific talent issues that are often overlooked, attempting to see how to resolve them. These included the appropriateness of various prompting techniques, talent movement, verbal communication, and nonverbal communication cues such as body language, makeup, and eye contact with the camera.

We emphasized how important it is to carefully choose the items that will appear in front of the camera. The positive-negative criteria (PNC) technique was presented as a way to approach each camera setup to maximize the positive and eliminate the negative. And we looked at a hierarchy of subject matter interests.

Turning to the camera and its various functions, we saw the importance of making camera movements gradual, smooth, and studied. We took up the subject of imaging from an aesthetic viewpoint, considering in turn an "energetic approach" to both staging and imaging, the importance of the dynamic center, vectors, composition, visual economy (strong design), color use and harmony, and perspective.

When we considered lighting, we focused on fundamental issues as well as on those that contribute to production value. These include lighting backgrounds, using reflectors, becoming sensitive to and aware of light, using diffused and/or specular light, and using color and contrast.

The images we put on the screen communicate.

Notes

1. Hickson, Mark L., III, and Don W. Stacks, *Nonverbal Communication: Studies and Applications,* 2nd ed. (Dubuque, IA: Wm. C. Brown, 1989), 288.
2. Lawlor, Robert, *Sacred Geometry: Philosophy and Practice* (New York: Crossroad, 1982), 44.
3. Ibid.
4. Arnheim, Rudolf, *Visual Thinking* (Berkeley: University of California Press, 1969).
5. Zettl, Herbert, *Sight, Sound, Motion: Applied Media Aesthetics,* 2nd ed. (Belmont, CA: Wadsworth, 1990).
6. Pearce, W. Barnett, *Communication and the Human Condition* (Carbondale: Southern Illinois University Press, 1989).
7. Arnheim, Rudolf, *The Power of the Center: A Study of Composition in the Visual Arts* (Berkeley: University of California Press, 1988), 13.
8. Ibid., 4.
9. Zettl, *Sight, Sound, Motion,* 120–121.
10. David, William, *The Harmonics of Sound, Color & Vibration* (Marina del Rey, CA: DeVorss & Company, 1980), 20–21.

Suggested Readings

Arnheim, Rudolf. *Visual Thinking.* Berkeley: University of California Press, 1969.

Bloomer, Carolyn. *Principles in Visual Perception.* New York: Van Nostrand Reinhold, 1976.

David, William. *The Harmonics of Sound, Color & Vibration.* Marina del Rey, CA: DeVorss & Company, 1980.

Dewey, John. *Art as Experience.* New York: Minton, Balch & Company, 1934.

Fast, Julius. *Body Language.* New York: M. Evans & Company, 1970.

Franck, Fredrick. *The Zen of Seeing.* New York: Vintage, 1973.

Guggenheimer, Richard. *Creative Vision.* New York: Harper & Row, 1960.

Hickson, Mark L., and Don W. Stacks. *Nonverbal Communication: Studies and Applications,* 2nd ed. Dubuque, IA: Wm. C. Brown, 1989.

Lawlor, Robert. *Sacred Geometry: Philosophy and Practice.* New York: Crossroad, 1982.

Verderber, Rudolph, and Kathleen Verderber. *Inter-Act,* 5th ed. Belmont, CA: Wadsworth, 1989.

Zettl, Herbert. *Sight, Sound, Motion: Applied Media Aesthetics,* 2nd ed. Belmont, CA: Wadsworth, 1990.

CHAPTER 14

Postproduction Values

· ·

Your decisions of what to use and what not, what to emphasize and what not, and exactly how to put everything together for the screen are influenced by your communications intent, the target audience, the medium requirements, and by your personal style.[1]

—Herbert Zettl

In Chapter 2 we discussed postproduction as the final element in the overall production process. The areas we addressed included the posting design, organizing the original video rolls, edit decision lists, mixing and sweetening the audio and music, and some off- and on-line editing strategies. Our examination focused on the mechanics of editing.

In this chapter we turn to the creative, communication aspects of the postproduction process, focusing on the critical thinking and decision-making parameters that contribute to effectively presenting a message or telling a story. These decisions transform editing techniques into values, which can ensure that the communication objective will be met. Although we can readily see how the picture and sound portions of a program communicate, we seldom think about how editing itself also communicates.

Before we begin, it's important to note that, although a script is usually intended to be precise and complete, no script is. After the scenes have been shot, we have a more complete picture of the whole program. It is then easier to see alternative ways of editing to best realize our communication objective.

In the case of lecture-style programs such as training, documentary, and other informational presentations, the script might be loosely structured to allow the director the opportunity to "find" some of the content in the production process. Dramas, however, are almost always more tightly scripted because the dialogue and action must be planned, so the story will be preserved. Nonetheless, the drama editor's challenge is to see how and if the energy in the script matches that on the screen. Additionally, the editor must cover and sometimes repair scenes where the shooting decisions proved to cause problems or where new decisions must be made.

People approach editing differently depending on the program scale, genre (documentary, drama, art), format, available technology, and personal circumstances. Even the person who makes editing decisions varies. In small productions the producer-director-cameraperson is also likely to do the editing or make the decisions. In corporate production studios and small production companies, where roles are more differentiated, it's customary for the director to make edit decisions in collaboration with an editor. In large-scale projects the director might insist on first or final cut decisions or both. And, in some instances, the director will turn the footage over to a trusted editor to do the first assembly, reserving the right to make final decisions on the fine cut (or master). The director has overall responsibility for the creative aspects of the production.

A typical professional-level editing process flows something like this:

- Time-code each original roll and make a "window dub."
- Log the scenes on each roll (using the dubs).
- Prepare an EDL for a rough-cut or first assembly using the script and logs.
- Evaluate the rough-cut and restructure the EDL accordingly.
- Prepare a second, third, and fourth assembly if necessary.
- Prepare the final on-line EDL.
- Do the audio/music/sound effects mix and sweetening.
- Prepare the master (fine-cut) program.

An editor has practiced her craft well when every transition occurs without a technical intrusion—nothing seems out of place or jars the viewer's sensibility and his attention shifts imperceptibly and as designed. An editor has practiced her art well when the content flows naturally from one scene to another, each scene contributing to the logical or emotional flow of the piece. As a result of appropriate transitions, viewers more closely attend to what is happening on the screen. Scene placement and pacing result in the generation of meaning and emotional experience.

Although the craft of video editing can be mastered by learning techniques and conventions, the art, which is highly intuitive and subjective, is developed through substantial experience working in front of the camera as well as over the editing console. Over time the process of handling creative challenges results in an ability to quickly analyze scene relationships, to know the appropriate elements to use, to see their effective placement, and to structure cinematic time and space in such a way that the communication objective is realized.

To understand the communication values editing contributes to a production, we'll examine a variety of factors focusing on two major types of presentations: informational and dramatic. But before we can take up those subjects, we will examine the basic editing techniques and what they contribute to communication.

The Grammar of Editing

· ·

Three structural areas of editing need to be learned: *transitions, continuity,* and *tempo.* These are the tools the editor uses to communicate.

Transitions

Shots exist in relation to other shots. When considering scene placement, it's necessary to find out what comes before and after the shot in question. At the junctures where every shot begins and ends, a transition occurs that carries definite communication implications. Every shot must have a communication purpose. It must in some way contribute to the dynamics of the sequence in which it is just one element. The transitions at the in- and out-points must also contribute to this dynamic to be appropriate. Does it carry the energy, or flow, forward? Does it blend gracefully? Or should it abruptly change the pace or establish a new time or place?

The cut   A cut is an instantaneous shift of the viewer's attention. A **jump cut** occurs when the incoming scene is an abrupt change that makes no sense: for instance, a cut from a speaker to another shot of the same speaker ten seconds later. The slight head and shoulder shift would call attention to the edit, so jump cuts are usually covered with another picture. To cover a jump cut the editor uses a **cutaway,** which could be anything related to the subject matter, such as scenes that illustrate what is being said. A cutaway that's used in interviews is the **reversal,** where the camera shows the interviewer listening to the interviewee.

An editing error is the **scene-on-scene** cut, where two scenes are so close to each other compositionally that the transition appears unmotivated. Such would be the case if the shot changed only slightly or when there was little distance between multiple cameras. The convention is to *vary the shots,* cutting between dissimilar viewpoints. It's generally more appropriate to cut from a wide shot to a close-up (or vice versa) than from wide to wide or from medium to medium.

Cuts can be "soft," where the transition is between shots that contain the same subject matter, or "hard," where completely unrelated content is abruptly juxtaposed. A regular series of cuts creates a "staccato" tempo, for example, a montage of construction site close-ups cut to the loud and constant beat of a pile driver. The sound motivates the cuts. Another example is the tempo of people interacting in a group. Our attention moves to each person as he or she speaks. We usually like to see the person talking, but often in dramas editors will show us faces other than that of the person speaking. Conversation and reactions can motivate cuts, as can mood and dramatic intensity, the fatigue factor, special visual effects, speech pacing, atmosphere, and so on. But cuts generally should not call attention to themselves.

The fade   Beginning directors often confuse the *fade* with the *dissolve,* especially when calling these shots in the control room. There is a major difference between them, and one should use these terms deliberately. A *fade* always involves black. Either the picture fades up from black or down to black. A fade is never a transi-

Cutting Conventions

- Cut on the action (actor or camera). When a car is going to travel out of the frame, cut before it disappears. When a zoom-in cuts to another shot, cut before the zoom ends. When an actor goes through a door, cut before the door closes behind her.

- Cut to the reaction, just before the person speaks.

- Cut at the end of a sentence or at a pause point when cutting to a different speaker.

- Cut midsentence when going to a reaction shot of someone listening to or watching the speaker.

- Cut at the end of a musical phrase or on the beat within a phrase.

- In a drama, do not cut on musical beats.

- When cutting between camera movements, use similar speed movements if they are cut together (slow zoom-in to slow zoom-in, not slow zoom to fast zoom).

- Begin wide (or long), then cut to a medium shot, then to a close-up.

- When cutting between camera movements (pan, tilt, zoom), keep the motion going in the same general direction. Do not pan right and then cut to a pan left. Do not zoom-in and then cut to a zoom-out.

- As emotional interest increases, move the shot closer to the subject. As intensity decreases, move the shot farther away.

- The length of a scene (shot) is ideally the shortest amount of time it takes to convey the point of the scene. Never saturate viewers with a shot. As soon as you know they've got it, move on. To hold a shot is to call attention to it.

- Vary the composition from scene to scene. Don't cut from a medium shot to a medium or a wide to a wide unless they are very different. Cutting between two shots that are very similarly composed (a scene-on-scene) confuses the audience.

- To change screen direction, use a completely different shot (or motion) between the shift. On a series of screen-right pans, before cutting to a shot that is a pan left, insert a shot that is not a pan at all (a zoom or tilt). And do not cut from a pan to a stationary shot. Let the pan stop and then cut.

- The cutting tempo should match the sensibility of the sequence (action). Heightened interest calls for fast cuts; slow action motivates longer cuts; sensitivity calls for dissolves.

- Eliminate any nonmotivated camera movements such as camera jerks, unsteady pans, tilts, or zooms.

tion from one picture to another, although it can be a segue from one sequence to another as when a fade-out (to black) is followed immediately by a fade-in.

The fade-in implies the beginning and the fade-out implies the end. Fades are generally used at the beginning and end of programs. Even when used within programs, the fade signals the beginning and ending of sequences or stories. When a fade-out/fade-in occurs quickly in a program, it is sometimes referred to as a **cross-fade.** Time, space, content, or a combination of these shifts completely.

The dissolve A **dissolve** is a transition from one image to another that never shows black—one image blends into another. It is a gradual transition that often signals a change in time, space, or both. A dissolve always begins with an image that is being replaced by another. During the dissolve a third image—the combination of the first and second images—is created. It disappears as the second image replaces the first.

Two separate rolls of video are required to make dissolves, in order to accomplish the overlap. This necessitates three VTRs: one to play the A roll, another to play the B roll, and a third to record their alternating scenes. More often than not, the coordination of the three machines is handled by an edit controller—a computer that, when programmed according to time-code locations, automatically performs the dissolve at a specified rate. A less costly, and less accurate, method is to prepare A and B roll tapes timed to alternate according to the desired order. These are then "rolled" together with their signals input into a switcher that outputs video to a recorder. The fader bar on the switcher is used to effect the dissolves.

In terms of energy, dissolves should be used when the content sensibility is graceful or sensitive because they can be stretched out in length. In addition to gradually moving the viewer's attention from scene to scene, dissolves create a third image, which often establishes an interesting visual relationship between the first two images. The motivation for a dissolve could be shifting time, space, content, or mood.

The wipe A **wipe** is a transition involving a shape that sweeps across or within the frame, taking one image off as it brings another one on. It changes images directionally. Production switchers have symbols that display the various available directions. The editor can wipe pictures horizontally, vertically, and diagonally. Circle, star, and square wipes have a zoomlike movement that takes the image into or out of the frame as the fader bar is moved up or down.

The wipe signals the viewer that a distinct transition in time and/or space is occurring. Wipes usually occur rather quickly. Although the transitional "message" is similar to that of the cut and the dissolve, going from one shot to another, the wipe differs in its visual sweeping motion across the screen. It's erasing one viewpoint while writing another. Instead of relating image to image as a dissolve does, the wipe separates them. The energy of the wipe is direct and pronounced. It creates distance between one event and another.

Continuity

Continuity consists of threads that weave the presentation together into a unified whole. The most obvious continuity device is the convention of beginning a sequence with a wide shot, cutting to a medium shot and finally to a close-up: wide, medium, close-up. This deductive arrangement establishes the setting first, then brings the audience's attention to focus increasingly on the primary character(s) or other subject matter. A wide-to-tight zoom-in does essentially the same thing within a single shot.

People commonly divide character actions into a series of separate shots that, when edited together, give the impression of one continuous movement. This **matched action** provides continuity of movement between scenes while providing different perspectives. It also gives the editor more options for controlling mood and pacing.

In a wide shot we might see a manager pick up her phone and call for a report. The next shot could show an employee putting down the phone, hunting for the report, and leaving her desk to briskly walk to the manager's office. Another shot might shift the perspective to a medium view of the employee approaching the manager's office as she stops and fidgets with her hair (to make a good impression). The same action will have been shot several times from different angles so the editor can cut at exactly the place where the hands and feet are in the proper place with respect to the preceding shot. The action could be divided into several shots from many different angles. As long as the action matches the cuts, viewers will see it as one continuous movement.

When a shot contains movement across the screen from left to right, the editor will look for shots to maintain the same **screen direction**. When screen characters or subject matter move left to right, cutting to a right to left movement would be a violation of screen direction. If this was necessary for some reason, the editor would insert a nondirectional shot between these opposite directional movements, for instance, a close-up.

In physics, for every action, there is an equal and opposite reaction. The same is true for editing—action motivates reaction. To shift the audience's attention, we can have a character look in a particular direction. This justifies the next scene being a **reaction shot**, a view of what the character sees. Directors commonly have a character make a statement (action) and then cut to the facial expression of the listener (reaction) so viewers will know how the comment was received. Consider using reaction shots whenever the subject matter needs emphasis or when an emotion should be elicited.

Cutaways are another continuity device, used to shift the viewer's attention away from repetitious shots. In informational programs cutaways are used to illustrate what is being said. They are also used to cover audio edits that would otherwise appear to be jump cuts. In dramatic programs cutaways shift the viewer's attention to secondary action that may be happening simultaneously. At a dinner party sequence we might cut away to see the late arrival fixing a flat tire, for instance. Or a singer might be performing and we'll cut away to her smiling boyfriend in the audience. In this latter instance the cutaway is also a reaction shot.

Regardless of the transition used, the editor must always consider the dynamics of the picture composition and its related geometries. **Matching compositions**, sometimes used as a creative continuity technique, should be considered at every transition. If the outgoing scene's dynamic center is on the left side of the screen, it's usually not good practice to cut to a scene where the center is on the right. However, it might be appropriate when doing a dissolve because the dissolve involves a direct visual relationship. It would tie the two scenes together.

For instance, a rowboat placed screen left but moving to the right might dissolve into a sunset where the sun is placed screen right. During the dissolve the boat would appear to be moving into the sun. A cut from the boat (screen left) to the sun (screen right) would jar the viewer's sensibility too much. Ideally you should provide *balance* and *graceful equilibrium* to keep the viewer's perceptions flowing naturally. This also communicates to the audience that these relationships are intentional.

Montage, as a continuity device, involves the use of several brief shots that express and often emphasize a single meaning or emotion. A montage shifts attention from the general presentation to highlight a particular idea or feeling. In informational programs it illustrates a point. A montage of pollution shots might be used to convey industrial greed; a montage of old illustrated manuscripts could convey traditional belief systems. In dramatic presentations montages are sometimes used to mark the passage of time or to detail a particular event. Think of a montage as providing visual evidence or proof for what is being expressed. It does this by showing several images that create a single, unified meaning.

Tempo

The tempo of a sequence is controlled by the pacing of the action within the shot, the scene length, and the rate at which the shots change (quick cuts, slow dissolves). Sometimes you will determine the tempo by the pace of music or speech, but tempo is more commonly motivated by the action or emotion of the sequence. Before you can edit any program, you must understand its action and emotional dynamics.

To help a program achieve the communication objective, you can prepare an *emotional flowchart* (Figure 14.1) in the preproduction phase. With it you can plot the intended peaks and valleys of the viewer's emotional experience. Then the scenes are shot according to this plan. The editor will select shots that deliver these emotions appropriately, also using action, scene length, and transitions. The editor can use the flowchart to learn as much as possible about the dynamics of each sequence as well as the overall strategy.

Standard practice in editing is to shorten the *scene length* as the emotional intensity and/or action increases and to lengthen scenes as these decrease. A highly active sequence, such as a chase, calls for quick cuts and up-tempo music. Intense emotions such as rage and excitement also suggest fast cuts. Conversely, sensitivity motivates a slow tempo constructed of longer scenes, soft music, and dissolves.

The editor controls the pace of the action by varying the length of shots. A series of lengthy, low-action shots might set the stage for a **crash cut,** high-energy sequence. Once you know what a sequence is building toward, you can order and pace the shots to achieve the desired effect. Every sequence ideally should be fashioned to create some kind of emotion or provide varieties of experience. Shots that are relatively the same in length for no reason invite audience boredom.

Music is one of the strongest and most direct ways of manipulating tempo and thereby creating emotion in a video. It provides entertainment. Viewers may enjoy a program more if it contains music. Select music that has a direct relationship to

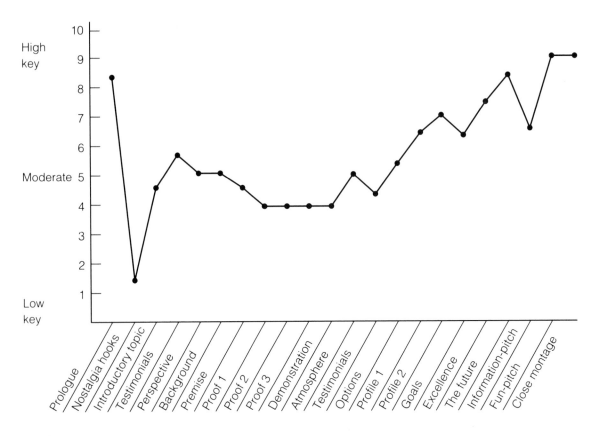

FIGURE 14.1
Emotional Flowchart

An emotional flowchart for each sequence of a program. "High" and "low key" refer to the relative emotional peaks and valleys the director plans for the program. In a drama, the sequences are identified either by scene numbers or by brief descriptions as shown here for a sales presentation. By preparing such a chart in the preproduction phase, the director can shoot accordingly, and the editor can quickly see the emotional flow of the design—especially the relationship between sequences.

the emotions involved, particularly in tempo. Editors try to see music and images as parts of the program as a whole rather than as independent elements featured alternatively within a program.

Cutting on the beat calls attention to the tempo itself, as is appropriate for music videos and sequences intended to make the audience move with the tempo, tapping their feet and so on. This is why editors of dramatic programs rarely use this technique. When you don't want to emphasize the tempo, you should cut based on elements other than the beat.

Speech patterns also affect tempo. A slow-paced speaker suggests longer scene length, whereas a fast-paced speaker prompts shorter scenes. For a soft voice use dissolve transitions and for a harsh voice use cuts. Pauses, repeats, silences, and nonfluent speech are often cut out, but in some instances you can make use of them—especially breaths between statements—to maintain a natural feeling and to contribute to the emotional sensibility. Because we usually want our screen characters to appear articulate, intelligent, and fluent, we should try to achieve balance.

In dramatic works dialogue strongly influences the tempo, but selected reaction shots and other inserts can be held longer or can be shortened to modify the pace within a scene. Silences should also be considered. They can be very powerful, especially for reaction shots, when you cut between characters as they glance meaningfully at one another.

Dialogue overlapping, when a speaker's voice is heard before he is seen, is an effective way to control continuity as well as scene tempo. The audio cues the audience that they are about to see the speaker, which sets up anticipation. We like to know what's coming next. But continuity between scenes can jump as well as flow logically.

A writer might devote a page or two to describing a setting or character whereas a producer can show it in a matter of seconds. In "real time" it would take hours to show a job hunter moving from interview to interview across town. But that tempo can be considerably shortened by jumping to the essentials and cutting out peripherals (elevator trips, lunch, traffic jams). *Cinematic time* reduces real-time activities by showing only what's essential to the communication. The tempo of life is speeded up, or slowed down, depending on the requirements of the sequence.

The duration of every shot then is related to its purpose. The rule of cinematic time suggests that a scene should be held only long enough for its purpose to be communicated. As soon as the viewer will get the message, go to the next shot (even if the shot is beautiful or you are attached to it).

Cinematic space operates the same way. Instead of seeing a character traverse the distance between two events, the camera cuts from one to the other and the distance covered is implied. Cinematic time and space can also be altered in real time, thanks to slow motion and high-speed technologies. For example, we can watch a flower bud open in five seconds on film even though it may have taken days to occur naturally. And we can dwell on the details of an Olympic high dive for twenty seconds or more when the plunge may actually have lasted only ten seconds. As editors we can provide extra time and attention for elements so we can communicate and entertain.

Editing Informational Content

Because their purposes differ significantly, the editing requirements for informational and dramatic presentations will be discussed separately here. In this section we'll examine some of the factors involved in editing information-oriented presentations to create interest, clarity, focus, and meaning. As we've seen, incorporating emotion and entertainment values into informational programs is a good way to sustain an audience's interest. So, although we're separating these approaches to see how they are handled differently, you will probably integrate them when you edit a program.

The editor's first task is to select the scenes to be used (and to put aside those that won't).

Scene Selection Criteria

The elements of informational (lecture-style) programs or segments will probably include lip-sync sound bites of individuals speaking or interacting; narration, on camera or using voice-over; cutaways and B roll illustrative visuals; character generated graphics; and perhaps talk elements if panel, studio-wrap, or call-in segments are involved. In programs where the voice content carries the primary communication, the editor will deal with voice considerations first. When pictures are primary, they are dealt with first.

Exclude poor-quality scenes   Eliminate poor talent performances, bad sound, picture problems such as glitches or dropouts, and anything that could interfere with the shot as a communication element. Of course, if the shot has a dropout but the audio is excellent, the scene can still be used. And sometimes the audio is bad but the picture usable. On the log sheet note scenes with unusable audio or picture. You will already have made a preliminary evaluation of the scenes during the logging process, but evaluation continues in more detail as you consider the most appropriate in- and out-points of each.

Sense the speaker's energy   Is the speaker's tempo fast or slow? Dull or enthusiastic? Flowing or broken? The pacing of the edits should generally match the talent's personality tempo so the flow feels natural. You would probably have worked on voice pacing during shooting, but the editor can manipulate and refine the tempo.

Attend to fluency   On camera people often pause to think, stammer, and use assorted conversational utterances such as "er" or "you know." These should be eliminated where possible to make the speaker sound more fluent and credible, but be careful not to clip the beginning or end of a word. Verbal redundancies, slurs, and the like should usually be eliminated. But if they must remain, make them a part of the natural flow of the sequence so they're not emphasized. By including an occasional "you know," the presentation will be more realistic. The context of the sequence will help you make these choices.

Maintain the flow   When there are several speakers juxtaposed in a sequence, cut the material as if one person were talking. Pauses that are too long or too short between speakers seem choppy and viewers will become aware of the editing. Breaths between speakers and sentences are important pacing cues. Ideally the audience should align their breathing with that of the speaker(s) they are watching, however subtly, because it creates a deeper resonance and draws them into the presentation.

Create a performance   When you're using a narrator, whether in the recording studio or on location, mark her script to help her perform her lines instead of merely reading them. Have the narrator punch and diminish key words and phrases. Make sure there are clean breaks between paragraphs. Build in edit points. And pay attention to the energy of the narrator's personal style as she reads/performs to keep it consistent with the mood you want. The performance should make you feel what you want the audience to feel and think what you want the audience to think. Retake the performance until it does. Then make the edits (sound and picture) consistent with this pacing.

Select the best content   A photographer once told me that the difference between an amateur and a professional is that an amateur shows you all the pictures he took but a professional only shows the few that are outstanding. An audience doesn't want or need to see everything you have; they want the substance, the essence. Selecting the *best* content means you use only the material that has the highest communication value in terms of content and quality.

Consider the context   Every shot is related to what comes before it and what will come after it. When you know the emotional or informational requirements of a sequence, placement will become apparent. But the context determines whether the shot relates well in a particular position.

Consider the composition   Do the compositions blend well from shot to shot? Or is the viewer's attention jumping across the screen and back again? As we said earlier, each shot placement decision should involve how the compositions work between scenes as well as within them.

Consider the energy   Every video image, no matter what the subject matter, has energy characteristics: a dynamic of sight, sound, and motion that reaches out from the screen to attract an audience. First, when you look at your footage to consider how best to structure a sequence, how do you process your experience with the material? Does it appeal to your mind or imagination? Does it stimulate you to *think* about the subject? If so, the energy is cerebral—a "head approach," which triggers thoughts and ideas. A "heart approach" evokes a mood or specific *feelings.*

You have to use the approach, or a combination, that is consistent with the way you want to affect your audience and that directly relates to your communication objective. The head approach involves the use of sights, sounds, and motions to express ideas, information, data, or other cognitive experiences. The heart approach expresses beliefs, moods, attitudes, or values that touch the emotions and can open up the viewer to the subject matter. Which is more appropriate to your objective? Is the approach consistent with your audience definition and with how you want them to experience your presentation? Does your footage clearly operate at one or a combination of these levels? How subtle or powerful should that energy be? How does that compare with what you have? What can be done though editing to bring these into alignment?

When I complete a sequence, I always play it back entirely, putting myself in the viewer's position to determine its energy level. Do you remember the positive-negative criteria (PNC) method of scene analysis referred to in the shooting process? I also apply it during the editing process. I first want to *feel* the experience. Do the shots combine to create the feeling I want? Is there another option that would convey the mood or feeling even better? I engage my own emotions and quiet my mind, avoiding analysis and criticism. Then I make notes, usually a string of one-word descriptions of the mood.

Then I look at the sequence again, this time using my analytical mind and stilling my emotions so I can critically examine the accuracy of the content and the quality of the picture and sound. Is there any element (word, sound, image, motion) that distracts from the sequence's purpose? From this exercise I know immediately whether I'm off the track and, if so, I rearrange the sequence accordingly. The primary benefit of using the PNC method in the editing process is that it integrates critical thinking and intuitive perception.

Scene Management

Informational-format programs often run long because they involve people talking. Some applications are *very* long, such as in the videos increasingly used to document seminars, conferences, and conventions. But you will still have more material than you can use. How does an editor manage vast amounts of video and find the best way of putting it together? At the conclusion of the week-long Soviet-American Citizens' Summit in Washington, D.C., we had no script and eighty hours of tape that had to be condensed into a one-hour show. It's more common to end up with twelve or more hours of tape to edit into a one-hour program. In one project we ended up with over a hundred rolls of videotape.

Lengthy informational projects require substantial organization so you can identify the most appropriate scenes and then decide on their placement and pacing within the program format. The following methodology simplifies the process:

Step 1. Time-code the originals and make window dubs   Each original tape is dubbed onto another tape (usually ¾ in. or VHS). Most systems are configured so that time-code information is recorded on an assigned audio track on the original reel as the dub is made. Simultaneously, time-code numbers are burned into the picture of the dub (not the original) in a little window. In this way the time-code numbers on the original (located on the audio track) are in perfect alignment with those visible on the dub reel.

Step 2. Transcribe the audio   Make an audio cassette recording of each video roll. Then, while listening to each audiocassette, type its words on either a typewriter or a computer. This printed hard copy is referred to as a *transcription*. You should create a double-spaced, *typed* transcription of every tape. It doesn't have to be spelled or punctuated correctly. The objective is to get an accurate account of what each speaker said.

Step 3. Select the "keepers"   Read the transcription pages and decide which statements you like best. From the emotional flowchart I've prepared (with the client, if there is one), I can create a program outline to determine the format and content sequencing. Then, with a yellow highlighter, I mark the sentences of the transcript that I think best meet our objectives. I also make hash marks (/) to indicate possible in- and out-points because they sometimes occur in the middle of a sentence (Figure 14.2).

00:37:53:09

(MT:) Bucky, //when you mention receiving letters from children other than American writing to you about why doesn't the world work, it brings up to me the question and granted it may be a large question// *00:37:53:20 (:20)* and we don't have a whole lot of time, but briefly, from both you and Barbara // *00:38:19:24* what would the world look like if it was working for everyone from your vantage point?

(BF:) Very beautiful. The way it looked when you were a little child and saw your first sunlight. Beautiful, ~~raindrops~~ *like dew on the garden.*

(BMH:) I think Bucky's right, it would be very beautiful and the way I've tried to imagine it, it's taking all our potentials and imagine them working fully. The personal as well as technological. And what I've seen is that we would be in a state of whole-centered, Christ-consciousness as a new norm. Everyone would be experiencing the love of each other as themselves. We would be in an earth-space or Universal environment. We would be restoring this Earth. We would be extending our environment into space. We would be building new worlds in space. We would be traveling to far-distant galaxies. We would be probably in a

(continued)

FIGURE 14.2
Transcription "Keepers"

Gray highlighting and hash marks indicate the in- and out-points, the sentences to be used or at least considered. Time-code numbers are associated with each of these, and the durations are set in parentheses.

Step 4. Note the time-code numbers of the "keepers" Take the transcript and, with a VCR, play the time-coded window dubs for each roll. When you come to a section of audio that you have highlighted, write down the time-code numbers above the in- and out-points. Do this in pencil. Time each section by subtracting the time-code numbers (out-point minus in-point) to derive a duration for each piece no matter how short. Put durations in parentheses. The object is to be able to identify the in- and out-points for each sound bite and to know its roll number and duration.

Step 5. Construct a script There are two methods for constructing a script for the audio (voice) linear master.

Method 1: Cut out all the sentences and paragraphs you have highlighted and

Universe full of Life and find we are just being born to a universal com-

munity. I think through our biological revolution and our healing powers

we'd find that we do not need to get disease, that we can heal ourselves,

and eventually we can regenerate our bodies and have extended lives so

that we will choose to die and we will choose to live on and we will not

(1.05)   00:39:24:13   //(scan lines – take out)

die like animals, choicelessly, I believe that when our information

revolution is complete with mass communications, cybernetics, robotics,

00:39:33:20

that it will be just like //Jesus said, Look at the lilies in the field,

how they grow, and they toil not. That work as we know it will pass

away…the whole planet will have a nervous system that makes it possible

for the crops to be monitored and food to be distributed and the physical

work will be done by exquisite intelligence of human and machine and we

will be free to discover what it means to be fully human. And a child

born when all of that is working would be a citizen of the Cosmos. You

know it's said we only use 5 to 10% of our potential. We are going

through the final exam.

FIGURE 14.2
Transcription "Keepers" *(continued)*

numbered. Lay them out on a table and move them around to obtain the sequence
you like. Type any missing statements, including narration, and include them.
Strips that relate to a common theme should be laid out together so you can see
where the same subject has been discussed elsewhere. This ensures that you don't
duplicate material, and it helps to identify the best expression of a particular topic.

Be sure to indicate the roll number on the strip. This is the only way you'll
know where to find the audio on your video rolls. Eventually you will end up with a
sequence of paper strips that you then tape onto 8½ × 11 sheets of paper. Photocopy these pages (on the "light" setting) so the yellow highlighter marks will disappear. You then have a script that's ready for the rough-cut (Figure 14.3).

Method 2: Instead of cutting out the statements you want to keep, transfer a
summary of their information onto three-by-five-inch cards (Figure 14.4). This pro-

B & B4

BF: 00:37:28:15

The criteria we have on our planet right now of success is making money, being a realist, and that is to make money. And we have to realize that making money and making sense are diametrically opposed. We are going to have to have a humanity who DARES to realize it's transcendental to making money.

(:25)

Those are the kinds of tests we're really up against, dear fellow, in a very, very big way, as to whether truth is what counts, or is it a man-made criteria like *money* ... an enormous test we're coming into.

00:37:58:08

B & B9 **MT** 00:37:53:09

, when you mention receiving letters from children other than American writing to you about why doesn't the world work,

00:37:53:20

(:20) it brings up to me the question, and granted it may be a large question

(continued)

FIGURE 14.3
Paper (Scene/Sentence) Cuts

Strips of the selected scenes or sentences are cut from the transcription and taped, in sequence, to another sheet. The roll number and duration of each is indicated in the left margin. After you assemble these mock-ups and determine the total program time, photocopy them so the yellow highlighter marks disappear. The result is an edit script that can be used to prepare an EDL.

00:38;19;24
what would the world look like
if it was working for everyone from your vantage point?

BF: Very beautiful. The way it looked when you were a little child and saw your first sunlight. Beautiful, ~~raindrops~~ *like dew on the garden.*

BMH: I think Bucky's right, it would be very beautiful and the way I've tried to imagine it, it's taking all our potentials and imagine them working fully. The personal as well as technological. And what I've seen is that we would be in a state of whole-centered, Christ-consciousness as a new norm. Everyone would be experiencing the love of each other as themselves. We would be in an earth-space or Universal environment. We would be restoring this Earth. We would be extending our environment into space. We would be building new worlds in space. We would be traveling to far-distant galaxies. We would be probably in a Universe full of Life and find we are just being born to a universal community. I think through our biological revolution and our healing powers we'd find that we do not need to get disease, that we can heal ourselves, and eventually we can regenerate our bodies and have extended lives so that we will choose to die and we will choose to live on and we will not die like animals, *(1:05)*
00:39:24:13
choicelessly,

B & B9

(1:05)

FIGURE 14.3
Paper (Scene/Sentence) Cuts *(continued)*

FIGURE 14.4
"Keeper" Cards *(at right)*
These three-by-five-inch cards contain the necessary information for every scene. The cards were developed from the transcript pages. In some instances it is easier and quicker to work with these cards than to work with an edit script in 8½ × 11 form. Each card represents one scene and indicates the transition to the next.

```
00:37:28:15                A + V      CAMERA 3
                    (BUCKY SPEAKS TO M.T.)

          (:25)      "The criteria we have on...


                     ... we're coming into."
00:37:53:08

CUT TO
                                              24.
```

```
00:37:53:09                A + V       CAMERA 1
                    (M.T. TO BUCKY)

          (:20)  "When you mention...


00:37:53:20 ... may be a large question."

CUT TO
                                              25.
```

```
00:38:19:24                A + V       CAMERA 1
                    (M.T. → B.F. → B.M.H.)

          (1:05) "... what would the world...


00:39:24:13 ... like animals, choicelessly."

DISS. TO
                                              26.
```

cedure will help you remember the material and it's easy to lay out the "keeper cards" to determine proper sequence. Method 2 works somewhat better than Method 1 because it's quicker to reference "in" and "out" cue words than it is to read the complete strips. It's also quicker than cutting and pasting last-minute changes.

Step 6. Time the script   Total the lengths of the sound bites you have selected to determine the approximate running time of the program. If the time is greater than your limit, you need to eliminate some material. Eliminate weaker scenes until the time is within your limit. Don't forget to allow time for titles and credits. And include time for any entertainment sequences—interludes that break up the monotony of people talking.

Step 7. Write and record any wraparound material   If the format calls for a host wraparound, these segments also need to be shot and incorporated into the rough-cut. If the wraparound will be live, and the rest of the material is prepackaged, the approximate time of each wrap segment needs to be estimated and included in the program's total time.

Step 8. Prepare a (rough-cut) linear master   Using either the script pages, the three-by-five-inch cards, or an EDL derived from them, assemble a rough-cut audio linear master by recording each scene in order. Because this is an off-line procedure, and this is the first assembly, use cuts for every transition. Mark places that need a dissolve or other effect (wipes, fades, CG) on the EDL, script, or cards.

Step 9. Screen the result   When all the words are laid down on video along with their associated pictures, do a PNC evaluation. Make any changes in the audio content that are necessary and then assess where video inserts, cutaways, or other B roll material should go. Make extended rigorous notes on these details. For some projects you'll have to insert the cutaways so the client can evaluate the rough-cut.

Step 10. Prepare an edit decision list   With your cards and/or script sheets, you are now ready to prepare an EDL (see Figure 2.29 in Chapter 2). At this point you can choose either (1) to go directly to the on-line process to make your final program master or (2) to prepare a second assembly. People sometimes produce third, fourth, and fifth assemblies before going to the on-line process. In these additional assemblies, you might want to edit in the music and the dissolves and other transitions to give the work print a more finished look. You should make these decisions based on how confident you are about the program and on whether or not a client or employer requires it. When your assembly is satisfactory, simply create a final EDL.

Step 11. Do on-line editing   Take your original video rolls, the rough-cut, and your EDL to the on-line facility and assemble the program master. If your program includes audio (music or effects) from other sources, these tracks will be needed at this time. If an audio mix session including sweetening is necessary, it should be done in advance of this on-line session or you'll have to return to finish the master.

Editing Dramatic Content

Stories communicate through *empathy* and *energy*. The emotional flowchart, therefore, must be very specific so that every sequence will contain the desired mood or feeling or contribute to building it. Effective informational programming depends on substantive information, credible presenters, logical development, and an interesting or entertaining presentation, but dramatic programs depend on the emotional impact of the characters, setting, and action.

Scene Selection Criteria

The elements of a dramatic presentation are likely to include lip sync (dialogue), visuals, sound effects, CG graphics, and music. In addition to learning the entire story and its planned emotional flow, as with lecture-style material, the first task is to eliminate scenes that exhibit poor quality, inadequate performances, and action that doesn't match or other incongruities.

Mood/atmosphere   Use the emotional flowchart to know what mood or feeling the sequence needs to convey or set up. Which combination of visual and sound elements should be used? Those that create *empathy*. Remember, we need to put on the screen the emotion we want our audience to feel, and we have to make it believable. If we want the audience to feel sad, then we'll show our screen characters feeling sad and support this mood with appropriately sad music, keeping the cutting pace slow and the scene length long.

Map the sequence in advance to find out which elements work together to carry the desired emotion. When you know the primary carrier of the scene's communication and mood, look at the other available elements as possible contributors. Then decide on the best combination given the purpose of the sequence. Every shot and technique used must be motivated or justified by carrying some story element. That is, it must contribute to establishing the setting, developing the characters, or moving the plot forward.

Lighting controls, diffusers, and toned filters are often used to create a texture or atmosphere to further enhance the sensibility of the setting. And the editor must look at these elements carefully. For instance, if the camera operator forgot to put on a diffusion filter for a shot to be part of a diffused sequence, the shot must be rejected or reshot.

Setting   A wide shot establishes the setting or environment in which the characters are found usually at the beginning of the program and at the beginning of each new sequence. Dramas often begin with as wide a perspective as possible such as an aerial view of a city or landscape. When the cinematic time and/or space changes, an establishing shot orients viewers to the new environment. Once a setting has been established, however, there is no need to reestablish it every time we come back to it. Often "environmentals" are used within a sequence to help set up the action or strengthen the atmosphere.

The setting can be emphasized through the use of landscape, appropriate architecture, decorations, textural props, strong geometries, and in particular lighting.

In addition to looking realistic, the setting should bear some relationship to the characterization or action. Think of your characters as being products of their environments.

Character   Select shots that communicate what the characters are thinking or feeling. As much as possible, use visuals to carry the character's expression before using his or her words. A smile, a head turn, a penetrating stare, or a glance can often communicate emotion more powerfully than words. Naturally these responses must be motivated in some way. Directors anticipate this during shooting by allowing the action to demonstrate what the character thinks or feels. That's why so much emphasis is placed on close-ups (CUs).

One technique, the *double cut*, takes advantage of the strength of visual communication with back and forth reaction shots between two characters. A man makes a statement. Cut to the woman's reaction. Cut back to his reaction. Cut to her response. The pause in dialogue creates dramatic tension. We tend to keep our characters talking but the silences are equally communicative.

Point of view   The way we are shown a character also communicates. As emotional intensity increases, the shots should become increasingly tighter, and vice versa. For instance, a series of medium shots of an interaction can set up a dramatic moment to cut to a close-up of some detail, such as a gun being pulled from a purse or an unexpected expression. The point of view (POV) relates equally to the nature of the shot (wide, medium, close-up) and the camera position (angle). The motivation for each perspective should be to shift the audience's attention appropriate to the purpose of the sequence.

Continuity   As we've discussed, it is important to have the audience identify with the screen character(s). Continuity is one of the primary means by which this is accomplished. When the audience's attention moves forward in a natural, logical flow, viewers see and understand the characters' motives, making it easy to relate to them. Continuity breaks when logic isn't sustained, when attention is shifted to technique, or when the character's behavior is not believable.

Continuity is always motivated by the sequence's purpose and directionality. If a sequence needs to show a boating accident, it should begin with a wide shot of the boat. The next logical shot would show the people on the boat, not the harbor or the seagulls. The next cut could be to another boat, if one is involved; the engine room, if that's where the accident will occur; or a couple talking near the rail— something that relates to where the sequence is going. In the latter case, the next shot should be closer yet to the action—the couple talking so we can hear their conversation. If what they're saying is important we'd cut back and forth to catch their dialogue. Then the man excitedly looks over the side of the boat, so the next shot needs to show us what he's seen (by his reaction), and nothing else, not even the other character's reaction. Now we're set up to see the accident, a man overboard, a smaller boat as it rams the hull, or whatever.

Throughout the sequence each shot motivates the next: wide, medium, close-up. When the next sequence occurs, you should follow the same procedure for the *normal* pacing. When we need to create tension or suspense or lead up to an abrupt change within or between sequences, the pacing and shot angles should be altered accordingly. Each shot still needs to be motivated by the previous shot; it's just the nature of the motivation that you have changed. Although the director shot the script as written, the editor may see ways of combining and timing the provided shots to help the sequence achieve its purpose while maintaining continuity.

Tempo The tempo of a sequence also follows from its purpose and must be determined by the amount of time a shot remains on the screen. When the action is slow or the emotion gentle, scenes should usually be longer. When the action is fast or exciting, scenes should usually be shorter. If you want to build from slow to fast, or from gentle to excited, the sequence should begin with a series of lengthy shots shifting to gradually shorter shots, and vice versa.

When surprise is needed, lengthy, slow-paced shots lead up to a series of quick cuts and up-tempo music. Suspense begins with somber music that builds in intensity as well as lengthy shots leading to progressively shorter ones. Long-held shots send a signal to the audience that something is about to happen, as the normal convention is to change shots frequently. To find a sequence's tempo, think of cuts as abrupt shifts of attention, and then pace them according to the nature of the mood involved.

Narrative Techniques

There are many ways to combine elements depending on your purpose. The following are some of the specific techniques editors use to make stories effective.

To create excitement:

- Use cuts rather than dissolves
- Make quick cuts (shortened scene length)
- Cut on the beat of the music
- Use up-tempo music
- Use upbeat dialogue
- Make cuts progressively shorter
- Maximize visual and aural variety

To create atmosphere:

- Emphasize textural qualities, especially with lighting, filters, fog
- Use unconventional angles
- Use longer scene lengths and pace appropriately
- Maintain and emphasize scene *tonality* (darks transition into darks and lights to lights)
- Use sound effects to enhance the atmosphere and increase the illusion of depth or presence
- Blend images gradually (dissolves)
- Make dialogue tempo and quality match the atmosphere
- Maintain visual consistency throughout the sequence

To create meaning:

- Use dialogue but don't have the characters give speeches for you
- Use wide shots to convey information
- Show facial reactions to action or emotional expressions
- Use matched action to maintain continuous flow
- Use cutaways to compress time, hide jump cuts, shift attention, and illustrate
- Juxtapose shots—when two shots are put together they create a third meaning, so relate shots purposefully
- Build a montage to illustrate or lend importance
- Use appropriate music
- Use music *stingers* (abrupt highlights) to accentuate or emphasize ideas, actions, or feelings
- Repeat images and sounds for emphasis

To create suspense:

- Hold shots and pace them to create tension (dissolve, dissolve, dissolve, dissolve, cut or CU, CU, CU, CU, CU, wide)
- Use the progression wide, medium, medium, medium, medium, CU
- Use lengthy shots to progress to a succession of short cuts
- Use shots that set up anticipation; delay the expected
- Use shots that generate questions
- Use appropriate music
- Use music stingers to highlight tensions
- Boost the level of sound effects so they predominate

Narrative Strategies

In Chapter 11, "Storytelling," we made a distinction between stories that are told and stories that are shown. From the perspective of the drama editor, when you *tell* a story, it will rely on the words and expression of the teller, a narrator. As with informational-format editing, you must try to structure the scenes so the words used (content), how they are spoken, and their pacing relate to the emotional flow of the piece as well as the message being communicated. The other elements (music, sound effects, and images) should support what is said.

When you *show* a story, it will emphasize the characters as personalities, focusing on their interaction and dialogue including the actions, behaviors, and events that move the story forward. In these instances, the editor must try to maintain the appropriate pacing of the primary elements (character, dialogue, action) while using supporting elements (music, sound effects, POV) to convince the viewer of the reality of the situation, setting, and time. We expect viewers not only to listen to and watch what the characters say and do, we also expect them to *empathize* with the characters and their circumstances.

Parallel Cutting

The classic example of **parallel cutting** is a girl on a raft floating toward a giant waterfall. Shots of her distress are intercut with shots of a hero coming to her rescue. The editor cuts back and forth between the girl's worsening situation and the hero getting into a good position to rescue her.

Parallel cutting is intended to make the audience's attention alternate between two or more places or events. In another case we might see shots of carpenters building theater sets. We hear the voice of their supervisor. Next, and parallel to this, we cut to the costume shop, where actors are being fitted and costumes are being sewn. Then we cut to the public relations office, where ticket sales are being analyzed. Each shot carries its own sensibility according to the respective characters and settings, related to the theme: how a stage production is organized.

In parallel cutting moving from one setting to another instantaneously is appropriate. Viewers find meaning by assuming that the shots relate.

Convergence Cutting

Let's use the above example to move the program forward a bit and have the actions converge. Cut from the box office activity to dressing room activity, just before show time. Cut to the orchestra pit, where musicians are tuning their instruments. Cut to the audience coming in and being seated. Cut to a lighting technician who adjusts a spotlight, then to the booth where the audio board is being "tweaked." Cut to actors in costume getting into position. The conductor lifts the baton, the music begins, the curtain rises, and the audience applauds—convergence.

From disparate times and places, all the people we saw now come together to perform. The convergence scene, as in the rafting example, rewards the viewer by confirming expectations.

In **convergence cutting,** the pacing generally increases imperceptibly until the separate actions come together. To use this technique you must keep the viewer's attention and interest on each separate action until the convergence becomes obvious. The longer you can delay the expected, the more powerful the payoff will be when it occurs.

Although we've used action to motivate the cutting in the examples of parallel and convergence cutting, we could also use dialogue to motivate the juxtapositions. Consider a corporate drama where the CEO discusses her vision of the company's future. Parallel to this we could show middle managers and other employees giving their views on where the company will be in ten years. We could also edit the statements (from the top to the bottom of the corporate ladder) to create a *convergence of viewpoint* (rather than of action).

Counterpoint

Elements are said to be in **counterpoint** when they are opposed, as when slow music is positioned against fast cuts or when slow dissolves are used against rapid drum beats. The *60 Minutes* segment called "point-counterpoint" juxtaposed opposing viewpoints. This is an effective dramatic strategy because we find meaning in conflict and contrast.

Example: Your assignment is to design a commercial promoting a political candidate's position on the issue of homelessness. Option 1 (informational, head approach): Put your candidate on camera and let him give his views on the subject. Option 2 (argumentative, head approach): Have the candidate debate with someone, perhaps an opponent. Option 3 (heart approach): Use dramatic counterpoint to contrast the "have-nots" with the "haves." Intercut the pictures and dialogue of street people playing cards with the pictures and dialogue of people playing cards in a wealthy suburb. Music and sound effects in each environment enhance the contrast. Close with the candidate handing out blankets to people on the street. Which option do you think is more powerful?

Counterpoint editing brings together opposite content or production elements. You create meaning through the contrast or conflict between them.

Flashback/Flashforward

The *flashback* is a common way of showing a character's background. It takes the audience to a prior event in the character's life. Toned images, diffusion, dissolves, costumes, wipes, and sometimes just a severe time-location shift cue the audience that they are seeing a past event. *Flashforward* uses the same kind of cues to transport the viewer into a future time and place. These jumps into history or the future give the storyteller options for communicating the character's background or dreams that relate to the cinematic present. These strategies strengthen the story's context by showing how events led to the present and where they might be going. Although flashbacks and flashforwards are usually designed into a script, at times the editor will see their appropriateness when not planned in advance and will be able to use existing footage to create them.

Music and Sound Effects

Music and sound effects strongly contribute to the communication experience. Music can provide a direct emotional experience, establish an atmosphere, shift a context, or regulate the level of intensity of a particular scene. When music is set against appropriate images, the combination multiplies the effect. Sound effects draw the audience into the events on the screen. They are largely responsible for our ease in identifying with the action.

Sources

The producer has two options for acquiring music and sound effects: using prerecorded material from libraries or recording them originally. There are a number of companies (listed in trade magazines) that sell or lease their music and effects libraries. Most production facilities have acquired one or more of these and, for a "needle-drop" fee, allow producers to identify and use selections.

The alternative is to find people who can compose and produce original music or effects. This can be extremely expensive, but it can also be less expensive if you have connections. Some composers and musicians are eager to find opportunities to get exposure for their work, especially if they are attracted to your project. You can compensate them in a variety of ways: by giving them copies of the video with rights to publish the music as a separate product, a partnership in the venture, screen credit, or deferred payment of their expenses and fees until revenues are generated. With original music you have maximum control, which can result in the best possible match between the picture and other elements.

Creating sound effects is another matter. It's difficult to get the variety of sounds that are usually needed, and the quality of original recordings is never quite as good as the prerecorded library effects, which have been heavily "sweetened." For this reason, aside from large-scale productions, most producers rely on libraries for sound effects, creating only those that are specific to their needs and not likely to be found in a prerecorded library.

Music Contributions

Music not only provides emotion and an entertainment context, it also contributes to communication. You can show the audience what a character is thinking or feeling through the music's pitch, tempo, or both. Music *informs* the audience what the character is experiencing. Low tones evoke low feelings; high, bright tones evoke bright feelings. A slow pace implies low intensity; a fast pace implies high intensity.

Music *creates a visceral response* so we can more closely identify with characters. We stop breathing for an instant when there is silence; our heart beats to the music's tempo; our muscles tense and loosen with its various levels of intensity; our thoughts shift instantaneously.

Music also *provides transitions* between moods. A single violin note, a *stinger,* can provide a transition between a quiet scene and a busy scene. To transition to a tragic scene, you could use a violin note low in tone, perhaps somewhat discordant. A single sound, positioned at just the right instant, tells us which emotional direction we're going to take.

The same devices can and should be applied to documentaries, training, and other nondramatic presentations. Everything we've discussed about music here applies in any genre or format.

Music *signals style changes.* A chase scene in New York sounds different from a chase scene in San Francisco; so should the music. Would the music to *Rocky* adapt well to *The Karate Kid?* The music in each case matches the sensibility of the subject matter. Brassy horn instruments are needed to express the contrasting textures of pain and triumph that characterize Rocky's urban experience. Flute, reeds, and strings are more appropriate to the oriental, thoughtful inner strength of Miagi and his pupil Danielsan.

Music *underscores* action as it rises or falls. As the screen action builds the music also builds, becoming louder, brighter, faster, or a combination of these. When the action declines the music becomes quieter, softer, or slower. The music matches whatever emotion is on the screen, often signaling it in advance by seconds.

Music can also *establish the pace* or flow of a piece. It can quicken, shorten, build, or decline and even shift styles or textures instantaneously.

Music can also *unify segments or a whole program* by providing a theme and variations on it to be used throughout. These themes become familiar by the end of the program, so that hearing them again creates a strong memory of the program. Think of one of your favorite musicals.

Special Effects and Graphics

In video and television, *special effects* are image-manipulation techniques primarily created during the on-line editing session. *Graphics,* for the most part, are on-screen stationary elements including words, bar charts, graphs, and other illustrations that use bold designs, color, words, and textures. When these images are generated by a computer other than a character generator, they are referred to as *computer graphics.* The movement of these elements is referred to as *animation.*

Special Effects

A *freeze frame* occurs when a single frame (field) of video is held on the screen. The freeze communicates that the action has stopped at a significant point: to end a program or sequence, to highlight something special about the image, to hold it so it can be seen longer. A **frame store,** or still store, is a device often used in broadcasting to hold a frame in a computer's memory indefinitely. The image can be manipulated, perhaps by adding an identification tag or logo, and then recalled whenever needed.

A **super** is created by the overlap (superimposition) of two (or more) images. Graphics can be supered over pictures and pictures can be supered over one another. Supers create a relationship between the images involved. Viewers assume that the director wants them to enjoy or explore this relationship. For example, when we super a close-up of a drummer's hands over his facial expression, we put the sound and the emotion in close proximity so nothing is left to the imagination. When we super a picture of a burning American flag over a picture of the Constitution, we show a direct, present relationship as opposed to a sequential one (as when the scenes are cut together as isolated shots).

Slow motion allows the viewer time to experience the details of an action that might otherwise go by too fast. It emphasizes the action and allows the observer to analyze the action, as done in a close race.

A *squeeze zoom* refers to editing technologies that can either expand (zoom-out) or compress (zoom-in) the picture size. The director can use the effect to add or diminish emphasis, juxtapose several different shots on the screen simultaneously, or dedicate areas of the screen to certain elements. The *aspect ratio*—the relationship of horizontal to vertical (4:3 in video)—can also be altered to create a rectangle of any other proportion.

A *page turn* is a sophisticated wipe that looks like a page being turned as one scene replaces another, much as in a book. Page turns can be accomplished in any direction, even beginning in a corner. They are appropriate transitions for conveying the sensibility of a book in the unfolding of a story.

Flips and tumbles allow the editor to flip (vertical axis) or tumble (horizontal axis) an image 360 degrees continuously or as many times as desired. We see this effect often in local commercials because it adds variety to an otherwise boring presentation. It's more appropriate to use it in animating screen elements to perform stunts not otherwise possible, for instance, flipping a logo from back to front, tumbling a series of scenes onto a geometric shape, or showing a mirror image. The communication value of flips and tumbles derives from their motion in relation to the scene's purpose.

The *mosaic* effect is achieved by transforming an image into its component *pixels,* or building blocks. Although the effect is interesting, its communication value is limited by the specific block nature of its design. Occasionally the mosaic is used as a way to hide a face or other pictorial element to protect a person's identity.

Electronic *paint* systems now permit the complete manipulation of still images. Anything that can be photographed or drawn can be visually modified in color, shape, size, texture, lighting, and much more. The communication value, again, depends on the nature of the image and its purpose.

Whenever a new electronic technique becomes available, we expand our communication potential, our creative capability, and our ability to visualize our dreams. Usually, because of its novelty, the special effect becomes overused and a cliché. In the midst of the current imaging environment it's critically important to keep these capabilities in perspective as tools for communicating. People communicate. And if we communicate poorly, it doesn't matter how many machines we have access to or how expensive they are.

The use of *computer generated imagery* signals the audience that the producer has some connection with high-tech, high-skill, high-budget, and intensive "personpower." It associates the producer with these values, which can be rewarding. It can and does attract business. But the substance lies in what such images can do to stimulate and create meaning, value, and positive experience for an audience. This makes clients want to return.

Computer imagery can too quickly call attention to technique. The use of special effects, therefore, must be grounded in a genuine communication purpose. If an effect leads to increased clarity or meaning, its use is well justified. Just as a cut or dissolve must be motivated, so must the use of any effects.

Graphics

Graphics usually include titles, credits, and illustrative diagrams or charts that supplement the content. These can be derived either from flat art, which is then photographed on a camera stand, or by using a character generator (CG), which serves as a typewriter (and potentially much more) for the video screen.

To communicate effectively, graphics must relate to the program content by providing necessary information, details, emphasis, or style. Additionally, their appearance should match the tone, texture, or sensibility of the piece. Font styles, letter height, letter color, background color, outline, drop shadow, and edging are just some of the ways graphics can be manipulated to do this. Their composition on the screen and their duration communicate. Should the letters be still? Should they crawl across the screen, roll up, or fade in and out? These considerations depend on the communication objective of the scene, sequence, and overall program look.

Titles appear at the beginning of a program, providing the program title and subtitle (if any). *Head credits* are also frequently used immediately after the title to indicate the principal creative participants (actors, writers, director, producer). In the titles, "stars" come first, followed by others in descending order according to their contribution (the more important come last). In films the director is last. In television the producer is last.

Credits, or end credits, are also displayed in descending order of importance, reserving till the end those who made the greatest contribution (and usually the most money). At the very end are references to the production and distribution companies. Finally the copyright notice appears along with any restrictions against duplication if needed. This ordering is a convention that is often ignored in favor of approaches that emphasize style or practical concerns. An example would be when you anticipate the end credits being cut short or not shown at all. In this case you might want to put the more important credits at the beginning of the program where they will definitely be shown.

In informational programs it's common practice to super the name and title of a speaker when he or she appears for the first time. Using a CG, these words are **keyed** into the lower third of the picture rather than being superimposed. Whereas a super puts one image on top of another, a "key" electronically cuts a hole in the background image where the words fit. The letters become opaque against the background, allowing the director to change their color or to insert other visuals within the letter area.

Charts, graphs, and other illustrations can be shown as separate elements, keyed into parts of another image, or supered over them. You will make this decision based on the relationships involved and how they communicate.

Summary

We began this chapter by noting that editing itself communicates, that the craft involves several technical controls best learned through experience, that editing becomes an art when it becomes intuitive, and that scripts vary in their accuracy and completeness, requiring the editor to constantly reevaluate the structural possibilities.

Because our focus was on communication aspects of editing, we based our discussion on the grammar of the controls involved. Transitions, including cuts, fades, dissolves, and wipes, cue the viewer about the flow of content including its time and space characteristics.

Continuity is partly determined by the shots selected and their placement in a given context. The viewer's attention follows a particular path depending on these juxtapositions, which are regulated by a deductive presentation that establishes the setting and then brings in the details (wide to medium to close-up). Matching action creates the illusion of continuous movement between shots; screen direction keeps attention moving naturally; reaction shots show the effect of some behavior or action; cutaways provide viewers with fresh perspectives; matching compositions contribute to the flow between scenes; and montage allows attention to dwell on a particular subject or theme.

Tempo control is specified in the emotional flowchart, which is an analysis of the varying levels of intensity of each sequence. Music, speech patterns, dialogue overlapping, and the modification of cinematic time and space are the tools the editor uses to control tempo.

With this grammatical foundation we next applied these tools to editing informational presentations. We examined the criteria for scene selection including speaker energy and fluency, performance values, context, and picture dynamics. Because the organization of material, especially large quantities of material, affects communication, we examined a way to manage scenes so the best material emerges out of all that's available.

Then we applied our editing grammar to dramatic content to show how mood, atmosphere, setting, character, point of view, continuity, and tempo relate to telling and showing a story. We then discussed certain narrative techniques and strategies. Parallel cutting divides attention between two or more events or subjects; convergence cutting brings two or more separate actions or subjects together for a purpose; counterpoint combines content or techniques in opposition or in conflict; flashback directs attention backward in time; and flashforward directs attention forward in time.

We examined the importance and contribution of music and sound effects to establishing a mood, setting a tempo, and highlighting or underscoring a subject, character, or action. Finally we looked at the meanings and contexts involved in a variety of special effects and graphics.

How a program is edited communicates.

Notes

1. Zettl, Herbert, *Sight, Sound, Motion,* 2nd ed. (Belmont, CA: Wadsworth, 1990), 299.

Suggested Readings

Anderson, Gary. *Video Editing and Post-Production: A Professional Guide,* 2nd ed. White Plains, NY: Knowledge Industry Publications, 1988.

Rosenblum, Ralph. *When the Shooting Stops . . . the Cutting Begins: A Film Editor's Story.* New York: Viking Press, 1979.

Shetter, Michael D. *Videotape Editing: A Guide to Communicating with Pictures and Sound.* Elk Grove, IL: Swiderski Electronics Incorporated, 1982.

PART **VI**

DOING IT RIGHT

. . . .

S oon after I began my
first job in television,
I was surprised to learn
that there wasn't going
to be any training, not even
some orientation about how the
industry works or what the company would expect. I wasn't told
about what to do or what not to
do. Although it was nice to be
left alone, I had a lot of policy
question. Answers to these
questions could have helped me
substantially.

As a cinematographer, my job
was to shoot and edit commercials. Some spots were scripted
by advertising agencies; others
were solely up to me in terms of
presentation. I soon found myself
in situations where I was "selling" products to the public, products that I didn't particularly
respect. In some instances I
made products look and function

better than their original design,
and I photographed business
owners who made fools of themselves in front of the camera.
Being quite naive, I simply produced the spots and enjoyed the
opportunity to be creative.

Occasionally I was asked to
shoot in-house corporate pieces
and specials and documentaries
for local broadcast. My creativity
was further challenged and I felt
privileged that I had been asked.
But in another context I also sat
in on program design meetings
about which I didn't feel good.

In one instance we were asked
to produce a program on a topic
that was important to the program director's mother and to
slant it toward her opinion. In another the company decided to
ignore the ascertainment survey
(community sampling to determine local interests) in favor of
doing a program that promoted a
news anchor instead.

In another situation five other
crew members and I worked
from 6:30 a.m. until 2:30 a.m.
the next morning (twenty hours)
for a commercial producer who

allowed us to take only bathroom breaks. He had lunch and a steak dinner brought in for himself and the client. They ate in front of us while we worked. We had nothing to eat for twenty hours. He responded to our complaints: "When I say we're done, we're done—and then you can break for as long as you like." This man's hateful attitude, abusive manner, and foul language caused two people simply to leave the set. It was the worst shoot I've ever been on and I would have quit too, had I not been assigned to "stick it out" by my boss, whom I respected.

Then, when this series of spots won a national advertising award, the client and this producer accepted it. Each of them received a plaque and their picture in a trade magazine for a fine job. None of us who actually did the work even received a mention.

I cite these instances as examples of some of the more common types of ethical issues that confront media professionals every day. These personal, judgment, and decision-making concerns color the production experience itself and the quality of the work we do.

But we must look at some larger issues as well: What if telling a story discredits a person or ruins his life? What if a person commits suicide as a result of a decision you made? What if telling the truth will get you fired?

Part VI consists of only one chapter not because it doesn't relate to other areas of video communication but because it relates to *everything* else in this book. You can't read a newspaper or watch television today without seeing that our society has been and continues to struggle with ethics issues. It appears that money, power, acquisition, and status have become ends that many attempt to achieve no matter what the means or cost to others.

Supreme Court Justice Potter Stewart, in conversation with Fred Friendly, media critic and educator, said:

> *You're all mixed up about the difference between what you have a right to do (under the First Amendment—which is almost anything), and* the right thing to do.

We would do well to keep this idea before us as an inspiration. It's not so hard to make a video; it's a bit harder to make it work, and harder yet to make it good. But the greater challenge is one we face every day—doing it right. "Right" in this context doesn't refer to the quality of the program but to the quality of character we bring to the process.

CHAPTER 15

Ethics, Integrity, Initiative

· ·

What you are speaks so loudly

that I cannot hear what you say.

—Ralph Waldo Emerson

t's 7:30 a.m., Saturday. You're busy unloading video equipment because you're late and your partner called in sick. You've got to set up everything and get audio and video levels so the client can shoot as soon as he arrives with the talent at 9 a.m. You've just unpacked a camera with a charged battery. Just then you hear two gunshots. You run to the second-story window. Across the street a person falls in front of a bank as an assailant runs to a car with money dropping all around. With the camera still in your hand, you run out of the building. Twenty- and fifty-dollar bills are all over the place and a man is lying face down in a pool of blood. He's not moving. Nobody else is in sight. What do you do? Take pictures of the scene for the police and the evening news? Grab a handful of bills first? Run to a phone and dial 911? See for yourself how badly the person is injured and then call? Yell and scream for help? Or go back to unloading the equipment because it's none of your business and you're late? Write down your course of action, in sequence, before reading on.

In this chapter we'll look at this and other kinds of situations for the purpose of understanding ethics, how it works, and some of the different kinds of ethical systems. We'll focus on some specific ethical issues that apply to both nonbroadcast and broadcast environments. We'll also explore the nature of integrity and responsibility, both of which are crucial to an informed perspective on ethics. Finally, I want to offer a brief story about one of my former students that illustrates the value of initiative. Our concern in this chapter is essentially with how ethics, integrity, and initiative are relevant and contribute to increased program effectiveness.

Ethics

. . . .

Ethics is a discipline within which people evaluate "right" or "wrong" with respect to some basis or principle(s). We observe how we (or others) behave and put a value on the behavior between extreme right or extreme wrong, attributing it to some motive. People generally do things for a reason, even when their action is spontaneous, unconscious, or reactive. We consider ethical what people "ought" to do or the "right thing." Although doing the right thing will be interpreted by each individual in each situation, most people would agree that it includes not harming anyone else. To be ethical is to be guided by principles that contribute to one's own good but not at the expense of another. This requires being true to oneself and these principles in practice.

How Ethics Work

Behavior reflects loyalty. In the situation above, if the first choice was to shoot videotape for the evening news before calling for help, the operative principles would probably be to build a professional reputation and possibly make some money. If the choice was to dial 911, one is loyal to a concern for human life. To take the money while no one was looking would suggest loyalty to self above others as the operative principle. To ignore the situation entirely might indicate that job responsibility comes before anything else, possibly even human life, or that there was fear of what might happen as a consequence of getting involved. *Who* are you responsible to? *What* are you responsible for?

Each behavior indicates a personal *identification* with certain principles. Now what about this situation? What if you were on the third floor and saw the whole thing. You saw me stuff the money in my camera bag, shoot pictures of the scene, and then run to the phone booth to make a call. Your story to the police would suggest that I'm guilty of robbery. But later, as you sit in the courtroom listening to my story and why I made the choices I did, the picture might be different. I could make the case that I took the money because I wanted to prevent it from being stolen by others. I could also make the case that I already saw the man was dead and felt there was no sense calling for help until the money had been secured and the site documented on video for the record. Instead of being indicted I would be rewarded, and the local TV station would consider me a hero and perhaps offer me a job. As you can see, each situation can be viewed in many ways depending on viewpoint and interpretation.

Although my behavior may be judged as right or wrong by others, I alone know the reason I acted as I did. My decision reveals my loyalty. Conclusions reached by others do matter, however, as the jury may find me guilty and send me to prison. Whether or not someone else is looking, our behavior indicates a loyalty to positive or negative principles that are already in place. This loyalty provides motivation to act in a certain way. Even when others can't see our principles, we usually know what they are. Guilt feelings let us know when we have acted contrary to our own values. The study of ethics increases our sensitivity to right and wrong by helping us to be "in touch" with the principles operative in our lives. It also reminds us that, whatever the project, whatever the scope, we are never alone in the consequences of our decisions or actions.

Kinds of Ethics

What should be the basis for our moral and ethical reasoning? Civil law? Scripture? The circumstances of each situation? Doing what promotes the best for the greatest number? In exploring these questions I came across an article by Reverend G. Bradford Hall, Jr., of Palm Desert, California, which appeared in the September–October 1988 issue of the *Broadcast Financial Journal*. "Thinking Ethically in a Morally Chaotic World" does such an excellent job of synthesizing contemporary ethical thinking that I will reprint his comments here. We'll learn the difference between **situation** and **character ethics,** among other things.

THINKING ETHICALLY IN A MORALLY CHAOTIC WORLD

My reading and experience lead me to cite three basic categories of authority upon which we base most of our moral reasoning:

RULES. Most often thought of as God's rules, but in a more secular context often called by philosophers natural law. We will ask the question: Are there rules and, if so, where are they to be found? And, once we locate them, are these rules clear and generally agreed upon standards to make our moral decisions?

SITUATIONS. This second criterion of authority says in part that often the moral situation we find ourselves in and the consequences of a person's action are sufficient authority upon which to base moral decisions. Indeed, some situations may even override the rules.

INDIVIDUAL CHARACTER. This third category allows the distinct possibility that there resides in each person a deep sense of what is right and what is wrong, and that sense can be developed and enhanced by developing and enhancing our character and developing virtues.

Let's explore each category in some detail.

Rule Ethics

I believe most of us make a basic assumption that there are rules which serve as standards for moral or ethical decision making. But, the question is which ones, what rules do we cite and what makes them valid for all to follow?

A. One primary source of rules for Western humanity comes from our religious background. Whether we are Muslim, Jew or Christian we are to do whatever God commands us to do, and the source of these divine commands is our Holy Scriptures (Koran, Hebrew Scriptures, or New Testament) commonly accepted as the revealed word of God. Often these scriptural commands come to us with the caveat "as interpreted by proper religious authority" (Church denomination, Rabbinic school or Muslim Sect).

Now, while we all know that scriptures contain clear and commonly accepted rules of behavior (e.g., Ten Commandments, Golden Rule, Sermon on the Mount), most students of scripture do not understand or use the Bible as an all inclusive moral cookbook, a definitive list of exactly what's right and what's wrong for every situation.

This is so because scriptures also contain old cultural or tribal laws which are more related to ancient situations than fundamental rules of behavior and, therefore, they just don't make much sense in this 20th Century time and culture. For example:

- In the list of rules in Deuteronomy (21:18) we read that children who are stubborn and disobey their parents are to be taken to the city gates—there to be stoned. This may have had some meaning in Bronze Age tribal culture, but surely is to be rejected today as a rule to follow.

- In much of the Old Testament we can make a clear assumption that polygamy was an acceptable practice in Old Testament times (classic example—Solomon had 700 wives, 300 concubines). Yet today, we accept a rule of monogamy.

- In Paul's letter to Timothy he makes a clear point that slaves must obey their masters with honor (I Timothy 6). Yet, today we know that slavery is against all of what we understand to be right and good in this world.

So when we use Holy Scriptures as a source of authority, we must somehow or other interpret which rules or commands of God are applicable, which scriptural rules transcend time and culture, and which rules reflect only the situation of the early times when they were written. Even the Ten Commandments are open to interpretation. For when Moses said, "Thou shalt not steal," he did not foresee the possibility of manipulating common stocks on the open market. And when he said "Thou shalt not kill," he did not envision the possibility of amniocentesis—testing babies in their mother's womb—which could tell us that a baby might be horribly deformed before birth. When he said "Honor thy Father and Mother" he did not envision surrogate motherhood.

B. Along with Divine Commandments found in scriptures, a second source of rules is called natural law. It is a source of rules for those people who are not specifically religious (remember that good ethical behavior does not necessarily depend on us being religious). Natural law is also the place where most philosophers (Plato, Aristotle, Kant) ground their source of rules authority.

The 18th Century philosopher Immanuel Kant articulated this criterion quite well. He said that humans have a unique capacity to act according to innate metaphysical laws of nature. Doing your duty and promoting goodwill would naturally align you with these laws that exist as nature's categorical imperatives. Just as there are standards in scriptures, so there are natural categorical standards for being human.

Now while we all agree on the need for standards of rules, whether divine or natural, it is not always clear which ones. Rules by their very nature raise some conflicts for us who try to live by them, questions of discernment, interpretation and application. For example, we accept the basic fact that rules cannot be broken, and that thou shalt not kill is valid both as Scriptural command and as nature's law. Yet, it is likely that more than half of us accept the civil law of capital punishment, or the killing of another person in self-defense, or the bombing of terrorists who seem to follow different rules than we do.

Another problem that arises in rules ethics is what I call the floating rule. There is a wonderful story about a man who went to work in a ruler factory making yardsticks. The supervisor gave him the basic yard by which he was to measure and make his product. A few days later the whole factory had to shut down when quality control discovered some of the yardsticks were growing. They quickly found out that the new man was using the last yardstick he made to measure the next one up, while the basic yard was gathering dust on the table. The application of rules can be a tricky business.

Probably the greatest difficulty occurs in **rule ethics** when two rules conflict and we are not sure which to go by. The most poignant example of this is in Hugo's monumental story *Les Miserables,* when Jean Valjean steals a loaf of bread in order to keep his sister's child from dying. The court of the times followed its legal counsel and declared that the rule against stealing took precedence over a man's commitment to feed his family, and so Valjean was thrown into jail for 19 years.

We continue to face this difficult ethical problem of competing rules in many of our current day medical ethics issues. Surely quadriplegic Elizabeth Bouvia and her doctors struggled with the right thing to do. Doctors followed a rule in hospitals to keep people alive and wished to force-feed this woman, so stricken with cerebral palsy and arthritis that she was totally unable to care for herself. She wished to pull the feeding tube and allow herself a natural death. So, rules about hospitals forcing a person to do something against their will, and the right for individuals to refuse treatment all must be sorted out in court. In complicated medical issues as this one it is very difficult to sort our priorities amongst conflicting rules. And we are suddenly aware that rules are more like rudders than anchors.

Given all the problems of agreement on which rules are valid and difficulties of application and interpretation, modern ethicists have been led to a second category of ethics called situation ethics or consequential ethics.

Situation Ethics

This second source of authority is sometimes called consequential ethics because it refers to ethical decisions which are made based more on the consequences of our actions than on external rules. Something is right or wrong depending on how it affects ourselves or others.

At its simplest level an act is ethically right if it promotes my best long term interests. Called ego ethics, it is best articulated by that archetype of American rugged individualists, Benjamin Franklin, who said, "We can all get ahead on our own initiative." "Anyone can be president if they really try hard enough." His ethic was based on popular aphorisms which focus on the self:

- A penny saved is . . .
- A stitch in time . . .
- God helps those who . . .
- Plow deep while sluggards sleep.

There are, of course, immediate problems that arise from a consequential ethic based on the self. How do we verify that an action is indeed in our best long term interest and, second, how can we identify a standard so that everyone's ego might be satisfied at one time without conflict? The latest variation of the ego ethic of self-fulfillment is that 1960's lifestyle known as "Me-ism" which says, "Do anything you want as long as you don't hurt anyone else, or do whatever makes you feel good." Another variation is "Just do the loving thing," which makes the rather bold assumption that your loving thing is the same as my loving thing.

The second and more useful version of consequential ethics is based on the promotion of everyone's best interests. Called utilitarianism, it says "Always act so as to produce the greatest possible ratio of good to evil for as many people as possible" (i.e., the most good for the most people).

Developed in America by Thomas Jefferson and in England by John Stuart Mill, utilitarians say that what is intrinsically good or right will promote the greatest happiness for all. Often utilitarians use a quite mathematical approach in deciding the rightness or wrongness of an action (calculus). Total good (happiness) minus total bad (unhappiness) equals the net utility. Take robbery for instance: the good for the robber is $+1$, the bad for the robbee and family and society is -10. The net effect is -9.

Therefore, the net negative consequence leads society to establish laws against robbery. The issue is not so much that the act of robbery itself is wrong as it is the results of robbery producing negative consequences. While this is a bit oversimplified, situation ethics is based primarily on empirical data at hand and deals more with the end result than the means of getting there.

Utilitarianism (consequential ethics) is the basis of most of our social, political and economic systems of laws. It works because it:

- resolves conflicts of interest (most good for most people)
- excludes individual selfish motives (ego)
- establishes uniform standards for all (which are changeable as the situation changes)

But there are some problems too:

- The question of who gets to do the arithmetic or determine net utility makes a difference. In the 18th and 19th centuries American landowners decided on the best utility for all and unabashedly supported the economic system of slavery.
- How we define good and bad also becomes a touchy issue. What's good for the goose is not always good for the gander. Good in first world nations is not always the same as good that exists or is needed in third world countries (Africa).
- We cannot always be sure of the ultimate consequences of our actions. No matter how hard we try we humans do indeed have limited vision.

An example:
In 1945 the decision to drop the atomic bomb was based primarily on the net effect of lives saved. It would end the war early and produce the lowest net loss of life on both sides. It was, in fact, a classical situation ethics decision.

Now in the (1990's) we are faced with nuclear proliferation, a potential world-wide holocaust and disastrous accidents such as the nuclear meltdown in Russia. I wonder if we would have developed and used a nuclear bomb in 1945 if we knew then what we know now. The ultimate consequences of our actions are not always so clear as we like to think.

Another difficulty with situation ethics is that some actions are wrong no matter what net happiness or utility is calculated. Principles of justice often transcend net consequences.

When basic rules do not seem to be available and when the situation gets so murky that it's hard to calculate the consequences (utility) we are often thrown into a moral dilemma. This dilemma appropriately leads us to a third source of moral behavior called individual or character ethics.

Character (Personal) Ethics

We begin with a story. A contractor wanted to give a government official a sports car in thanks for a closed contract. The official objected saying, "Sir, a gift is against the rules; common decency and my basic sense of honor would never permit me to accept a free gift like that." The contractor then said, "I quite understand. Suppose we do this. I'll sell you the sports car for $10." The official thought for a moment then responded, "In that case I'll take two."

Something is obviously wrong here. These men have somehow or other met the basic rules involved; indeed, the situation is ambiguous at best. Yet, we know that this is a questionable moral decision on both sides. It has to do, of course, with character.

An individual's character is a third source of authority along with rules and situations to help us make tough moral decisions. Called in scripture the law that is written in our hearts, called conscience in psychology, character ethics says that who we are often determines what we will do. Like Pinocchio we all seem to have a Jimminy Cricket whispering in our ears and banging his umbrella of guilt upon our heads. So how do we define character?

In philosophical terms character is best understood by the word "virtue," for a person's character is defined by the possession of certain virtues, like honesty and patience. Ancient Greek philosophers like Plato and Aristotle considered personal virtues to have a greater priority than rules. In fact, the word "ethic" comes from the Greek word "ethos" which means character. Rules exist, said Plato, only to fill in for a person's lack of character or certain virtues. Indeed, he said, a completely virtuous person has no need for rules whatsoever. [Remember Justice Potter Stewart's distinction between what we have a right to do and doing the right thing?]

1. The particular virtue most often used as a basis for personal ethic is love. When we call upon love as a resource we must be clear about what we mean by love. Love is not a feeling, and it is not a sentimental cover for doing whatever makes you or me or another person feel better, and it's not being nice. Love is an active word, more a verb than noun, and has more to do with will than feeling. Basically, love is a force which turns negatives into positives. For example:

- Love turns passive avoidance of evil into the active doing of good.
- Love turns "live and let live" into love by helping others to live.
- Love translates the rule of don't kill into the command to help everyone, even your enemies.
- Love turns not getting involved into getting involved.

2. What really counts in using our individual character as a source of moral authority is not being wise enough or smart enough to figure out complicated ethical problems. Knowledge is not necessarily a primary virtue in this resource. What counts is being personally strong enough, and having the character to want to act ethically with all our heart and mind and soul, regardless of the consequences. Character, said one writer, is what you do in the dark!

An experience which helped me understand this [occurred] near the end of my flying career. I remember that we installed a new navigation system in our Navy airplanes. It was called Inertial Navigation and was based on a spinning gyroscope, kind of like a sophisticated top, which would spin constantly and always keep its balance. No matter how we turned the airplane, regardless of stormy weather or dark nights, that gyroscope always pointed north and kept track of where we were. I never again feared getting lost on those long over water flights in the Arctic Ocean.

Just as it was hard to get lost with that wonderful inertial navigation system, it is hard to go wrong with a well-working inner system of balanced virtues. A well developed character acts as a kind of moral gyroscope for us, which keeps us steady and always homing in on the North Star we call Truth.

3. How do we get started thinking and acting morally in character ethics? . . . The best way to begin to use and develop our virtues is to begin. It's called the "grace of doing one thing" (Stanley Hauerwas).

- You do not have to do everything—that's the sin of pride.
- You should not do nothing—for that is the sin of sloth.
- But do take the time to do one thing, that will develop your character and help you act morally and become a moral person. . . .

One ethicist (Stanley Hauerwas) says it this way: "I do not have to think about doing everything or nothing; I do not have to begin by solving the problems of the world. Instead I can take the time to do one thing that might lead myself and another closer to peace and joy. In accepting the 'grace of doing one thing' we begin to alter the pattern of our lives, and ultimately the fabric of our society." . . .

It is clear that there are no simple answers. We must draw from our natural law and scriptures some foundation stones—rules—which give direction to life and are relevant for all time. It's the bedrock upon which we will build the rest of our moral life. Then from real life situations we must design a reasoned approach that takes into account the ambiguities of life and which allows doubt, healthy dialogue and struggle to take place. This situation ethic is the architecture, the framing and superstructure of our moral life. And from deep within, we must look to our inner gyroscope and develop those virtues of character which will guide us along the way through the moral maze. This is the finishing touch—the windows, the color and decor of our moral house. Character is what makes the difference between a plain ordinary house and a moral home that [like a work of art] we are proud to show to all.[1]

Selected Ethical Issues

After we read a piece like this, our resolve is strengthened so that, when faced with a tough decision, we think we'll know the right thing to do and do it. However, it's quite different to be faced with a situation where ethical action is demanded and to decide to act ethically. We can easily forget about ethics in the face of seemingly easy reward or payoff.

As an industry, broadcasting has been an ethical battleground since its founding. Significant issues such as copyright infringement, business versus service, excesses in children's commercials, journalists' objectivity versus subjectivity, privacy, truth in advertising, and tabloid or "trash" TV continue to generate heated debate. And although they may not be as visible, ethical issues in related nonbroadcast contexts are equally challenging.

Manipulation Versus Coercion

Throughout this text you've encountered numerous techniques for manipulating others. Any time you use these techniques you will want to give some thought to the power you're exercising so you'll be fully aware of not only how but why you're doing what you're doing. We manipulate (persuade) others to get our way. This is a necessary part of human interaction because we are interdependent and not totally self-sufficient.

Persuasion becomes coercion when we don't allow people a choice. In the course of producing a training tape, one client wrote a script that carried the tone of a general giving orders. This man was used to giving directives, but in video viewers will reject and ridicule such an approach. It wasn't easy to change the client's mind. But finally he agreed to change the context from that of what employees had to do to that of what he recommended they do in order to get the job done well. Afterward he was still uneasy about the fact that he could not force the employees to do what he wanted them to do.

An audience recognizes when they are being coerced into something when they are not given choices or the opportunity to think for themselves. We have the responsibility also to allow people choice when we assert our views. And then there is more openness to our views because people realize we are not trying to coerce them. The context instead becomes that of a mutual search for the truth or for the best outcome.

Truth

In the movie *Broadcast News* we saw a relationship disintegrate because the anchorman staged a reaction shot of himself in tears to heighten the impact of his news story. Some in the group I saw the movie with thought it was all right to do this because his story was more powerful when staged and contributed to increasing public awareness. But the point brought out by the director in the movie was that news should be factually true. To incorporate a faked shot for dramatic effect is unethical; the end does not justify the means. Where do you think the anchorman's loyalty lies? Was anyone harmed by his action?

And what about situations where people are noticeably hurt by the telling of some truth? On many occasions people have committed suicide because they learned a reporter was going to air their story. There's even a monthly newsletter on journalism ethics called *FineLine,* which presents these and other kinds of situations. Another, more modestly priced periodical is *Media & Values,* which focuses primarily on television. An excellent group that emphasizes ethics in all media is the Association for Responsible Communication, which has periodic workshops all over the country, an annual national conference, and a newsletter that alone is worth the cost of membership. Addresses for these are provided at the end of this chapter.

As producers we need to be sensitive to the fact that things are not always as they appear and what we might assume to be a simple matter of professional choice for us could possibly also ruin someone else's life. This is why we do content checks whenever we doubt our information's accuracy; why we check our sources to be sure we've been told the truth and given all the facts available; why we get release forms signed by anyone we direct in front of a camera; and why we generally show a newly completed program to the people who are in it before releasing it to the public. We want to be sure that our presentation of the truth does not seriously conflict with others' perceptions. And if it does, we need to fully understand why so our decisions can be conscious and ethical.

One person's truth can be another's crime. And we must often ask: Truth at what cost? We must be determined to be aware of everyone who may be influenced by our communication and to deal openly with them so we can make responsible decisions. We should address this simple question throughout our productions: Is there anything about this program or subject matter that will harm anyone?

Decision Making

Everyone in the media is faced with choices that affect the lives of others. For instance, who decides what should be in a program? In broadcasting we call this person a "gatekeeper." He or she can be a news director, program manager, station manager, sales manager, client, or advertiser. This person makes decisions about what will air and what will not, in spite of the fact that someone else wrote the material.

In nonbroadcast environments the issue is often more politically based. Who has the authority to approve scripts (content)? Who has the final say over the edit? Who is in the best position to know what a program should say? Who knows the most about the topic? It could be a different individual for each of these questions.

In a corporate structure the pecking order is usually clear; there is usually no contest. But I have been involved in corporate situations where the person in charge was the least qualified to make content decisions and yet insisted on doing so anyway. Some programs fail as a result of this kind of ego attachment.

What do you do when your (unqualified) superior holds the right to creative and content approval? Is it worth a fight? This is where character (or personal) ethics becomes involved. A strategy one friend uses successfully is to get the boss away from the office, take a walk in a natural setting (i.e., meet as people instead of as coworkers), and talk it over. Open and frank communication can often resolve conflicts. But you need to decide for yourself on the right thing to do, whatever the potential outcome.

Another choice is whether to use copyrighted material (audio or video or both) without getting permission. "But it's just a four-second shot; nobody will recognize it; it's not worth bothering about." Or is it?

- *Choice:* To use the best talent available or put a friend in a role because you like her?
- *Choice:* To spend petty cash allocated for props on a small party for the cast and crew? You'll have receipts. The money was spent in the context of the production.
- *Choice:* To cover up a minor accident with a camera you've rented. You dropped it hard in the course of shooting. It doesn't appear damaged except for a ding in the base that nobody will notice. It still makes pictures. Should you report the accident to the rental house?
- *Choice:* To include content that you know is not accurate or valid when reshooting would cost time and money?

- *Choice:* To lie to gain permission to enter and shoot an event?
- *Choice:* To provide a story because the audience has a right to know even when it infringes on someone's privacy?

Ethical decisions, large or small, ought to be made for the right motive. A natural consequence of ethical decisions is a lack of harm. By definition, the ethical decision harms no one. If it does, then it's not ethical.

Limited Versus Expanded Vision

In Chapter 3, "Consciousness," we looked at the desirability of expanding one's perspective as a way to encompass a wider view of a program's content. Not having a wider vision can have ethical implications.

For instance, managers of institutional and corporate video departments usually have freedom to spend their budgets as they see fit as long as the expenses in various categories (supplies, equipment, maintenance) can be justified. Because the department is our responsibility, we have the impression that it is the most important department. We plead for larger budgets and spend all we get because we tend to look at the good of the department without considering the good of the parent institution. I've seen two video departments in major institutions completely disbanded because the managers consistently made decisions that were good for the departments but unfavorable to their organizations.

On the personal level, independent producers can severely mark up production expenses to make more money. But if they do, they'll probably lose repeat business. An alternative would be to cultivate a relationship with the client first. Then, before the job, negotiate together what the expenses will be. When you write out and mutually agree upon a rate in advance, you safeguard friendships and reduce embarrassment over miscommunication or misjudgments.

In terms of content, if we simply provide our viewers with the information we have at hand without doing research, we may shortchange them by not fully expanding their awareness of the subject. One supervisor I've worked with allocated funds to produce a program he personally wanted done. He then chose to limit the public's fuller, more balanced, understanding of the topic. We focused on X, Y, and Z without even mentioning A, B, C, and D, which were equally important.

Professionalism

We sometimes have a tendency to mask ethical decisions behind "professionalism." Professional contexts sometimes create their own ethical standards that have more weight than personal contexts, implying that the business cause is higher and grander than any personal agenda we might have. In American society, we often feel like we have little power outside our organizational affiliations. Many people have to place their loyalty in an institutional framework. This gives them a clear identity.

But what does it mean to be a professional in video? Some people think it means earning more than 50% of their incomes from video. Others who freelance often feel that a professional is one who is capable of producing a high-quality product.

Michael Bayles,[2] writing specifically about professional ethics, cites more rigorous requirements: To be professional, one

- Must have extensive training in the field.
- Must have training that includes a significant intellectual component.
- Must have trained ability that provides an important service to society.
- May be expected to have credentials, be involved in an organization of like-minded members, and have some autonomy with regard to making decisions.

In both broadcast and nonbroadcast industries, although I've found little talk about the definition of a *professional,* there is a lot of discussion about who does or does not do *professional work.* This implies that program quality is more highly regarded than credentials. While I applaud the attention given to production quality, we also need to include in the term *professional* a requirement to assume responsibility not only for the corporate or other affiliation but, more important, for *oneself,* so that decisions and behavior are qualified by higher principles (above those of any institution or ego need). Here are a few examples of some common situations that evidence a lack of "genuine" professionalism:

- Showing up later than promised, or sometimes not at all, without calling to inform anyone.
- Seizing an opportunity to make connections (holding up production time) by talking with the client or celebrities when not part of the job.
- Pilfering small items: gaffer tape, pen-type flashlights, batteries, lavaliere microphones.
- Abusing equipment: creating nicks and scrapes, not removing adhesives, coiling cables improperly (which causes shorts), transporting cameras without cases to absorb shock.
- Finding excuses for not carrying heavy equipment cases.
- Showing off one's knowledge to the client by criticizing what's being done (the "I know better syndrome").
- Ordering the most expensive item on the menu because the company is picking up the tab.
- Laying back while others work hard.
- Padding expenses.
- Shooting people without their permission or not asking permission to enter someone's property to set up for a shot.

A professional is one who is "aware" on many levels and takes personal responsibility for every detail of her performance. This means

- Making decisions that maximize the quality of the program.
- Ensuring that every component of the content is true or at least accurate to the best of your knowledge.
- Being sensitive to others and their property—treating both as you would have them treat you or your property.
- Being considerate of the needs of others.
- Being meticulous about details that relate to money matters: getting receipts for

everything; getting value for dollars spent; saving the client/company as much as is reasonable; conserving materials (videotape, gaffer tape, lamps).

- Communicating openly and honestly.
- Providing honest effort for honest return.
- Respecting the environments in which you work by not littering or polluting and by leaving an area (interior or exterior) as good as if not better than you found it.

These kinds of qualities reveal strength of character, which, in turn, gives confidence that, when faced with a major ethical decision, you are likely to do the right thing. Ethical behavior comes not from a singular challenge but from a life lived by a pattern of high principles.

Communication Strategies

As we've seen, you can approach communicating a message in many ways. Some may be more ethical than others, and you must decide. If your purpose is to produce a tape on woman-battering so men with this problem will seek help from a social agency (your client), which strategy would you use?

1. Show hidden camera footage of actual batterings.

2. Show actors playing the parts of victim and assailant.

3. Interview real victims and batterers (men and women) showing their faces.

4. Interview real victims but protect their identities.

Which of these strategies would you prefer as the predominant one, given that all would communicate the message to the target audience? Before reading on write down which option you prefer and why.

Under the First Amendment you have a right to use any one or a combination of these strategies. The right to privacy may be infringed if you don't obtain permission. But which, for you, is the right thing to do? Notice that your choice again relates to your loyalty. Identify that loyalty now. What does it reveal about where your consciousness is qualified?

Consider that strategy 1, in addition to communicating that woman-battering is wrong, might also produce fear in the viewer. Will that fear assist her in seeking help or will it stop her? Certainly the emotions created in the viewer, by identification and empathy, will be stronger, but might that not be the problem in the first place, high-pitched, out-of-control emotion? Often television and movie producers show the negative side of an issue to promote change. Many war movies are justified on this basis. But often the opposite occurs for the audience—the "wrong" is glorified and made glamorous. Was the purpose accomplished or has something else occurred?

In strategy 3 there seems to be a privacy problem. But is this really a problem? It is because you are actually asking these people to play the role of victim again, to be victims of possible public ridicule. Although viewers might respond to seeing the actual victims of this violence, couldn't the message be even more powerfully communicated by silhouette lighting that carries a completely different contextual message to the viewer—that this subject is so difficult that we (being responsible producers) chose to protect these people from any further victimization?

What is the right choice keeping in mind the need to accomplish your purpose? And what if the purpose itself requires infringement of someone else's rights? What if your client's purpose was specifically to embarrass or frighten these victims into seeking help? Or what if a friend of yours will give you a lot of money to shoot people in this situation with a hidden camera, without their knowledge, so he could add music and create an "art" video? Isn't that a kind of pornography? What's the right thing to do then?

Integrity

Knowing what's right is different from doing what's right, which takes integrity. Although this is logical, it is also difficult to put into practice. I think of "yes-men," who, when asked if they agree, always do because the boss or client is always right. But we know that genuine, authentic participation requires that we say what we really think. If your viewpoint doesn't coincide with the client's and you lose the job, so be it.

When we display integrity, it calls for respect and invites others to model it. When a director has script integrity, she is as faithful as possible to the writer's intention and not just to the words on the page. When a production team has integrity, it is bold, vigorous, and synergistic. When a special effect has integrity, it fits perfectly within the context provided; there is a flow and a rightness about it. Lack of integrity is a weakness and it blocks potential and vigor.

So how does one bring integrity into a production? First, by providing a living example of it, and, second, by speaking about it openly when there's an ethical question or breakdown, which is the perfect time to announce your organization's commitment to integrity.

This is normally the leader's role and responsibility, but the commitment can come from anyone. Integrity should be talked about openly or the people around you won't know that it's part of what's expected and encouraged. I like what James Ritscher, a management consultant, has to say about it: "Ultimately, integrity comes down to a fundamental question: 'Which is more important to me: my relationship with myself or my business success?'"[3] This is the keynote of an increasing number of progressive businesses, large and small: "Doing good is good business."

At different times we have a duty to our families, clients, employers, organizations, colleagues, friends, society, country, planet, and a god we may choose. But none of these can or will be served well if we don't continuously acknowledge our primary duty to ourselves—to be true to who we are and what we know to be right and act on it.

What we communicate internally—whether in dreams, fantasies, fears or aspirations—are to some degree written large upon the billboards, headlines, screens, and ads of our civilization. In this sense, "Inside Media" becomes "Inside Me."[1]

—Thomas W. Cooper

Initiative

As we have seen, integrity creates a challenge for us to be true to ourselves and to invest truth and principles in our communication. *Initiative* requires that we *take appropriate action.* It also implies that the action we take is socially responsible. Watch any newscast if you think your gifts and talent are not desperately needed at this point in human history. The work we do can make a difference.

My students usually get excited when I tell a story about a former student and a friend, John Thai. I tell it every semester as an example of initiative because I see too many students taking classes simply to meet their requirements, get a diploma, or meet someone else's expectations.

Dinh Xuan Thai, or John, was a fortunate Vietnamese refugee, one of the boat people who found his way to the United States through the generosity of a sponsor in Cincinnati. He came to this country alone and didn't speak the language. I met John on the first day of "Video Production and Technology," our introductory class. After class he asked, in very broken English, if it was true that being in the class meant he could use the equipment. His eyes lit up when I explained that the complete studio and remote equipment was available for scheduling as long as he was enrolled in a television course.

He explained to me as best he could that he had been using some of the video equipment at a local cable access facility, had taken their instruction, and he was "very much wanting to learn to make television." In our classes we emphasize that television/video production is a subject you learn by *doing* as well as *listening* and *thinking.* So we encourage students to get as much experience as possible, any way they can.

This usually amounts to internships, part-time jobs, assignment work, and volunteering in our studio. Some students do this, others don't. John decided to make a career of it.

John almost literally "camped out" in our studio. Whenever others on the staff and I would come in—weekends, evenings, Christmas vacation, 3:00 a.m.—John was there shooting, editing, or checking out equipment. He constantly asked questions about how to route audio from here to there, what kind of connector he needed, what we thought of his footage, how to use the **newsmat** and insert CG in the same shot. He spent hours playing with the switcher or the cameras set up on magazine pictures or his coat. Before the semester ended John was doing work equivalent to our advanced students on his own in addition to the assignments.

I got to know John quickly because our studio manager kept sending him to my office for special permissions. He created program ideas faster than he could pull crews together to help shoot them. When and where did this guy sleep or eat? John became what we call a "studio rat." Video access to him was like saying to any other college student there's free pizza over in student union twenty-four hours a day.

John took and excelled in all of our courses including an internship. Before he graduated he had produced a drama, several full-length documentaries, PSAs, experimental programs, promotional tapes, and who knows what else. Most of these aired on cable access, and some aired on local commercial stations. (He wasn't at all shy about talking to people he didn't know.) His resume was equally weighted with academic and professional work experience. One day I asked, "John where do you get your drive?" He responded that his dream was to help his people and to bring the Vietnamese and American peoples together in closer understanding and friendship, which in America is easy because there's so much you can do, so much good equipment and everybody wants to help.

Four years ago he paid us a visit to introduce his new (and beautiful) bride, who is a partner in his business. He has started and developed a successful television production company in Los Angeles. At last count he had thirty-four employees who are kept very busy doing work all over the world. I visited the Thais a year later, even borrowed some equipment. Their studio was large and very active. He didn't have much time to talk because they were in the process of bidding on a multimillion-dollar project. When John was in my class he was twenty-two years old. Seven years later John is realizing his dream.

Who you are, what you do, and how you do it communicate.

Notes

1. Hall, G. Bradford, Jr., "Thinking Ethically in a Morally Chaotic World." *Broadcast Financial Journal,* September– October 1988, 6. Reprinted by permission of the author.
2. Bayles, Michael D., *Professional Ethics,* 2d ed. (Belmont, CA: Wadsworth, 1989), 8.
3. Ritscher, James A., "Spiritual Leadership," in *Transforming Leadership: From Vision to Results,* ed. John D. Adams (Alexandria, VA: Miles River Press, 1986), 76.

Suggested Readings

Adams, John D., ed. *Transforming Leadership: From Vision to Results.* Alexandria, VA: Miles River Press, 1986.

Christians, Clifford. *Media Ethics: Cases and Moral Reasoning,* 2nd ed. New York: Longman, 1987.

Fink, Conrad. *Media Ethics.* New York: McGraw-Hill, 1988.

Harman, Willis, and Howard Rheingold. *Higher Creativity: Liberating the Unconscious for Breakthrough Insights.* New York: Jeremy Tarcher, 1984.

Jaksa, James A., and Michael S. Pritchard. *Communication Ethics: Methods of Analysis.* Belmont, CA: Wadsworth, 1988.

Rivers, William, and Wilbur Schramm. *Responsibility in Mass Communication.* New York: Harper & Row, 1969.

Addresses

Association for Responsible Communication
25000 Glen Ivy Road
Corona, California 91719

FineLine (newsletter for journalists)
600 East Main Street
Louisville, Kentucky 40202-9723

Integrity (newsletter)
Box 9
100 Mile House
British Columbia, Canada VOK 2EO

Media & Values (magazine)
1962 South Shenandoah
Los Angeles, California 90034

Summation

· ·

Whether and how well a system is managed communicates.

How you produce a program communicates.

Your consciousness communicates.

The medium you choose communicates.

How communication tools are used communicates.

How you design a project communicates

The audience we select communicates.

The content we choose and how we use it communicate.

How and whether a program is organized communicates.

How we persuade an audience communicates.

The stories we tell, and how we tell them, communicate.

The sound of a program communicates.

The images we put on the screen communicate.

How a program is edited communicates.

Who you are, what you do, and how you do it communicate.

To be true to a practice I have recommended in this book, ending as you begin, I want to conclude with a quote from another television pioneer and visionary (do you remember General Sarnoff's statement about television technology far outdistancing our capacity to use it?). In a 1957 speech (RTNDA) Edward R. Murrow concluded:

This instrument can teach, it can illuminate; yes, it can even inspire. But it can do so only to the extent that humans are determined to use it to those ends. Otherwise it is merely wires and lights in a box. There is a great and perhaps decisive battle to be fought against ignorance, intolerance and indifference. This weapon of television could be useful.

Appendixes

APPENDIX **A** TREATMENT

Hurricane!
(Cineworks, Inc.)

Video

I. Introduction

The film opens with an excerpt from a TV interview with Neil Frank. He gestures with his hands.

Cut to man sitting in his car with his family, on a bridge clogged with traffic.

Cut back to Neil Frank with a colleague at a satellite terminal. Cut away to a satellite image of a well-defined hurricane, then to Neil Frank talking to us on camera.

Cut to trees thrashing about violently, a house falling apart in the wind, surf crashing, etc. *Fade in title:*

B&W stills from Galveston aftermath.

Footage from Hurricane *Camile,* cars piled up bumper to bumper on a highway, and scenes of massive destruction in the aftermath.

Stills and motion pictures from East Pakistan: the devastated landscape, bodies piled into enormous heaps.

Audio

NEIL FRANK
We just can't tell where the hurricane is going to go. We don't know what that "river of wind" is doing out there.

MAN
I'm concerned because we've been sitting here for an hour now. I think there's an accident up there on the bridge.

NEIL FRANK (to colleague)
I don't think it's really changing direction, I think it's going to correct back to the west. What did the MFM indicate . . .

NEIL FRANK
In the fairy tale, the boy cried wolf and there was no wolf. But here there is a wolf. It's just a question of whether he'll appear at your door or your neighbor's.

Hurricane!

NARRATOR
The hurricane unleashes the tremendous power stored in the tropical ocean—generating as much energy in an hour as twenty atomic bombs. It can disrupt, even destroy, entire cities.

September 8th, 1900, the worst natural disaster in U.S. history. Residents of Galveston, Texas, were caught by surprise as a hurricane swept a deadly dome of sea water over the island. 6,000 perished.

On September 17, 1969, 200,000 residents of Mississippi fled the most powerful hurricane ever measured. Hurricane Camile *killed 300 and wrecked an entire coastline, leaving a legacy of dislocation and chaos.*

The following year, one of the biggest natural disasters of all time struck East Pakistan, now Bangladesh. A hurricane, known as a typhoon in Asia, swept over tiny delta islands in the Bay of Bengal. 300,000 or more drowned.

Video	*Audio*

Video

Coastal scenes: A citizen opens a newspaper and finds a hurricane awareness flier; people swimming along Galveston's 15-foot seawall, evacuation markers along a boulevard.

Slow pans of houses, condos, and trailers on the beachfronts.

People, old and young, by the water, walking along a beach promenade.

Pan of busy Hurricane Center, the central area crammed with satellite consoles, maps, computer terminals. People working.

Cut to Neil Frank at work, conferring with colleagues, putting out a bulletin, etc.

Cut to a satellite image of Hurricane *Gloria* in its early stages, advancing across the Atlantic and reaching maturity.

Cut to Neil Frank on Camera.

Audio

In the U.S., states and local communities have made elaborate plans to evacuate coastal areas. The roadways are marked with evacuation routes, and a network of shelters stands ready. Awareness of the hurricane threat has never been higher.

And yet, our coastlines may be more vulnerable than ever to a major disaster.

Over 42 million people live in coastal counties from Maine to Mexico—the fastest-growing areas of the country. Communities are expanding onto barrier islands and peninsulas. Vacation and retirement centers are springing up all along the beaches.

At the center of the readiness equation is the National Hurricane Center in Miami. Meteorologists here analyze information about approaching hurricanes and issue warnings to the public. They feed an array of information into computer models that predict the movement of storms toward land. And they are linked to satellites that track them in the most remote regions of the ocean.

But the factors that influence hurricane movements are among the deepest mysteries in meteorology. These forecasters know how unpredictable the hurricane can be, so they depend on a public relations blitz aimed at getting people out of the way.

Neil Frank joined the Hurricane Center in 1961, and became its director in 1974. Few scientists have attracted as much public attention, and few have generated as much controversy.

September 22nd, 1985: A swirling mass of rain clouds drifted across the Atlantic. The winds picked up and formed a tightening spiral. Hurricane Gloria *became one of eleven Atlantic storms that year strong enough to receive a name.*

NEIL FRANK

A storm can go up the east coast and start to accelerate in its forward speed. In 1938 we had a devastating hurricane that was moving at 60 miles per hour when it crossed New England. And if you have a hurricane developing out near the Bahamas and it's moving that fast, you may not have much time to tell some folks to get out of the way. And we have places where it's just going to take too long to get everybody to safety.

Video	*Audio*
More satellite imagery.	NARRATOR
	Several days later, Gloria *angled north of Cuba. Air Force planes flying into its core recorded winds at 120 miles per hour, and air pressures lower than any measured in the Atlantic. Hurricane* Gloria *was soon known as the "storm of the century."*
Reporter on camera, then cut to surf pounding over the seawall and boardwalk.	TV REPORTER
	We're here live on the boardwalk in Atlantic City. Officials are getting ready to close down the casinos for the first time since they were built here. . . .

APPENDIX **B** PRODUCTION BUDGET

The Evolving Earth **BUDGET SUMMARY**

(1) Salaries & Wages		$ 28,125.
(2) Fringe Benefits		(−)
(3) Consultant Fees		10,700.
(4) Travel		44,840.
(5) Supplies & Materials		29,544.
(6) Services (Technical & Professional)		130,075.
(7) Other		55,095.
	PRODUCTION:	$298,379.
(A) Educational Materials		20,000.
(B) Publicity Campaign		70,000.
(C) Contingency (4% × $298,379.)		11,935.
	TOTAL PROJECT:	$400,314.

FUNDING STRATEGY

Production	$298,379.
**Educational Materials	20,000.
1) Study/Teachers Guides	
2) School releases	
***Publicity Campaign	70,000.
Regional and National	
Contingency	11,935.
	$400,314.

DIRECT COSTS   SUBTOTAL   TOTAL

1. Salaries and Wages:
   PROJECT DIRECTOR-EXECUTIVE PRODUCER-
   FILM DIRECTOR David L. Smith (6.75 full-time months)
   (9 months × $3125.) $28,125. $28,125.   (1)

2. Fringe Benefits: (none)   (2)

3. Consultant Fees:
   Beatrice Bruteau   30 days × $200./day   6,000.
   H. James Birx   7 days × $150./day   1,050.
   James Somerville   15 days × $150./day   2,250.
   Bernard Towers   7 days × $200./day   1,400.   10,700.   (3)

4. Travel Costs: (*Foreign Travel)
   Local Mileage: David Smith $ 100.
                  Marty Ducheny   80.
                  Patrick Griffin   100.
                  Cynthia Allen   80.
                                                           ($ 360.)

   Air Fares:
      New York   2 pass.   3 days $ 306.
      Cincinnati   2 pass.   3 wks.   1,400.
      Buffalo, NY   3 pass.   1 day   492.
      Cincinnati   1 pass.   1 day   694.
      Wash., DC   1 pass.   5 days   700.
      DC-Phila.   3 pass.   2 days   1,100.
      New York   3 pass.   14 days   700.
      Arizona   5 pass.   5 days   1,800.
      Los Angeles   4 pass.   12 days   1,800.
     *France   4 pass.   12 days   4,700.
      Cincinnati   3 pass.   1 day   405.
      Boston   2 pass.   3 days   592.
      New York   2 pass.   3 days   306.
      Tucson   3 pass.   2 days   1,584.
      New York   3 pass.   3 days   683.
                                                           ($17,262.)

   Ground Transportation:
   (car rentals, taxi, etc.)
      New York   (taxi 3 days) $ 80.
      Wash., DC   (taxi 5 days)   50.
      DC-Phila.   (car rental in Phila. 1 day)   60.
      New York   (car: $420./wk. × 2 wks.)   840.
      Arizona   (car: $294./wk. × 1 wk.)
                    (van: $310./wk. × 1 wk.) (Hertz)   604.
      Los Angeles   (car: $60./day × 12)   720.
                    (van: $425./wk. × 2 wks.)   850.
     *France   (7 pass. wagon 8 days—nonconsecutive)   382.
                    (car: 4 days × $45./day)   180.

DIRECT COSTS			SUBTOTAL	TOTAL
Boston	(taxi, bus for 3 days)		40.	
New York	(taxi, bus for 3 days)		60.	
Tucson	(6 pass. wagon for 1 day)		52.	
New York	(taxi, 3 days)		180.	
			($ 4,098.)	
Per Diem (lodging, meals, personal)				
New York	2 persons 2 days × $100.		$ 400.	
Cincinnati	2 persons:			
	1 4 days × $70.		280.	
	1 15 days × $73.		1,095.	
Buffalo	3 persons 1 day × $20.		60.	
Cincinnati	1 person (Narrator)			
	1 night		100.	
	4 persons 8 days × $15.		480.	
Wash., DC	1 person 5 days × $80.		400.	
DC-Phila.	3 persons 2 days × $80.		480.	
New York	4 persons 14 days × $100.		5,600.	
	1 person (Narrator) 1 night		150.	
Arizona	4 persons 5 days × $80.		1,600.	
	1 person (Narrator) 3 days × $100.		300.	
Los Angeles	3 persons 12 days × $80.		2,880.	
	1 person 12 days × $25. (PG)		300.	
	1 person 12 days × $100.		1,200.	
*France	2 persons 12 days × $80.		1,920.	
	1 person 7 days × $100. (Narrator)		700.	
	3 persons 7 days × $70.			
	(French camera crew)		1,470.	
Cincinnati	3 persons 1 day × $70.		210.	
Boston	2 persons 3 days × $90.		540.	
New York	2 persons 3 days × $100.		600.	
Tucson	3 persons 2 days × $80.		480.	
New York	3 persons 3 days × $100.		900.	
			($22,145.)	
Entrance/Other Fees:				
Location permissions (France) 3 × $50.			$ 150.	
Boat pass for 5 persons × $3.			15.	
			($ 165.)	
Location Expenses:				
(Petty cash for unexpected—based on $100./month)			300.	
Location box lunches (8 days × $40.)			240.	
Hospitality ($30. × 9 trips)			270.	
			($ 810.)	44,840. (4)

5. Supplies and Materials:
Office Rental (Cinti.) $554./mo. × 9 mo.
    (incl. 3 offices & workroom) $ 4,986.

DIRECT COSTS	SUBTOTAL	TOTAL
Office Supplies ($100./mo. × 9)	$ 900.	
Office Equipment Rental ($290./mo. × 9 mo.—		
3 desks/files/chairs/tables/shelves)	2,610.	
Typewriter Rental (2 units) (9 mo. × $110./mo.)	990.	
Printing and Duplicating		
(letterheads/envelopes/labels/scripts)	400.	
Xeroxing ($85./mo. × 9)	765.	
Postage & Shipping ($125./mo. × 9)	1,125.	
Express Mail ($9.35 × 9 times)	113.	
Telephone (Installation of 3 phones, 2 lines—$125. service	1,125.	
charge × 9)		
(MCI Long Dist. Service—saves 25% min.-$420./mo.		
× 9 mo.)	3,780.	
Misc. Film Supplies (light meter/tools/changing		
bag/maint.)	500.	
Editing Supplies (leaders/tape/gloves/glue, etc.)	600.	
Audiocassette Tapes (Transcriptions—Maxwell C-60s		
48 × $1.25)	60.	
Production Insurance (Hold Harmless/Basic Produc-		
tion/Litigation Liability—Commercial Union Ins.)	3,000.	
Graphic Materials (Map)	80.	
Scenic Materials (Bk., Monitor Set)	260.	
Costumes (Presenter clothing items)	500.	
Film Stock (Eastman Neg. 7247) (15:1 ratio = 75 rolls,		
400 ft. × $61. each)	4,575.	
Videotape Stock (¾″)		
1 60-min. MBU (Hearing Impaired Master)	25.	
40 20-min. UCA (for review/editing) × $20.	800.	
10 60-min. UCA (total prog.) × $24.	240.	
¼″ Audio Tape (40, 5″ rolls × $6.50 each)	260.	
16 mm Full Coat (Magnetic Tape) (40,000 ft. at .03/ft.)	1,200.	
35 mm Full Coat (Magnetic Tape) (5,000 ft. at .07/ft.)	350.	29,544. (5)

6. Services: Technical

16 mm Original Film Processing		
(Deluxe NY—30,000 ft. × .081)	$ 2,430.	
Work Printing (30,000 ft. × .128)	3,840.	
Answer Printing (2,000 ft. × .289 A&B = $578. + fades		
$20, and dissolves $320.)	918.	
CRI Printing Master (Liquid Gate) (2,000 ft. × 1.0173)	2,035.	
Check Print from CRI (2,000 ft. × .12)	240.	
Release Prints (7 prints × $220.)		
1 for PBS (incl. Hearing Impaired)		
1 for National Endowment/Humanities		
1 for Films for the Humanities		
1 for Project Director		
3 for International film competitions	1,540.	
Opticals		
Titles/Supers/Title preparations/Credit Crawl/3 optical		
zooms	6,500.	

Negative Cutting (Conforming)
    Film House (56 hrs. × $20./hr.) $ 1,120.
Animation
    Creative Union, Tree of Life, and Synergizing Earth
       SEQs   10,000.
    Map and Anamatics of Stills   1,800.
Audio Transfers ¼″ to Full Coat (25 hrs. × $40./hr.)   1,000.
Audio Mix
    (12 hrs. × $160./hr.)   1,920.
Photocopying (Teilhard archival stills—70 × $9.50 each)   665.
Transfers: 16 mm Interlock to ¾″ Videotape
    (15 hrs. × $64./hr.)   960.

Services: Professional
Producer $21,600.
    (30 wks. × $720./wk. full-time)
Associate Producer   12,000.
    (16 wks. × $750./wk)
Unit I Manager (LA)   3,375.
    (15 days × $225./day)
Unit II Manager (NY)   8,000.
    (40 days × $200./day)
Production Assistants   1,250.
    (25 days × $50./day)
Researcher (Archival)   750.
    (5 days × $150./day)
Production Secretary-Bookkeeper   10,400.
    (40 wks. × $260./wk.)
Teilhard Voice (flat fee)   1,000.
Music Producer (flat fee)   2,000.
"Name" Presenter (flat fee based on 15 total days and
    $100./day)   13,500.
Synthesizer Music Producer (flat fee)   2,000.
Lighting Director
    (15 days × $250./day)   3,750.
    France: (5 days × $200./day)   1,000.
Grips (15 days × $180./day)   2,700.
    France: (5 days × $180./day)   900.
Cinematographer (30 days × $400./day)   12,000.
    France: (5 days × $400./day)   2,000.
Audio Technician (30 days × $225./day)   6,750.
    France: (6 days × $225./day)   1,350.
Assistant Camera (17 days × $150./day)   2,550.
    France: (5 days × $150./day)   750.
Graphic Artist (4 wks. × $400./wk.)   1,600.
Still Photographer (20 days × $70./day)   1,400.
Set Designer (flat fee)   400.
Legal Services (30 hrs. × $75./hr.)   2,250.
Accounting Services (flat fee)   2,000.
    (Fiscal Agent)

DIRECT COSTS	SUBTOTAL	TOTAL
Film Editor	$12,000.	
(12 wks. × $1000./wk.)		
Assistant Film Editor	800.	
(2 wks. × $400./wk.)	————	130,075. (6)

7. Other Expenses:

	SUBTOTAL
Screen Actor's Guild (5% Presenter)	$ 600.
Screen Actor's Guild (5% Teilhard's voice)	50.
TV Studio with Monitors	
(5 days × $800./day)	4,000.
Recording Studio (Narration & Teilhard Voice—	
15 hrs. × $100.)	1,500.
Cameraprompter Rental ($75./day × 12 days)	900.
Prompter rolls (8 rolls × $21./roll)	168.
Microphone Rental	
Sennheiser 416 (30 days × $30./day)	900.
ECM 50s (30 days × $18./day)	540.
Wireless System (4 days × $48./day)	192.
Lighting Rentals	
5 units (14 days × $60./day)	840.
HVs (3 days × $500./day)	1,500.
Cables & Accessories	200.
Videocassette Player & Monitor	
(8 mo. × $550./mo.)	4,400.
Camera System (complete)	
Arri 16-SR (25 days × $293./day)	7,325.
Arri S (15 days × $160./day)	2,400.
TV sync (3 × $200./day)	600.
Nagra 4.2 + QGX (25 days × $75./day)	1,875.
Camera Support Equipment	
Tripod & Head (35 days × $40./day)	1,400.
Stindt Dolly (6 days × $55./day)	330.
Dolly Track (130 ft. × $1.00/ft.)	130.
High Hat (30 days × $5.00/day)	150.
Zoom Motor (J-4) (30 days × $35./day)	1,050.
Video Facilities	
Transfer 15 hrs. 16 mm film to ¾″ (15 hrs. × $65./hr.)	975.
Preparation & Mastering for PBS (KOCE) (flat fee)	2,000.
Control Room & Character Generator	
(Hearing Impaired Master)	
(4 hrs. setup × $100./hr.)	400.
(2 hrs. production × $800./hr.)	1,600.
(1 60 min. 1″ roll Tape Stock)	110.
(1 60 min. ¾″ dub)	35.
Music Facilities	
Music Library (flat fee)	675.
Power Generator (3 days × $100./day)	300.
Lens Rental	
12-120 Angenieux (30 days × $50./day)	1,500.
8 mm 2.4 Distagon (10 days × $22./day)	220.

DIRECT COSTS	SUBTOTAL	TOTAL
5.7 Angenieux (5 days × $22./day)	$ 110.	
25 mm f0.95 Angenieux (3 days × $15./day)	45.	
300 mm Nikkor (3 days × $22./day)	66.	
50 mm Zeiss Planar (8 days × $15./day)	120.	
Filters		
Star (26 days × $5./day)	130.	
Fog/Diffusion (26 days × $7.50/day)	195.	
Conversion (26 days × $2.50/day)	65.	
Gaffer Kit Supplies (Tape & Connectors)	134.	
Grip Kit Supplies		
4 × 4 reflections w/stands		
(14 days × $9.50)	133.	
Misc. (dots, scrims)		
(14 days × $8.00)	112.	
Aerial Services		
Arizona desert (2 hrs. × $100./hr.)	200.	
Verdun Battlefield		
(1 hr. × $200./hr.)	200.	
Audio Recording Studio Magno-Sound NY		
Mixing (12 hrs. × $160./hr.)	1,920.	
Editing Facility—Flatbed		
(12 wks. × $200./wk.)	2,400.	
Archival/Stock/Newsreel Film Purchase		
(8 min. × $1000./min.)	8,000.	
Film Royalties	1,200.	
Stock Stills (70 × $10./each)	700.	
Competition Entry Fees (5 at $100./each)	500.	55,095. (7)

(A) **   Production of Press Releases, Study Guides, Teachers
         Guides, etc., to promote the sale and rental of the film
         to nontheatrical markets $20,000.

(B) ***National Publicity Campaign to inform the public, in-
         cluding media (all) factual press kits, PBS press and
         promotional materials (national program guide, station
         outreach, slides, etc.), reviews by syndicated writers,
         regional exposure (color mailout, interviews on radio
         and TV, press conference, screenings, etc.) $70,000   90,000.

(C) Contingency—4% (of Production) × $298,379.   11,935.

NOTE: The ruled lines have been omitted from this budget to save space in the grant proposal of which it was a part.

APPENDIX **C**   RENTAL AGREEMENT

Xavier University Television Center

Terms and Conditions

THE FOLLOWING TERMS ARE AGREED TO BY THE RENTER OF ANY AND ALL
EQUIPMENT RENTED OR LEASED FROM XAVIER UNIVERSITY TELEVISION
CENTER, THE OWNER.

POLICIES

1. Rental charges accrue from the time equipment is removed from the Xavier University Television Center until the time it is returned. No allowances will be made because of time periods in which the equipment was in the renter's possession but not actually used. Renter understands that renter's liability begins as soon as the equipment leaves Xavier University Television Center's actual possession. Delays in shipping will always be chargeable to the renter.
2. All rental prices are computed on a daily basis. (A day being any 24-hour period.) A weekend is charged as one day. The weekly rate is four times the daily rate.
3. Equipment returned late will be charged one full day's rental for each 24-hour period not returned.
4. Renter acknowledges he/she has examined and tested the equipment and that equipment is in good working order at the time of the beginning of the rental. The equipment is accepted "as is" and no warranties or representations are made, of any type or nature whatsoever, expressed or implied, for the performance of cameras, services, equipment supplies, or equipment rented. No claim for liability of any kind shall be made by the renter arising out of the alleged failure of the equipment to be in good working order. Renter specifically acknowledges and understands that owner assumes no responsibility whatsoever and makes no promises or representations whatsoever for the performance of the equipment.
5. In the event of loss or damage to the leased equipment, renter agrees to repair or replace same and to pay the owner a rental for such period of time, until such lost or damaged equipment shall be replaced, together with all costs and expenses of such repair or replacement. Standards to be determined by Xavier University Television Center.
6. Acceptance of return of ordered equipment does not waive claims against renter for latent or hidden damage to equipment.
7. The renter agrees to keep and maintain all rental equipment in good condition and assumes full responsibility for all equipment and supplies until rented items are returned. Rental fee shall be payable until the rental equipment is actually returned and until payment in full is received for lost or damaged rental equipment.
8. In the event of any loss, the value of leased equipment shall be that listed in the manufacturer's current user price list effective at time of loss.
9. Renter agrees to pay for all lamp replacements.
10. Renter shall not lease or loan the equipment described herein to any other persons, firms, or corporations, and the equipment shall at all times remain under the immediate and actual control and direction of the renter. Renter agrees not to remove cover, deface, or alter any tag, serial number, or nameplate.
11. Renters shall not remove equipment from state without prior permission from Xavier University Television Center.
12. Owner at all times has the option to terminate this agreement on 24 hours' notice by certified mail or personal service; renter shall return equipment to owner's premises in the same condition as when first rented at renter's risk and expense.

INSURANCE

1. The renter, at their own expense, shall arrange insurance coverage against loss or damage of equipment at its full value. Proof of insurance is required by Xavier University Television Center.

TERMS

1. Payment of all invoices is due within 10 days. Payments not received within ten days will be subject to 1½% service charge per month.

SOUND EFFECTS LOG   Page _____

REEL/ SOURCE	DESCRIPTION	WORK PRINT		MASTER		LENGTH
		IN	OUT	IN	OUT	

APPENDIX **E** VALS™ 2 TYPOLOGY

The VALS 2 typology, developed by the Values and Lifestyles Program at SRI International, is a new psychographic system for segmenting American consumers and predicting consumer behavior.

For over a decade, the Values and Lifestyles Program has been the leader in psychographic consumer segmentation. Its insights have helped countless advertisers, advertising agencies, and media companies improve the effectiveness of their marketing. Now, building on its years of research into consumer attitudes and life-styles, the VALS Program has created VALS 2, a new typology of American consumers.

VALS 2 is built on a conceptual framework that is called self-orientation, and a new definition of resources.

Self-Orientation

Consumers pursue and acquire products, services, and experiences that provide satisfaction and give shape, substance, and character to their identities. They are motivated by one of three powerful self-orientations—principle, status, or action. Principle-oriented consumers are guided in their choices by their beliefs or principles, rather than by feelings, events, or desire for approval. Status-oriented consumers are heavily influenced by the actions, approval, and opinions of others. Action-oriented consumers are guided by a desire for social or physical activity, variety, and risk-taking. Each VALS 2 segment has distinctive attitudes, life-styles, and life goals according to its members' self-orientation.

Resources

Resources, in the VALS 2 system, refers to the full range of psychological, physical, demographic, and material means and capacities consumers have to draw upon. This dimension is a continuum ranging from minimal to abundant. It encompasses education, income, self-confidence, health, eagerness to buy, intelligence, and energy level. Resources generally increase from adolescence through middle-age, while they decrease with extreme age, depression, financial reverses, and physical or psychological impairment.

Network of Distinctive Interconnected Segments

Using these two dimensions—self-orientation and resources—VALS defined eight segments of consumers who have different attitudes and exhibit distinctive behavior and decision-making patterns. The segments are balanced in size, so that each truly represents a viable target. VALS 2 is a network of interconnected segments. Neighboring types have similar characteristics and can be combined in varying ways to suit particular marketing purposes. The overall system is highly flexible and predictive of consumer behavior.

THE VALS™ 2 NETWORK

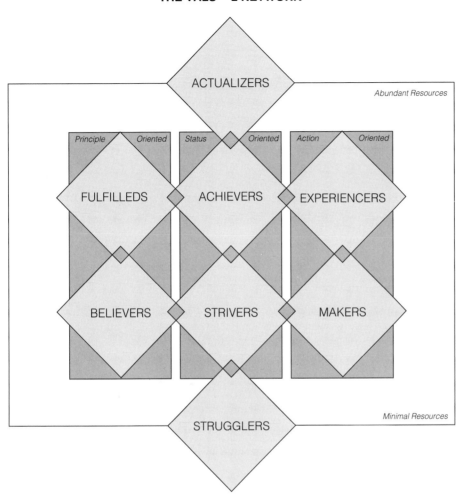

Actualizers

Actualizers are successful, sophisticated, active, "take-charge" people with high self-esteem and abundant resources. They are interested in growth and seek to develop, explore, and express themselves in a variety of ways—sometimes guided by principle, and sometimes by a desire to have an effect, to make a change. Image is important to Actualizers, not as evidence of status or power, but as an expression of their taste, independence, and character. Actualizers are among the established and emerging leaders in business and government, yet they continue to seek challenges. They have a wide range of interests, are concerned with social issues, and are open to change. Their lives are characterized by richness and diversity. Their possessions and recreation reflect a cultivated taste for the finer things in life.

Fulfilleds and Believers: Principle-Oriented

Principle-oriented consumers seek to make their behavior consistent with their views of how the world is or should be.

Fulfilleds are mature, satisfied, comfortable, reflective people who value order, knowledge, and responsibility. Most are well educated, and in, or recently retired from, professional occupations. They are well informed about world and national events and are alert to opportunities to broaden their knowledge. Content with their careers, families, and station in life, their leisure activities tend to center on their homes. Fulfilleds have a moderate respect for the status quo, institutions of authority, and social decorum, but are open-minded about new ideas and social change. Fulfilleds tend to base their decisions on strongly held principles and consequently appear calm and self-assured. While their incomes allow them many choices, Fulfilleds are conservative, practical consumers; they look for functionality, value, and durability in the products they buy.

Believers are conservative, conventional people with concrete beliefs based on traditional, established codes: family, church, community, and the nation. Many Believers express moral codes that are deeply rooted and literally interpreted. They follow established routines, organized in large part around their homes, families, and social or religious organizations to which they belong. As consumers, they are conservative and predictable, favoring American products and established brands. Their education, income, and energy are modest but sufficient to meet their needs.

Achievers and Strivers: Status-Oriented

Status-oriented consumers have or seek a secure place in a valued social setting. They make choices to enhance their position or to facilitate their move to another, more desirable group. Strivers look to others to indicate what they should be and do, whereas Achievers, more resourceful and active, seek recognition and self-definition through achievements at work and in their families.

Achievers are successful career- and work-oriented people who like to, and generally do, feel in control of their lives. They value structure, predictability, and stability over risk, intimacy, and self-discovery. They are deeply committed to their work and their families. Work provides them a sense of duty, material rewards, and prestige. Their social lives reflect this focus and are structured around family, church, and business. Achievers live conventional lives, are politically conservative, and respect authority and the status quo. Image is important to them. As consumers, they favor established products and services that demonstrate their success to their peers.

Strivers seek motivation, self-definition, and approval from the world around them. They are striving to find a secure place in life. Unsure of themselves and low on economic, social, and psychological resources, Strivers are deeply concerned about the opinions and approval of others. Money defines success for Strivers, who don't have enough of it, and often feel that life has given them a raw deal. Strivers are easily bored and impulsive. Many of them seek to be stylish. They emulate those who own more impressive possessions, but what they wish to obtain is generally beyond their reach.

Experiencers and Makers: Action-Oriented

Action-oriented consumers like to affect their environment in tangible ways. Makers do so primarily at home and at work, Experiencers in the wider world. Both types are intensely involved.

Experiencers are young, vital, enthusiastic, impulsive, and rebellious. They seek variety and excitement, savoring the new, the offbeat, and the risky. Still in the process of formulating life values and patterns of behavior, they quickly become enthusiastic about new possibilities but are equally quick to cool. At this stage in their lives, they are politically uncommitted, uninformed, and highly ambivalent about what they believe. Experiencers combine an abstract disdain for conformity and authority with an outsider's awe of other's wealth, prestige, and power. Their energy finds an outlet in exercise, sports, outdoor recreation, and social activities. Experiencers are avid consumers and spend much of their income on clothing, fast food, music, movies, and video.

Makers are practical people who have constructive skills and value self-sufficiency. They live within a traditional context of family, practical work, and physical recreation and have little interest in what lies outside that context. Makers experience the world by working on it—building a house, raising children, fixing a car, or canning vegetables—and have sufficient skill, income, and energy to carry out their projects successfully. Makers are politically conservative, suspicious of new ideas, respectful of governmental authority and organized labor, but resentful of government intrusion on individual rights. They are unimpressed by material possessions other than those with a practical or functional purpose (e.g., tools, pickup trucks, or fishing equipment).

Strugglers

Strugglers' lives are constricted. Chronically poor, ill-educated, low-skilled, without strong social bonds, aging, and concerned about their health, they are often despairing and passive. Because they are so limited, they show evidence of a strong self-orientation, but are focused on meeting the urgent needs of the present moment. Their chief concerns are for security and safety. Strugglers are cautious consumers. They represent a very modest market for most products and services, but are loyal to favorite brands.

PSYCHOLOGICAL CHARACTERISTICS

Actualizers

Optimistic
Self-confident
Involved
Outgoing
Growth oriented

Fulfilleds	**Achievers**	**Experiencers**
Mature	Moderate	Extraverted
Satisfied	Goal oriented	Unconventional
Reflective	Conventional	Active
Open-minded	Deliberate	Impetuous
Intrinsically motivated	In control	Energetic

Believers	**Strivers**	**Makers**
Traditional	Dissatisfied	Practical
Conforming	Unsure	Self-sufficient
Cautious	Alienated	Constructive
Moralistic	Impulsive	Committed
Settled	Approval seeking	Satisfied

Strugglers

Powerless
Narrowly focused
Risk averse
Burdened
Conservative

SOURCE: SRI International.

CONSUMER CHARACTERISTICS

Actualizers

Enjoy the "finer things"
Receptive to new products,
technologies, distribution
Skeptical of advertising
Frequent readers of a wide
variety of publications
Light TV viewers

Fulfilleds

Little interest in image
or prestige
Above-average consumers of
products for the home
Like educational and public
affairs programming
Read widely
and often

Achievers

Attracted to premium
products
Prime target for variety of
products
Average TV watchers
Read business, news,
and self-help
publications

Experiencers

Follow fashion and fads
Spend much of disposable
income on socializing
Buy on impulse
Attend to advertising
Listen to rock music

Believers

Buy American
Slow to change habits
Look for bargains
Watch TV more than average
Read retirement,
home and garden,
and general interest
magazines

Strivers

Image conscious
Limited discretionary income,
but carry credit balances
Spend on clothing and
personal care products
Prefer TV
to reading

Makers

Shop for comfort,
durability, value
Unimpressed by luxuries
Buy the basics
Listen to radio
Read auto, home mechanics,
fishing, outdoors
magazines

Strugglers

Brand loyal
Use coupons and watch
for sales
Trust advertising
Watch TV often
Real tabloids and
women's
magazines

SOURCE: SRI International.

LIFESTYLE CHARACTERISTICS

Actualizers

Value personal growth
Wide intellectual interests
Varied leisure activities
Well informed; concerned
with social issues
Highly social
Politically active

Fulfilleds

Moderately active
in community and politics
Leisure centers on home
Value education and travel
Health conscious
Politically moderate
and tolerant

Achievers

Lives center on
career and family
Have formal social relations
Avoid excess change
or stimulation
May emphasize work at
expense of recreation
Politically conservative

Experiencers

Like the new,
offbeat, and risky
Like exercise, socializing,
sports, and outdoors
Concerned about image
Unconforming, but admire
wealth, power, and fame
Politically apathetic

Believers

Respect rules and
trust authority figures
Enjoy settled, comfortable,
predictable existence
Socialize within family and
established groups
Politically conservative
Reasonably well
informed

Strivers

Narrow interests
Easily bored
Somewhat isolated
Look to peer group for
motivation and approval
Unconcerned about health
or nutrition
Politically apathetic

Makers

Enjoy outdoors
Prefer "hands-on" activities
Spend leisure with family and
close friends
Avoid joining organizations,
except unions
Distrust politicians,
foreigners, and
big business

Strugglers

Limited interests
and activities
Prime concerns are safety
and security
Burdened with health problems
Conservative and traditional
Rely on organized
religion

SOURCE: SRI International.

Descriptive Titles	Nicknames
Educated, Affluent Executives and Professionals in Elite Metro Suburbs	Blue Blood Estates Money & Brains Furs & Station Wagons
Pre- and Post-Child Families and Singles in Upscale, White Collar Suburbs	Pools & Patios Two More Rungs Young Influentials
Upper-Middle, Child Raising Families in Outlying, Owner Occupied Suburbs	Young Suburbia Blue-Chip Blues
Educated, White Collar Singles and Ethnics in Upscale, Urban Areas	Urban Gold Coast Bohemian Mix Black Enterprise New Beginnings
Educated, Young, Mobile Families in Exurban Satellites and Boom Towns	God's Country New Homesteaders Towns & Gowns
Middle-Class, Post-Child Families in Aging Suburbs and Retirement Areas	Levitown, U.S.A. Gray Power Rank & File
Mid-Scale, Child-Raising Blue Collar Families in Remote Suburbs and Towns	Blue-Collar Nursery Middle America Coalburg & Corntown
Mid-Scale Families, Singles and Elders in Dense, Urban Row and High-Rise Areas	New Melting Pot Old Yankee Rows Emergent Minorities Single City Blues
Rural Towns and Villages Amidst Farms and Ranches Across Agrarian Mid-America	Shotguns & Pickups Agri-Business Grain Belt
Mixed Gentry and Blue Collar Labor in Low-Mid Rustic, Mill and Factory Towns	Golden Ponds Mines & Mills Norma Rae-Villa Smalltown Downtown
Landowners, Migrants and Rustics in Poor Rural Towns, Farms, and Uplands	Back-Country Folks Share Croppers Tobacco Roads Hard Scrabble
Mixed, Unskilled Service and Labor in Aging, Urban Rows and High-Rise Areas	Heavy Industry Downtown Dixie-Style Hispanic Mix Public Assistance

SOURCE: Claritas Incorporated.

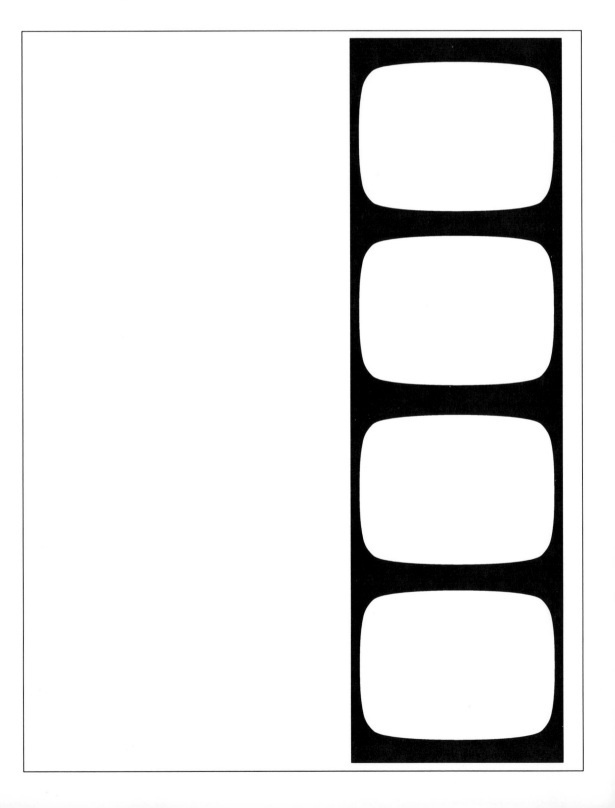

SHOOTING/EDITING SCRIPT

NARRATIVE

CUT/DISS TO:

CUT/DISS TO:

CUT/DISS TO:

CUT/DISS TO:

Glossary

· ·

A/B roll An editing process that results in dissolves. The A roll usually contains audio as well as video and the B roll contains the visuals that are inserted over a voice. A/B roll editing can be done mechanically by placing alternating scenes on two different rolls of videotape and then dissolving between the two using the fader bar on a switcher. It is more common to do A/B roll editing with an edit controller that electronically synchronizes and coordinates two or more VTRs to accomplish the dissolves. The term is derived from film production, which labels reels "A" and "B" in preparation for printing (which combines the film scenes from two rolls onto one).

Analogies Brief comparisons in which a subject is said to be like something else.

Anecdotes Brief stories people tell to illustrate a point. They usually relate to the teller's life experience.

A roll The roll of film or videotape that predominantly carries the audio portion of a program.

Aspect ratio The mathematical relationship between the vertical and horizontal planes of a rectangle. In television the aspect ratio is expressed as 4:3. There are four units of horizontal and three units

of vertical dimension to the average standard television screen.

Audience A group of people who share a common (usually entertaining) experience. Theater audiences come together for a performance whereas video audiences may view individually.

Audience definition A way to describe an audience in specific terms of use to a producer, advertiser, or market researcher.

Audience needs analysis An investigation into a variety of audience-related issues to determine the best way to structure and present a message.

Brainstorming An interactive and interpersonal technique used to generate a quantity of ideas that relate to a central theme.

B roll A term used to designate cutaways or images that go over the words being spoken by an announcer or narrator. Also the roll of film or videotape that predominantly carries the video pictures (as opposed to the sound).

CCD (chip-type) camera A light-sensitive, transistorized, charge-coupled device that transforms optical images into electrical impulses. CCD chips are an alternative to camera tubes, which serve the same purpose. The primary advantage of the chip over the tube is that the tube may burn due to overexposure to high-intensity light.

Character ethics An approach to ethics in which the quality of one's character (as opposed to codes or other laws established by institutions) becomes a reference for making decisions.

Character generator A keyboard-operated device (usually a computer) that puts letters and words on a video screen.

Cinematic time/space A reference to screen time and space relationships that can differ significantly from real time and space. Cinematic time can be collapsed or expanded by juxtaposing scenes with different time references. Cinematic space can alter distances, perspectives, and spatial relationships either by editing or special effects techniques.

Cinema verité Literally, "cinema truth," where there is little or no directing of the action in front of the camera. The camera is only used to observe whatever is naturally occurring.

Circular argument Evidence that is based on other evidence that is based on other evidence (and so on).

Color harmony The placement of colors in a frame that are all closely related to the same area of the color spectrum. Reds, greens, blues, neutrals, and earth tones are expressions of color harmony. When an image mostly contains reds, and a green-blue (cyan, which is the opposite of red) is introduced, color harmony is destroyed. Sometimes color harmony is appropriate and at other times color discordance is appropriate.

Communication objective The content of what you have to say. The communication objective is the answer to the question: What do we want the audience to "get"? What will the video communicate?

Consciousness For our purposes here, it refers to the quality of our being and thinking as exhibited by what we are able to incorporate into a program, including the qualitative manner in which we proceed.

Content Everything contained within a program, especially the subject matter and its presentation.

Content system The content of a program considered as a whole. What the program contains in the way of information, inspiration, entertainment, or the like.

Context Every communication carries a context, a set of surrounding circumstances that influence the message and how it is expressed to its audience or receiver. The context is often understood intuitively and emotionally rather than from some overt explanation of it.

Continuity A presentational or content element that continues throughout a program to unify its message or theme.

Convergence cutting An editing technique that shows different actions (in time and/or place) that, through some relationship, are brought closer and closer until they come together. For example, scenes of a dog on a raft approaching a waterfall are intercut with scenes of a helicopter pilot who diverts his mission to rescue the dog after seeing it in trouble.

Counterpoint When production elements or content expression is in conflict or disagreement. In this technique the director uses elements that are opposite each other to create meaning. Very fast, high-key music played over a slow, sensitive dissolve montage of a flower is an example.

Crash cut A cut that is very abrupt in its change of action and/or emotion—from the fury and noise of the stock exchange floor to a Japanese tea ceremony or vice versa.

Cross-fade A fade-out followed by a fade-in within a program, for instance, when one story ends and another begins.

Cutaway A scene different from the one associated with a sound track when a picture replaces the first scene showing something related to the audio content.

Cybernetics The science and study of machines, particularly those involving memory ability such as computers.

Deductive To deduce, to move from the general to the particular. Cutting from a wide shot to close-ups is deductive editing. The opposite is inductive editing.

Demographics The science and study of human vital statistics usually with the intent to quantify an audience or market.

Denouement The very last scenes of a drama that occur after the climax. The intent is to bring the story line to completion, to fully answer any remaining questions and satisfy the audience that the characters "live happily ever after."

Description Words and images that show the qualities or characteristics of the subject matter.

Dissolve A gradual editing transition from one scene to another.

Double cut An editing technique that lets the actor's expressions rather than his words carry emotional cues. A character makes a comment, and the next shot is the listener's reaction. The editor then cuts back to the person who made the comment to see his expression—and cuts back to the listener reacting again before going to another comment. The shot changes several times, surveying expressions and reactions before the dialogue continues.

Dynamic center The area of a picture where the potency of the action is at its highest. On a television screen this center is more often a "field" of interacting image elements. It's the center of interest.

Edit decision list (EDL) A listing of all scenes, in sequence, with their time-code in- and out-points specified. The EDL is used to perform on-line editing.

Electronic news gathering (ENG) An approach to shooting video in which the camera is used on one shoulder and the VTR is strung over the other shoulder including a mike and light attached to the camera. The objective is to make the equipment as portable as possible to enable the videographer to get in, get the shots, and get out fast.

Empathy Putting oneself in the place of the other to imagine what it is like to be the other. Feeling *with* another. Sympathy is feeling *for* another.

Entropy The tendency of all matter (if left to natural forces alone) to move in the direction of disorder, chaos, and eventual destruction.

Equifinality Every element of a system has equal opportunity to affect the final outcome of its functioning. Basically, if any one element is changed, the entire system is also changed.

Equivocation False reasoning based on a loose or ambiguous definition of terms.

False analogy An analogy that doesn't work because one of the elements is out of relationship to what it is being measured against. The similarity is not true or accurate.

Feedback Information returned to a system to communicate about the system performance, thereby causing it to alter its behavior in order to operate according to established criteria.

Flashback/flashforward A part of a story that refers to a past/future event. In video viewers are given a cue (usually visual) to orient them to the past/future.

Focus group A means of gathering information. Members of a target audience (with very specific characteristics) meet to learn about a product or service. They respond to questions to help the product developers understand more about what works and what doesn't work with respect to their effectiveness.

Foley The technique of audio recording footsteps and other environmental sounds to be mixed into the audio portion of a program.

Frame store A technique and an electronic capability that captures one frame of video and holds it indefinitely. A frame from a program can be held, manipulated, and then replayed. TV talk shows often use a frame store technique to create IDs to be used later in the same program. Also referred to as "still store" in some shops.

Gantt chart A bar chart that plots time against some kind of activity to indicate the overall time frame involved.

Grazing Using a remote control unit to change TV channels, thereby continuing to sample program offerings instead of just watching one channel— continuous channel changing.

Headroom The positioning of the top of the talent's head in relation to the top of the frame.

Hook The technique of showing viewers a sampling of the most dynamic and interesting images as the first program element to "hook" their attention.

Hue The designation of a color: blue, green, magenta, and so on.

Inductive A way to organize content from the particular to the general. A series of close-ups of cockpit dials and the roar of a jet engine cut to a wide shot of the plane beginning to move is inductive editing. The opposite would be deductive organization.

Information Data that make a difference (to someone).

Integrity An act or state of being true. Equipment, considered as a system, has integrity when all its parts work, that is, are true to their design. Individuals with integrity are true to their understanding of what is good for them.

Interlude A change of pace between similar presentation styles. A song is an interlude between people speaking. A person speaking is an interlude between a series of songs.

Jump cut A cut from a person speaking to the same person a minute later when the camera angle, zoom, and talent are unchanged between shots. The head and sholders may jump at the edit point even though the audio track may make sense. Jump cuts are usually covered by a cutaway or reversal.

Keying The electronic cutting in of one image over another as when words are "keyed" into a scene.

Layoff The postproduction process of taking the audio (usually speech) track off the linear master to mix and "sweeten" it with music and effects tracks. When all this has been done in sync and an audio mix completed, the audio is then laid back onto the video master.

Life-style The behavior patterns that constitute an individual's common way of being and relating to others and the environment.

Light meter A light-measuring instrument used mostly by still photographers to determine exposure. Most meters, because they read luminance values, can also be used for television lighting purposes.

Linear master The first step in assembling a video rough-cut master is to lay down, in proper sequence, the scenes containing the element (audio or video) that will determine program length.

Log sheets Information relating to a particular roll (or reel) of tape. Includes reel number, scene, take, evaluation, timing, and a description of what the scene looks like. By referring to log sheets the director knows what is on the reel and where to find it.

Luminance A measurement of light intensity or brightness (obtained by using a light meter). In film and television environments the unit of measurement is usually footcandles.

Market A specified group of individuals who represent a potential for sales.

Matching action Combining (usually with a cut) two scenes so the action looks like one continuous, natural movement. For example, a shot of a person approaching a doorway match cuts to the person entering the room.

Medium Any device, process, or technology that extends some human capability.

Message An idea or perspective that is shared and has meaning.

Moiré pattern Irregular, wavy, ripplelike lines on TV screens resulting from interference between lines on the subject matter (e.g., clothing) and the scan lines of the electronic signal.

Montage A series or sequence of scenes edited together to make a single statement. An animal montage would consist of a series of shots of animals.

Mosaic A term applied to a computerized special effect that shows an image broken down into its pixels. Each pixel is a rectangular representation of a point on the screen. These points can be enlarged so the pixels create a mosaic pattern—like floor tiles—or reduced so they are no longer visible.

Motion control A technique achieved using a sophisticated combination of mechanical and computerized machines to accomplish complex and exactly repeatable camera moves.

Motive The reason someone does something.

Narration Content that tells a story.

Neg-entropy The opposite of entropy; those acts that sustain a system and contribute to its future functioning.

Nemesis The person or power the hero of a story must overcome to succeed in accomplishing the goal.

Newsmat The brand name of an electronic keying technology. It is commonly used to key in pictures over the shoulder of a news anchor as she introduces a story.

Off-line editing Using video equipment to make edit decisions. "Off-line" means that the equipment is not connected to other editing components used to finalize (post) the program by creating a program master. The purpose of off-lining is merely to make the edit decisions that will be used later (on-line) to make the master tape. Sometimes, as in news, a video is off-lined only. That is, the compilation of scenes as they are sequenced will be the final "product."

On-line editing The process of using an edit decision list (EDL) to record scenes onto a master tape using equipment components that allow for special transitions, effects, graphics, and so on. To work "on-line" is to use equipment that is interconnected to maximize capabilities as the program is finalized (posted).

Organizing principle Design concepts relating to how a system's parts are structured so that together they function as a whole.

Packing A process of resetting the videotape tension on its cassette or roll. The tape is fast-forwarded to the end and then rewound to the head. Professionals always pack a virgin tape before using it because it maximizes the quality of the recording overall.

Page turn A term applied to a special effect that simulates the look of a page turning. Page turns can be accomplished horizontally, vertically, or diagonally across the screen and are used predominately as wipes.

Parallel cutting An editing technique that shows viewers two or more distinct events, usually involving different locations and time frames. The editor shows one and then the other to establish a relationship that will eventually be revealed.

Parody A genre in which the style of a work is closely imitated by another, for instance, a corporate celebration that uses the Academy Awards format and style to present awards to employees.

Persona A fictitious person designed to create a mental image to carry certain characteristics forward in memory. It is easier to remember a personality type than it is to remember a list of characteristics.

Persuasion The attempt to change the attitude or opinion of another.

Pixel The smallest element of an electronic image that can be resolved. By using a computer to enlarge an image graphically, pixels can be small or large rectangles of visual information.

Plot The events of a story and how they unfold: what, where, and when.

Point of view (POV) This phrase designates in scripts the position of the camera as if the actor were standing in that place. It is the perspective the audience will see when they identify with the screen character.

Positioning Placing an image, idea, or feeling in the audience's minds that bears a positive (or at least comfortable) association or relationship to what is already there.

Post house A term used for postproduction facilities. Post houses service producers by providing on-line editing equipment and other computerized technologies used in the final steps of creating a program.

Preliminary outline The first outline of a program idea.

Previsualization The act of visualizing what scenes and sequences of the program will look like before anything is shot. Directors often previsualize the next day's shooting the night before so that, when it is time to shoot, they know how cameras should be positioned and so on. Everything should be mentally worked out before it is written down.

Primacy The idea that the order of presentation has an influence on effectiveness; specifically, the message presented first has the persuasive advantage.

Prime lens A fixed, focal-length lens. (Not a zoom lens, which has a variable focal length.) Prime lenses have higher resolving power than zoom lenses.

Process A sequential progression of actions that lead to a result. A process orientation means there is more emphasis on the steps taken than on the accomplishment of the goal that results from the process.

Production The process of creating the audio and visual elements of a video or television program.

Production needs analysis A determination of the many needs required by the program content, including the personnel, that when combined will make production flow smoothly.

Production switcher A device that permits several video inputs (from cameras, VTRs, character generators, and so on) to be combined, manipulated, and output to program and preview monitors for the purpose of creating a desired program sequence. Although the switcher may be used as a way to build sequences, its primary use is to facilitate the video switching of program elements during a program, for the length of the program. Switchers carry only the video signal, never the audio.

Program A finished, complete video experience ready for delivery to its intended audience.

Program needs analysis An assessment of the program needs; those relating to content and presentation including format, actors, and locations.

Project In the context of this book, this term refers to the overall effort to design and produce a video program from start to finish. A program idea becomes a project when funds are allocated to realize it.

Prologue An introduction to a program that sets the tone; the scenes that precede and lead into and through the program titles.

Promotional gifts Items such as T-shirts, mugs, pens, fans, jackets, and jewelry that contain a logo and are given away in contexts where some promotional value is hoped for in return.

Proposal A document submitted to a funding source requesting money to produce a program. It contains a description of the program and its use, a time frame, a budget, and resumes of key participants. Proposals are most often prepared for foundations and other entities that provide funding on a not-for-profit basis.

Prospectus A document submitted to potential investment partners or other businesses to obtain production financing. It contains the same information as a proposal but also delineates specific financial terms and agreements between the participants. A prospectus is prepared for businesses and other entities that may provide production funds in a for-profit context.

Proxemics The study of space between people and how it influences interaction and communication.

Psychographics Research into the qualitative decisions people make as part of an audience or market. How do they like the product? How does it make them feel? What effect does its use have on them?

Reaction shot A shot of the face of the person who responds or otherwise listens to or observes a speaker. A reaction could express any emotion.

Receiver The person or persons who receive a message or other communication. In the video context these people are referred to as "viewers."

Recency The idea that the order of presenting content has some influence on its effectiveness; specifically, that the message given last will be remembered best because it is closest to the time when recall will be required or solicited.

Repeat Sounds and images repeated in a program either for effect or to give emphasis and thereby create a memory of the content.

Rerecording Speech recorded in a studio and timed exactly to the speech that was recorded on location to replace inferior quality with excellent quality. The actor watches a monitor while listening to his own voice (through headphones) and speaks into a microphone. Several takes are needed to perfect the sync, but audio editing permits words to be moved slightly in either direction.

Resonance Vibrational empathy; a deep connection between people who have a common vision or purpose that, if directed and applied properly, can lead to heightened effectiveness (of interaction and product).

Reveal A theatrical technique that teases the audience until the moment is appropriate to reveal a particular element.

Reversal A cutaway shot of an interviewer listening to the person she is interviewing. It allows for the expression of a response and technically provides a cutaway option to cover a jump cut.

Rough-cut A trial edit of a program to determine whether the sequencing, timing, and content work as they should. A rough-cut is usually done with time-code numbers so afterward the numbers associated with the in- and out-points of each scene can be easily copied onto an edit decision list for final editing of the program master.

Rule ethics An approach to ethics that bases moral decisions on codes (civil or religious), laws, or other rules that have been established by others.

Safety (print or copy) The first copy of a freshly created master, which is often retained by the facility where postproduction work occurred. If the other master is destroyed or lost, the safety copy will then serve as the master from which release prints can be made.

Saturation The amount of white (light) that is added to a hue (color) to make it pale or rich. Light pink is actually a low-saturation red because it contains a lot of white light and very little red.

Scene-on-scene An editing mistake that shows a transition from one scene to another that too closely resembles the first. The transition appears (and is) unmotivated. The error is corrected by varying the shot between transitions.

Screen direction The direction of the action within a frame.

Script breakdown Itemizing all production elements that will be involved to facilitate scheduling and budget preparation.

Secondary audience Individuals who watch a program that was designed more specifically to be seen by others; that is, people outside the target audience.

Second law of thermodynamics A law of physics relating to heat: For any closed system (unit of matter and energy) differences in concentration and temperature tend to disappear and are replaced by randomness and uniformity. Notice that the temperature of your room tends toward uniformity rather than zones of hot and cold.

Setup The storyteller, writer, or director stages a situation so the audience is unaware of what is about to happen; they are being set up for the experience to come. Any experience can be made more powerful by setting up the audience, a device that takes advantage of emotional contrast.

Simulations Trying something out to see whether it works. Simulations help viewers see what something would be like.

Situation ethics An approach to ethics that considers the uniqueness of each situation as an influence on ethical decisions and behavior. Life is not black and white; each situation imposes special circumstances that must be taken into consideration.

SMPTE The acronym for the organization that sets technical standards for the film and television industries: Society of Motion Picture and Television Engineers.

Social system All the people involved in a program production taken as a whole.

Squeeze zoom A special effect that reduces or expands an image within the frame. The resulting image can be positioned anywhere on the screen and its aspect ratio changed as desired.

Still store Another name for frame store; the electronic capturing of a single field of video for later use.

Stinger A sharp musical beat or note that highlights or accents a particular screen action.

Storyboard A script that contains TV frames with illustrations so the reader can quickly see what the shot should look like. Storyboards specify visuals so there is no doubt what the writer-producer had in mind.

Super Superimposition; the combining of two shots so that they are simultaneously equally visible on the screen.

Sweetening A postproduction procedure for improving the quality of the audio track.

Switcher An electronic device that receives video signals from several different sources (cameras, CG) and then permits the operator to move and manipulate the signals so they can appear on the program monitor (which shows what is being aired or taped).

Sympathy Feeling for another; being sad or happy for his experience.

Sync Synchronize; the exact timing of video signals between systems (cameras, recorders) so the signals are sent and received in a lockstep manner. Sync keeps the picture steady.

Synergy A mode of interacting cooperatively so the outcome (of a synergistic group) is greater than the sum of its parts (i.e., greater than what would have been accomplished had the individuals worked in their own ways).

System An interacting assemblage of parts designed to function together for a purpose.

Talent release form A form signed by people that gives the producer rights to use their image and/or sound performance.

Target audience An audience identified and characterized as recipients for a particular message or communication experience.

Technical system All the pieces of equipment and the facilities used in a production taken together as a whole.

TelePrompTer A two-way mirror device attached to a camera that enables talent to read words on a screen placed in front of the lens. The TelePrompTer allows the talent to maintain good eye contact with the lens (viewers) while reading the script. Extensively used in newscasts.

Theme The primary, often universal statement that a story makes about the human condition.

Time-code A standard (established by SMPTE) for numbering every frame of video. The time-code can be placed on an audio track or an address track or invisibly interlaced in the video track by a device called a time-code writer. Another device (often the same piece of equipment), the time-code reader, makes the numbers (hours, minutes, seconds, frames) visible in a small "window" superimposed over the picture. The time-code is used to specify the location of any portion of the tape for editing purposes. It is also the only way A/B roll editing can be done with perfect frame accuracy because edit controllers rely on time-code numbers for all internal commands.

Transcription A typed draft, or hard copy, of words that were originally recorded on audiotape or videotape.

Transition A movement of attention from one area to another; a bridge between content areas.

Treatment A highly visual description of program content designed to interest others in the idea.

TV-safe A specific, central area of a TV screen in which all TV receivers (in a facility or at home) are certain to receive the picture elements without anything being cut off. Directors and camera operators keep the dynamic action of a scene within the TV-safe area so none of the image is cut off on different sets.

Vectors Lines of force usually created by lighting. Every image has vectors. Simply follow the lines of the subject matter and extend imaginary lines in these directions to see how they intersect. These lines direct viewers' attention. The objective is to keep viewers' attention within the frame as long as possible rather than having them follow vectors outside the frame.

Verisimilitude A quality of rightness within a story. Things feel right, appropriate; they make sense.

Video tape recorder (VTR) A machine that records video (and audio) in any format other than VHS. A VHS recorder is a video cassette recorder (VCR).

Visual analogy Pictures that make an analogy. For example, scenes of an assembly line are used to communicate the linear manner in which a company plans its projects.

Visual economy Showing as few visual elements as possible in any given image while providing enough information for the audience to "get" the point of it. If a shot concerns hands, visual economy dictates that nothing else in the frame distracts the viewers from the hands.

Visualization Seeing with the imagination; mental imaging.

Walk and talk The coordinated movement of subject (person talking) and camera; the talent walks as she talks (on camera).

Waveform monitor An electronic device that displays and measures the relative luminance values of a video picture.

Window dub A copy of video footage that also contains a window displaying time-code numbers so that any scene can be identified and located exactly later.

Wipe A transition where one image is swept off the screen as another is "wiped" on. Wipes can occur in a variety of patterns depending on the capability of the switcher.

INDEX